Toyota Corolla Automotive Repair Manual

by Jay Storer
and John H Haynes
Member of the Guild of Motoring Writers

Models covered:

Toyota Corolla models
2003 through 2011
Does not include information specific to XRS models

(1Q5 - 92037)

ABCDE
FGHIJ
KLMN

Haynes Publishing Group
Sparkford Nr Yeovil
Somerset BA22 7JJ England

Haynes North America, Inc
861 Lawrence Drive
Newbury Park
California 91320 USA

Acknowledgements

Wiring diagrams provided exclusively for Haynes North America,
Inc. by Solution Builders. Technical writers who contributed to this
project are Jay Storer and Ralph Rendina.

A book in the Haynes Automotive Repair Manual Series

Printed in the U.S.A.

ISBN-13: 978-1-56392-978-6

ISBN-10: 1-56392-978-3

Library of Congress Control Number 2012932141

While every attempt is made to ensure that the information in this manual is correct, no liability can be accepted by the authors or publishers
for loss, damage or injury caused by any errors in, or omissions from,
the information given.

Contents

Haynes mechanic and photographer with a 2005 Toyota Corolla

About this manual

Its purpose

The purpose of this manual is to help you get the best value from your vehicle. It can do so in several ways. It can help you decide what work must be done, even if you choose to have it done by a dealer service department or a repair shop; it provides information and procedures for routine maintenance and servicing; and it offers diagnostic and repair procedures to follow when trouble occurs.

We hope you use the manual to tackle the work yourself. For many simpler jobs, doing it yourself may be quicker than arranging an appointment to get the vehicle into a shop and making the trips to leave it and pick it up. More importantly, a lot of money can be saved by avoiding the expense the shop must pass on to you to cover its labor and overhead costs. An added benefit is the sense of satisfaction and accomplishment that you feel after doing the job yourself.

Using the manual

The manual is divided into Chapters. Each Chapter is divided into numbered Sections, which are headed in bold type between horizontal lines. Each Section consists of consecutively numbered paragraphs.

At the beginning of each numbered Section you will be referred to any illustrations which apply to the procedures in that Section. The reference numbers used in illustration captions pinpoint the pertinent Section and the Step within that Section. That is, illustration 3.2 means the illustration refers to Section 3 and Step (or paragraph) 2 within that Section.

Procedures, once described in the text, are not normally repeated. When it's necessary to refer to another Chapter, the reference will be given as Chapter and Section number. Cross references given without use of the word "Chapter" apply to Sections and/or paragraphs in the same Chapter. For example, "see Section 8" means in the same Chapter.

References to the left or right side of the vehicle assume you are sitting in the driver's seat, facing forward.

Even though we have prepared this manual with extreme care, neither the publisher nor the author can accept responsibility for any errors in, or omissions from, the information given.

NOTE

A **Note** provides information necessary to properly complete a procedure or information which will make the procedure easier to understand.

CAUTION

A **Caution** provides a special procedure or special steps which must be taken while completing the procedure where the Caution is found. Not heeding a Caution can result in damage to the assembly being worked on.

WARNING

A **Warning** provides a special procedure or special steps which must be taken while completing the procedure where the Warning is found. Not heeding a Warning can result in personal injury.

Introduction to the Toyota Corolla

The Toyota Corolla models covered by this manual are four-door sedans.

The transversely-mounted inline four-cylinder engine used in these vehicles is equipped with electronic fuel injection.

The engine drives the front wheels through either a five-speed manual transaxle or a four-speed automatic transaxle via independent driveaxles.

Independent suspension, featuring coil spring/strut damper units, is used on the front of the vehicle. The rack-and-pinion steering unit is mounted behind the engine with power-assist on most models. The rear suspension uses coil-over shock absorber assemblies, connected to a pressed-steel beam-type axle.

The brakes are disc at the front and drums at the rear, with power-assist standard. An Anti-lock Brake System (ABS) is available on all models, with optional Electronic Brake Distribution (EBD) for better traction and handling.

Vehicle identification numbers

Modifications are a continuing and unpublicized process in vehicle manufacturing. Since spare parts manuals and lists are compiled on a numerical basis, the individual vehicle numbers are essential to correctly identify the component required.

Vehicle Identification Number (VIN)

This very important identification number is stamped on the firewall in the engine compartment, on a plate attached to the dashboard inside the windshield on the driver's side of the vehicle and, on some models, on the Vehicle Safety Certification label in the driver's door opening (see illustration). The VIN also appears on the Vehicle Certificate of Title and Registration. It contains information such as where and when the vehicle was manufactured, the model year and the body style.

Manufacturer's Certification Regulation label

The manufacturer's Certification Regulation label is attached to the driver's side door end or post. The plate contains the name of the manufacturer, the month and year of production, the Gross Vehicle Weight Rating (GVWR), the Gross Axle Weight Rating (GAWR) and the certification statement (see illustration).

VIN model year codes

One particularly important piece of information found within the VIN is the model year code. Counting from the left, the model year code designation is the 10th character in the VIN.

On all models covered by this manual, the model year codes are:

3	2003
4	2004
5	2005
6	2006
7	2007
8	2008
9	2009
A	2010
B	2011

Engine and transaxle identification numbers

The engine code number can be found on a pad on the rear side of the block (see illustration). The transaxle identification number is located on a plate attached to the top of the transaxle case (see illustration), or stamped on the transaxle housing.

The Vehicle Identification Number (VIN) is visible through the driver's side of the windshield

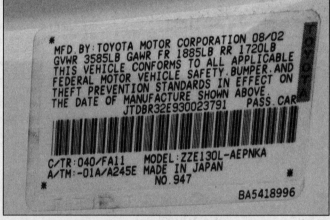

Manufacturer's Certification Regulation label

Location of the engine identification number

Location of the transaxle identification number

Buying parts

Replacement parts are available from many sources, which generally fall into one of two categories - authorized dealer parts departments and independent retail auto parts stores. Our advice concerning these parts is as follows:

Retail auto parts stores: Good auto parts stores will stock frequently needed components which wear out relatively fast, such as clutch components, exhaust systems, brake parts, tune-up parts, etc. These stores often supply new or reconditioned parts on an exchange basis, which can save a considerable amount of money. Discount auto parts stores are often very good places to buy materials and parts needed for general vehicle maintenance such as oil, grease, filters, spark plugs, belts, touch-up paint, bulbs, etc. They also usually sell tools and general accessories, have convenient hours, charge lower prices and can often be found not far from home.

Authorized dealer parts department: This is the best source for parts which are unique to the vehicle and not generally available elsewhere (such as major engine parts, transmission parts, trim pieces, etc.).

Warranty information: If the vehicle is still covered under warranty, be sure that any replacement parts purchased - regardless of the source - do not invalidate the warranty!

To be sure of obtaining the correct parts, have engine and chassis numbers available and, if possible, take the old parts along for positive identification.

Maintenance techniques, tools and working facilities

Maintenance techniques

There are a number of techniques involved in maintenance and repair that will be referred to throughout this manual. Application of these techniques will enable the home mechanic to be more efficient, better organized and capable of performing the various tasks properly, which will ensure that the repair job is thorough and complete.

Fasteners

Fasteners are nuts, bolts, studs and screws used to hold two or more parts together. There are a few things to keep in mind when working with fasteners. Almost all of them use a locking device of some type, either a lockwasher, locknut, locking tab or thread adhesive. All threaded fasteners should be clean and straight, with undamaged threads and undamaged corners on the hex head where the wrench fits. Develop the habit of replacing all damaged nuts and bolts with new ones. Special locknuts with nylon or fiber inserts can only be used once. If they are removed, they lose their locking ability and must be replaced with new ones.

Rusted nuts and bolts should be treated with a penetrating fluid to ease removal and prevent breakage. Some mechanics use turpentine in a spout-type oil can, which works quite well. After applying the rust penetrant, let it work for a few minutes before trying to loosen the nut or bolt. Badly rusted fasteners may have to be chiseled or sawed off or removed with a special nut breaker, available at tool stores.

If a bolt or stud breaks off in an assembly, it can be drilled and removed with a special tool commonly available for this purpose. Most automotive machine shops can perform this task, as well as other repair procedures, such as the repair of threaded holes that have been stripped out.

Flat washers and lockwashers, when removed from an assembly, should always be replaced exactly as removed. Replace any damaged washers with new ones. Never use a lockwasher on any soft metal surface (such as aluminum), thin sheet metal or plastic.

Fastener sizes

For a number of reasons, automobile manufacturers are making wider and wider use of metric fasteners. Therefore, it is important to be able to tell the difference between standard (sometimes called U.S. or SAE) and metric hardware, since they cannot be interchanged.

All bolts, whether standard or metric, are sized according to diameter, thread pitch and length. For example, a standard 1/2 - 13 x 1 bolt is 1/2 inch in diameter, has 13 threads per inch and is 1 inch long. An M12 - 1.75 x 25 metric bolt is 12 mm in diameter, has a thread pitch of 1.75 mm (the distance between threads) and is 25 mm long. The two bolts are nearly identical, and easily confused, but they are not interchangeable.

In addition to the differences in diameter, thread pitch and length, metric and standard bolts can also be distinguished by examining the bolt heads. To begin with, the distance across the flats on a standard bolt head is measured in inches, while the same dimension on a metric bolt is sized in millimeters (the same is true for nuts). As a result, a standard wrench should not be used on a metric bolt and a metric wrench should not be used on a standard bolt. Also, most standard bolts have slashes radiating out from the center of the head to denote the grade or strength of the bolt, which is an indication of the amount of torque that can be applied to it. The greater the number of slashes, the greater the strength of the bolt. Grades 0 through 5 are commonly used on automobiles. Metric bolts have a property class (grade) number, rather than a slash, molded into their heads to indicate bolt strength. In this case, the higher the number, the stronger the bolt. Property class numbers 8.8, 9.8 and 10.9 are commonly used on automobiles.

Strength markings can also be used to distinguish standard hex nuts from metric hex nuts. Many standard nuts have dots stamped into one side, while metric nuts are marked with a number. The greater the number of

dots, or the higher the number, the greater the strength of the nut.

Metric studs are also marked on their ends according to property class (grade). Larger studs are numbered (the same as metric bolts), while smaller studs carry a geometric code to denote grade.

It should be noted that many fasteners, especially Grades 0 through 2, have no distinguishing marks on them. When such is the case, the only way to determine whether it is standard or metric is to measure the thread pitch or compare it to a known fastener of the same size.

Standard fasteners are often referred to as SAE, as opposed to metric. However, it should be noted that SAE technically refers to a non-metric fine thread fastener only. Coarse thread non-metric fasteners are referred to as USS sizes.

Since fasteners of the same size (both standard and metric) may have different

strength ratings, be sure to reinstall any bolts, studs or nuts removed from your vehicle in their original locations. Also, when replacing a fastener with a new one, make sure that the new one has a strength rating equal to or greater than the original.

Tightening sequences and procedures

Most threaded fasteners should be tightened to a specific torque value (torque is the twisting force applied to a threaded component such as a nut or bolt). Overtightening the fastener can weaken it and cause it to break, while undertightening can cause it to eventually come loose. Bolts, screws and studs, depending on the material they are made of and their thread diameters, have specific torque values, many of which are noted in the Specifications at the beginning of each Chapter. Be sure to follow the torque recommendations closely. For fasteners not assigned a

Grade 1 or 2   Grade 5   Grade 8

Bolt strength marking (standard/SAE/USS; bottom - metric)

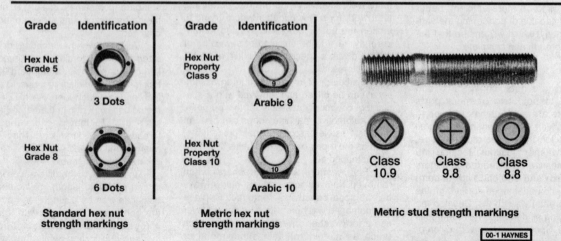

Grade   Identification   Grade   Identification

Hex Nut Grade 5   3 Dots

Hex Nut Grade 8   6 Dots

Hex Nut Property Class 9   Arabic 9

Hex Nut Property Class 10   Arabic 10

Class 10.9   Class 9.8   Class 8.8

Standard hex nut strength markings   **Metric hex nut strength markings**   **Metric stud strength markings**

00-1 HAYNES

specific torque, a general torque value chart is presented here as a guide. These torque values are for dry (unlubricated) fasteners threaded into steel or cast iron (not aluminum). As was previously mentioned, the size and grade of a fastener determine the amount of torque that can safely be applied to it. The figures listed here are approximate for Grade 2 and Grade 3 fasteners. Higher grades can tolerate higher torque values.

Fasteners laid out in a pattern, such as cylinder head bolts, oil pan bolts, differential cover bolts, etc., must be loosened or tightened in sequence to avoid warping the component. This sequence will normally be shown in the appropriate Chapter. If a specific pattern is not given, the following procedures can be used to prevent warping.

Initially, the bolts or nuts should be assembled finger-tight only. Next, they should be tightened one full turn each, in a crisscross or diagonal pattern. After each one has been tightened one full turn, return to the first one and tighten them all one-half turn, following the same pattern. Finally, tighten each of them one-quarter turn at a time until each fastener has been tightened to the proper torque. To loosen and remove the fasteners, the procedure would be reversed.

Component disassembly

Component disassembly should be done with care and purpose to help ensure that

Metric thread sizes	Ft-lbs	Nm
M-6	6 to 9	9 to 12
M-8	14 to 21	19 to 28
M-10	28 to 40	38 to 54
M-12	50 to 71	68 to 96
M-14	80 to 140	109 to 154
Pipe thread sizes		
1/8	5 to 8	7 to 10
1/4	12 to 18	17 to 24
3/8	22 to 33	30 to 44
1/2	25 to 35	34 to 47
U.S. thread sizes		
1/4 - 20	6 to 9	9 to 12
5/16 - 18	12 to 18	17 to 24
5/16 - 24	14 to 20	19 to 27
3/8 - 16	22 to 32	30 to 43
3/8 - 24	27 to 38	37 to 51
7/16 - 14	40 to 55	55 to 74
7/16 - 20	40 to 60	55 to 81
1/2 - 13	55 to 80	75 to 108

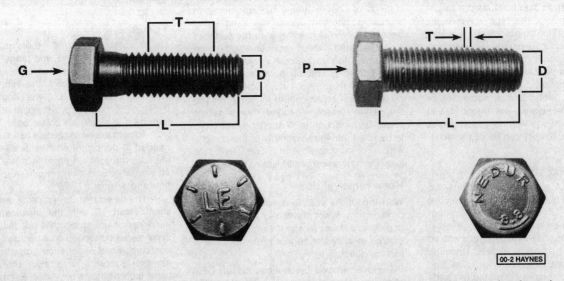

Standard (SAE and USS) bolt dimensions/grade marks

G	Grade marks (bolt strength)
L	Length (in inches)
T	Thread pitch (number of threads per inch)
D	Nominal diameter (in inches)

Metric bolt dimensions/grade marks

P	Property class (bolt strength)
L	Length (in millimeters)
T	Thread pitch (distance between threads in millimeters)
D	Diameter

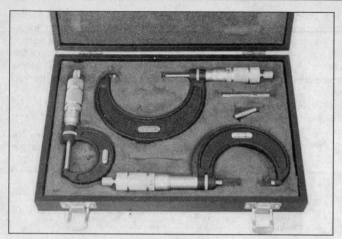

Micrometer set

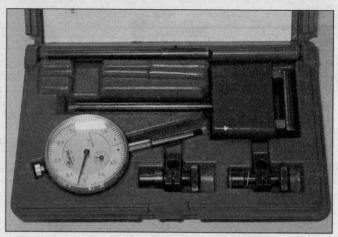

Dial indicator set

the parts go back together properly. Always keep track of the sequence in which parts are removed. Make note of special characteristics or marks on parts that can be installed more than one way, such as a grooved thrust washer on a shaft. It is a good idea to lay the disassembled parts out on a clean surface in the order that they were removed. It may also be helpful to make sketches or take instant photos of components before removal.

When removing fasteners from a component, keep track of their locations. Sometimes threading a bolt back in a part, or putting the washers and nut back on a stud, can prevent mix-ups later. If nuts and bolts cannot be returned to their original locations, they should be kept in a compartmented box or a series of small boxes. A cupcake or muffin tin is ideal for this purpose, since each cavity can hold the bolts and nuts from a particular area (i.e. oil pan bolts, valve cover bolts, engine mount bolts, etc.). A pan of this type is especially helpful when working on assemblies with very small parts, such as the carburetor, alternator, valve train or interior dash and trim pieces. The cavities can be marked with paint or tape to identify the contents.

Whenever wiring looms, harnesses or connectors are separated, it is a good idea to identify the two halves with numbered pieces of masking tape so they can be easily reconnected.

Gasket sealing surfaces

Throughout any vehicle, gaskets are used to seal the mating surfaces between two parts and keep lubricants, fluids, vacuum or pressure contained in an assembly.

Many times these gaskets are coated with a liquid or paste-type gasket sealing compound before assembly. Age, heat and pressure can sometimes cause the two parts to stick together so tightly that they are very difficult to separate. Often, the assembly can be loosened by striking it with a soft-face hammer near the mating surfaces. A regular hammer can be used if a block of wood is placed between the hammer and the part. Do

not hammer on cast parts or parts that could be easily damaged. With any particularly stubborn part, always recheck to make sure that every fastener has been removed.

Avoid using a screwdriver or bar to pry apart an assembly, as they can easily mar the gasket sealing surfaces of the parts, which must remain smooth. If prying is absolutely necessary, use an old broom handle, but keep in mind that extra clean up will be necessary if the wood splinters.

After the parts are separated, the old gasket must be carefully scraped off and the gasket surfaces cleaned. Stubborn gasket material can be soaked with rust penetrant or treated with a special chemical to soften it so it can be easily scraped off. **Caution:** *Never use gasket removal solutions or caustic chemicals on plastic or other composite components.* A scraper can be fashioned from a piece of copper tubing by flattening and sharpening one end. Copper is recommended because it is usually softer than the surfaces to be scraped, which reduces the chance of gouging the part. Some gaskets can be removed with a wire brush, but regardless of the method used, the mating surfaces must be left clean and smooth. If for some reason the gasket surface is gouged, then a gasket sealer thick enough to fill scratches will have to be used during reassembly of the components. For most applications, a non-drying (or semi-drying) gasket sealer should be used.

Hose removal tips

Warning: *If the vehicle is equipped with air conditioning, do not disconnect any of the A/C hoses without first having the system depressurized by a dealer service department or a service station.*

Hose removal precautions closely parallel gasket removal precautions. Avoid scratching or gouging the surface that the hose mates against or the connection may leak. This is especially true for radiator hoses. Because of various chemical reactions, the rubber in hoses can bond itself to the metal spigot that the hose fits over. To remove

a hose, first loosen the hose clamps that secure it to the spigot. Then, with slip-joint pliers, grab the hose at the clamp and rotate it around the spigot. Work it back and forth until it is completely free, then pull it off. Silicone or other lubricants will ease removal if they can be applied between the hose and the outside of the spigot. Apply the same lubricant to the inside of the hose and the outside of the spigot to simplify installation.

As a last resort (and if the hose is to be replaced with a new one anyway), the rubber can be slit with a knife and the hose peeled from the spigot. If this must be done, be careful that the metal connection is not damaged.

If a hose clamp is broken or damaged, do not reuse it. Wire-type clamps usually weaken with age, so it is a good idea to replace them with screw-type clamps whenever a hose is removed.

Tools

A selection of good tools is a basic requirement for anyone who plans to maintain and repair his or her own vehicle. For the owner who has few tools, the initial investment might seem high, but when compared to the spiraling costs of professional auto maintenance and repair, it is a wise one.

To help the owner decide which tools are needed to perform the tasks detailed in this manual, the following tool lists are offered: *Maintenance and minor repair, Repair/overhaul* and *Special.*

The newcomer to practical mechanics should start off with the *maintenance and minor repair* tool kit, which is adequate for the simpler jobs performed on a vehicle. Then, as confidence and experience grow, the owner can tackle more difficult tasks, buying additional tools as they are needed. Eventually the basic kit will be expanded into the *repair and overhaul* tool set. Over a period of time, the experienced do-it-yourselfer will assemble a tool set complete enough for most repair and overhaul procedures and will add tools from the special category when it is felt that the expense is justified by the frequency of use.

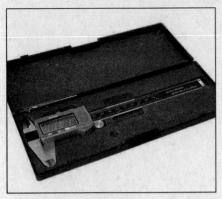

Dial caliper

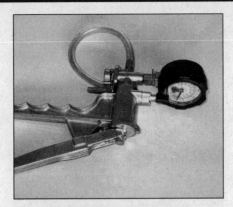

Hand-operated vacuum pump

Timing light

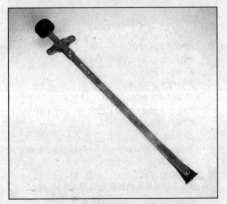

Compression gauge with spark plug hole adapter

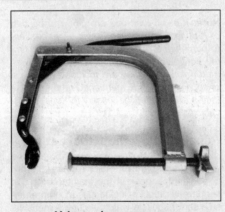

Damper/steering wheel puller

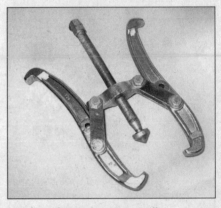

General purpose puller

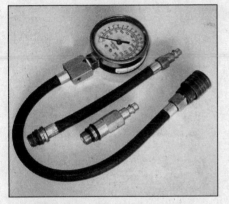

Hydraulic lifter removal tool

Valve spring compressor

Valve spring compressor

Ridge reamer

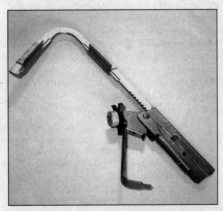

Piston ring groove cleaning tool

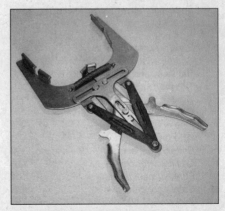

Ring removal/installation tool

Ring compressor

Cylinder hone

Brake hold-down spring tool

Torque angle gauge

Clutch plate alignment tool

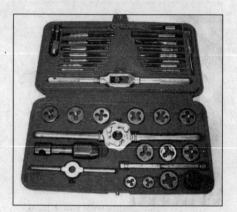

Tap and die set

Maintenance and minor repair tool kit

The tools in this list should be considered the minimum required for performance of routine maintenance, servicing and minor repair work. We recommend the purchase of combination wrenches (box-end and open-end combined in one wrench). While more expensive than open end wrenches, they offer the advantages of both types of wrench.

> Combination wrench set (1/4-inch to 1 inch or 6 mm to 19 mm)
> Adjustable wrench, 8 inch
> Spark plug wrench with rubber insert
> Spark plug gap adjusting tool
> Feeler gauge set
> Brake bleeder wrench
> Standard screwdriver (5/16-inch x 6 inch)
> Phillips screwdriver (No. 2 x 6 inch)
> Combination pliers - 6 inch
> Hacksaw and assortment of blades
> Tire pressure gauge
> Grease gun
> Oil can
> Fine emery cloth
> Wire brush
> Battery post and cable cleaning tool
> Oil filter wrench
> Funnel (medium size)
> Safety goggles
> Jackstands (2)
> Drain pan

Note: *If basic tune-ups are going to be part of routine maintenance, it will be necessary to purchase a good quality stroboscopic timing light and combination tachometer/dwell meter. Although they are included in the list of special tools, it is mentioned here because they are absolutely necessary for tuning most vehicles properly.*

Repair and overhaul tool set

These tools are essential for anyone who plans to perform major repairs and are in addition to those in the maintenance and minor repair tool kit. Included is a comprehensive set of sockets which, though expensive, are invaluable because of their versatility, especially when various extensions and drives are available. We recommend the 1/2-inch drive over the 3/8-inch drive. Although the larger drive is bulky and more expensive, it has the capacity of accepting a very wide range of large sockets. Ideally, however, the mechanic should have a 3/8-inch drive set and a 1/2-inch drive set.

> Socket set(s)
> Reversible ratchet
> Extension - 10 inch
> Universal joint
> Torque wrench (same size drive as sockets)
> Ball peen hammer - 8 ounce
> Soft-face hammer (plastic/rubber)
> Standard screwdriver (1/4-inch x 6 inch)

> Standard screwdriver (stubby - 5/16-inch)
> Phillips screwdriver (No. 3 x 8 inch)
> Phillips screwdriver (stubby - No. 2)
> Pliers - vise grip
> Pliers - lineman's
> Pliers - needle nose
> Pliers - snap-ring (internal and external)
> Cold chisel - 1/2-inch
> Scribe
> Scraper (made from flattened copper tubing)
> Centerpunch
> Pin punches (1/16, 1/8, 3/16-inch)
> Steel rule/straightedge - 12 inch
> Allen wrench set (1/8 to 3/8-inch or 4 mm to 10 mm)
> A selection of files
> Wire brush (large)
> Jackstands (second set)
> Jack (scissor or hydraulic type)

Note: *Another tool which is often useful is an electric drill with a chuck capacity of 3/8-inch and a set of good quality drill bits.*

Special tools

The tools in this list include those which are not used regularly, are expensive to buy, or which need to be used in accordance with their manufacturer's instructions. Unless these tools will be used frequently, it is not very economical to purchase many of them. A consideration would be to split the cost and use between yourself and a friend or friends. In addition, most of these tools can be obtained from a tool rental shop on a temporary basis.

This list primarily contains only those tools and instruments widely available to the public, and not those special tools produced by the vehicle manufacturer for distribution to dealer service departments. Occasionally, references to the manufacturer's special tools are included in the text of this manual. Generally, an alternative method of doing the job without the special tool is offered. However, sometimes there is no alternative to their use. Where this is the case, and the tool cannot be purchased or borrowed, the work should be turned over to the dealer service department or an automotive repair shop.

> *Valve spring compressor*
> *Piston ring groove cleaning tool*
> *Piston ring compressor*
> *Piston ring installation tool*
> *Cylinder compression gauge*
> *Cylinder ridge reamer*
> *Cylinder surfacing hone*
> *Cylinder bore gauge*
> *Micrometers and/or dial calipers*
> *Hydraulic lifter removal tool*
> *Balljoint separator*
> *Universal-type puller*
> *Impact screwdriver*
> *Dial indicator set*
> *Stroboscopic timing light (inductive pick-up)*
> *Hand operated vacuum/pressure pump*
> *Tachometer/dwell meter*
> *Universal electrical multimeter*
> *Cable hoist*
> *Brake spring removal and installation tools*
> *Floor jack*

Buying tools

For the do-it-yourselfer who is just starting to get involved in vehicle maintenance and repair, there are a number of options available when purchasing tools. If maintenance and minor repair is the extent of the work to be done, the purchase of individual tools is satisfactory. If, on the other hand, extensive work is planned, it would be a good idea to purchase a modest tool set from one of the large retail chain stores. A set can usually be bought at a substantial savings over the individual tool prices, and they often come with a tool box. As additional tools are needed, add-on sets, individual tools and a larger tool box can be purchased to expand the tool selection. Building a tool set gradually allows the cost of the tools to be spread over a longer period of time and gives the mechanic the freedom to choose only those tools that will actually be used.

Tool stores will often be the only source of some of the special tools that are needed, but regardless of where tools are bought, try to avoid cheap ones, especially when buying screwdrivers and sockets, because they won't last very long. The expense involved in replacing cheap tools will eventually be greater than the initial cost of quality tools.

Care and maintenance of tools

Good tools are expensive, so it makes sense to treat them with respect. Keep them clean and in usable condition and store them properly when not in use. Always wipe off any dirt, grease or metal chips before putting them away. Never leave tools lying around in the work area. Upon completion of a job, always check closely under the hood for tools that may have been left there so they won't get lost during a test drive.

Some tools, such as screwdrivers, pliers, wrenches and sockets, can be hung on a panel mounted on the garage or workshop wall, while others should be kept in a tool box or tray. Measuring instruments, gauges, meters, etc. must be carefully stored where they cannot be damaged by weather or impact from other tools.

When tools are used with care and stored properly, they will last a very long time. Even with the best of care, though, tools will wear out if used frequently. When a tool is damaged or worn out, replace it. Subsequent jobs will be safer and more enjoyable if you do.

How to repair damaged threads

Sometimes, the internal threads of a nut or bolt hole can become stripped, usually from overtightening. Stripping threads is an all-too-common occurrence, especially when working with aluminum parts, because aluminum is so soft that it easily strips out.

Usually, external or internal threads are only partially stripped. After they've been cleaned up with a tap or die, they'll still work. Sometimes, however, threads are badly damaged. When this happens, you've got three choices:

1) *Drill and tap the hole to the next suitable oversize and install a larger diameter bolt, screw or stud.*

2) *Drill and tap the hole to accept a threaded plug, then drill and tap the plug to the original screw size. You can also buy a plug already threaded to the original size. Then you simply drill a hole to the specified size, then run the threaded plug into the hole with a bolt and jam nut. Once the plug is fully seated, remove the jam nut and bolt.*

3) *The third method uses a patented thread repair kit like Heli-Coil or Slimsert. These easy-to-use kits are designed to repair damaged threads in straight-through holes and blind holes. Both are available as kits which can handle a variety of sizes and thread patterns. Drill the hole, then tap it with the special included tap. Install the Heli-Coil and the hole is back to its original diameter and thread pitch.*

Regardless of which method you use, be sure to proceed calmly and carefully. A little impatience or carelessness during one of these relatively simple procedures can ruin your whole day's work and cost you a bundle if you wreck an expensive part.

Working facilities

Not to be overlooked when discussing tools is the workshop. If anything more than routine maintenance is to be carried out, some sort of suitable work area is essential.

It is understood, and appreciated, that many home mechanics do not have a good workshop or garage available, and end up removing an engine or doing major repairs outside. It is recommended, however, that the overhaul or repair be completed under the cover of a roof.

A clean, flat workbench or table of comfortable working height is an absolute necessity. The workbench should be equipped with a vise that has a jaw opening of at least four inches.

As mentioned previously, some clean, dry storage space is also required for tools, as well as the lubricants, fluids, cleaning solvents, etc. which soon become necessary.

Sometimes waste oil and fluids, drained from the engine or cooling system during normal maintenance or repairs, present a disposal problem. To avoid pouring them on the ground or into a sewage system, pour the used fluids into large containers, seal them with caps and take them to an authorized disposal site or recycling center. Plastic jugs, such as old antifreeze containers, are ideal for this purpose.

Always keep a supply of old newspapers and clean rags available. Old towels are excellent for mopping up spills. Many mechanics use rolls of paper towels for most work because they are readily available and disposable. To help keep the area under the vehicle clean, a large cardboard box can be cut open and flattened to protect the garage or shop floor.

Whenever working over a painted surface, such as when leaning over a fender to service something under the hood, always cover it with an old blanket or bedspread to protect the finish. Vinyl covered pads, made especially for this purpose, are available at auto parts stores.

Jacking and towing

Jacking

Warning: *The jack supplied with the vehicle should only be used for changing a tire or placing jackstands under the frame. Never work under the vehicle or start the engine while this jack is being used as the only means of support.*

The vehicle should be on level ground. Place the shift lever in Park, if you have an automatic, or Reverse if you have a manual transaxle. Block the wheel diagonally opposite the wheel being changed. Set the parking brake.

Remove the spare tire and jack from stowage. Remove the wheel cover and trim ring (if so equipped) with the tapered end of the lug nut wrench by inserting and twisting the handle and then prying against the back of the wheel cover. Loosen, but do not remove, the lug nuts (one-half turn is sufficient).

Place the scissors-type jack under the side of the vehicle and adjust the jack height until it fits between the notches in the vertical rocker panel flange nearest the wheel to be changed. There is a front and rear jacking point on each side of the vehicle **(see illustration)**.

Turn the jack handle clockwise until the tire clears the ground. Remove the lug nuts and pull the wheel off. Replace it with the spare.

Install the lug nuts with the beveled edges facing in. Tighten them snugly. Don't attempt to tighten them completely until the vehicle is lowered or it could slip off the jack. Turn the jack handle counterclockwise to lower the vehicle. Remove the jack and tighten the lug nuts in a diagonal pattern.

Install the cover (and trim ring, if used) and be sure it's snapped into place all the way around.

Stow the tire, jack and wrench. Unblock the wheels.

Towing

The manufacturer does not recommend towing except with a towing dolly under the front wheels. In an emergency the vehicle can be towed a short distance with a cable or chain attached to one of the towing eyelets located under the front or rear bumpers following the precautions above. The driver must remain in the vehicle to operate the steering and brakes (remember that power steering and power brakes will not work with the engine off).

The jack fits over the rocker panel flange, between the two notches (there are two jacking points on each side of the vehicle)

Booster battery (jump) starting

Observe these precautions when using a booster battery to start a vehicle:

a) *Before connecting the booster battery, make sure the ignition switch is in the Off position.*
b) *Turn off the lights, heater and other electrical loads.*
c) *Your eyes should be shielded. Safety goggles are a good idea.*
d) *Make sure the booster battery is the same voltage as the dead one in the vehicle.*
e) *The two vehicles MUST NOT TOUCH each other!*
f) *Make sure the transaxle is in Neutral (manual) or Park (automatic).*
g) *If the booster battery is not a maintenance-free type, remove the vent caps and lay a cloth over the vent holes.*

Connect the red jumper cable to the positive (+) terminals of each battery **(see illustration)**.

Connect one end of the black jumper cable to the negative (-) terminal of the booster battery. The other end of this cable should be connected to a good ground on the vehicle to be started, such as a bolt or bracket on the body.

Start the engine using the booster battery, then, with the engine running at idle speed, disconnect the jumper cables in the reverse order of connection.

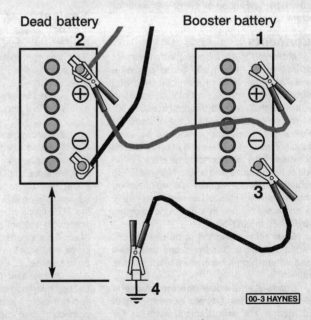

Make the booster battery cable connections in the numerical order shown (note that the negative cable of the booster battery is NOT attached to the negative terminal of the dead battery)

Automotive chemicals and lubricants

A number of automotive chemicals and lubricants are available for use during vehicle maintenance and repair. They include a wide variety of products ranging from cleaning solvents and degreasers to lubricants and protective sprays for rubber, plastic and vinyl.

Cleaners

Carburetor cleaner and choke cleaner is a strong solvent for gum, varnish and carbon. Most carburetor cleaners leave a dry-type lubricant film which will not harden or gum up. Because of this film it is not recommended for use on electrical components.

Brake system cleaner is used to remove brake dust, grease and brake fluid from the brake system, where clean surfaces are absolutely necessary. It leaves no residue and often eliminates brake squeal caused by contaminants.

Electrical cleaner removes oxidation, corrosion and carbon deposits from electrical contacts, restoring full current flow. It can also be used to clean spark plugs, carburetor jets, voltage regulators and other parts where an oil-free surface is desired.

Demoisturants remove water and moisture from electrical components such as alternators, voltage regulators, electrical connectors and fuse blocks. They are non-conductive and non-corrosive.

Degreasers are heavy-duty solvents used to remove grease from the outside of the engine and from chassis components. They can be sprayed or brushed on and, depending on the type, are rinsed off either with water or solvent.

Lubricants

Motor oil is the lubricant formulated for use in engines. It normally contains a wide variety of additives to prevent corrosion and reduce foaming and wear. Motor oil comes in various weights (viscosity ratings) from 0 to 50. The recommended weight of the oil depends on the season, temperature and the demands on the engine. Light oil is used in cold climates and under light load conditions. Heavy oil is used in hot climates and where high loads are encountered. Multi-viscosity oils are designed to have characteristics of both light and heavy oils and are available in a number of weights from 0W-20 to 20W-50.

Gear oil is designed to be used in differentials, manual transmissions and other areas where high-temperature lubrication is required.

Chassis and wheel bearing grease is a heavy grease used where increased loads and friction are encountered, such as for wheel bearings, balljoints, tie-rod ends and universal joints.

High-temperature wheel bearing grease is designed to withstand the extreme temperatures encountered by wheel bearings in disc brake equipped vehicles. It usually contains molybdenum disulfide (moly), which is a dry-type lubricant.

White grease is a heavy grease for metal-to-metal applications where water is a problem. White grease stays soft under both low and high temperatures (usually from -100 to +190-degrees F), and will not wash off or dilute in the presence of water.

Assembly lube is a special extreme pressure lubricant, usually containing moly, used to lubricate high-load parts (such as main and rod bearings and cam lobes) for initial start-up of a new engine. The assembly lube lubricates the parts without being squeezed out or washed away until the engine oiling system begins to function.

Silicone lubricants are used to protect rubber, plastic, vinyl and nylon parts.

Graphite lubricants are used where oils cannot be used due to contamination problems, such as in locks. The dry graphite will lubricate metal parts while remaining uncontaminated by dirt, water, oil or acids. It is electrically conductive and will not foul electrical contacts in locks such as the ignition switch.

Moly penetrants loosen and lubricate frozen, rusted and corroded fasteners and prevent future rusting or freezing.

Heat-sink grease is a special electrically non-conductive grease that is used for mounting electronic ignition modules where it is essential that heat is transferred away from the module.

Sealants

RTV sealant is one of the most widely used gasket compounds. Made from silicone, RTV is air curing, it seals, bonds, waterproofs, fills surface irregularities, remains flexible, doesn't shrink, is relatively easy to remove, and is used as a supplementary sealer with almost all low and medium temperature gaskets.

Anaerobic sealant is much like RTV in that it can be used either to seal gaskets or to form gaskets by itself. It remains flexible, is solvent resistant and fills surface imperfections. The difference between an anaerobic sealant and an RTV-type sealant is in the curing. RTV cures when exposed to air, while an anaerobic sealant cures only in the absence of air. This means that an anaerobic sealant cures only after the assembly of parts, sealing them together.

Thread and pipe sealant is used for sealing hydraulic and pneumatic fittings and vacuum lines. It is usually made from a Teflon compound, and comes in a spray, a paint-on liquid and as a wrap-around tape.

Chemicals

Anti-seize compound prevents seizing, galling, cold welding, rust and corrosion in fasteners. High-temperature ant-seize, usually made with copper and graphite lubricants, is used for exhaust system and exhaust manifold bolts.

Anaerobic locking compounds are used to keep fasteners from vibrating or working loose and cure only after installation, in the absence of air. Medium strength locking compound is used for small nuts, bolts and screws that may be removed later. High-strength locking compound is for large nuts, bolts and studs which aren't removed on a regular basis.

Oil additives range from viscosity index improvers to chemical treatments that claim to reduce internal engine friction. It should be noted that most oil manufacturers caution against using additives with their oils.

Gas additives perform several functions, depending on their chemical makeup. They usually contain solvents that help dissolve gum and varnish that build up on carburetor, fuel injection and intake parts. They also serve to break down carbon deposits that form on the inside surfaces of the combustion chambers. Some additives contain upper cylinder lubricants for valves and piston rings, and others contain chemicals to remove condensation from the gas tank.

Miscellaneous

Brake fluid is specially formulated hydraulic fluid that can withstand the heat and pressure encountered in brake systems. Care must be taken so this fluid does not come in contact with painted surfaces or plastics. An opened container should always be resealed to prevent contamination by water or dirt.

Weatherstrip adhesive is used to bond weatherstripping around doors, windows and trunk lids. It is sometimes used to attach trim pieces.

Undercoating is a petroleum-based, tar-like substance that is designed to protect metal surfaces on the underside of the vehicle from corrosion. It also acts as a sound-deadening agent by insulating the bottom of the vehicle.

Waxes and polishes are used to help protect painted and plated surfaces from the weather. Different types of paint may require the use of different types of wax and polish. Some polishes utilize a chemical or abrasive cleaner to help remove the top layer of oxidized (dull) paint on older vehicles. In recent years many non-wax polishes that contain a wide variety of chemicals such as polymers and silicones have been introduced. These non-wax polishes are usually easier to apply and last longer than conventional waxes and polishes.

Conversion factors

Length (distance)
Inches (in)	X 25.4	= Millimeters (mm)	X 0.0394	= Inches (in)
Feet (ft)	X 0.305	= Meters (m)	X 3.281	= Feet (ft)
Miles	X 1.609	= Kilometers (km)	X 0.621	= Miles

Volume (capacity)
Cubic inches (cu in; in^3)	X 16.387	= Cubic centimeters (cc; cm^3)	X 0.061	= Cubic inches (cu in; in^3)
Imperial pints (Imp pt)	X 0.568	= Liters (l)	X 1.76	= Imperial pints (Imp pt)
Imperial quarts (Imp qt)	X 1.137	= Liters (l)	X 0.88	= Imperial quarts (Imp qt)
Imperial quarts (Imp qt)	X 1.201	= US quarts (US qt)	X 0.833	= Imperial quarts (Imp qt)
US quarts (US qt)	X 0.946	= Liters (l)	X 1.057	= US quarts (US qt)
Imperial gallons (Imp gal)	X 4.546	= Liters (l)	X 0.22	= Imperial gallons (Imp gal)
Imperial gallons (Imp gal)	X 1.201	= US gallons (US gal)	X 0.833	= Imperial gallons (Imp gal)
US gallons (US gal)	X 3.785	= Liters (l)	X 0.264	= US gallons (US gal)

Mass (weight)
Ounces (oz)	X 28.35	= Grams (g)	X 0.035	= Ounces (oz)
Pounds (lb)	X 0.454	= Kilograms (kg)	X 2.205	= Pounds (lb)

Force
Ounces-force (ozf; oz)	X 0.278	= Newtons (N)	X 3.6	= Ounces-force (ozf; oz)
Pounds-force (lbf; lb)	X 4.448	= Newtons (N)	X 0.225	= Pounds-force (lbf; lb)
Newtons (N)	X 0.1	= Kilograms-force (kgf; kg)	X 9.81	= Newtons (N)

Pressure
Pounds-force per square inch (psi; lbf/in^2; lb/in^2)	X 0.070	= Kilograms-force per square centimeter (kgf/cm^2; kg/cm^2)	X 14.223	= Pounds-force per square inch (psi; lbf/in^2; lb/in^2)
Pounds-force per square inch (psi; lbf/in^2; lb/in^2)	X 0.068	= Atmospheres (atm)	X 14.696	= Pounds-force per square inch (psi; lbf/in^2; lb/in^2)
Pounds-force per square inch (psi; lbf/in^2; lb/in^2)	X 0.069	= Bars	X 14.5	= Pounds-force per square inch (psi; lbf/in^2; lb/in^2)
Pounds-force per square inch (psi; lbf/in^2; lb/in^2)	X 6.895	= Kilopascals (kPa)	X 0.145	= Pounds-force per square inch (psi; lbf/in^2; lb/in^2)
Kilopascals (kPa)	X 0.01	= Kilograms-force per square centimeter (kgf/cm^2; kg/cm^2)	X 98.1	= Kilopascals (kPa)

Torque (moment of force)
Pounds-force inches (lbf in; lb in)	X 1.152	= Kilograms-force centimeter (kgf cm; kg cm)	X 0.868	= Pounds-force inches (lbf in; lb in)
Pounds-force inches (lbf in; lb in)	X 0.113	= Newton meters (Nm)	X 8.85	= Pounds-force inches (lbf in; lb in)
Pounds-force inches (lbf in; lb in)	X 0.083	= Pounds-force feet (lbf ft; lb ft)	X 12	= Pounds-force inches (lbf in; lb in)
Pounds-force feet (lbf ft; lb ft)	X 0.138	= Kilograms-force meters (kgf m; kg m)	X 7.233	= Pounds-force feet (lbf ft; lb ft)
Pounds-force feet (lbf ft; lb ft)	X 1.356	= Newton meters (Nm)	X 0.738	= Pounds-force feet (lbf ft; lb ft)
Newton meters (Nm)	X 0.102	= Kilograms-force meters (kgf m; kg m)	X 9.804	= Newton meters (Nm)

Vacuum
Inches mercury (in. Hg)	X 3.377	= Kilopascals (kPa)	X 0.2961	= Inches mercury
Inches mercury (in. Hg)	X 25.4	= Millimeters mercury (mm Hg)	X 0.0394	= Inches mercury

Power
Horsepower (hp)	X 745.7	= Watts (W)	X 0.0013	= Horsepower (hp)

Velocity (speed)
Miles per hour (miles/hr; mph)	X 1.609	= Kilometers per hour (km/hr; kph)	X 0.621	= Miles per hour (miles/hr; mph)

Fuel consumption*
Miles per gallon, Imperial (mpg)	X 0.354	= Kilometers per liter (km/l)	X 2.825	= Miles per gallon, Imperial (mpg)
Miles per gallon, US (mpg)	X 0.425	= Kilometers per liter (km/l)	X 2.352	= Miles per gallon, US (mpg)

Temperature
Degrees Fahrenheit = (°C x 1.8) + 32

Degrees Celsius (Degrees Centigrade; °C) = (°F - 32) x 0.56

*It is common practice to convert from miles per gallon (mpg) to liters/100 kilometers (l/100km), where mpg (Imperial) x l/100 km = 282 and mpg (US) x l/100 km = 235

DECIMALS to MILLIMETERS

Decimal	mm	Decimal	mm
0.001	0.0254	0.500	12.7000
0.002	0.0508	0.510	12.9540
0.003	0.0762	0.520	13.2080
0.004	0.1016	0.530	13.4620
0.005	0.1270	0.540	13.7160
0.006	0.1524	0.550	13.9700
0.007	0.1778	0.560	14.2240
0.008	0.2032	0.570	14.4780
0.009	0.2286	0.580	14.7320
		0.590	14.9860
0.010	0.2540		
0.020	0.5080		
0.030	0.7620		
0.040	1.0160	0.600	15.2400
0.050	1.2700	0.610	15.4940
0.060	1.5240	0.620	15.7480
0.070	1.7780	0.630	16.0020
0.080	2.0320	0.640	16.2560
0.090	2.2860	0.650	16.5100
		0.660	16.7640
0.100	2.5400	0.670	17.0180
0.110	2.7940	0.680	17.2720
0.120	3.0480	0.690	17.5260
0.130	3.3020		
0.140	3.5560		
0.150	3.8100		
0.160	4.0640	0.700	17.7800
0.170	4.3180	0.710	18.0340
0.180	4.5720	0.720	18.2880
0.190	4.8260	0.730	18.5420
		0.740	18.7960
0.200	5.0800	0.750	19.0500
0.210	5.3340	0.760	19.3040
0.220	5.5880	0.770	19.5580
0.230	5.8420	0.780	19.8120
0.240	6.0960	0.790	20.0660
0.250	6.3500		
0.260	6.6040		
0.270	6.8580	0.800	20.3200
0.280	7.1120	0.810	20.5740
0.290	7.3660	0.820	21.8280
		0.830	21.0820
0.300	7.6200	0.840	21.3360
0.310	7.8740	0.850	21.5900
0.320	8.1280	0.860	21.8440
0.330	8.3820	0.870	22.0980
0.340	8.6360	0.880	22.3520
0.350	8.8900	0.890	22.6060
0.360	9.1440		
0.370	9.3980		
0.380	9.6520		
0.390	9.9060		
		0.900	22.8600
0.400	10.1600	0.910	23.1140
0.410	10.4140	0.920	23.3680
0.420	10.6680	0.930	23.6220
0.430	10.9220	0.940	23.8760
0.440	11.1760	0.950	24.1300
0.450	11.4300	0.960	24.3840
0.460	11.6840	0.970	24.6380
0.470	11.9380	0.980	24.8920
0.480	12.1920	0.990	25.1460
0.490	12.4460	1.000	25.4000

FRACTIONS to DECIMALS to MILLIMETERS

Fraction	Decimal	mm	Fraction	Decimal	mm
1/64	0.0156	0.3969	33/64	0.5156	13.0969
1/32	0.0312	0.7938	17/32	0.5312	13.4938
3/64	0.0469	1.1906	35/64	0.5469	13.8906
1/16	0.0625	1.5875	9/16	0.5625	14.2875
5/64	0.0781	1.9844	37/64	0.5781	14.6844
3/32	0.0938	2.3812	19/32	0.5938	15.0812
7/64	0.1094	2.7781	39/64	0.6094	15.4781
1/8	0.1250	3.1750	5/8	0.6250	15.8750
9/64	0.1406	3.5719	41/64	0.6406	16.2719
5/32	0.1562	3.9688	21/32	0.6562	16.6688
11/64	0.1719	4.3656	43/64	0.6719	17.0656
3/16	0.1875	4.7625	11/16	0.6875	17.4625
13/64	0.2031	5.1594	45/64	0.7031	17.8594
7/32	0.2188	5.5562	23/32	0.7188	18.2562
15/64	0.2344	5.9531	47/64	0.7344	18.6531
1/4	0.2500	6.3500	3/4	0.7500	19.0500
17/64	0.2656	6.7469	49/64	0.7656	19.4469
9/32	0.2812	7.1438	25/32	0.7812	19.8438
19/64	0.2969	7.5406	51/64	0.7969	20.2406
5/16	0.3125	7.9375	13/16	0.8125	20.6375
21/64	0.3281	8.3344	53/64	0.8281	21.0344
11/32	0.3438	8.7312	27/32	0.8438	21.4312
23/64	0.3594	9.1281	55/64	0.8594	21.8281
3/8	0.3750	9.5250	7/8	0.8750	22.2250
25/64	0.3906	9.9219	57/64	0.8906	22.6219
13/32	0.4062	10.3188	29/32	0.9062	23.0188
27/64	0.4219	10.7156	59/64	0.9219	23.4156
7/16	0.4375	11.1125	15/16	0.9375	23.8125
29/64	0.4531	11.5094	61/64	0.9531	24.2094
15/32	0.4688	11.9062	31/32	0.9688	24.6062
31/64	0.4844	12.3031	63/64	0.9844	25.0031
1/2	0.5000	12.7000	1	1.0000	25.4000

Safety first!

Regardless of how enthusiastic you may be about getting on with the job at hand, take the time to ensure that your safety is not jeopardized. A moment's lack of attention can result in an accident, as can failure to observe certain simple safety precautions. The possibility of an accident will always exist, and the following points should not be considered a comprehensive list of all dangers. Rather, they are intended to make you aware of the risks and to encourage a safety conscious approach to all work you carry out on your vehicle.

Essential DOs and DON'Ts

DON'T rely on a jack when working under the vehicle. Always use approved jackstands to support the weight of the vehicle and place them under the recommended lift or support points.

DON'T attempt to loosen extremely tight fasteners (i.e. wheel lug nuts) while the vehicle is on a jack - it may fall.

DON'T start the engine without first making sure that the transmission is in Neutral (or Park where applicable) and the parking brake is set.

DON'T remove the radiator cap from a hot cooling system - let it cool or cover it with a cloth and release the pressure gradually.

DON'T attempt to drain the engine oil until you are sure it has cooled to the point that it will not burn you.

DON'T touch any part of the engine or exhaust system until it has cooled sufficiently to avoid burns.

DON'T siphon toxic liquids such as gasoline, antifreeze and brake fluid by mouth, or allow them to remain on your skin.

DON'T inhale brake lining dust - it is potentially hazardous (see *Asbestos* below).

DON'T allow spilled oil or grease to remain on the floor - wipe it up before someone slips on it.

DON'T use loose fitting wrenches or other tools which may slip and cause injury.

DON'T push on wrenches when loosening or tightening nuts or bolts. Always try to pull the wrench toward you. If the situation calls for pushing the wrench away, push with an open hand to avoid scraped knuckles if the wrench should slip.

DON'T attempt to lift a heavy component alone - get someone to help you.

DON'T *rush or take unsafe shortcuts to finish a job.*

DON'T allow children or animals in or around the vehicle while you are working on it.

DO wear eye protection when using power tools such as a drill, sander, bench grinder, etc. and when working under a vehicle.

DO keep loose clothing and long hair well out of the way of moving parts.

DO make sure that any hoist used has a safe working load rating adequate for the job.

DO get someone to check on you periodically when working alone on a vehicle.

DO carry out work in a logical sequence and make sure that everything is correctly assembled and tightened.

DO keep chemicals and fluids tightly capped and out of the reach of children and pets.

DO remember that your vehicle's safety affects that of yourself and others. If in doubt on any point, get professional advice.

Steering, suspension and brakes

These systems are essential to driving safety, so make sure you have a qualified shop or individual check your work. Also, compressed suspension springs can cause injury if released suddenly - be sure to use a spring compressor.

Airbags

Airbags are explosive devices that can **CAUSE** injury if they deploy while you're working on the vehicle. Follow the manufacturer's instructions to disable the airbag whenever you're working in the vicinity of airbag components.

Asbestos

Certain friction, insulating, sealing, and other products - such as brake linings, brake bands, clutch linings, torque converters, gaskets, etc. - may contain asbestos or other hazardous friction material. Extreme care must be taken to avoid inhalation of dust from such products, since it is hazardous to health. If in doubt, assume that they do contain asbestos.

Fire

Remember at all times that gasoline is highly flammable. Never smoke or have any kind of open flame around when working on a vehicle. But the risk does not end there. A spark caused by an electrical short circuit, by two metal surfaces contacting each other, or even by static electricity built up in your body under certain conditions, can ignite gasoline vapors, which in a confined space are highly explosive. Do not, under any circumstances, use gasoline for cleaning parts. Use an approved safety solvent.

Always disconnect the battery ground (-) cable at the battery before working on any part of the fuel system or electrical system. Never risk spilling fuel on a hot engine or exhaust component. It is strongly recommended that a fire extinguisher suitable for use on fuel and electrical fires be kept handy in the garage or workshop at all times. Never try to extinguish a fuel or electrical fire with water.

Fumes

Certain fumes are highly toxic and can quickly cause unconsciousness and even death if inhaled to any extent. Gasoline vapor falls into this category, as do the vapors from some cleaning solvents. Any draining or pouring of such volatile fluids should be done in a well ventilated area.

When using cleaning fluids and solvents, read the instructions on the container carefully. Never use materials from unmarked containers.

Never run the engine in an enclosed space, such as a garage. Exhaust fumes contain carbon monoxide, which is extremely poisonous. If you need to run the engine, always do so in the open air, or at least have the rear of the vehicle outside the work area.

The battery

Never create a spark or allow a bare light bulb near a battery. They normally give off a certain amount of hydrogen gas, which is highly explosive.

Always disconnect the battery ground (-) cable at the battery before working on the fuel or electrical systems.

If possible, loosen the filler caps or cover when charging the battery from an external source (this does not apply to sealed or maintenance-free batteries). Do not charge at an excessive rate or the battery may burst.

Take care when adding water to a non maintenance-free battery and when carrying a battery. The electrolyte, even when diluted, is very corrosive and should not be allowed to contact clothing or skin.

Always wear eye protection when cleaning the battery to prevent the caustic deposits from entering your eyes.

Household current

When using an electric power tool, inspection light, etc., which operates on household current, always make sure that the tool is correctly connected to its plug and that, where necessary, it is properly grounded. Do not use such items in damp conditions and, again, do not create a spark or apply excessive heat in the vicinity of fuel or fuel vapor.

Secondary ignition system voltage

A severe electric shock can result from touching certain parts of the ignition system (such as the spark plug wires) when the engine is running or being cranked, particularly if components are damp or the insulation is defective. In the case of an electronic ignition system, the secondary system voltage is much higher and could prove fatal.

Hydrofluoric acid

This extremely corrosive acid is formed when certain types of synthetic rubber, found in some O-rings, oil seals, fuel hoses, etc. are exposed to temperatures above 750-degrees F (400-degrees C). The rubber changes into a charred or sticky substance containing the acid. *Once formed, the acid remains dangerous for years. If it gets onto the skin, it may be necessary to amputate the limb concerned.*

When dealing with a vehicle which has suffered a fire, or with components salvaged from such a vehicle, wear protective gloves and discard them after use.

Troubleshooting

Contents

This section provides an easy reference guide to the more common problems which may occur during the operation of your vehicle. These problems and their possible causes are grouped under headings denoting various components or systems, such as Engine, Cooling system, etc. They also refer you to the chapter and/or section which deals with the problem.

Remember that successful troubleshooting is not a mysterious art practiced only by professional mechanics. It is simply the result of the right knowledge combined with an intelligent, systematic approach to the problem. Always work by a process of elimination, starting with the simplest solution and working through to the most complex - and never overlook the obvious. Anyone can run the gas tank dry or leave the lights on overnight, so don't assume that you are exempt from such oversights.

Finally, always establish a clear idea of why a problem has occurred and take steps to ensure that it doesn't happen again. If the electrical system fails because of a poor connection, check the other connections in the system to make sure that they don't fail as well. If a particular fuse continues to blow, find out why - don't just replace one fuse after another. Remember, failure of a small component can often be indicative of potential failure or incorrect functioning of a more important component or system.

Engine

1 Engine will not rotate when attempting to start

1 Battery terminal connections loose or corroded (Chapter 1).
2 Battery discharged or faulty (Chapter 1).
3 Automatic transaxle not completely engaged in Park (Chapter 7) or clutch not completely depressed (Chapter 8).
4 Broken, loose or disconnected wiring in the starting circuit (Chapters 5 and 12).
5 Starter motor pinion jammed in flywheel ring gear (Chapter 5).
6 Starter solenoid faulty (Chapter 5).
7 Starter motor faulty (Chapter 5).
8 Ignition switch faulty (Chapter 12).
9 Starter pinion or flywheel teeth worn or broken (Chapter 5).

2 Engine rotates but will not start

1 Fuel tank empty.
2 Battery discharged (engine rotates slowly) (Chapter 5).
3 Leaking fuel injector(s), faulty fuel pump, pressure regulator, etc. (Chapter 4).
4 Fuel not reaching fuel rail (Chapter 4).
5 Ignition components damp or damaged (Chapter 5).
6 Worn, faulty or incorrectly gapped spark plugs (Chapter 1).

7 Broken, loose or disconnected wires at the ignition coil(s) or faulty coil(s) (Chapter 5).
8 Faulty camshaft or crankshaft position sensor (Chapter 6).
9 Theft Deterrent System problem.

3 Engine hard to start when cold

1 Battery discharged or low (Chapter 1).
2 Malfunctioning fuel system (Chapter 4).
3 Injector(s) leaking (Chapter 4).
4 Faulty coolant temperature sensor (Chapter 6).

4 Engine hard to start when hot

1 Air filter clogged (Chapter 1).
2 Fuel not reaching the fuel injection system (Chapter 4).
3 Corroded battery connections, especially ground (Chapter 1).

5 Starter motor noisy or excessively rough in engagement

1 Pinion or flywheel gear teeth worn or broken (Chapter 5).
2 Starter motor mounting bolts loose or missing (Chapter 5).

6 Engine starts but stops immediately

1 Loose or faulty electrical connections at coil(s) or alternator (Chapter 5).
2 Insufficient fuel reaching the fuel injector(s) (Chapters 1 and 4).
3 Vacuum leak at the gasket between the intake manifold/plenum and throttle body (Chapters 1 and 4).

7 Oil puddle under engine

1 Oil pan gasket and/or oil pan drain bolt washer leaking (Chapter 2).
2 Oil pressure sending unit leaking (Chapter 2).
3 Valve cover leaking (Chapter 2).
4 Engine oil seals leaking (Chapter 2).
5 Timing chain cover leaking (Chapter 2).

8 Engine lopes while idling or idles erratically

1 Vacuum leakage (Chapters 2 and 4).
2 Air filter clogged (Chapter 1).
3 Fuel pump not delivering sufficient fuel to the fuel injection system (Chapter 4).
4 Leaking head gasket (Chapter 2).

5 Timing chain and/or sprockets worn (Chapter 2).
6 Camshaft lobes worn (Chapter 2).

9 Engine misses at idle speed

1 Spark plugs worn or not gapped properly (Chapter 1).
2 Faulty ignition coil (Chapter 5).
3 Vacuum leaks (Chapter 1).
4 Fault in engine management system (Chapter 6).
5 Uneven or low compression (Chapter 2).

10 Engine misses throughout driving speed range

1 Fuel filter clogged and/or impurities in the fuel system (Chapter 1).
2 Low fuel output at the injector(s) (Chapter 4).
3 Faulty or incorrectly gapped spark plugs (Chapter 1).
4 Fault in engine management system (Chapter 6).
5 Faulty emission system components (Chapter 6).
6 Low or uneven cylinder compression pressures (Chapter 2).
7 Weak or faulty ignition system (Chapter 5).
8 Vacuum leak in fuel injection system, intake manifold/plenum, air control valve or vacuum hoses (Chapter 4).

11 Engine stumbles on acceleration

1 Spark plugs fouled (Chapter 1).
2 Fuel injection system faulty (Chapter 4).
3 Fuel filter clogged (Chapters 1 and 4).
4 Fault in engine management system (Chapter 6).
5 Intake manifold or plenum air leak (Chapters 2 and 4).

12 Engine surges while holding accelerator steady

1 Intake air leak (Chapter 4).
2 Fuel pump faulty (Chapter 4).
3 Loose fuel injector wire harness connectors (Chapter 4).
4 Defective ECM or information sensor (Chapter 6).

13 Engine stalls

1 Fuel filter clogged and/or water and impurities in the fuel system (Chapter 4).
2 Ignition components damp or damaged (Chapter 5).
3 Faulty emissions system components (Chapter 6).

4   Faulty or incorrectly gapped spark plugs (Chapter 1).
5   Vacuum leak in the fuel injection system, intake manifold or vacuum hoses (Chapters 2 and 4).
6   Valve clearances incorrectly set (Chapter 1).

14   Engine lacks power

1   Fault in engine management system (Chapter 6).
2   Faulty or incorrectly gapped spark plugs (Chapter 1).
3   Fuel injection system malfunction (Chapter 4).
4   Faulty coil(s) (Chapter 5).
5   Brakes binding (Chapter 9).
6   Automatic transaxle fluid level incorrect (Chapter 1).
7   Clutch slipping (Chapter 8).
8   Fuel filter clogged and/or impurities in the fuel system (Chapter 4).
9   Low or uneven cylinder compression pressures (Chapter 2).
10   Obstructed exhaust system (Chapter 4).

15   Engine backfires

1   Emission control system not functioning properly (Chapter 6).
2   Fault in engine management system (Chapter 6).
3   Faulty secondary ignition system (cracked spark plug insulator, faulty ignition coil) (Chapters 1 and 5).
4   Fuel injection system malfunction (Chapter 4).
5   Vacuum leak at fuel injector(s), intake manifold, air control valve or vacuum hoses (Chapters 2 and 4).
6   Valve clearances incorrectly set and/or valves sticking (Chapter 1).

16   Pinging or knocking engine sounds during acceleration or uphill

1   Incorrect grade of fuel.
2   Fault in engine management system (Chapter 6).
3   Fuel injection system faulty (Chapter 4).
4   Improper or damaged spark plugs (Chapter 1).
5   Vacuum leak (Chapters 2 and 4).
6   Defective knock sensor (Chapter 6).

17   Engine runs with oil pressure light on

1   Low oil level (Chapter 1).
2   Idle rpm below specification (Chapter 4).
3   Short in wiring circuit (Chapter 12).

4   Faulty oil pressure sender (Chapter 2).
5   Worn engine bearings and/or oil pump (Chapter 2).

18   Engine diesels (continues to run) after switching off

1   Excessive engine operating temperature (Chapter 3).
2   Fault in engine management system (Chapter 6).

Engine electrical system

19   Battery will not hold a charge

1   Drivebelt or tensioner defective (Chapter 1).
2   Battery electrolyte level low (Chapter 1).
3   Battery terminals loose or corroded (Chapter 1).
4   Alternator not charging properly (Chapter 5).
5   Loose, broken or faulty wiring in the charging circuit (Chapter 5).
6   Short in vehicle wiring (Chapter 12).
7   Internally defective battery (Chapters 1 and 5).

20   Alternator light fails to go out

1   Faulty alternator or charging circuit (Chapter 5).
2   Alternator drivebelt defective or out of adjustment (Chapter 1).
3   Alternator voltage regulator inoperative (Chapter 5).

21   Alternator light fails to come on when key is turned on

1   Warning light bulb defective (Chapter 12).
2   Fault in the printed circuit, dash wiring or bulb holder (Chapter 12).

Fuel system

22   Excessive fuel consumption

1   Dirty or clogged air filter element (Chapter 1).
2   Fault in engine management system (Chapter 6).
3   Emissions systems not functioning properly (Chapter 6).
4   Fuel injection system not functioning properly (Chapter 4).

5   Low tire pressure or incorrect tire size (Chapter 1).

23   Fuel leakage and/or fuel odor

1   Leaking fuel feed or return line (Chapters 1 and 4).
2   Tank overfilled.
3   Evaporative canister filter clogged (Chapters 1 and 6).
4   Fuel injection system not functioning properly (Chapter 4).

Cooling system

24   Overheating

1   Insufficient coolant in system (Chapter 1).
2   Water pump defective (Chapter 3).
3   Radiator core blocked or grille restricted (Chapter 3).
4   Thermostat faulty (Chapter 3).
5   Electric coolant fan blades broken or cracked (Chapter 3).
6   Radiator cap not maintaining proper pressure (Chapter 3).
7   Fault in engine management system (Chapter 6).

25   Overcooling

1   Faulty thermostat (Chapter 3).
2   Inaccurate temperature gauge sending unit (Chapter 3)

26   External coolant leakage

1   Deteriorated/damaged hoses; loose clamps (Chapters 1 and 3).
2   Water pump defective (Chapter 3).
3   Leakage from radiator core or coolant reservoir bottle (Chapter 3).
4   Engine drain or water jacket core plugs leaking (Chapter 2).

27   Internal coolant leakage

1   Leaking cylinder head gasket (Chapter 2).
2   Cracked cylinder bore or cylinder head (Chapter 2).

28   Coolant loss

1   Too much coolant in system (Chapter 1).
2   Coolant boiling away because of overheating (Chapter 3).
3   Internal or external leakage (Chapter 3).
4   Faulty radiator cap (Chapter 3).

29 Poor coolant circulation

1 Inoperative water pump (Chapter 3).
2 Restriction in cooling system (Chapters 1 and 3).
3 Drivebelt or tensioner defective (Chapter 1).
4 Thermostat sticking (Chapter 3).

Clutch

30 Pedal travels to floor - no pressure or very little resistance

1 Master or release cylinder faulty (Chapter 8).
2 Hose/pipe burst or leaking (Chapter 8).
3 Connections leaking (Chapter 8).
4 No fluid in reservoir (Chapter 8).
5 If fluid level in reservoir rises as pedal is depressed, master cylinder center valve seal is faulty (Chapter 8).
6 If there is fluid on dust seal at master cylinder, piston primary seal is leaking (Chapter 8).
7 Broken release bearing or fork (Chapter 8).

31 Fluid in area of master cylinder dust cover and on pedal

Rear seal failure in master cylinder (Chapter 8).

32 Fluid on release cylinder

Release cylinder plunger seal faulty (Chapter 8).

33 Pedal feels spongy when depressed

Air in system (Chapter 8).

34 Unable to select gears

1 Faulty transaxle (Chapter 7).
2 Faulty clutch disc (Chapter 8).
3 Release lever and bearing not assembled properly (Chapter 8).
4 Faulty pressure plate (Chapter 8).
5 Pressure plate-to-flywheel bolts loose (Chapter 8).

35 Clutch slips (engine speed increases with no increase in vehicle speed)

1 Clutch plate worn (Chapter 8).

2 Clutch plate is oil soaked by leaking rear main seal (Chapter 8).
3 Clutch plate not seated. It may take 30 or 40 normal starts for a new one to seat.
4 Warped pressure plate or flywheel (Chapter 8).
5 Weak diaphragm spring (Chapter 8).
6 Clutch plate overheated. Allow to cool.

36 Grabbing (chattering) as clutch is engaged

1 Oil on clutch plate lining, burned or glazed facings (Chapter 8).
2 Worn or loose engine or transaxle mounts (Chapters 2 and 7).
3 Worn splines on clutch plate hub (Chapter 8).
4 Warped pressure plate or flywheel (Chapter 8).
5 Burned or smeared resin on flywheel or pressure plate (Chapter 8).

37 Transaxle rattling (clicking)

1 Release lever loose (Chapter 8).
2 Clutch plate damper spring failure (Chapter 8).
3 Low engine idle speed (Chapter 1).

38 Noise in clutch area

1 Release fork improperly installed (Chapter 8).
2 Faulty bearing (Chapter 8).

39 Clutch pedal stays on floor

1 Clutch master cylinder piston binding in bore (Chapter 8).
2 Broken release bearing or fork (Chapter 8).

40 High pedal effort

1 Piston binding in bore (Chapter 8).
2 Pressure plate faulty (Chapter 8).
3 Incorrect size master or release cylinder (Chapter 8).

Manual transaxle

41 Knocking noise at low speeds

1 Worn driveaxle constant velocity (CV) joints (Chapter 8).
2 Worn side gear shaft counterbore in differential case (Chapter 7A).*

42 Noise most pronounced when turning

Differential gear noise (Chapter 7A).*

43 Clunk on acceleration or deceleration

1 Loose engine or transaxle mounts (Chapters 2 and 7A).
2 Worn differential pinion shaft in case.*
3 Worn side gear shaft counterbore in differential case (Chapter 7A).*
4 Worn or damaged driveaxle inner CV joints (Chapter 8).

44 Clicking noise in turns

Worn or damaged outer CV joint (Chapter 8).

45 Vibration

1 Rough wheel bearing (Chapters 1 and 10).
2 Damaged driveaxle (Chapter 8).
3 Out of round tires (Chapter 1).
4 Tire out of balance (Chapters 1 and 10).
5 Worn CV joint (Chapter 8).

46 Noisy in neutral with engine running

1 Damaged input gear bearing (Chapter 7A).*
2 Damaged clutch release bearing (Chapter 8).

47 Noisy in one particular gear

1 Damaged or worn constant mesh gears (Chapter 7A).*
2 Damaged or worn synchronizers (Chapter 7A).*
3 Bent reverse fork (Chapter 7A).*
4 Damaged fourth speed gear or output gear (Chapter 7A).*
5 Worn or damaged reverse idler gear or idler bushing (Chapter 7A).*

48 Noisy in all gears

1 Insufficient lubricant (Chapters 1 and 7A).
2 Damaged or worn bearings (Chapter 7A).*
3 Worn or damaged input gear shaft and/or output gear shaft (Chapter 7A).*

49 Slips out of gear

1   Worn or improperly adjusted linkage (Chapter 7A).
2   Transaxle loose on engine (Chapter 7A).
3   Shift linkage does not work freely, binds (Chapter 7A).
4   Input gear bearing retainer broken or loose (Chapter 7A).*
5   Worn shift fork (Chapter 7A).*

50 Leaks lubricant

1   Side gear shaft seals worn (Chapter 7).
2   Excessive amount of lubricant in transaxle (Chapters 1 and 7A).
3   Loose or broken input gear shaft bearing retainer (Chapter 7A).*
4   Input gear bearing retainer O-ring and/or lip seal damaged (Chapter 7A).*

51 Locked in gear

Lock pin or interlock pin missing (Chapter 7A).*

Although the corrective action necessary to remedy the symptoms described is beyond the scope of this manual, the above information should be helpful in isolating the cause of the condition so that the owner can communicate clearly with a professional mechanic.

Automatic transaxle

Note: *Due to the complexity of the automatic transaxle, it is difficult for the home mechanic to properly diagnose and service this component. For problems other than the following, the vehicle should be taken to a dealer or transaxle shop.*

52 Fluid leakage

1   Automatic transaxle fluid is a deep red color. Fluid leaks should not be confused with engine oil, which can easily be blown onto the transaxle by air flow.
2   To pinpoint a leak, first remove all built-up dirt and grime from the transaxle housing with degreasing agents and/or steam cleaning. Then drive the vehicle at low speeds so air flow will not blow the leak far from its source. Raise the vehicle and determine where the leak is coming from. Common areas of leakage are:
a) *Pan (Chapters 1 and 7)*
b) *Dipstick tube (Chapters 1 and 7)*
c) *Transaxle oil lines (Chapter 7)*
d) *Speed sensor (Chapter 7)*
e) *Differential drain plug (Chapters 1 and 7B)*

53 Transaxle fluid brown or has a burned smell

Transaxle fluid overheated (Chapter 1).

54 General shift mechanism problems

1   Chapter 7, Part B, deals with checking and adjusting the shift linkage on automatic transaxles. Common problems which may be attributed to poorly adjusted linkage are:
a) *Engine starting in gears other than Park or Neutral.*
b) *Indicator on shifter pointing to a gear other than the one actually being used.*
c) *Vehicle moves when in Park.*
2   Refer to Chapter 7B for the shift linkage adjustment procedure.

55 Transaxle will not downshift with accelerator pedal pressed to the floor

Problem with the transmission electronic control system (Chapter 7B).

56 Engine will start in gears other than Park or Neutral

Neutral start switch malfunctioning (Chapter 7B).

57 Transaxle slips, shifts roughly, is noisy or has no drive in forward or reverse gears

There are many probable causes for the above problems, but the home mechanic should be concerned with only one possibility - fluid level. Before taking the vehicle to a repair shop, check the level and condition of the fluid as described in Chapter 1. Correct the fluid level as necessary or change the fluid and filter if needed. If the problem persists, have a professional diagnose the cause.

Driveaxles

58 Clicking noise in turns

Worn or damaged outboard CV joint (Chapter 8).

59 Shudder or vibration during acceleration

1   Excessive toe-in (Chapter 10).

2   Incorrect spring heights (Chapter 10).
3   Worn or damaged inboard or outboard CV joints (Chapter 8).
4   Sticking inboard CV joint assembly (Chapter 8).

60 Vibration at highway speeds

1   Out of balance front wheels and/or tires (Chapters 1 and 10).
2   Out of round front tires (Chapters 1 and 10).
3   Worn CV joint(s) (Chapter 8).

Brakes

Note: *Before assuming that a brake problem exists, make sure that:*
a) *The tires are in good condition and properly inflated (Chapter 1).*
b) *The front end alignment is correct (Chapter 10).*
c) *The vehicle is not loaded with weight in an unequal manner.*

61 Vehicle pulls to one side during braking

1   Incorrect tire pressures (Chapter 1).
2   Front end out of alignment (have the front end aligned).
3   Front or rear tires not matched to one another.
4   Restricted brake lines or hoses (Chapter 9).
5   Malfunctioning drum brake or caliper assembly (Chapter 9).
6   Loose suspension parts (Chapter 10).
7   Excessive wear of brake shoe or pad material or disc/drum on one side.

62 Noise (high-pitched squeal when the brakes are applied)

Disc brake pads worn out. The noise comes from the wear sensor rubbing against the disc (does not apply to all vehicles). Replace pads with new ones immediately (Chapter 9).

63 Brake roughness or chatter (pedal pulsates)

1   Excessive lateral runout (Chapter 9).
2   Uneven pad wear (Chapter 9).
3   Defective disc (Chapter 9).

64 Excessive brake pedal effort required to stop vehicle

1   Malfunctioning power brake booster (Chapter 9).

2 Partial system failure (Chapter 9).
3 Excessively worn pads or shoes (Chapter 9).
4 Piston in caliper or wheel cylinder stuck or sluggish (Chapter 9).
5 Brake pads or shoes contaminated with oil or grease (Chapter 9).
6 New pads or shoes installed and not yet seated. It will take a while for the new material to seat against the disc or drum.

65 Excessive brake pedal travel

1 Partial brake system failure (Chapter 9).
2 Insufficient fluid in master cylinder (Chapters 1 and 9).
3 Air trapped in system (Chapters 1 and 9).

66 Dragging brakes

1 Incorrect adjustment of brake light switch (Chapter 9).
2 Master cylinder pistons not returning correctly (Chapter 9).
3 Restricted brakes lines or hoses (Chapters 1 and 9).
4 Incorrect parking brake adjustment (Chapter 9).

67 Grabbing or uneven braking action

1 Malfunction of proportioning valve (Chapter 9).
2 Malfunction of power brake booster unit (Chapter 9).
3 Binding brake pedal mechanism (Chapter 9).

68 Brake pedal feels spongy when depressed

1 Air in hydraulic lines (Chapter 9).
2 Master cylinder mounting bolts loose (Chapter 9).
3 Master cylinder defective (Chapter 9).

69 Brake pedal travels to the floor with little resistance

1 Little or no fluid in the master cylinder reservoir caused by leaking caliper piston(s) (Chapter 9).
2 Loose, damaged or disconnected brake lines (Chapter 9).

70 Parking brake does not hold

Parking brake linkage improperly adjusted (Chapters 1 and 9).

Suspension and steering systems

Note: *Before attempting to diagnose the suspension and steering systems, perform the following preliminary checks:*

a) *Tires for wrong pressure and uneven wear.*
b) *Steering universal joints from the column to the rack and pinion for loose connectors or wear.*
c) *Front and rear suspension and the rack and pinion assembly for loose or damaged parts.*
d) *Out-of-round or out-of-balance tires, bent rims and loose and/or rough wheel bearings.*

71 Vehicle pulls to one side

1 Mismatched or uneven tires (Chapter 10).
2 Broken or sagging springs (Chapter 10).
3 Wheel alignment (Chapter 10).
4 Front brake dragging (Chapter 9).

72 Abnormal or excessive tire wear

1 Wheel alignment (Chapter 10).
2 Sagging or broken springs (Chapter 10).
3 Tire out of balance (Chapter 10).
4 Worn strut or shock absorber (Chapter 10).
5 Overloaded vehicle.
6 Tires not rotated regularly.

73 Wheel makes a thumping noise

1 Blister or bump on tire (Chapter 10).
2 Improper strut or shock absorber action (Chapter 10).

74 Shimmy, shake or vibration

1 Tire or wheel out-of-balance or out-of-round (Chapter 10).
2 Loose or worn wheel bearings (Chapters 1, 8 and 10).
3 Worn tie-rod ends (Chapter 10).
4 Worn balljoints (Chapters 1 and 10).
5 Excessive wheel runout (Chapter 10).
6 Blister or bump on tire (Chapter 10).
7 Loose wheel lug nuts.

75 Hard steering

1 Lack of lubrication at balljoints, tie-rod ends and rack and pinion assembly (Chapter 10).
2 Front wheel alignment (Chapter 10).
3 Low tire pressure(s) (Chapters 1 and 10).

76 Poor returnability of steering to center

1 Lack of lubrication at balljoints and tie-rod ends (Chapter 10).
2 Binding in balljoints (Chapter 10).
3 Binding in steering column (Chapter 10).
4 Lack of lubricant in steering gear assembly (Chapter 10).
5 Front wheel alignment (Chapter 10).

77 Abnormal noise at the front end

1 Lack of lubrication at balljoints and tie-rod ends (Chapters 1 and 10).
2 Damaged strut mounting (Chapter 10).
3 Worn control arm bushings or tie-rod ends (Chapter 10).
4 Loose stabilizer bar (Chapter 10).
5 Loose wheel nuts.
6 Loose suspension bolts (Chapter 10)

78 Wander or poor steering stability

1 Mismatched or uneven tires (Chapter 10).
2 Lack of lubrication at balljoints and tie-rod ends (Chapters 1 and 10).
3 Worn strut assemblies (Chapter 10).
4 Loose stabilizer bar (Chapter 10).
5 Broken or sagging springs (Chapter 10).
6 Wheels out of alignment (Chapter 10).

79 Erratic steering when braking

1 Wheel bearings worn (Chapter 10).
2 Broken or sagging springs (Chapter 10).
3 Leaking wheel cylinder or caliper (Chapter 9).
4 Warped discs or drums (Chapter 9).

80 Excessive pitching and/or rolling around corners or during braking

1 Loose stabilizer bar (Chapter 10).
2 Worn strut/shock absorber or mountings (Chapter 10).
3 Broken or sagging springs (Chapter 10).
4 Overloaded vehicle.

81 Suspension bottoms

1 Overloaded vehicle.
2 Worn struts or shock absorbers (Chapter 10).
3 Incorrect, broken or sagging springs (Chapter 10).

82 Cupped tires

1 Front wheel or rear wheel alignment

(Chapter 10).
2   Worn struts or shock absorbers (Chapter 10).
3   Wheel bearings worn (Chapter 10).
4   Excessive tire or wheel runout (Chapter 10).
5   Worn balljoints (Chapter 10).

83 Excessive tire wear on outside edge

1   Inflation pressures incorrect (Chapter 1).
2   Excessive speed in turns.
3   Front end alignment incorrect (excessive toe-in). Have professionally aligned.
4   Suspension arm bent or twisted (Chapter 10).

84 Excessive tire wear on inside edge

1   Inflation pressures incorrect (Chapter 1).
2   Front end alignment incorrect (toe-out). Have professionally aligned.
3   Loose or damaged steering components (Chapter 10).

85 Tire tread worn in one place

1   Tires out of balance.
2   Damaged or buckled wheel. Inspect and replace if necessary.
3   Defective tire (Chapter 1).

86 Excessive play or looseness in steering system

1   Wheel bearing(s) worn (Chapter 10).
2   Tie-rod end loose (Chapter 10).
3   Steering gear loose or worn (Chapter 10).
4   Worn or loose steering intermediate shaft (Chapter 10).

87 Rattling or clicking noise in steering gear

1   Steering gear loose (Chapter 10).
2   Steering gear defective.

Notes

Notes

Chapter 1
Tune-up and routine maintenance

Contents

Specifications

Recommended lubricants and fluids

Note: *Listed here are manufacturer recommendations at the time this manual was written. Manufacturers occasionally upgrade their fluid and lubricant specifications, so check with your local auto parts store for current recommendations.*

Engine oil

Type .... API "Certified for gasoline engines"

Viscosity .... See accompanying charts

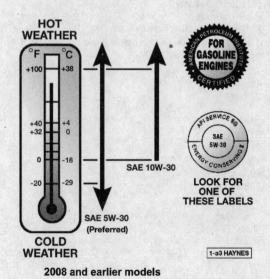

2008 and earlier models

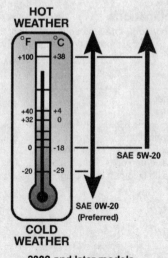

2009 and later models

Recommended engine oil viscosity

Recommended lubricants and fluids

Fuel	Unleaded gasoline, 87 octane or higher
Engine coolant	Toyota Genuine Long Life Coolant or equivalent
Automatic transaxle fluid	Toyota ATF Type T-IV automatic transmission fluid
Manual transaxle lubricant	API GL-5 75W-90 gear oil
Brake fluid	DOT 3 brake fluid
Clutch fluid	DOT 3 brake fluid
Power steering system	DEXRON III automatic transmission fluid

Capacities*

Engine oil (with filter change)	
2008 and earlier models	3.9 qts
2009 and later models	4.4 qts
Coolant	6.9 qts
Transaxle (drain and refill)	
Automatic	3.2 qts
Manual	2.0 to 2.6 qts

*All capacities approximate. Add as necessary to bring up to appropriate level.

Ignition system

Spark plug type	
2008 and earlier models	Denso SK16R11 or NGK IFR5-A11
2009 and later models	SC20HR11
Gap (all)	0.043 inch
Firing order	1-3-4-2

Cooling system

Thermostat rating fully open	203-degrees F

Clutch pedal

Freeplay	3/16 to 5/8 inch
Height	5.3 to 5.7 inches

FRONT OF VEHICLE ↓

①② ③ ④

92036-2B SPECS HAYNES

Cylinder numbering diagram

Brakes

Disc brake pad thickness (minimum)	3/32 inch
Drum brake shoe lining thickness (minimum)	1/16 inch
Parking brake adjustment	6 to 9 clicks

Suspension and steering

Steering wheel freeplay limit	1.2 inches
Balljoint allowable movement	0 inch

Engine

Valve clearance (cold) (2008 and earlier models only)	
Intake	0.006 to 0.010 inch
Exhaust	0.010 to 0.014 inch

Torque specifications

Ft-lbs (unless otherwise indicated)

Note: *One foot-pound (ft-lb) of torque is equivalent to 12 inch-pounds (in-lbs) of torque. Torque values below approximately 15 ft-lbs are expressed in inch-pounds, since most foot-pound torque wrenches are not accurate at these smaller values.*

Wheel lug nuts	76
Spark plugs	18
Seat bolts/nuts	27
Drivebelt tensioner	
To cylinder head	21
To block	51
Engine oil pan drain plug	27
Engine oil filter cap (2009 and later models)	18
Automatic transaxle pan bolts	48 in-lbs
Automatic transaxle fluid pan drain plug	156 in-lbs

Typical engine compartment components (engine cover removed)

1	Engine oil dipstick	6	Ignition coils	11	Battery
2	Drivebelt	7	PCV valve	12	Automatic transaxle dipstick
3	Fuse/relay block	8	Oil filler cap	13	Coolant reservoir
4	Windshield washer fluid reservoir	9	Brake fluid reservoir	14	Radiator cap
5	Power steering fluid reservoir	10	Air filter housing	15	Upper radiator hose

Typical engine compartment underside components

1	Driveaxle boot	4	Steering gear boot	7	Radiator drain fitting
2	Automatic transaxle drain plug	5	Engine oil drain plug	8	Engine oil filter
3	Catalytic converter	6	Front suspension strut unit	9	Front disc brake caliper

Typical rear underside components

1	Gas tank filler pipe	5	Gas tank
2	Muffler	6	Rear brake assembly
3	Shock absorber/coil spring assembly	7	Rear axle beam
4	Exhaust system		

1 Toyota Corolla Maintenance schedule

The maintenance intervals in this manual are provided with the assumption that you, not the dealer, will be doing the work. These are the minimum maintenance intervals recommended by the factory for vehicles that are driven daily. If you wish to keep your vehicle in peak condition at all times, you may wish to perform some of these procedures even more often. Because frequent maintenance enhances the efficiency, performance and resale value of your car, we encourage you to do so. If you drive in dusty areas, tow a trailer, idle or drive at low speeds for extended periods or drive for short distances (less than four miles) in below freezing temperatures, shorter intervals are also recommended.

When your vehicle is new, it should be serviced by a factory authorized dealer service department to protect the factory warranty. In many cases, the initial maintenance check is done at no cost to the owner.

Every 250 miles or weekly, whichever comes first

Check the engine oil level (Section 4)
Check the engine coolant level (Section 4)
Check the windshield washer fluid level (Section 4)
Check the brake fluid level (Section 4)
Check the power steering fluid level (Section 4)
Check the automatic transaxle fluid level (Section 4)
Check the tires and tire pressures (Section 5)

Every 3000 miles or 3 months, whichever comes first

All items listed above plus:
Change the engine oil and oil filter (Section 6)

Every 7500 miles or 6 months, whichever comes first

Inspect (and replace, if necessary) the windshield wiper blades (Section 7)
Check the clutch pedal for proper freeplay (Section 8)
Check and service the battery (Section 9)
Check the engine drivebelt (Section 10)
Inspect (and replace if, necessary) all underhood hoses (Section 11)
Check the cooling system (Section 12)
Rotate the tires (Section 13)
Check the seat belts (Section 14)

Every 15,000 miles or 12 months, whichever comes first

All items listed above plus:
Inspect the brake system (Section 15)*
Replace the air filter (Section 16)
Inspect the fuel system (Section 17)
Check the manual transaxle lubricant level (Section 18)
Inspect the suspension and steering components (Section 19)*

Check the driveaxle boots (Section 19)
Replace the cabin air filter (Section 20)

Every 30,000 miles or 24 months, whichever comes first

All items listed above plus:
Change the brake fluid (Section 21)
Check (and replace, if necessary) the spark plugs (Section 22)
Service the cooling system (drain, flush and refill) (Section 23)
Inspect the evaporative emissions control system (Section 24)
Inspect the exhaust system (Section 25)
Change the automatic transaxle fluid and filter and differential lubricant (Section 26)**
Change the manual transaxle lubricant (Section 27)**
Check and replace if necessary the PCV valve (Section 28)

Every 60,000 miles or 48 months, whichever comes first

Check and adjust the valve clearances (2008 and earlier models) (Section 29)

This item is affected by "severe" operating conditions as described below. If your vehicle is operated under "severe" conditions, perform all maintenance indicated with an asterisk (*) at 3000 mile/3 month intervals. Severe conditions are indicated if you mainly operate your vehicle under one or more of the following conditions:

Operating in dusty areas
Towing a trailer
Idling for extended periods and/or low speed operation
Operating when outside temperatures remain below freezing and when most trips are less than 4 miles

** If operated under one or more of the following conditions, change the manual or automatic transaxle fluid and differential lubricant every 15,000 miles:

In heavy city traffic where the outside temperature regularly reaches 90-degrees F (32-degrees C) or higher
In hilly or mountainous terrain
Frequent trailer pulling

2   Introduction

This chapter is designed to help the home mechanic maintain the Toyota Corolla for peak performance, economy, safety and long life.

Included is a master maintenance schedule, followed by sections dealing specifically with each item on the schedule. Visual checks, adjustments, component replacement and other helpful items are included. Refer to the **accompanying illustrations** of the engine compartment and the underside of the vehicle for the location of various components.

Servicing your Corolla in accordance with the mileage/time maintenance schedule and the following Sections will provide it with a planned maintenance program that should result in a long and reliable service life. This is a comprehensive plan, so maintaining some items but not others at the specified service intervals will not produce the same results.

As you service your Corolla, you will discover that many of the procedures can - and should - be grouped together because of the nature of the particular procedure you're performing or because of the close proximity of two otherwise unrelated components to one another.

For example, if the vehicle is raised for any reason, you should inspect the exhaust, suspension, steering and fuel systems while you're under the vehicle. When you're rotating the tires, it makes good sense to check the brakes and wheel bearings since the wheels are already removed.

Finally, let's suppose you have to borrow or rent a torque wrench. Even if you only need to tighten the spark plugs, you might as well check the torque of as many critical fasteners as time allows.

The first step of this maintenance program is to prepare yourself before the actual work begins. Read through all sections pertinent to the procedures you're planning to do, then make a list of and gather together all the parts and tools you will need to do the job. If it looks as if you might run into problems during a particular segment of some procedure, seek advice from your local parts counterperson or dealer service department.

3   Tune-up general information

The term *tune-up* is used in this manual to represent a combination of individual operations rather than one specific procedure.

If, from the time the vehicle is new, the routine maintenance schedule is followed closely and frequent checks are made of fluid levels and high wear items, as suggested throughout this manual, the engine will be kept in relatively good running condition and the need for additional work will be minimized.

More likely than not, however, there will be times when the engine is running poorly due to lack of regular maintenance. This is even more likely if a used vehicle, which has not received regular and frequent maintenance checks, is purchased. In such cases, an engine tune-up will be needed outside of the regular routine maintenance intervals.

The first step in any tune-up or engine diagnosis to help correct a poor running engine would be a cylinder compression check. A check of the engine compression (Chapter 2 Part B) will give valuable information regarding the overall performance of many internal components and should be used as a basis for tune-up and repair procedures. If, for instance, a compression check indicates serious internal engine wear, a conventional tune-up will not help the running condition of the engine and would be a waste of time and money.

The following series of operations are those most often needed to bring a generally poor running engine back into a proper state of tune.

Minor tune-up

Check all engine related fluids (Section 4)
Clean, inspect and test the battery
(Section 9)
Check the drivebelt (Section 10)
Check all underhood hoses (Section 11)
Check the cooling system (Section 12)
Check the air filter (Section 16)
Replace the spark plugs (Section 24)

Major tune-up

All items listed under Minor tune-up, plus . . .

Replace the air filter (Section 16)
Check the fuel system (Section 17)
Check the charging system (Chapter 5)

4   Fluid level checks (every 250 miles or weekly)

1   Fluids are an essential part of the lubrication, cooling, brake, clutch and other systems. Because these fluids gradually become depleted and/or contaminated during normal operation of the vehicle, they must be periodically replenished. See *Recommended lubricants and fluids* and *Capacities* at the beginning of this Chapter before adding fluid to any of the following components. **Note:** *The vehicle must be on level ground before fluid levels can be checked.*

Engine oil

Refer to illustrations 4.2, 4.4 and 4.6

2   The engine oil level is checked with a dipstick located at the front of the engine **(see illustration)**. The dipstick extends through a metal tube from which it protrudes down into the engine oil pan.

3   The oil level should be checked before the vehicle has been driven, or about 5 minutes after the engine has been shut off. If the oil is checked immediately after driving the vehicle, some of the oil will remain in the upper engine components, producing an inaccurate reading on the dipstick.

4   Pull the dipstick from the tube and wipe all the oil from the end with a clean rag or paper towel. Insert the clean dipstick all the way back into its metal tube and pull it out again. Observe the oil at the end of the dipstick. At its highest point, the level should be between the two dimples **(see illustration)**.

5   It takes one quart of oil to raise the level from the lower dimple to the upper dimple on the dipstick. Do not allow the level to drop below the lower dimple or oil starvation may

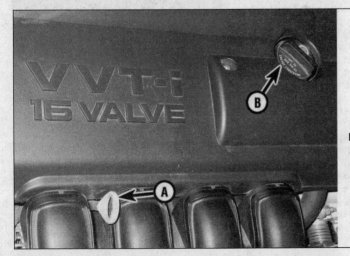

4.2 The engine oil dipstick (A) is located at the front of the engine - the oil filler cap (B) is in the valve cover

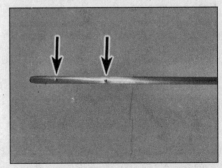

4.4 On 1998 and later models, the engine oil dipstick has two dimples - keep the oil level at or near the upper dimple

4.6 The threaded oil filler cap is located on the valve cover - always make sure the area around the opening is clean before unscrewing the cap to prevent dirt from contaminating the engine

4.8 The coolant reservoir is at the right side of the radiator - make sure the coolant level is between the Low and Full marks on the reservoir

cause engine damage. Conversely, overfilling the engine (adding oil above the upper dimple) may cause oil fouled spark plugs, oil leaks or oil seal failures.

6   Remove the threaded cap from the valve cover to add oil **(see illustration)**. Use a funnel to prevent spills. After adding the oil, install the filler cap hand tight. Start the engine and look carefully for any small leaks around the oil filter or drain plug. Stop the engine and check the oil level again after it has had sufficient time to drain from the upper block and cylinder head galleys.

7   Checking the oil level is an important preventive maintenance step. A continually dropping oil level indicates oil leakage through damaged seals, from loose connections, or past worn rings or valve guides. If the oil looks milky in color or has water droplets in it, a cylinder head gasket may be blown. The engine should be checked immediately. The condition of the oil should also be checked. Each time you check the oil level, slide your thumb and index finger up the dipstick before wiping off the oil. If you see small dirt or metal particles clinging to the dipstick, the oil should be changed (see Section 6).

Engine coolant

Refer to illustration 4.8

Warning: *Do not allow antifreeze to come in contact with your skin or painted surfaces of the vehicle. Flush contaminated areas immediately with plenty of water. Don't store new coolant or leave old coolant lying around where it's accessible to children or pets - they're attracted by its sweet smell and may drink it. Ingestion of even a small amount of coolant can be fatal! Wipe up garage floor and drip pan spills immediately. Keep antifreeze containers covered and repair cooling system leaks as soon as they're noticed.*

8   All vehicles covered by this manual are equipped with a pressurized coolant recovery system. A white coolant reservoir located

at the right side of the radiator in the engine compartment is connected by a hose to the base of the radiator filler neck **(see illustration)**. If the coolant heats up during engine operation, coolant can escape through a pressurized filler cap, then through a connecting hose into the reservoir. As the engine cools, the coolant is automatically drawn back into the cooling system to maintain the correct level.

9   The coolant level should be checked regularly. It must be between the Full and Low lines on the tank. The level will vary with the temperature of the engine. When the engine is cold, the coolant level should be at or slightly above the Low mark on the tank. Once the engine has warmed up, the level should be at or near the Full mark. If it isn't, allow the fluid in the tank to cool, then remove the cap from the reservoir and add coolant to bring the level up to the Full line. Use only the coolant listed in this Chapter's Specifications, or its equivalent. Do not use supplemental inhibitor additives. If only a small amount of coolant is required to bring the system up to the proper level, water can be used. However, repeated additions of water will dilute the recommended antifreeze and water solution. In order to maintain the proper ratio of antifreeze and water, it is advisable to top up the coolant level with the correct mixture.

10   If the coolant level drops within a short time after replenishment, there may be a leak in the system. Inspect the radiator, hoses, engine coolant filler cap, drain plugs, air bleeder plugs and water pump. If no leak is evident, have the radiator cap pressure tested by your dealer. **Warning:** *Never remove the radiator cap or the coolant recovery reservoir cap when the engine is running or has just been shut down, because the cooling system is hot. Escaping steam and scalding liquid could cause serious injury.*

11   If it is necessary to open the radiator cap, wait until the system has cooled completely, then wrap a thick cloth around the cap and

turn it to the first stop. If any steam escapes, wait until the system has cooled further, then remove the cap.

12   When checking the coolant level, always note its condition. It should be relatively clear. If it is brown or rust colored, the system should be drained, flushed and refilled. Even if the coolant appears to be normal, the corrosion inhibitors wear out with use, so it must be replaced at the specified intervals.

13   Do not allow antifreeze to come in contact with your skin or painted surfaces of the vehicle. Flush contacted areas immediately with plenty of water.

Windshield washer fluid

Refer to illustration 4.14

14   Fluid for the windshield washer system is stored in a plastic reservoir which is located on the right side of the engine compartment **(see illustration)**. In milder climates, plain water can be used to top up the reservoir, but

4.14 The windshield washer fluid reservoir is located in the right front corner of the engine compartment

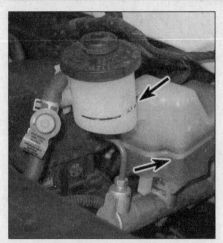

4.17 The brake fluid level should be kept between the MIN and MAX marks on the translucent plastic reservoir

4.25 The power steering fluid reservoir is located near the right shock tower in the engine compartment

4.29 The power steering fluid level is checked by looking through the plastic reservoir

the reservoir should be kept no more than two-thirds full to allow for expansion should the water freeze. In colder climates, the use of a specially designed windshield washer fluid, available at your dealer and any auto parts store, will help lower the freezing point of the fluid. Mix the solution with water in accordance with the manufacturer's directions on the container. Do not use regular antifreeze. It will damage the vehicle's paint.

Battery electrolyte

15   On models not equipped with a sealed battery, remove the filler/vent cap and check the electrolyte level. It must be between the upper and lower levels. If the level is low, add distilled water. Install and securely retighten the cap. **Caution:** *Overfilling the cells may cause electrolyte to spill over during periods of heavy charging, causing corrosion or damage.*

Brake and clutch fluid

Refer to illustration 4.17

16   The brake master cylinder is mounted on the front of the power booster unit in the engine compartment. The clutch master cylinder on vehicles with manual transaxles is connected by a hose to the brake master cylinder.

17   To check the fluid level, simply look at the MAX and MIN marks on the reservoir **(see illustration)**. The level should be at or near the maximum fill line.

18   If the level is low, wipe the top of the reservoir cover with a clean rag to prevent contamination of the brake or clutch system before lifting the cover.

19   Add only the specified brake fluid to the reservoir (refer to *Recommended lubricants and fluids* at the front of this chapter or to your owner's manual). Mixing different types of brake fluid can damage the system. **Warning:** *Use caution when filling the reservoir - brake fluid can harm your eyes and damage painted surfaces. Do not use brake fluid that has been opened for more than one year*

(even if the cap has been on) or has been left open. Brake fluid absorbs moisture from the air. Excess moisture can cause a dangerous loss of braking.

20   While the reservoir cap is removed, inspect the master cylinder reservoir for contamination. If deposits, dirt particles or water droplets are present, the fluid in the brake system should be changed (see Section 21 for the brake fluid replacement procedure or Chapter 8 for the clutch hydraulic system bleeding procedure).

21   After filling the reservoir to the proper level, make sure the lid is properly seated to prevent fluid leakage and/or system pressure loss.

22   The brake fluid in the master cylinder will drop slightly as the brake pads at each wheel wear down during normal operation. If the master cylinder requires repeated replenishing to keep it at the proper level, this is an indication of leakage in the brake system, which should be corrected immediately. Check all brake lines and connections, along with the calipers, wheel cylinders and booster (see Section 15 for more information).

23   If, upon checking the master cylinder fluid level, you discover the reservoir empty or nearly empty, the brake and clutch systems must be diagnosed immediately (see Chapters 8 and 9).

Power steering fluid

Refer to illustrations 4.25 and 4.29

24   Unlike manual steering, the power steering system relies on fluid which may, over a period of time, require replenishing.

25   The fluid reservoir for the power steering pump is located on the passenger's side inner fender panel, just below the windshield washer fluid reservoir **(see illustration)**.

26   For the check, the front wheels should be pointed straight ahead and the engine should be off.

27   Use a clean rag to wipe off the reservoir cap and the area around the cap. This will

help prevent any foreign matter from entering the reservoir during the check.

28   Twist off the cap and check the temperature of the fluid at the end of the dipstick with your finger.

29   View the level of power steering fluid through the translucent reservoir **(see illustration)**. At no time should the fluid level drop below the upper mark for each heat range.

30   If additional fluid is required, pour the specified type directly into the reservoir, using a funnel to prevent spills.

31   If the reservoir requires frequent fluid additions, all power steering hoses, hose connections, the power steering pump and the rack and pinion assembly should be carefully checked for leaks.

Automatic transaxle fluid

Refer to illustrations 4.35a and 4.35b

32   The level of the automatic transaxle fluid should be carefully maintained. Low fluid level can lead to slipping or loss of drive, while overfilling can cause foaming, loss of fluid and transaxle damage.

33   The transaxle fluid level should only be checked when the transaxle is hot (at its normal operating temperature). If the vehicle has just been driven over 10 miles (15 miles in a frigid climate), and the fluid temperature is 160 to 175-degrees F, the transaxle is hot. **Caution:** *If the vehicle has just been driven for a long time at high speed or in city traffic in hot weather, or if it has been pulling a trailer, an accurate fluid level reading cannot be obtained. Allow the fluid to cool down for about 30 minutes.*

34   If the vehicle has not just been driven, park the vehicle on level ground, set the parking brake and start the engine. While the engine is idling, depress the brake pedal and move the selector lever through all the gear ranges, beginning and ending in Park.

35   With the engine still idling, remove the dipstick from its tube **(see illustration)**. Check the level of the fluid on the dipstick **(see illus-**

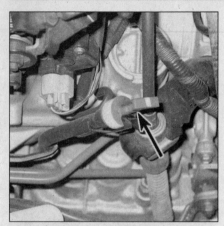

4.35a The automatic transaxle dipstick is located in a tube which extends forward from the transaxle

4.35b If the automatic transaxle fluid is cold, the level should be between the two lower notches; if it's at operating temperature, the level should be between the two upper notches

5.2 A tire tread depth indicator should be used to monitor tire wear - they are available at auto parts stores and service stations and cost very little

tration) and note its condition.

36   Wipe the fluid from the dipstick with a clean rag and reinsert it back into the filler tube until the cap seats.

37   Pull the dipstick out again and note the fluid level. If the transaxle is cold, the level should be in the COLD or COOL range on the dipstick. If it is hot, the fluid level should be in the HOT range. If the level is at the low side of either range, add the specified automatic transmission fluid through the dipstick tube with a funnel.

38   Add just enough of the recommended fluid to fill the transaxle to the proper level. It takes about one pint to raise the level from the low mark to the high mark when the fluid is hot, so add the fluid a little at a time and keep checking the level until it is correct.

39   The condition of the fluid should also be checked along with the level. If the fluid at the end of the dipstick is black or a dark reddish brown color, or if it emits a burned smell, the fluid should be changed (see Section 26). If you are in doubt about the condition of the fluid, purchase some new fluid and compare the two for color and smell.

5   Tire and tire pressure checks (every 250 miles or weekly)

Refer to illustrations 5.2, 5.3, 5.4a, 5.4b and 5.8

1   Periodic inspection of the tires may spare you from the inconvenience of being stranded with a flat tire. It can also provide you with vital information regarding possible problems in the steering and suspension systems before major damage occurs.

2   Normal tread wear can be monitored with a simple, inexpensive device known as a tread depth indicator **(see illustration)**. When the tread depth reaches the specified minimum, replace the tire(s).

3   Note any abnormal tread wear **(see illustration)**. Tread pattern irregularities such as cupping, flat spots and more wear on one side than the other are indications of front end alignment and/or balance problems. If any of these conditions are noted, take the vehicle to a tire shop or service station to correct the problem.

UNDERINFLATION

CUPPING

Cupping may be caused by:
• Underinflation and/or mechanical irregularities such as out-of-balance condition of wheel and/or tire, and bent or damaged wheel.
• Loose or worn steering tie-rod or steering idler arm.
• Loose, damaged or worn front suspension parts.

OVERINFLATION

5.3 This chart will help you determine the condition of your tires, the probable cause(s) of abnormal wear and the corrective action necessary

INCORRECT TOE-IN OR EXTREME CAMBER

FEATHERING DUE TO MISALIGNMENT

5.4a If a tire loses air on a steady basis, check the valve core first to make sure it's snug (special inexpensive wrenches are commonly available at auto parts stores)

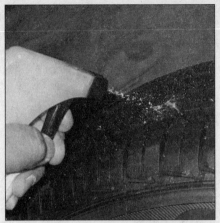

5.4b If the valve core is tight, raise the corner of the vehicle with the low tire and spray a soapy water solution onto the tread as the tire is turned slowly - slow leaks will cause small bubbles to appear

5.8 To extend the life of your tires, check the air pressure at least once a week with an accurate gauge (don't forget the spare!)

4   Look closely for cuts, punctures and embedded nails or tacks. Sometimes a tire will
hold its air pressure for a short time or leak
down very slowly even after a nail has embedded itself into the tread. If a slow leak persists,
check the valve stem core to make sure it is
tight **(see illustration)**. Examine the tread for
an object that may have embedded itself into
the tire or for a "plug" that may have begun to
leak (radial tire punctures are repaired with a
plug that is installed in a puncture). If a puncture
is suspected, it can be easily verified by spraying a solution of soapy water onto the puncture
area **(see illustration)**. The soapy solution will
bubble if there is a leak. Unless the puncture is
inordinately large, a tire shop or gas station can
usually repair the punctured tire.
5   Carefully inspect the inner sidewall of
each tire for evidence of brake fluid leakage. If
you see any, inspect the brakes immediately.
6   Correct tire air pressure adds miles to
the lifespan of the tires, improves mileage
and enhances overall ride quality. Tire pressure cannot be accurately estimated by looking at a tire, particularly if it is a radial. A tire
pressure gauge is therefore essential. Keep
an accurate gauge in the glovebox. The pressure gauges fitted to the nozzles of air hoses
at gas stations are often inaccurate.
7   Always check tire pressure when the
tires are cold. "Cold," in this case, means the
vehicle has not been driven over a mile in the
three hours preceding a tire pressure check.
A pressure rise of four to eight pounds is not
uncommon once the tires are warm.
8   Unscrew the valve cap protruding from
the wheel or hubcap and push the gauge
firmly onto the valve **(see illustration)**. Note
the reading on the gauge and compare this fig-
ure to the recommended tire pressure shown
on the tire placard on the left door. Be sure to
reinstall the valve cap to keep dirt and moisture out of the valve stem mechanism. Check
all four tires and, if necessary, add enough air
to bring them up to the recommended pressure levels.
9   Don't forget to keep the spare tire

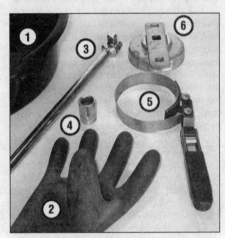

6.2 These tools are required when changing the engine oil and filter

1   **Drain pan** - *It should be fairly shallow in
depth, but wide in order to prevent spills*
2   **Rubber gloves** - *When removing the
drain plug and filter, it is inevitable that
you will get oil on your hands (the gloves
will prevent burns)*
3   **Breaker bar** - *Sometimes the oil drain
plug is pretty tight and a long breaker
bar is needed to loosen it*
4   **Socket** - *To be used with the breaker
bar or a ratchet (must be the correct size
to fit the drain plug)*
5   **Filter wrench** - *This is a metal band-
type wrench, which requires clearance
around the filter to be effective*
6   **Filter wrench** - *This type fits on the
bottom of the filter and can be turned
with a ratchet or beaker bar (different
size wrenches are available for different
types of filters)*

inflated to the specified pressure (consult your
owner's manual). Note that the air pressure
specified for the compact spare is significantly
higher than the pressure of the regular tires.

6   Engine oil and oil filter change (every 3000 miles or 3 months)

Refer to illustrations 6.2, 6.7, 6.12 and 6.14
1   Frequent oil changes are the best preventive maintenance the home mechanic can
give the engine, because aging oil becomes
diluted and contaminated, which leads to premature engine wear.
2   Make sure that you have all the necessary tools before you begin this procedure
(see illustration). You should also have
plenty of rags or newspapers handy for mopping up any spills.
3   Access to the underside of the vehicle
is greatly improved if the vehicle can be lifted
on a hoist, driven onto ramps or supported by
jackstands. **Warning:** *Do not work under a
vehicle which is supported only by a bumper,
hydraulic or scissors-type jack.*
4   If this is your first oil change, get under
the vehicle and familiarize yourself with the
location of the oil drain plug. The engine and
exhaust components will be warm during the
actual work, so try to anticipate any potential
problems before the engine and accessories
are hot.
5   Park the vehicle on a level spot. Start the
engine and allow it to reach its normal operating temperature (the needle on the temperature gauge should be at least above the
bottom mark). Warm oil and sludge will flow
out more easily. Turn off the engine when it's
warmed up. Remove the filler cap in the rear
cam cover.
6   Raise the vehicle and support it on
jackstands. **Warning:** *To avoid personal
injury, never get beneath the vehicle when it
is supported by only by a jack. The jack provided with your vehicle is designed solely for
raising the vehicle to remove and replace the
wheels. Always use jackstands to support the
vehicle when it becomes necessary to place
your body underneath the vehicle.*
7   Being careful not to touch the hot exhaust
components, place the drain pan under the
drain plug in the bottom of the pan and remove

6.7 Use a proper size box-end wrench or socket to remove the oil drain plug and avoid rounding it off

6.12 The oil filter points straight down from the engine block

6.14 Lubricate the oil filter gasket with clean engine oil before installing the filter on the engine

the plug **(see illustration)**. You may want to wear gloves while unscrewing the plug the final few turns if the engine is really hot.

8   Allow the old oil to drain into the pan. It may be necessary to move the pan farther under the engine as the oil flow slows to a trickle. Inspect the old oil for the presence of metal shavings and chips.

9   After all the oil has drained, wipe off the drain plug with a clean rag. Even minute metal particles clinging to the plug would immediately contaminate the new oil.

10   Clean the area around the drain plug opening, reinstall the plug and tighten it to the torque listed in this Chapter's Specifications.

11   Move the drain pan into position under the oil filter.

12   Loosen the oil filter **(see illustration)** by turning it counterclockwise with the filter wrench. **Note:** *2008 and earlier models use a traditional spin-on type filter. 2009 and later models use a cartridge-type filter.* If you're working on a 2009 or later model, remove the old filter element from the cap, clean the cap, then install a new filter element. Also install a new O-ring on the cap.

13   With a clean rag, wipe off the mounting surface on the block. If a residue of old oil is allowed to remain, it will smoke when the block is heated up. It will also prevent the new filter from seating properly. Also make sure that the none of the old gasket remains stuck to the mounting surface. It can be removed with a scraper if necessary.

14   Compare the old filter with the new one to make sure they are the same type. Smear some engine oil on the rubber gasket or O-ring of the new filter and screw it into place **(see illustration)**. Because overtightening the filter will damage the gasket, do not use a filter wrench to tighten the filter. Tighten it by hand following the directions on the canister or packing box. If you're working on a 2009 or later model, tighten the filter cap to the torque listed in this Chapter's Specifications.

15   Remove all tools, rags, etc. from under the vehicle, being careful not to spill the oil in the drain pan, then lower the vehicle.

16   Add new oil to the engine through the oil filler cap in the valve cover. Use a funnel to prevent oil from spilling onto the top of the engine. **Caution:** *Don't push the funnel into the engine as this will bend the inner baffle and could cause enegine damage.* Pour three quarts of fresh oil into the engine. Wait a few minutes to allow the oil to drain into the pan, then check the level on the oil dipstick (see Section 4 if necessary). If the oil level is at or near the F mark, install the filler cap hand tight, start the engine and allow the new oil to circulate.

17   Allow the engine to run for about a minute. While the engine is running, look under the vehicle and check for leaks at the oil pan drain plug and around the oil filter. If either is leaking, stop the engine and tighten the plug or filter slightly.

18   Wait a few minutes to allow the oil to trickle down into the pan, then recheck the level on the dipstick and, if necessary, add enough oil to bring the level to the F mark.

19   During the first few trips after an oil change, make it a point to check frequently for leaks and proper oil level.

20   The old oil drained from the engine cannot be reused in its present state and should be discarded. Check with your local refuse disposal company, disposal facility or environmental agency to see if they will accept the oil for recycling. Don't pour used oil into drains or onto the ground. After the oil has cooled, it can be drained into a suitable container (capped plastic jugs, topped bottles, milk cartons, etc.) for transport to one of these disposal sites.

Maintenance Required light resetting

21   Turn the ignition key to the On position and depress the button to the right of the speedometer until the odometer is displayed.

22   Turn the ignition key to the Off position.

23   Depress the button again and hold it, then turn the ignition key to the On position. Hold the button in the depressed position for five seconds.

24   The odometer should indicate "000000" and the MAINT REQD light should turn off.

7   Windshield wiper blade inspection and replacement (every 7500 miles or 6 months)

Refer to illustrations 7.5, 7.6 and 7.7

1   The windshield wiper and blade assembly should be inspected periodically for damage, loose components and cracked or worn blade elements.

2   Road film can build up on the wiper blades and affect their efficiency, so they should be washed regularly with a mild detergent solution.

3   The action of the wiping mechanism can loosen bolts, nuts and fasteners, so they should be checked and tightened, as necessary, at the same time the wiper blades are checked.

4   If the wiper blade elements are cracked, worn or warped, or no longer clean adequately, they should be replaced with new ones.

5   Remove the wiper blade assembly from the arm by pushing on the release lever, then

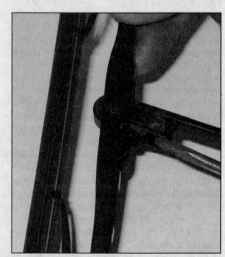

7.5 Push on the release lever and slide the wiper assembly down out of the hook in the end of the wiper arm

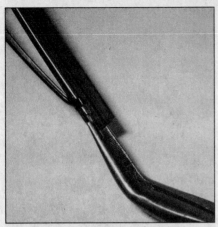

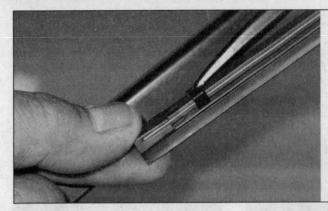

7.7 Slide the element into place until the cutouts seat into the locking claw

7.6 After detaching the end of the element, slide it out of the end of the frame

sliding the assembly down and out of the hook in the end of the arm **(see illustration)**.

6   Squeeze the end of the wiper element and pull it out of the wiper frame **(see illustration)**.

7   Insert the new element end without the cutouts into the wiper frame. Slide the element fully into place, then seat the protrusions in the end of the frames to secure it **(see illustration)**.

8   Clutch pedal freeplay check and adjustment (every 7500 miles or 6 months)

Refer to illustration 8.1

1   Peel back the carpet and check the clutch pedal height **(see illustration)**. If pedal

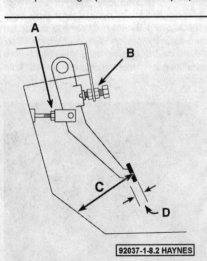

92037-1-8.2 HAYNES

8.1 Clutch pedal height and freeplay measuring points and adjustments

A   Pedal freeplay adjustment point
B   Pedal height adjustment point
C   Pedal height measurement point
D   Freeplay measurement point

height is incorrect, loosen the locknut and turn the stopper bolt until the height is correct. Tighten the locknut.

2   Press down lightly on the clutch pedal and measure the distance that it moves freely before the clutch resistance is felt. The freeplay should be within the specified limits. If it isn't, it must be adjusted.

3   Loosen the locknut on the pedal end of the clutch pushrod **(see illustration 8.1)**.

4   Turn the pushrod until pedal freeplay is correct.

5   Tighten the locknut.

6   After adjusting the pedal freeplay, check the pedal height again, adjusting it if necessary.

9   Battery check, maintenance and charging (every 7500 miles or 6 months)

Refer to illustrations 9.1, 9.6a, 9.6b, 9.7a, 9.7b and 9.8

Warning: *Certain precautions must be followed when checking and servicing the battery. Hydrogen gas, which is highly flammable, is always present in the battery cells, so keep lighted tobacco and all other open flames and sparks away from the battery. The electrolyte inside the battery is actually dilute sulfuric acid, which will cause injury if splashed on your skin or in your eyes. It will also ruin clothes and painted surfaces. When removing the battery cables, always detach the negative cable first and hook it up last!*

1   A routine preventive maintenance program for the battery in your vehicle is the only way to ensure quick and reliable starts. But before performing any battery maintenance, make sure that you have the proper equipment necessary to work safely around the battery **(see illustration)**.

2   There are also several precautions that should be taken whenever battery maintenance is performed. Before servicing the battery, always turn the engine and all accessories off and disconnect the cable from the negative terminal of the battery.

3   The battery produces hydrogen gas, which is both flammable and explosive. Never create a spark, smoke or light a match around the battery. Always charge the battery in a

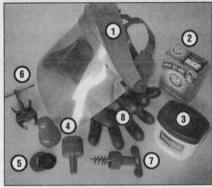

9.1 Tools and materials required for battery maintenance

1   ***Face shield/safety goggles*** - *When removing corrosion with a brush, the acidic particles can easily fly up into your eyes*

2   ***Baking soda*** - *A solution of baking soda and water can be used to neutralize corrosion*

3   ***Petroleum jelly*** - *A layer of this on the battery posts will help prevent corrosion*

4   ***Battery post/cable cleaner*** - *This wire brush cleaning tool will remove all traces of corrosion from the battery posts and cable clamps*

5   ***Treated felt washers*** - *Placing one of these on each post, directly under the cable clamps, will help prevent corrosion*

6   ***Puller*** - *Sometimes the cable clamps are very difficult to pull off the posts, even after the nut/bolt has been completely loosened. This tool pulls the clamp straight up and off the post without damage*

7   ***Battery post/cable cleaner*** - *Here is another cleaning tool which is a slightly different version of number 4 above, but it does the same thing*

8   ***Rubber gloves*** - *Another safety item to consider when servicing the battery; remember that's acid inside the battery*

ventilated area.

4   Electrolyte contains poisonous and corrosive sulfuric acid. Do not allow it to get in your eyes, on your skin on your clothes. Never ingest it. Wear protective safety glasses when working near the battery. Keep children away

9.6a Battery terminal corrosion usually appears as light, fluffy powder

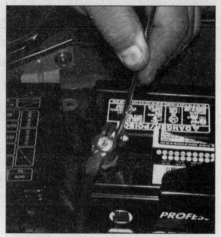

9.6b Removing a cable from the battery post with a wrench - sometimes a pair of special battery pliers are required for this procedure if corrosion has caused deterioration of the nut hex (always remove the ground (-) cable first and hook it up last!)

9.7a When cleaning the cable clamps, all corrosion must be removed (the inside of the clamp is tapered to match the taper on the post, so don't remove too much material)

from the battery.

5   Note the external condition of the battery. If the positive terminal and cable clamp on your vehicle's battery is equipped with a rubber protector, make sure that it's not torn or damaged. It should completely cover the terminal. Look for any corroded or loose connections, cracks in the case or cover or loose hold-down clamps. Also check the entire length of each cable for cracks and frayed conductors.

6   If corrosion, which looks like white, fluffy deposits (see illustration) is evident, particularly around the terminals, the battery should be removed for cleaning. Loosen the cable clamp bolts with a wrench, being careful to remove the ground cable first, and slide them off the terminals (see illustration). Then disconnect the hold-down clamp bolt and nut, remove the clamp and lift the battery from the engine compartment.

7   Clean the cable clamps thoroughly with a battery brush or a terminal cleaner and a solution of warm water and baking soda (see illustration). Wash the terminals and the top of the battery case with the same solution but

make sure that the solution doesn't get into the battery. When cleaning the cables, terminals and battery top, wear safety goggles and rubber gloves to prevent any solution from coming in contact with your eyes or hands. Wear old clothes too - even diluted, sulfuric acid splashed onto clothes will burn holes in them. If the terminals have been extensively corroded, clean them up with a terminal cleaner (see illustration). Thoroughly wash all cleaned areas with plain water.

8   Make sure that the battery tray is in good condition and the hold-down nut and bolt are tight (see illustration). If the battery is removed from the tray, make sure no parts remain in the bottom of the tray when the battery is reinstalled. When reinstalling the hold-down clamp bolt or nut, do not overtighten it.

9   Information on removing and installing the battery can be found in Chapter 5. Information on jump starting can be found at the

front of this manual. For more detailed battery checking procedures, refer to the *Haynes Automotive Electrical Manual.*

Cleaning

10   Corrosion on the hold-down components, battery case and surrounding areas can be removed with a solution of water and baking soda. Thoroughly rinse all cleaned areas with plain water.

11   Any metal parts of the vehicle damaged by corrosion should be covered with a zinc-based primer, then painted.

Charging

Warning: *When batteries are being charged, hydrogen gas, which is very explosive and flammable, is produced. Do not smoke or allow open flames near a charging or a recently charged battery. Wear eye protection when near the battery during charging. Also, make sure the charger is unplugged before connecting or disconnecting the battery from the charger.*

9.7b Regardless of the type of tool used to clean the battery posts, a clean, shiny surface should be the result

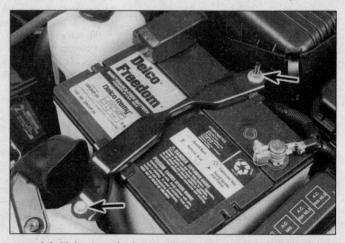

9.8 Make sure the battery clamp nut and bolt are tight

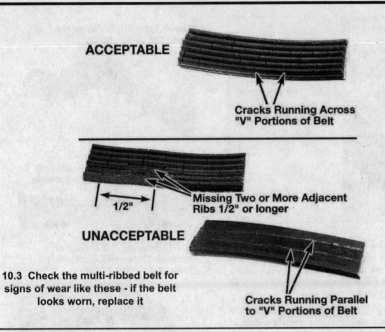

ACCEPTABLE

Cracks Running Across "V" Portions of Belt

1/2"

Missing Two or More Adjacent Ribs 1/2" or longer

UNACCEPTABLE

Cracks Running Parallel to "V" Portions of Belt

10.3 Check the multi-ribbed belt for signs of wear like these - if the belt looks worn, replace it

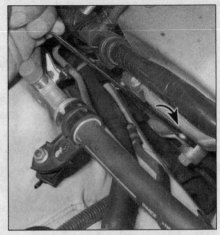

10.4 To release the tension on the drivebelt, place a long wrench or socket and ratchet on the hex-shaped boss, then turn the tensioner clockwise

12   Slow-rate charging is the best way to restore a battery that's discharged to the point where it will not start the engine. It's also a good way to maintain the battery charge in a vehicle that's only driven a few miles between starts. Maintaining the battery charge is particularly important in the winter when the battery must work harder to start the engine and electrical accessories that drain the battery are in greater use.

13   It's best to use a one or two-amp battery charger (sometimes called a "trickle" charger). They are the safest and put the least strain on the battery. They are also the least expensive. For a faster charge, you can use a higher amperage charger, but don't use one rated more than 1/10th the amp/hour rating of the battery. Rapid boost charges that claim to restore the power of the battery in one to two hours are hardest on the battery and can damage batteries not in good condition. This type of charging should only be used in emergency situations.

14   The average time necessary to charge a battery should be listed in the instructions that come with the charger. As a general rule, a trickle charger will charge a battery in 12 to 16 hours.

10   Drivebelt check and replacement (every 7500 miles or 6 months)

Check

Refer to illustration 10.3

1   The alternator, power steering pump, water pump and air-conditioning compressor are all driven by one serpentine belt. Because of their composition and the stresses they are subjected to, drivebelts stretch and deteriorate as they get older. They must therefore be inspected periodically.

2   The serpentine belt has no adjustment for tension, as with older systems with multiple V-belts. The engine has a tensioner that automatically applies the right belt tension and compensates for belt stretch over time.

3   With the engine off, open the hood and locate the drivebelt. With a flashlight, check the belt for separation of the adhesive rubber on both sides of the core, core separation from the belt side, a severed core, separation of the ribs from the adhesive rubber, cracking or separation of the ribs, and torn or worn ribs or cracks in the inner ridges of the ribs (see illustration). Also check for fraying and glazing, which gives the belt a shiny appearance. Both sides of the belt should be inspected, which means you will have to twist the belt to check the underside. Use your fingers to feel the belt where you can't see it. If any of the above conditions are evident, replace the belt (go to Step 4).

Replacement

Refer to illustrations 10.4, 10.5a and 10.5b

4   Rotate the belt tensioner clockwise to release the tension, then slip the belt off the pulleys (see illustration). Slowly release the tensioner.

5   Route the new belt over the pulleys (see illustrations), again rotating the tensioner to allow the belt to be installed, then release the belt tensioner.

6   Make sure the belt is properly centered in the pulleys.

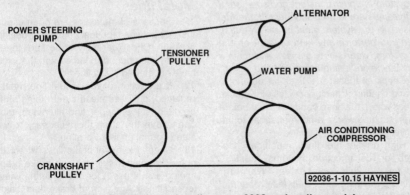

POWER STEERING PUMP

ALTERNATOR

TENSIONER PULLEY

WATER PUMP

AIR CONDITIONING COMPRESSOR

CRANKSHAFT PULLEY

92036-1-10.15 HAYNES

10.5a Drivebelt routing diagram - 2008 and earlier models

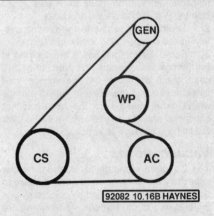

GEN

WP

CS

AC

92082 10.16B HAYNES

10.5b Drivebelt routing diagram - 2009 and later models

10.7 The drivebelt tensioner is retained by a nut and a bolt

Check for a chafed area that could fail prematurely.

Check for a soft area indicating the hose has deteriorated inside.

Overtightening the clamp on a hardened hose will damage the hose and cause a leak.

Check each hose for swelling and oil-soaked ends. Cracks and breaks can be located by squeezing the hose.

Drivebelt tensioner replacement

Refer to illustration 10.7

7   To replace a tensioner that can't properly tension the belt, or one that exhibits binding or a worn-out bearing/pulley, remove the drivebelt (see Step 4) then unscrew the mounting bolt and nut **(see illustration)**.

8   Installation is the reverse of the removal procedure. Tighten the fasteners to the torque values listed in this Chapter's Specifications.

9   Install the drivebelt (see Steps 5 and 6).

11   Underhood hose check and replacement (every 7500 miles or 6 months)

Caution: *Replacement of air conditioning hoses must be left to a dealer service department or air conditioning shop that has the equipment to depressurize the system safely. Never remove air conditioning components or hoses until the system has been depressurized.*

General

1   High temperatures in the engine compartment can cause the deterioration of the rubber and plastic hoses used for engine, accessory and emission systems operation. Periodic inspection should be made for cracks, loose clamps, material hardening and leaks.

2   Information specific to the cooling system hoses can be found in Section 12.

3   Some, but not all, hoses are secured to the fittings with clamps. Where clamps are used, check to be sure they haven't lost their tension, allowing the hose to leak. If clamps aren't used, make sure the hose has not expanded and/or hardened where it slips over the fitting, allowing it to leak.

Vacuum hoses

4   It's quite common for vacuum hoses, especially those in the emissions system, to be color coded or identified by colored stripes molded into them. Various systems require hoses with different wall thickness, collapse resistance and temperature resistance. When replacing hoses, be sure the new ones are made of the same material.

5   Often the only effective way to check a hose is to remove it completely from the vehicle. If more than one hose is removed, be sure to label the hoses and fittings to ensure correct installation.

6   When checking vacuum hoses, be sure to include any plastic T-fittings in the check. Inspect the fittings for cracks and the hose where it fits over the fitting for distortion, which could cause leakage.

7   A small piece of vacuum hose (1/4-inch inside diameter) can be used as a stethoscope to detect vacuum leaks. Hold one end of the hose to your ear and probe around vacuum hoses and fittings, listening for the "hissing" sound characteristic of a vacuum leak. **Warning:** *When probing with the vacuum hose stethoscope, be very careful not to come into contact with moving engine components such as the drivebelt, cooling fan, etc.*

Fuel hose

Warning: *Gasoline is extremely flammable, so take extra precautions when you work on any part of the fuel system. Don't smoke or allow open flames or bare light bulbs near the work area, and don't work in a garage where a gas-type appliance (such as a water heater or a clothes dryer) is present. Since gasoline is carcinogenic, wear latex gloves when there's a possibility of being exposed to fuel, and, if you spill any fuel on your skin, rinse it off immediately with soap and water. Mop up any spills immediately and do not store fuel-soaked rags where they could ignite. The fuel system is under constant pressure, so, if any fuel lines are to be disconnected, the fuel pressure in the system must be relieved first. When you perform any kind of work on the fuel system, wear safety glasses and have a Class B type fire extinguisher on hand.*

8   Check all rubber fuel lines for deterioration and chafing. Check especially for cracks in areas where the hose bends and just before fittings, such as where a hose attaches to the fuel filter.

9   High quality fuel line, specifically designed for fuel injection systems, must be used for fuel line replacement. **Warning:** *Never use anything other than the proper fuel line for fuel line replacement.*

10   Spring-type clamps are commonly used

12.4 Hoses, like drivebelts, have a habit of failing at the worst possible time - to prevent the inconvenience of a blown radiator or heater hose, inspect them carefully as shown here

on fuel lines. These clamps often lose their tension over a period of time, and can be "sprung" during removal. Replace all spring-type clamps with screw clamps whenever a hose is replaced.

Metal lines

11   Sections of metal line are often used for fuel line between the fuel pump and fuel injection unit. Check carefully to be sure the line has not been bent or crimped and that cracks have not started in the line.

12   If a section of metal fuel line must be replaced, only seamless steel tubing should be used, since copper and aluminum tubing don't have the strength necessary to withstand normal engine vibration.

13   Check the metal brake lines where they enter the master cylinder and brake proportioning unit (if used) for cracks in the lines or loose fittings. Any sign of brake fluid leakage calls for an immediate thorough inspection of the brake system.

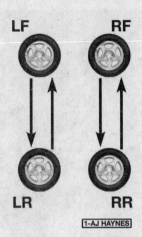

13.2 The recommended tire rotation pattern for these vehicles

12 Cooling system check (every 7500 miles or 6 months)

Refer to illustration 12.4

1 Many major engine failures can be attributed to a faulty cooling system. If the vehicle is equipped with an automatic transaxle, the cooling system also cools the transaxle fluid and thus plays an important role in prolonging transaxle life.

2 The cooling system should be checked with the engine cold. Do this before the vehicle is driven for the day or after the engine has been shut off for at least three hours.

3 Remove the radiator cap by turning it to the left until it reaches a stop. If you hear a hissing sound (indicating there is still pressure in the system), wait until it stops. Now press down on the cap with the palm of your hand and continue turning to the left until the cap can be removed. Thoroughly clean the cap, inside and out, with clean water. Also clean the filler neck on the radiator. All traces of corrosion should be removed. The coolant inside the radiator should be relatively transparent. If it's rust colored, the system should be drained and refilled (see Section 23). If the coolant level isn't up to the top, add additional antifreeze/coolant mixture (see Section 4).

4 Carefully check the large upper and lower radiator hoses along with the smaller diameter heater hoses which run from the engine to the firewall. Inspect each hose along its entire length, replacing any hose which is cracked, swollen or shows signs of deterioration. Cracks may become more apparent if the hose is squeezed **(see illustration)**. Regardless of condition, it's a good idea to replace hoses with new ones every two years.

5 Make sure that all hose connections are tight. A leak in the cooling system will usually show up as white or rust colored deposits on the areas adjoining the leak. If wire-type clamps are used at the ends of the hoses, it may be a good idea to replace them with more secure screw-type clamps.

6 Use compressed air or a soft brush to remove bugs, leaves, etc. from the front of the radiator or air conditioning condenser. Be careful not to damage the delicate cooling fins or cut yourself on them.

7 Every other inspection, or at the first indication of cooling system problems, have the cap and system pressure tested. If you don't have a pressure tester, most gas stations and repair shops will do this for a minimal charge.

13 Tire rotation (every 7500 miles or 6 months)

Refer to illustration 13.2

1 The tires should be rotated at the specified intervals and whenever uneven wear is noticed. Since the vehicle will be raised and the tires removed anyway, check the brakes (see Section 15) at this time.

2 Radial tires must be rotated in a specific pattern **(see illustration)**.

3 Refer to the information in *Jacking and towing* at the front of this manual for the proper procedures to follow when raising the vehicle and changing a tire. If the brakes are to be checked, do not apply the parking brake as stated. Make sure the tires are blocked to prevent the vehicle from rolling.

4 Preferably, the entire vehicle should be raised at the same time. This can be done on a hoist or by jacking up each corner and then lowering the vehicle onto jackstands placed under the frame rails. Always use four jackstands and make sure the vehicle is firmly supported.

5 After rotation, check and adjust the tire pressures as necessary and be sure to check the lug nut tightness.

6 For further information on the wheels and tires, refer to Chapter 10.

14 Seat belt check (every 7500 miles or 6 months)

1 Check the seat belts, buckles, latch plates and guide loops for obvious damage and signs of wear. Seat belts that exhibit fraying along the edges should be replaced.

2 Where the seat belt receptacle bolts to the floor of the vehicle, check that the bolts are secure.

3 See if the seat belt reminder light comes on when the key is turned to the Run or Start position. A chime should also sound.

15 Brake check (every 15,000 miles or 12 months)

Warning: *Dust created by the brake system is harmful to your health. Never blow it out with compressed air and don't inhale any of it. An approved filtering mask should be worn when working on the brakes. Do not, under any circumstances, use petroleum-based solvents to clean brake parts. Use brake system cleaner only!*

Note: *For detailed photographs of the brake system, refer to Chapter 9.*

1 In addition to the specified intervals, the brakes should be inspected every time the wheels are removed or whenever a defect is suspected. Any of the following symptoms could indicate a potential brake system defect: The vehicle pulls to one side when the brake pedal is depressed; the brakes make squealing or dragging noises when applied; brake travel is excessive; the pedal pulsates; brake fluid leaks, usually onto the inside of the tire or wheel.

2 The disc brake pads have built-in wear indicators which should make a high-pitched squealing or scraping noise when they are worn to the replacement point. When you hear this noise, replace the pads immediately or expensive damage to the discs can result.

3 Loosen the wheel lug nuts.

4 Raise the vehicle and place it securely on jackstands.

5 Remove the wheels (see *Jacking and towing* at the front of this book, or your owner's manual, if necessary).

Disc brakes

Refer to illustration 15.6

6 There are two pads - an outer and an inner - in each caliper. The pads are visible through small inspection holes in each caliper **(see illustration)**.

7 Check the pad thickness by looking at each end of the caliper and through the inspection hole in the caliper body. If the lining material is less than the thickness listed in this Chapter's Specifications, replace the pads. **Note:** *Keep in mind that the lining material is riveted or bonded to a metal backing plate and the metal portion is not included in this measurement.*

8 If it is difficult to determine the exact thickness of the remaining pad material by the

15.6 You will find an inspection hole like this in each caliper - placing a ruler across the hole should enable you to determine the thickness of remaining pad material for both inner and outer pads

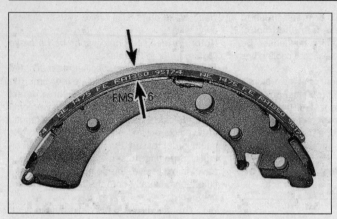

15.15 If the lining is bonded to the brake shoe, measure the lining thickness from the outer surface to the metal shoe, as shown here; if the lining is riveted to the shoe, measure from the lining outer surface to the rivet head

15.17 Carefully peel back the wheel cylinder boot and check for leaking fluid indicating that the cylinder must be replaced

above method, or if you are at all concerned about the condition of the pads, remove the caliper(s), then remove the pads for further inspection (refer to Chapter 9).

9   Once the pads are removed from the calipers, clean them with brake cleaner and re-measure them.

10   Measure the disc thickness with a micrometer to make sure that it still has service life remaining. If any disc is thinner than the specified minimum thickness, replace it (refer to Chapter 9). Even if the disc has service life remaining, check its condition. Look for scoring, gouging and burned spots. If these conditions exist, remove the disc and have it resurfaced (see Chapter 9).

11   Before installing the wheels, check all brake lines and hoses for damage, wear, deformation, cracks, corrosion, leakage, bends and twists, particularly in the vicinity of the rubber hoses at the calipers.

12   Check the clamps for tightness and the connections for leakage. Make sure that all hoses and lines are clear of sharp edges, moving parts and the exhaust system. If any of the above conditions are noted, repair, reroute or replace the lines and/or fittings as necessary (see Chapter 9).

Rear drum brakes

Refer to illustrations 15.15 and 15.17

13   To check the brake shoe lining thickness without removing the brake drums, remove the rubber plug from the backing plate and use a flashlight to inspect the linings. For a more thorough brake inspection, follow the procedure below.

14   Refer to Chapter 9 and remove the rear brake drums.

15   Note the thickness of the lining material on the rear brake shoes **(see illustration)** and look for signs of contamination by brake fluid and grease. If the lining material is within 1/16-inch of the recessed rivets or metal shoes, replace the brake shoes with new ones. The shoes should also be replaced if they are cracked, glazed (shiny lining surfaces) or

contaminated with brake fluid or grease. See Chapter 9 for the replacement procedure.

16   Check the shoe return and hold-down springs and the adjusting mechanism to make sure they're installed correctly and in good condition. Deteriorated or distorted springs, if not replaced, could allow the linings to drag and wear prematurely.

17   Check the wheel cylinders for leakage by carefully peeling back the rubber boots **(see illustration)**. If brake fluid is noted behind the boots, the wheel cylinders must be replaced (see Chapter 9).

18   Check the drums for cracks, score marks, deep scratches and hard spots, which will appear as small discolored areas. If imperfections cannot be removed with emery cloth, the drums must be resurfaced by an automotive machine shop (see Chapter 9 for more detailed information).

19   Install the brake drums.

20   Install the wheels and lug nuts.

21   Remove the jackstands and lower the vehicle.

22   Tighten the wheel lug nuts to the torque listed in this Chapter's Specifications.

Brake booster check

23   Sit in the driver's seat and perform the following sequence of tests.

24   With the brake fully depressed, start the engine - the pedal should move down a little when the engine starts.

25   With the engine running, depress the brake pedal several times - the travel distance should not change.

26   Depress the brake, stop the engine and hold the pedal in for about 30 seconds - the pedal should neither sink nor rise.

27   Restart the engine, run it for about a minute and turn it off. Then firmly depress the brake several times - the pedal travel should decrease with each application.

28   If your brakes do not operate as described above when the preceding tests are performed, the brake booster has failed. Refer to Chapter 9 for the replacement procedure.

Parking brake

29   Slowly pull up on the parking brake and count the number of clicks you hear until the handle is up as far as it will go. The adjustment is correct if you hear the specified number of clicks. If you hear more or fewer clicks, it's time to adjust the parking brake (refer to Chapter 9).

30   An alternative method of checking the parking brake is to park the vehicle on a steep hill with the parking brake set and the transaxle in Neutral (be sure to stay in the vehicle for this procedure). If the parking brake cannot prevent the vehicle from rolling, it is in need of adjustment (see Chapter 9).

16   Air filter replacement (every 15,000 miles or 12 months)

Refer to illustrations 16.2a and 16.2b

1   The air filter is located inside a housing at the left (driver's) side of the engine compartment.

2   To remove the air filter, release the spring clips that keep the two halves of the air cleaner housing together, then lift the cover

16.2a Detach the clips and separate the cover from the air cleaner housing

16.2b Hold the cover up out of the way and lift the element out

17.2 Use a small screwdriver to carefully pry out the old gasket - take care not to damage the cap

17.5 Inspect the filler hose for cracks and make sure the clamps are tight

up and remove the air filter element **(see illustrations)**.

3   Inspect the outer surface of the filter element. If it is dirty, replace it. If it is only moderately dusty, it can be reused by blowing it clean from the back to the front surface with compressed air. Because it is a pleated paper type filter, it cannot be washed or oiled. If it cannot be cleaned satisfactorily with compressed air, discard and replace it. While the cover is off, be careful not to drop anything down into the housing. **Caution:** *Never drive the vehicle with the air cleaner removed. Excessive engine wear could result and backfiring could even cause a fire under the hood.*

4   Wipe out the inside of the air cleaner housing.

5   Place the new filter into the air cleaner housing, making sure it seats properly.

6   Installation of the cover is the reverse of removal.

17 Fuel system check (every 15,000 miles or 12 months)

Refer to illustrations 17.2 and 17.5

Warning: *Gasoline is extremely flammable, so take extra precautions when you work on any part of the fuel system. Don't smoke or allow open flames or bare light bulbs near the work area, and don't work in a garage where a gas-type appliance (such as a water heater or a clothes dryer) is present. Since gasoline is carcinogenic, wear latex gloves when there's a possibility of being exposed to fuel, and, if you spill any fuel on your skin, rinse it off immediately with soap and water. Mop up any spills immediately and do not store fuel-soaked rags where they could ignite. The fuel system is under constant pressure, so, if any fuel lines are to be disconnected, the fuel pressure in the system must be relieved first. When you perform any kind of work on the fuel system, wear safety glasses and have a Class B type fire extinguisher on hand.*

1   If you smell gasoline while driving or after the vehicle has been sitting in the sun, inspect the fuel system immediately.

2   Remove the gas filler cap and inspect it for damage and corrosion. The gasket should have an unbroken sealing imprint. If the gasket is damaged or corroded, remove it and install a new one **(see illustration)**.

3   Inspect the fuel feed and return lines for cracks. Make sure that the threaded flare-nut type connectors which secure the metal fuel lines to the fuel injection system are tight.

4   Since some components of the fuel system - the fuel tank and part of the fuel feed and return lines, for example - are underneath the vehicle, they can be inspected more easily with the vehicle raised on a hoist. If that's not possible, raise the vehicle and support it securely on jackstands.

5   With the vehicle raised and safely supported, inspect the gas tank and filler neck for punctures, cracks and other damage. The connection between the filler neck and the tank is particularly critical. Sometimes a rubber filler neck will leak because of loose clamps or deteriorated rubber **(see illustration)**. These are problems a home mechanic can usually rectify. **Warning:** *Do not, under any circumstances, try to repair a fuel tank (except rubber components). A welding torch or any open flame can easily cause fuel vapors inside the tank to explode.*

6   Carefully check all rubber hoses and metal lines leading away from the fuel tank. Check for loose connections, deteriorated hoses, crimped lines and other damage. Carefully inspect the lines from the tank to the fuel injection system. Repair or replace damaged sections as necessary (see Chapter 4).

18 Manual transaxle lubricant level check (every 15,000 miles or 12 months)

1   The manual transaxle does not have a dipstick. To check the fluid level, raise the vehicle and support it securely on jackstands. On the lower front side of the transaxle housing, you will see a plug. Remove it. If the lubricant level is correct, it should be up to the lower edge of the hole.

2   If the transaxle needs more lubricant (if the level is not up to the hole), use a syringe or a gear oil pump to add more. Stop filling the transaxle when the lubricant begins to run out the hole.

3   Install the plug and tighten it securely. Drive the vehicle a short distance, then check for leaks.

19 Steering, suspension and driveaxle boot check (every 15,000 miles or 12 months)

Refer to illustrations 19.7 and 19.8

Note: *For detailed illustrations of the steering and suspension components, refer to Chapter 10.*

Steering and suspension check

With the wheels on the ground

1   With the vehicle stopped and the front wheels pointed straight ahead, rock the steering wheel gently back and forth. If freeplay **(see illustration)** is excessive, a front wheel bearing, main shaft yoke, intermediate shaft yoke, lower arm balljoint or steering system joint is worn or the steering gear is out of adjustment or broken. Refer to Chapter 10 for the appropriate repair procedure.

2   Other symptoms, such as excessive vehicle body movement over rough roads, swaying (leaning) around corners and binding as the steering wheel is turned, may indicate faulty steering and/or suspension components.

3   Check the shock absorbers by pushing down and releasing the vehicle several times at each corner. If the vehicle does not come back to a level position within one or two bounces, the shocks/struts are worn and must be replaced. When bouncing the vehicle up and down, listen for squeaks and noises from the suspension components. Additional information on suspension components can be found in Chapter 10.

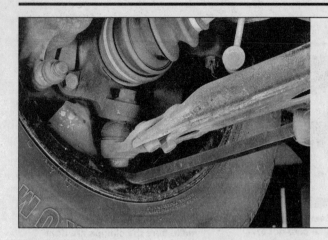

19.7 To check a balljoint for wear, try to move the control arm up and down with a prybar to make sure there is no play in the balljoint (if there is, replace it)

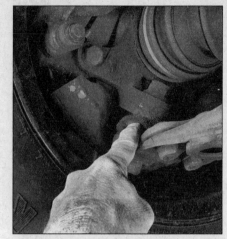

19.8 Push on the balljoint boot to check for damage

Under the vehicle

4   Raise the vehicle with a floor jack and support it securely on jackstands. See *Jacking and towing* at the front of this book for the proper jacking points.

5   Check the tires for irregular wear patterns and proper inflation. See Section 5 in this Chapter for information regarding tire wear and Chapter 10 for the wheel bearing replacement procedures.

6   Inspect the universal joint between the steering shaft and the steering gear housing. Check the steering gear housing for grease leakage or oozing. Make sure that the dust seals and boots are not damaged and that the boot clamps are not loose. Check the steering linkage for looseness or damage. Check the tie-rod ends for excessive play. Look for loose bolts, broken or disconnected parts and deteriorated rubber bushings on all suspension and steering components. While an assistant turns the steering wheel from side to side, check the steering components for free movement, chafing and binding. If the steering components do not seem to be reacting with the movement of the steering wheel, try to determine where the slack is located.

7   Move each control arm up and down with a pry bar **(see illustration)** to ensure that its balljoint has no play. If any balljoint does have play, replace it. See Chapter 10 for the balljoint replacement procedure.

8   Inspect the balljoint boots for damage and leaking grease **(see illustration)**. Replace the balljoints with new ones if they are damaged (see Chapter 10).

Driveaxle boot check

Refer to illustration 19.10

9   The driveaxle boots are very important because they prevent dirt, water and foreign material from entering and damaging the constant velocity (CV) joints. Oil and grease can cause the boot material to deteriorate prematurely, so it's a good idea to wash the boots with soap and water. Because it constantly pivots back and forth following the steering action of the front hub, the outer CV boot wears out sooner and should be inspected regularly.

10   Inspect the boots for tears and cracks as well as loose clamps **(see illustration)**. If there is any evidence of cracks or leaking lubricant, they must be replaced as described in Chapter 8.

20 Cabin air filter - replacement (every 15,000 miles or 12 months)

Refer to illustration 20.3

1   The covered models are equipped with a cabin air filter in the blower housing. The filter traps dust and pollen before the air enters the passenger compartment.

2   For access to the cabin air filter, remove the glove box (see Chapter 11).

3   Release the two clips on the filter door, open the door and remove the filter **(see illustration)**.

4   Installation is the reverse of the removal procedure.

21 Brake fluid change (every 30,000 miles or 24 months)

Warning: *Brake fluid can harm your eyes and damage painted surfaces, so use extreme caution when handling or pouring it. Do not use brake fluid that has been standing open or is more than one year old. Brake fluid absorbs moisture from the air. Excess moisture can cause a dangerous loss of braking effectiveness.*

1   At the specified intervals, the brake fluid should be drained and replaced. Since the brake fluid may drip or splash when pouring it, place plenty of rags around the master cylinder to protect any surrounding painted surfaces.

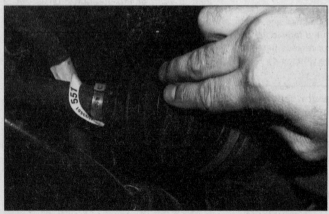

19.10 Flex the driveaxle boots by hand to check for cracks and/or leaking grease

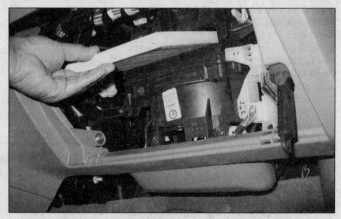

20.3 Open the cabin air filter door and slide the filter out

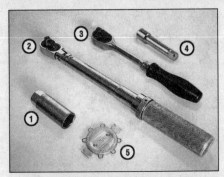

22.1 Tools required for changing spark plugs

1 **Spark plug socket** - *This will have special padding inside to protect the spark plug porcelain insulator*
2 **Torque wrench** - *Although not mandatory, use of this tool is the best way to ensure that the plugs are tightened properly*
3 **Ratchet** - *Standard hand tool to fit the plug socket*
4 **Extension** - *Depending on model and accessories, you may need special extensions and universal joints to reach one or more of the plugs*
5 **Spark plug gap gauge** - *This gauge for checking the gap comes in a variety of styles. Make sure the gap for your engine is included*

22.4a Spark plug manufacturers recommend using a wire-type gauge when checking the gap - if the wire does not slide between the electrodes with a slight drag, adjustment is required

22.4b To change the gap, bend the side electrode only, as indicated by the arrows, and be very careful not to crack or chip the porcelain insulator surrounding the center electrode

22.6 Engine cover fastener locations

2 Before beginning work, purchase the specified brake fluid (see *Recommended lubricants and fluids* at the beginning of this Chapter).
3 Remove the cap from the master cylinder reservoir.
4 Using a hand suction pump or similar device, withdraw the fluid from the master cylinder reservoir.
5 Add new fluid to the master cylinder until it rises to the line indicated on the reservoir.
6 Bleed the brake system as described in Chapter 9 at all four brakes until new and uncontaminated fluid is expelled from the bleeder screw. Be sure to maintain the fluid level in the master cylinder as you perform the bleeding process. If you allow the master cylinder to run dry, air will enter the system.
7 Refill the master cylinder with fluid and check the operation of the brakes. The pedal should feel solid when depressed, with no sponginess. **Warning:** *Do not operate the vehicle if you are in doubt about the effectiveness of the brake system.*

22 Spark plug check and replacement (every 30,000 miles or 24 months)

Refer to illustrations 22.1, 22.4a, 22.4b, 22.6, 22.10a and 22.10b

1 Spark plug replacement requires a spark plug socket which fits onto a ratchet wrench. This socket is lined with a rubber grommet to protect the porcelain insulator of the spark plug and to hold the plug while you insert it into the spark plug hole. You will also need a wire-type feeler gauge to check and adjust the spark plug gap and a torque wrench to tighten the new plugs to the specified torque **(see illustration).**
2 If you are replacing the plugs, purchase the new plugs, adjust them to the proper gap and then replace each plug one at a time. **Note:** *When buying new spark plugs, it's essential that you obtain the correct plugs for your specific vehicle. This information can be found in the Specifications Section at the beginning of this Chapter, on the Vehicle Emissions Control Information (VECI) label located on the underside of the hood or in the owner's manual. If these sources specify different plugs, purchase the spark plug type specified on the VECI label because that information is provided specifically for your engine.*
3 Inspect each of the new plugs for defects. If there are any signs of cracks in the porcelain insulator of a plug, don't use it.
4 Check the electrode gaps of the new plugs. Check the gap by inserting the wire gauge of the proper thickness between the electrodes at the tip of the plug **(see illustrations).** The gap between the electrodes should be identical to that listed in this Chap-ter's Specifications or on the VECI label. If the gap is incorrect, use the notched adjuster on the feeler gauge body to bend the curved side electrode slightly **(see illustration). Caution:** *Don't attempt to adjust the gap on a used iridium-coated plug.*
5 If the side electrode is not exactly over the center electrode, use the notched adjuster to align them. **Caution:** *If the gap of a new plug must be adjusted, bend only the base of the ground electrode - do not touch the tip.*

Removal

6 Remove the engine cover **(see illustration),** then remove the ignition coils (see Chapter 5).
7 If compressed air is available, blow any dirt or foreign material away from the spark plug area before proceeding.
8 Remove the spark plug.
9 Whether you are replacing the plugs at this time or intend to reuse the old plugs, compare each old spark plug with the chart on the inside back cover of this manual to determine the overall running condition of the engine.

Installation

10 Prior to installation, it's a good idea to coat the spark plug threads with anti-seize

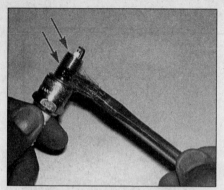

22.10a Apply a thin coat of anti-seize compound to the spark plug threads

22.10b A length of snug-fitting rubber hose will save time and prevent damaged threads when installing the spark plugs

23.4 On most models you will have to remove a cover for access to the radiator drain fitting located at the bottom of the radiator - before opening the valve, push a short section of 3/8-inch ID hose onto the plastic fitting to prevent the coolant from splashing

compound **(see illustration)**. Also, it's often difficult to insert spark plugs into their holes without cross-threading them. To avoid this possibility, fit a length of snug-fitting rubber hose over the end of the spark plug **(see illustration)**. The flexible hose acts as a universal joint to help align the plug with the plug hole. Should the plug begin to cross-thread, the hose will slip on the spark plug, preventing thread damage. Tighten the plug to the torque listed in this Chapter's Specifications.

11   Install the ignition coil.

12   Follow the above procedure for the remaining spark plugs.

---

23   Cooling system servicing (draining, flushing and refilling) (every 30,000 miles or 24 months)

Warning: *Do not allow engine coolant (antifreeze) to come in contact with your skin or painted surfaces of the vehicle. Rinse off spills immediately with plenty of water. Antifreeze is highly toxic if ingested. Never leave antifreeze lying around in an open container or in puddles on the floor; children and pets are attracted by it's sweet smell and may drink it. Check with local authorities on disposing of used antifreeze. Many communities have collection centers which will see that antifreeze*

is disposed of safely. Antifreeze is flammable under certain conditions - be sure to read the precautions on the container.

Note: *Non-toxic antifreeze is available at most auto parts stores. Although the antifreeze is non-toxic when fresh, proper disposal is still required.*

1   Periodically, the cooling system should be drained, flushed and refilled to replenish the antifreeze mixture and prevent formation of rust and corrosion, which can impair the performance of the cooling system and cause engine damage. When the cooling system is serviced, all hoses and the radiator cap should be checked and replaced if necessary.

Draining

Refer to illustrations 23.4 and 23.5

2   Apply the parking brake and block the wheels. If the vehicle has just been driven, wait several hours to allow the engine to cool down before beginning this procedure.

3   Once the engine is completely cool, remove the radiator cap.

4   Move a large container under the radiator drain to catch the coolant. Attach a 3/8-inch inner diameter hose to the drain fitting to direct the coolant into the container (some models are already equipped with a hose), then open the drain fitting (a pair of pliers may

be required to turn it) **(see illustration)**.

5   After the coolant stops flowing out of the radiator, move the container under the engine block drain plug **(see illustration)**. Loosen the plug and allow the coolant in the block to drain.

6   While the coolant is draining, check the condition of the radiator hoses, heater hoses and clamps (refer to Section 12 if necessary). Replace any damaged clamps or hoses.

Flushing

Refer to illustration 23.9

7   Once the system is completely drained, remove the thermostat from the engine (see Chapter 3). Then reinstall the thermostat housing without the thermostat. This will allow the system to be thoroughly flushed.

8   Tighten the radiator drain plug. Turn your heating system controls to Hot, so that the heater core will be flushed at the same time as the rest of the cooling system.

9   Disconnect the upper radiator hose from the radiator, then place a garden hose in the

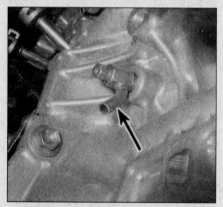

23.5 Attach a length of tubing to the spigot on the engine block drain, then loosen the drain bolt and allow the block to drain

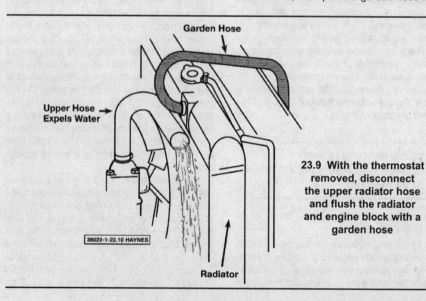

Garden Hose

Upper Hose Expels Water

Radiator

36022-1-22.10 HAYNES

23.9 With the thermostat removed, disconnect the upper radiator hose and flush the radiator and engine block with a garden hose

24.2 The charcoal canister is located above the rear suspension crossmember

upper radiator inlet and flush the system until the water runs clear at the upper radiator hose **(see illustration)**.

10   In severe cases of contamination or clogging of the radiator, remove the radiator (see Chapter 3) and have a radiator repair facility clean and repair it if necessary.

11   Many deposits can be removed by the chemical action of a cleaner available at auto parts stores. Follow the procedure outlined in the manufacturer's instructions. **Note:** *When the coolant is regularly drained and the system refilled with the correct antifreeze/water mixture, there should be no need to use chemical cleaners or descalers.*

12   Remove the overflow hose from the coolant recovery reservoir. Drain the reservoir and flush it with clean water, then reconnect the hose.

Refilling

13   Close and tighten the radiator drain. Install and/or tighten the block drain plug. Reinstall the thermostat (see Chapter 3).

14   Place the heater temperature control in the maximum heat position.

15   Slowly add new coolant (a 50/50 mixture of water and antifreeze) to the radiator until it's full. Squeeze the radiator hoses, then add more coolant, if possible. Add coolant to the reservoir up to the lower mark.

16   Install the radiator cap and run the engine in a well-ventilated area until the thermostat opens (coolant will begin flowing through the radiator and the upper radiator hose will become hot).

17   Turn the engine off and let it cool. Add more coolant mixture to bring the level back up to the lip on the radiator filler neck.

18   Squeeze the upper radiator hose to expel air, then add more coolant mixture if necessary. Reinstall the radiator cap.

19   Start the engine, allow it to reach normal operating temperature and check for leaks.

24 Evaporative emissions control system check (every 30,000 miles or 24 months)

Refer to illustration 24.2

1   The function of the evaporative emissions control system is to draw fuel vapors from the gas tank and fuel system, store them in a charcoal canister and then burn them during normal engine operation.

2   The most common symptom of a fault in the evaporative emissions control system is a strong fuel odor from the rear of the vehicle. If a fuel odor is detected, inspect the charcoal canister duct **(see illustration)** located under the rear of the vehicle, above the rear suspension crossmember. Check the canister and all hoses for damage and deterioration.

3   The evaporative emissions control system is explained in more detail in Chapter 6.

25 Exhaust system check (every 30,000 miles or 24 months)

Refer to illustration 25.4

1   With the engine cold (at least three hours after the vehicle has been driven), check the complete exhaust system from its starting point at the engine to the end of the tailpipe. This should be done on a hoist where unrestricted access is available.

2   Check the pipes and connections for evidence of leaks, severe corrosion or damage. Make sure that all brackets and hangers are in good condition and tight.

3   At the same time, inspect the underside of the body for holes, corrosion, open seams, etc. which may allow exhaust gases to enter the passenger compartment. Seal all body openings with silicone or body putty.

4   Rattles and other noises can often be traced to the exhaust system, especially the mounts and hangers. Try to move the pipes,

26.8a After loosening the front bolts, remove the rear transaxle pan bolts . . .

25.4 Be sure to check each exhaust system rubber hanger for damage

muffler and catalytic converter. If the components can come in contact with the body or suspension parts, secure the exhaust system with new mounts **(see illustration)**.

5   Check the running condition of the engine by inspecting inside the end of the tailpipe. The exhaust deposits here are an indication of engine state-of-tune. If the pipe is black and sooty or coated with white deposits, the engine is in need of a tune-up, including a thorough engine control system inspection.

26 Automatic transaxle fluid and filter change (every 30,000 miles or 24 months)

Refer to illustrations 26.8a, 26.8b, 26.9 and 26.11

1   At the specified time intervals, the automatic transaxle fluid should be drained and replaced.

2   Before beginning work, purchase the specified transmission fluid (see *Recommended fluids and lubricants* at the front of this Chapter).

3   Other tools necessary for this job include jackstands to support the vehicle in a raised position, wrenches, drain pan capable of holding at least four quarts, newspapers and clean rags.

4   The fluid should be drained immediately after the vehicle has been driven. Hot fluid is more effective than cold fluid at removing built up sediment. **Warning:** *Fluid temperature can exceed 350-degrees F in a hot transaxle. Wear protective gloves.*

5   After the vehicle has been driven to warm up the fluid, raise it and support it on jackstands for access to the transaxle and differential drain plugs.

6   Move the necessary equipment under the vehicle, being careful not to touch any of the hot exhaust components.

7   Place the drain pan under the drain plug in the transaxle pan and remove the drain plug. Be sure the drain pan is in position, as fluid will come out with some force. Once the fluid is drained, reinstall the drain plug securely.

8   Remove the front transaxle pan bolts, then loosen the rear bolts and carefully pry

26.8b . . . and allow the remaining fluid to drain out

26.9 Remove the filter bolts and lower the filter (be careful, there will be some residual fluid) - note that here one of the pan magnets is stuck to the filter (arrow); be sure to clean any magnets and return them to the pan

the pan loose with a screwdriver and allow the remaining fluid to drain (**see illustrations**). Once the fluid has drained, remove the bolts and lower the pan.

9   Remove the filter retaining bolts, disconnect the clip (some models) and lower the filter from the transaxle (**see illustration**). Be careful when lowering the filter as it contains residual fluid.

10   Place the new filter in position, connect the clip (if equipped) and install the bolts. Tighten the bolts securely.

11   Carefully clean the gasket surfaces of the fluid pan, removing all traces of old gasket material. Noting their location, remove the magnets, wash the pan in clean solvent and dry it. Be sure to clean and reinstall any magnets (**see illustration**).

12   Install a new gasket, place the fluid pan in position and install the bolts in their original positions. Tighten the bolts to the torque listed in this Chapter's Specifications.

13   Lower the vehicle.

14   With the engine off, add new fluid to the transaxle through the dipstick tube (see *Recommended fluids and lubricants* for the recommended fluid type and capacity). Use

a funnel to prevent spills. It is best to add a little fluid at a time, continually checking the level with the dipstick (see Section 4). Allow the fluid time to drain into the pan.

15   Start the engine and shift the selector into all positions from P through L, then shift into P and apply the parking brake.

16   With the engine idling, check the fluid level. Add fluid up to the Cool level on the dipstick.

27   Manual transaxle lubricant change (every 30,000 miles or 24 months)

1   Raise the vehicle and support it securely on jackstands.

2   Remove the filler plug and drain plug(s) and drain the fluid.

3   Reinstall the drain plug(s) and tighten securely.

4   Add new fluid until it is even with the lower edge of the filler hole. See *Recommended lubricants and fluids* for the specified lubricant type.

28   Positive Crankcase Ventilation (PCV) valve and hose check and replacement (every 30,000 miles or 24 months)

Refer to illustration 28.1

1   The PCV valve and hose is located in the valve cover. It's threaded into the left (driver's) end of the valve cover (**see illustration**).

2   Detach the hose, unscrew the valve from the cover, then reattach the hose to the valve.

3   With the engine idling at normal operating temperature, place your finger over the end of the valve. If there's no vacuum at the valve, check for a plugged hose or valve. Replace any plugged or deteriorated hoses.

4   Turn off the engine. Remove the PCV valve from the hose. Connect a clean piece of hose and blow through the valve from the valve cover (cylinder head) end. If air will not pass through the valve in this direction, replace it with a new one.

5   When purchasing a replacement PCV

26.11 Noting their locations, remove any magnets and wash them and the pan in solvent before reinstalling them

28.1 The PCV valve is threaded into the valve cover

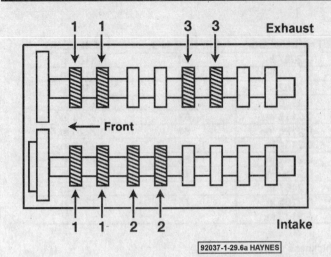

29.6a When the No. 1 piston is at TDC on the compression stroke, the valve clearance for the No. 1 and No. 3 cylinder exhaust valves and the No. 1 and No. 2 intake valves can be measured

29.6b Check the clearance for each valve with a feeler gauge of the specified thickness - if the clearance is correct, you should feel a slight drag on the gauge as you pull it out

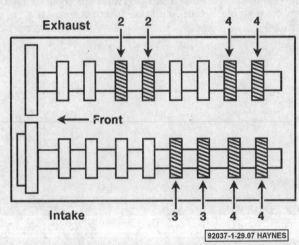

29.7 When the No. 4 piston is at TDC on the compression stroke, the valve clearance for the No. 2 and No. 4 exhaust valves and the No. 3 and No. 4 intake valves can be measured

29.9 Measure the thickness of each lifter head with a micrometer

valve, make sure it's for your particular vehicle and engine size. Compare the old valve with the new one to make sure they're the same.

29 Valve clearance check and adjustment (2008 and earlier models) (every 60,000 miles or 48 months)

Warning: *These models are equipped with airbags. Always disable the airbag system before working in the vicinity of any airbag system component to avoid the possibility of accidental deployment of the airbag(s), which could cause personal injury (see Chapter 12).*

Check

Refer to illustrations 29.6a, 29.6b and 29.7

1   Disconnect the negative cable from the battery.

2   Remove the ignition coils (see Chapter 5) and remove any other components that will interfere with valve cover removal.

3   Blow out the recessed area around the spark plug openings with compressed air, if available, to remove any debris that might fall into the cylinders, then remove the spark plugs (see Section 22).

4   Remove the valve cover (refer to Chapter 2A).

5   Refer to Chapter 2A and position the number 1 piston at TDC on the compression stroke.

6   Measure the clearances of the indicated valves with feeler gauges **(see illustrations)**. Record the measurements which are out of specification. They will be used later to determine the required replacement lifters.

7   Turn the crankshaft one complete revolution and realign the timing marks. Measure the remaining valves **(see illustration)**.

Adjustment

Refer to illustrations 29.9 and 29.10

8   If any of the valve clearances were out of adjustment, remove the camshaft(s) from over the lifter(s) that was/were out of the specified clearance range (see Chapter 2, Part B).

9   Measure the thickness of the lifter with a micrometer **(see illustration)**. To calculate the correct thickness of a replacement shim or lifter that will place the valve clearance within the specified value, use the following formula:

$N = T + (A - V)$
$T = thickness\ of\ the\ old\ shim\ or\ lifter$
$A = valve\ clearance\ measured$
$N = thickness\ of\ the\ new\ shim\ or\ lifter$
$V = desired\ valve\ clearance$ (see this Chapter's Specifications)

10   Select a lifter with a thickness as close as possible to the valve clearance calculated. The lifters are available in 35 sizes in increments of 0.0008-inch (0.020 mm), range in size from 0.1992-inch (5.060 mm) to 0.2260-inch (5.740 mm) **(see illustration)**. **Note:** *Through careful analysis of the lifter sizes needed to bring the out-of-specification valve*

LIFTER NO.	THICKNESS	LIFTER NO.	THICKNESS	LIFTER NO.	THICKNESS
06	0.1992 in.	30	0.2087 in.	54	0.2181 in.
08	0.2000 in.	32	0.2094 in.	56	0.2189 in.
10	0.2008 in.	34	0.2102 in.	58	0.2197 in.
12	0.2016 in.	36	0.2110 in.	60	0.2205 in.
14	0.2024 in.	38	0.2118 in.	62	0.2213 in.
16	0.2031 in.	40	0.2126 in.	64	0.2220 in.
18	0.2039 in.	42	0.2134 in.	66	0.2228 in.
20	0.2047 in.	44	0.2142 in.	68	0.2236 in.
22	0.2055 in.	46	0.2150 in.	70	0.2244 in.
24	0.2063 in.	48	0.2157 in.	72	0.2252 in.
26	0.2071 in.	50	0.2165 in.	74	0.2260 in.
28	0.2079 in.	52	0.2173 in.		

29.10 Valve lifter thickness chart

clearance within specification, it is often possible to simply move a lifter that has to come out anyway to another location requiring a lifter of that particular size, thereby reducing the number of new lifters that must be purchased.

11   Install the proper thickness lifter(s) in position, making sure to lubricate them with camshaft installation lube first. **Note:** *Apply the lubricant to the underside of the lifter where it contacts the valve stem, the walls of the lifter and the face of the lifter.*

12   Install the camshaft(s) (see Chapter 2A).
13   Recheck the valve clearances.
14   Installation of the spark plugs, valve cover, spark plug wires and boots (or ignition coils), etc. is the reverse of removal.

Notes

Notes

Chapter 2 Part A
Engine

Contents

Specifications

General

Engine type	DOHC, inline four-cylinder, four valves per cylinder
Engine designation	
2008 and earlier	1ZZ-FE
2009 and later	2ZR-FE
Cylinder numbers (drivebelt end-to-transaxle end)	1-2-3-4
Firing order	1-3-4-2
Displacement	
1ZZ-FE	1.8L
2ZR-FE	1.8L

Timing chain

Timing chain sprocket wear limit (minimum diameter)	
Camshaft sprocket(s) (w/chain)	
2003 and 2004	3.831 inches
2005 and later	3.811 inches
Crankshaft sprocket (w/chain)	
2003 and 2004	2.032 inches
2005 and later	2.008 inches
Timing chain stretch limit	
2003 and 2004 (16 pins)	4.827 inches
2005 and later (15 pins)	4.539 inches
Timing chain guide wear limit	0.039 inch

FRONT OF VEHICLE ① ② ③ ④

92036-2B SPECS HAYNES

Cylinder numbering

Cylinder head

Warpage limit (all machined surfaces)	0.0031 inch

Camshaft and lifters

Journal diameter	
No. 1 journal	1.3563 to 1.3569 inch
All others	0.9035 to 0.9041 inch
Bearing oil clearance	
Standard	0.0014 to 0.0028 inch
Service limit (maximum)	0.0039 inch

Camshaft and lifters (continued)

Runout limit.. 0.0012 inch
Thrust clearance (endplay)
  Standard... 0.0016 to 0.0037 inch
  Service limit (maximum)... 0.0043 inch
Lobe height
  Intake camshaft
    Standard .... 1.7454 to 1.7493 inches
    Service limit (minimum) .... 1.7394 inches
  Exhaust camshaft
    Standard .... 1.7229 to 1.7268 inches
    Service limit (minimum) .... 1.7169 inches
Valve lifter
  Diameter... 1.2191 to 1.2195 inches
  Bore diameter.. 1.2205 to 1.2215 inches
Lifter oil clearance
  Standard... 0.0009 to 0.0023 inch
  Service limit.. 0.0031 inch

Oil pump

Rotor-to-body clearance
  Standard
    2008 and earlier models .... 0.0102 to 0.0128 inch
    2009 and later models .... 0.005 to 0.007 inch
  Service limit.. 0.0128 inch
Rotor tip clearance
  Standard... 0.0016 to 0.0063 inch
  Service limit.. 0.0138 inch
Rotor side clearance
  Standard... 0.0010 to 0.0028 inch
  Service limit
    2008 and earlier models .... 0.0028 inch
    2009 and later models .... 0.006 inch

Torque specifications

Ft-lbs (unless otherwise indicated)

Note: *One foot-pound (ft-lb) of torque is equivalent to 12 inch-pounds (in-lbs) of torque. Torque values below approximately 15 ft-lbs are expressed in inch-pounds, since most foot-pound torque wrenches are not accurate at these smaller values.*

Camshaft bearing cap bolts
  2008 and earlier models
    Journal no. 1 17
    All others.. 120 in-lbs
  2009 and later models **(see illustration 8.42)**
    Camshaft bearing cap-to-cylinder head bolts 20
    Camshaft bearing cap-to-camshaft housing bolts .... 144 in-lbs
Camshaft sprocket bolts...................................... 40
Crankshaft pulley/vibration damper bolt 102
Cylinder head bolts
  2008 and earlier models
    Step 1 18
    Step 2 36
    Step 3 .... Tighten an additional 90-degrees (1/4 turn)
  2009 and later models
    Step 1 36
    Step 2 .... Tighten an additional 90-degrees (1/4 turn)
    Step 3 .... Tighten an additional 45-degrees (1/8 turn)
Drivebelt tensioner
  Bolt.. 51
  Nut 21
Engine mounts
  Passenger's side mount
    Mount-to-frame bolts.. 40
    Mount bracket-to engine mount bracket nuts/bolts....... 40
  Driver's side mount
    Mount-to-frame bolts.. 44
    Mount through-bolt.. 44
    Mount bracket (manual transaxle) 15

Torque specifications (continued)

Ft-lbs (unless otherwise indicated)

Engine mounts (continued)

Front and rear mounts

Front through-bolt to insulator	38

Rear through-bolt

2003 and 2004	64
2005 and later	48
Engine mount bracket-to timing chain cover bolts	35
Exhaust manifold nuts	27
Exhaust manifold brace bolts	36

Exhaust manifold heat shield bolts

2008 and earlier models	156 in-lbs
2009 and later models	108 in-lbs
Exhaust pipe-to-exhaust manifold bolts	32

Flywheel/driveplate bolts

Manual transaxle

Step 1	36
Step 2	Tighten an additional 90-degrees
Automatic transaxle	69
Intake manifold nuts/bracket bolts	22

Oil pump mounting bolts

2008 and earlier models	80 in-lbs
2009 and later models	16
Oil pump sprocket fastener (2009 and later models)	21
Oil pick-up/strainer nuts/bolts	80 in-lbs
Oil pan bolts	80 in-lbs
Timing chain guide bolts (stationary)	80 in-lbs
Timing chain tensioner pivot arm bolt	168 in-lbs

Timing chain cover bolts

2008 and earlier models

10 mm head	120 in-lbs
12 mm head	168 in-lbs

2009 and later models **(see illustrations 7.61a and 7.61b)**

Bolts A	19
Bolts B	38
Bolts C	38
Bolts D	84 in-lbs
Bolts E	19
Timing chain tensioner nuts/bolts	168 in-lbs

Valve cover bolts

2008 and earlier models

Perimeter bolts and nuts	80 in-lbs
Center two bolts	96 in-lbs
2009 and later models	84 in-lbs

1   General information

This Part of Chapter 2 is devoted to in-vehicle repair procedures. Information concerning engine removal and overhaul or re-placement can be found in Chapter 2, Part B.

The following repair procedures are based on the assumption that the engine is installed in the vehicle. If the engine has been removed from the vehicle and mounted on a stand, many of the steps outlined in this Part of Chapter 2 will not apply.

The Specifications included in this Part of Chapter 2 apply only to the procedures contained in this Part.

The four cylinder engines in the Corolla models covered by this manual are:

*2008 and earlier 1.8L engines,
designated 1ZZ-FE
2009 and later 1.8L engines,
designated 2ZR-FE*

The engines incorporate an aluminum cylinder block with a lower crankcase to strengthen the lower half of the block. All models use a Variable Valve Timing system to increase horsepower and decrease emissions.

2   Repair operations possible with the engine in the vehicle

Many major repair operations can be accomplished without removing the engine from the vehicle.

Clean the engine compartment and the exterior of the engine with some type of degreaser before any work is done. It will make the job easier and help keep dirt out of the internal areas of the engine.

Depending on the components involved, it may be helpful to remove the hood to improve access to the engine as repairs are performed (refer to Chapter 11 if necessary). Cover the fenders to prevent damage to the paint. Special pads are available, but an old bedspread or blanket will also work.

If vacuum, exhaust, oil or coolant leaks develop, indicating a need for gasket or seal replacement, the repairs can generally be made with the engine in the vehicle. The intake and exhaust manifold gaskets, oil pan gasket, crankshaft oil seals and cylinder head gasket are all accessible with the engine in place.

Exterior engine components, such as the intake and exhaust manifolds, the oil pan, the oil pump, the water pump, the starter motor, the alternator and the fuel system components can be removed for repair with the engine in place.

Since the cylinder head can be removed without pulling the engine, camshaft and valve component servicing can also be

3.5 A compression gauge can be used in the number one plug hole to assist in finding TDC

accomplished with the engine in the vehicle. Replacement of the timing chain and sprockets is also possible with the engine in the vehicle.

In extreme cases caused by a lack of necessary equipment, repair or replacement of piston rings, pistons, connecting rods and rod bearings is possible with the engine in the vehicle. However, this practice is not recommended because of the cleaning and preparation work that must be done to the components involved.

3   Top Dead Center (TDC) for number one piston - locating

Refer to illustrations 3.5 and 3.8

1   Top Dead Center (TDC) is the highest point in the cylinder that each piston reaches as it travels up the cylinder bore. Each piston reaches TDC on the compression stroke and again on the exhaust stroke, but TDC generally refers to piston position on the compression stroke.

2   Positioning the piston(s) at TDC is an essential part of many procedures such as valve timing, camshaft and timing chain/ sprocket removal.

3   Before beginning this procedure, be sure to place the transmission in Neutral and apply the parking brake or block the rear wheels. Disable the ignition system by disconnecting the primary electrical connectors at the ignition coils and remove the spark plugs (see Chapter 1). Also, remove the EFI fuse from the underhood fuse/relay block (this is only necessary if you will be using the starter to rotate the engine in the next step).

4   In order to bring any piston to TDC, the crankshaft must be turned using one of the methods outlined below. When looking at the front of the engine, normal crankshaft rotation is clockwise.

   a)   *The preferred method is to turn the crankshaft with a socket and ratchet attached to the bolt threaded into the front of the crankshaft. Turn the bolt in a clockwise direction only.*

   b)   *A remote starter switch, which may save some time, can also be used. Follow the instructions included with the switch. Once the piston is close to TDC, use a socket and ratchet as described in the previous paragraph.*

   c)   *If an assistant is available to turn the ignition switch to the Start position in short bursts, you can get the piston close to TDC without a remote starter switch. Make sure your assistant is out of the vehicle, away from the ignition switch, then use a socket and ratchet as described in Paragraph (a) to complete the procedure.*

5   Install a compression gauge in the number one spark plug hole **(see illustration)**. It should be a gauge with a screw-in fitting and a hose at least six inches long.

6   Rotate the crankshaft using one of the methods described above while observing for pressure on the compression gauge. The moment the gauge shows pressure indicates that the number one cylinder has begun the compression stroke.

7   Once the compression stroke has begun, TDC for the compression stroke is reached by bringing the piston to the top of the cylinder.

8   Continue turning the crankshaft until the notch in the crankshaft damper is aligned with the "TDC" or the "0" mark on the timing chain cover **(see illustration)**. At this point, the number one cylinder is at TDC on the compression stroke. If the marks are aligned but there was no compression, the piston was on the exhaust stroke; continue rotating the crankshaft 360-degrees (1-turn) and realign the marks. **Note:** *If a compression gauge is not available, you can simply place a blunt object over the spark plug hole and listen for compression as the engine is rotated. Once compression at the No.1 spark plug hole is noted the remainder of the Step is the same.*

9   After the number one piston has been positioned at TDC on the compression stroke, TDC for any of the remaining cylinders can be located by turning the crankshaft 180-degrees (clockwise) and following the firing order (refer to the Specifications). Rotating the engine 180-degrees past TDC #1 will put the engine at TDC compression for cylinder #3.

4   Valve cover - removal and installation

Removal

Refer to illustrations 4.2 and 4.6

1   Disconnect the cable from the negative terminal of the battery.

2   Remove the engine cover **(see illustration)**.

3   Disconnect the electrical connectors from the ignition coils, remove the nuts securing the wiring harness to the valve cover and position the ignition coil wiring harness aside. Then remove the ignition coil pack from each of the spark plugs (see Chapter 5).

4   On 2009 and later models, disconnect

3.8 Align the groove in the damper with the "0" mark on the timing chain cover

4.2 Remove the engine cover - upper arrows indicate plastic retaining clips, lower arrows indicate two retaining nuts

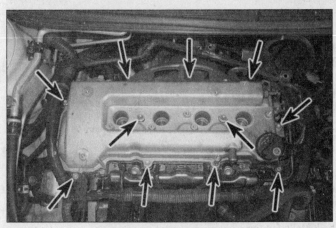

4.6 Valve cover fastener locations

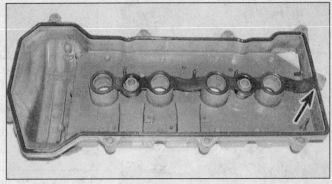

4.7 The valve cover gasket and the spark plug tube seals are incorporated into a single rubber O-ring-like seal (arrow) - press the gasket evenly into the grooves around the underside of the valve cover and the spark plug openings

the camshaft timing control valve assemblies and camshaft position sensor electrical connectors. Remove the mounting bolts for the control valves and sensors.

5   Detach the PCV hoses from the valve cover.

6   Remove the valve cover mounting bolts and nuts, then detach the valve cover and gasket from the cylinder head (see illustration). If the valve cover is stuck to the cylinder head, bump the end with a wood block and a hammer to jar it loose. If that doesn't work, try to slip a flexible putty knife between the cylinder head and valve cover to break the seal. Caution: *Don't pry at the valve cover-to-cylinder head joint or damage to the sealing surfaces may occur, leading to oil leaks after the valve cover is reinstalled.*

Installation

Refer to illustrations 4.7 and 4.8

7   Remove the valve cover gasket from the valve cover and clean the mating surfaces with lacquer thinner or acetone. Install a new rubber gasket, pressing it evenly into the grooves around the underside of the valve cover. Note: *Make sure the spark plug tube seals are in place on the underside of the valve cover before reinstalling it* (see illustration). The mating surfaces of the timing chain cover, the cylinder head and valve cover must be perfectly clean when the valve cover is installed. If there's residue or oil on the mating surfaces when the valve cover is installed, oil leaks may develop. On 2009 and later models, remove the O-rings from the No.1 camshaft bearing cap. Install a new rubber gasket (and O-rings on 2009 and later models), pressing it evenly into the grooves around the underside of the valve cover. Note: *Make sure the spark plug tube seals are in place on the underside of the valve cover before reinstalling it* (see illustration).

8   Apply RTV sealant at the timing chain cover-to-cylinder head joint, then install the valve cover and fasteners (see illustration).

9   Tighten the nuts/bolts to the torque listed in this Chapter's Specifications in three or four equal steps.

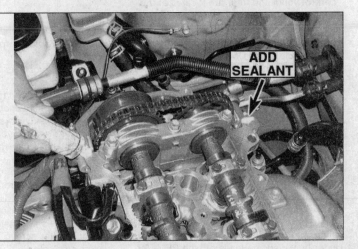

4.8 Apply sealant at the timing chain cover-to-cylinder head joint before installing the valve cover

ADD SEALANT

10   Reinstall the remaining parts, run the engine and check for oil leaks.

5   Variable Valve Timing (VVT) system - description and component check

Description

1   The VVT system is used on all models; a single Variable Valve Timing (VVT) system used on 2008 and earlier models, or the dual Variable Valve Timing (VVT-i) system used on 2009 and later models.

2   The VVT/VVT-i system varies intake (and exhaust on 2009 and later models) camshaft timing that is optimized for the driving conditions. Both systems achieve this by using engine oil pressure to advance or retard the controller on the front end of the intake camshaft on all models and also on the exhaust camshaft on 2009 and later models.

3   The VVT system on 2008 and earlier models consists of a CMP sensor, CKP sensor, camshaft timing oil control valve, Powertrain Control Module (PCM) and one controller (intake camshaft sprocket/actuator assembly). The dual VVT-i system, on 2009 and later models, consists of two CMP sensors, a

CKP sensor, two camshaft timing oil control valves, Powertrain Control Module (PCM) and two controllers (intake and exhaust camshaft sprocket/actuator assemblies).

4   Each controller consists of a timing rotor (for the VVT sensor), a housing with an impeller-type vane inside it, a lock pin and the actual timing chain sprocket for the intake camshaft. The vane is fixed on the end of the camshaft.

5   Once the VVT oil control valve is actuated by the PCM it directs the specified amount of oil pressure from the engine to advance or retard the camshaft sprocket/actuator assembly.

6   The camshaft sprocket/actuator assembly is equipped with an inner hub that is attached to the camshaft. The inner hub consists of a series of fixed vanes that use oil pressure as a wedge against the vanes to rotate the camshaft. The higher the oil pressure (or flow) the more the actuator assembly will rotate, thereby advancing or retarding the camshaft.

7   When oil is applied to the advance side of the vanes, the actuator can advance the camshaft up to 21-degrees in a clockwise direction. When oil is applied to the retard side of the vanes, the actuator will start to rotate the camshaft counterclockwise back to 0-degrees which is the normal position of

5.9a The Variable Valve Timing (VVT) oil control valve and filter are located at the front of the cylinder head

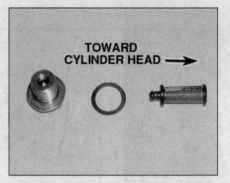

5.9b Whenever problems are suspected in the VVT system, check the oil control valve filter for clogging - note that the big end of the filter must be installed in the direction shown

head and check the operation of the control valve plunger. Using a pair of fused jumper wires, apply battery voltage to terminal No. 1 on the control valve, then apply ground to terminal No. 2 on the oil control valve. With battery voltage applied to the oil control valve, check for free movement of the plunger **(see illustration)**. The plunger should move out when voltage is applied and move back inward when voltage is not applied. If the oil control valve does not operate as described, replace the VVT oil control valve. Always use a new O-ring when reinstalling the control valve.

VVT camshaft sprocket/actuator assembly

12   The fourth and final check of the VVT system requires removing the valve cover, the intake camshaft and the camshaft sprocket/actuator assembly from the engine. Refer to Section 8 and perform Steps 1 through 10, removing the intake camshaft and sprocket from the engine only. Do not remove the exhaust camshaft or sprocket from the engine.

13   Clean the snout of the intake camshaft with lacquer thinner or acetone to remove all traces of oil from the front journals and the VVT oil control orifices. Apply vinyl tape over all the oil control orifices at the front of the camshaft, except the advance side oil port. Do not apply tape over the front of the camshaft were the sprocket fits.

14   Install the intake camshaft sprocket/actuator assembly onto the intake camshaft and tighten the bolt to 40 ft-lbs. Check that the actuator assembly will not rotate from the locked position. The locked position is a neutral position in which the actuator is placed during idle and no load conditions or when the VVT system is not activated by the PCM.

15   Apply 14 psi of air pressure to the advance side oil port and try to rotate the actuator assembly by hand. The actuator should rotate approximately 30-degrees in a counterclockwise direction from the locked position. Also check that it rotates freely with

the actuator during engine operation under no load or at idle. The PCM can also send a signal to the oil control valve to stop oil flow to both (advance and retard) passages to hold camshaft advance in its current position.

8   Under light engine loads, the VVT system will retard the camshaft timing to decrease valve overlap and stabilize engine output. Under medium engine loads, the VVT system will advance the camshaft timing to increase valve overlap, thereby increasing fuel economy and decreasing exhaust emissions. Under heavy engine loads at low RPM, the VVT system will advance the camshaft timing to help close the intake valve faster, which improves low to midrange torque. Under heavy engine loads at high RPM, the VVT system will retard the camshaft timing to slow the closing of the intake valve to improve engine horsepower.

Component checks

VVT oil control valve and filter

Refer to illustrations 5.9a, 5.9b, 5.10 and 5.11

Note 1: *A problem in the VVT oil control valve circuit will set a diagnostic* **trouble code** *and*

turn on the Check Engine light on the dash. Refer to Chapter 6 for accessing trouble codes.

Note 2: *Most problems in the VVT system are with the oil control valve and its filter. Regular engine oil and filter changes are necessary for trouble-free operation of the valve.*

Note 3: *Some checks and inspections of the VVT system require removal of the valve cover, the intake camshaft sprocket/actuator assembly and the intake camshaft.*

9   The first check of the VVT system components begins with removing the oil control valve filter from the cylinder head and check the filter/O-ring for clogging **(see illustrations)**. Clean and reinstall with a new O-ring. A clogged filter screen is often the cause of system problems.

10   The second and third check of the VVT system involve checking the operation of the oil control valve. Disconnect the electrical connector from the oil control valve and measure the resistance between the terminals of the control valve **(see illustration)**. There should be 6.9 to 7.9 ohms (approximately); if not, replace the VVT oil control valve.

11   If the resistance figures check out OK, remove the oil control valve from the cylinder

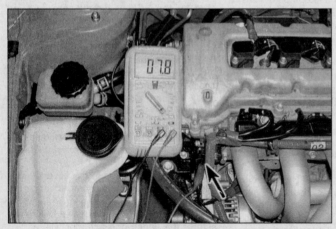

5.10 Measure the resistance between the terminals of the VVT oil control valve

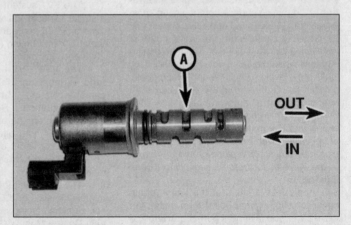

5.11 The oil control valve plunger (A) can be seen through the slots in the housing - the plunger should move outward when voltage is applied and inward when voltage is released

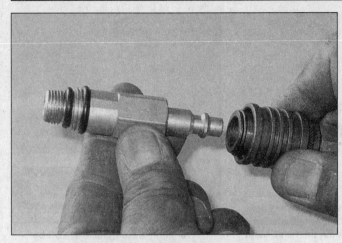

6.4 You'll need an air hose adapter to reach down into the spark plug tubes - they're commonly available from auto parts stores

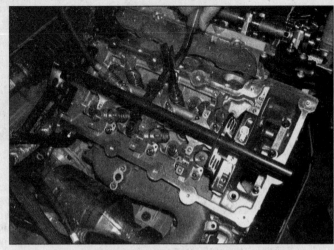

6.8a Compress the valve spring enough to release the keepers . . .

no obvious binding. **Note:** *It is critical to have an airtight seal between the air gun nozzle and the advance oil port hole to accomplish this task, as the lock pin in the actuator may not be forced out of its locating hole. If leakage at the air gun nozzle occurs, it may be necessary to apply a greater amount of air pressure to the advance side oil port in order to force the lock pin from the locating hole.*

16 If the actuator does not rotate freely as described, replace the intake camshaft sprocket/actuator assembly.

17 Reassembly is the reverse of removal.

6   Valve springs, retainers and seals - replacement

Refer to illustrations 6.4, 6.8a, 6.8b, 6.10, 6.15 and 6.17

Note: *Broken valve springs and defective valve stem seals can be replaced without removing the cylinder head. Two special tools and a compressed air source are normally required to perform this operation, so read through this Section carefully. The universal shaft-type valve spring compressor required*

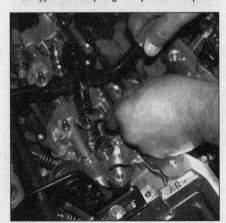

6.8b . . . and lift them out with a magnet or needle-nose pliers

for the tight valve spring pockets of this vehicle may not be available at all tool rental yards, so check on the availability before beginning the job.

1   Remove the valve cover (see Section 4). Refer to Section 7 and remove the timing chain, then refer to Section 8 and remove the camshafts and lifters from the cylinder head.

2   Remove the spark plug from the cylinder that has the defective component. If all of the valve stem seals are being replaced, all of the spark plugs should be removed.

3   Turn the crankshaft until the piston in the affected cylinder is at top dead center (TDC) on the compression stroke (see Section 3 for instructions). If you're replacing all of the valve stem seals, begin with cylinder number one and work on the valves for one cylinder at a time. Move from cylinder-to-cylinder following the firing order sequence (see the Specifications listed at the beginning of this Chapter).

4   Thread an adapter into the spark plug hole **(see illustration)** and connect an air hose from a compressed air source to it. Most auto parts stores can supply the air hose adapter. **Note:** *Many cylinder compression gauges utilize a screw-in fitting that may work with your air hose quick-disconnect fitting.*

5   Apply compressed air to the cylinder. The valves should be held in place by the air pressure. **Warning:** *If the cylinder isn't exactly at TDC, air pressure may force the piston down, causing the engine to quickly rotate. DO NOT leave a wrench on the crankshaft drive sprocket bolt or you may be injured by the tool.*

6   Stuff shop rags into the cylinder head holes around the valves to prevent parts and tools from falling into the engine.

7   Using a socket and a hammer, gently tap on the top of each valve spring retainer several times. This will break the bond between the valve keepers and the spring retainer and allow the keepers to separate from the valve spring retainer as the valve spring is compressed.

8   Use a valve spring compressor to compress the spring, then remove the keepers with small needle-nose pliers or a magnet **(see illustrations)**. **Note:** *Several different types of tools are available for compressing the valve springs with the head in place. Be sure to purchase or rent the "import type" that bolts to the top of the cylinder head. This type uses a support bar across the cylinder head for leverage as the valve spring is compressed. The lack of clearance surrounding the valve springs on these engines prohibits typical types of valve spring compressors from being used.*

9   Remove the valve spring and retainer. **Note:** *If air pressure fails to retain the valve in the closed position during this operation, the valve face or seat may be damaged. If so, the cylinder head will have to be removed for repair.*

10   Remove the old valve stem seals, noting differences between the intake and exhaust seals **(see illustration)**.

11   Wrap a rubber band or tape around the

6.10 A pair of pliers will be required to remove the valve seal from the valve guide

6.15 Using a deep socket and hammer, gently tap the new seals onto the valve guide only until seated

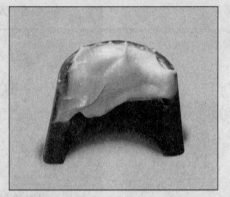

6.17 Apply a small dab of grease to each keeper as shown here before installation - it will hold them in place on the valve stem as the spring is released

7.7a Verify the engine is at TDC by observing the position of the camshaft sprocket marks (upper arrows) - they must be in a straight line and parallel with the top of the timing chain cover (lower arrow) (2008 and earlier models)

top of the valve stem so the valve won't fall into the combustion chamber, then release the air pressure.

12   Inspect the valve stem for damage. Rotate the valve in the guide and check the end for eccentric movement, which would indicate that the valve is bent.

13   Move the valve up-and-down in the guide and make sure it doesn't bind. If the valve stem binds, either the valve is bent or the guide is damaged. In either case, the head will have to be removed for repair.

14   Reapply air pressure to the cylinder to retain the valve in the closed position, then remove the tape or rubber band from the valve stem.

15   Lubricate the valve stem with engine oil and install a new seal on the valve guide (see illustration).

16   Install the valve spring and the spring retainer in position over the valve.

17   Compress the valve spring and carefully position the keepers in the groove. Apply a small dab of grease to the inside of each keeper to hold it in place (see illustration).

18   Remove the pressure from the spring tool and make sure the keepers are seated.

19   Disconnect the air hose and remove the adapter from the spark plug hole.

20   Install the camshaft, lifters, timing chain and the valve cover by referring to the appropriate Sections.

21   Install the spark plugs and the ignition coils.

22   Start and run the engine, then check for oil leaks and unusual sounds coming from the valve cover area.

7   Timing chain and sprockets - removal, inspection and installation

Note 1: *Special tools are required for this procedure. Read through the entire procedure and acquire the necessary tools and equipment before beginning work.*

Note 2: *On 2009 and later models, the manu-*

facturer recommends removing the engine and transaxle assembly to perform this procedure (see Chapter 2B).

Removal

Warning: *Wait until the engine is completely cool before beginning this procedure.*

Caution: *The timing system is complex, and severe engine damage will occur if you make any mistakes. Do not attempt this procedure*

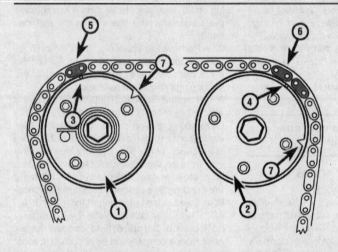

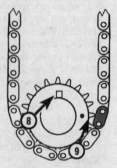

7.7b Camshafts and crankshaft TDC timing chain mark locations - 2009 and later 1.8L engines

1   *Exhaust camshaft sprocket*
2   *Intake camshaft sprocket*
3   *Exhaust camshaft sprocket timing mark*
4   *Intake camshaft sprocket timing mark*
5   *Timing chain orange colored link - exhaust*
6   *Timing chain orange colored links - intake*
7   *Index mark, not a timing mark*
8   *Crankshaft TDC keyway at 12 o'clock position*
9   *Crankshaft timing mark and timing chain yellow colored link*

42026-2B-06.17 HAYNES

7.9 If an engine support fixture is not available, the engine can be supported from below using a floor jack and a block of wood

7.11 Remove the drivebelt tensioner, the engine mount bracket and the crankshaft position sensor from the timing chain cover

unless you are highly experienced with this type of repair. If you are at all unsure of your abilities, be sure to consult an expert. Double-check all your work and be sure everything is correct before you attempt to start the engine. **Note:** *Special tools are required for this procedure. Read through the entire procedure and acquire the necessary tools and equipment before beginning work.*

All models

Refer to illustrations 7.7a, 7.7b, 7.9 and 7.11

1   Disconnect the cable from the negative battery terminal (see Chapter 5).

2   Remove the drivebelt (see Chapter 1) and the alternator (see Chapter 5).

3   Remove the windshield washer reservoir and valve cover (see Section 4).

4   With the parking brake applied and the rear wheels blocked, loosen the right front wheel lug nuts, then raise the front of the vehicle and support it securely on jackstands. Remove the right front wheel and the right splash shield from the wheel well.

5   Drain the cooling system (see Chapter 1).

6   While the coolant is draining, on 2008 and earlier models, remove the power steering pump from the engine without disconnecting the fluid lines (see Chapter 10). Tie the power steering pump to the body with a piece of wire and position it out of the way. On 2009 and later models, remove the cowl assembly (see Chapter 11) and windshield wiper motor and linkage (see Chapter 12).

7   Position the number one piston at TDC on the compression stroke (see Section 3). Confirm the engine is at TDC on the compression stroke by verifying that the timing mark on the crankshaft pulley/vibration damper is aligned with the "0" mark on the timing chain cover **(see illustration 3.8)** and the camshaft sprocket marks are aligned with the marks on the camshaft front bearing caps **(see illustrations)**. **Note:** *There are two sets of marks on the camshaft sprockets. The marks that align at TDC are for TDC reference only; the other two marks are used to align the sprockets with the timing chain during installation.*

8   Remove the crankshaft pulley/vibration damper, being careful not to rotate the engine from TDC (see Section 11). If the engine rotates off TDC during this step, reposition the engine back to TDC before proceeding.

9   Support the engine from above using an engine support fixture (available at rental yards), or from below using a floor jack. Use a wood block between the floor jack and the engine to prevent damage **(see illustration)**.

10   Remove the front exhaust pipe-to-manifold mounting bolts and the passenger side engine mount (see Section 18).

11   Remove the drivebelt tensioner (see Chapter 1) and the crankshaft position sensor (see Chapter 6) from the timing chain cover **(see illustration)**. Also remove the bolt securing the crankshaft position sensor wiring harness to the timing chain cover. On 2009 and later models, remove the steel oil pan (see Section 14).

2008 and earlier models

Refer to illustrations 7.13, 7.14a, 7.14b, 7.14c, 7.15 , 7.16 and 7.19

12   Remove the water pump.

13   Remove the timing chain tensioner from the rear side of the timing chain cover **(see illustration)**.

14   Remove the timing chain cover fasteners and pry the cover off the engine **(see illustrations)**.

7.13 Timing chain tensioner mounting nuts

7.14a Timing chain cover upper fasteners - this stud (A) will have to be removed with a Torx socket and tightened to 82 in-lbs during installation - 2008 and earlier models

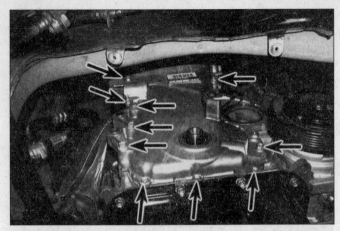

7.14b Timing chain cover lower fasteners - make a note of the fastener sizes, locations and lengths as you're removing them, as they must be installed back in their original position - 2008 and earlier models

7.14c Pry the timing chain cover off by the casting protrusion

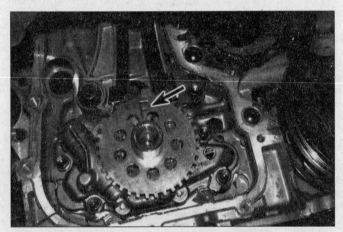

7.15 Slide the crankshaft position sensor reluctor ring off the crankshaft - note the "F" mark on the front (it must be facing outward upon installation)

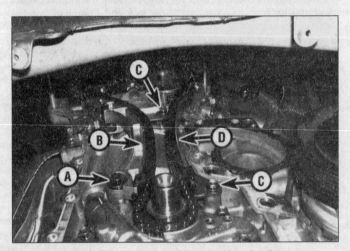

7.16 Timing chain guide mounting details

A	Pivot bolt	C Stationary chain guide mounting bolts
B	Tensioner pivot arm/ chain guide	D Stationary chain guide

7.19 Hold the lug on the camshaft with a wrench to keep it from rotating as the sprocket bolts are loosened - on the intake camshaft, loosen the center bolt securing the VVT sprocket to the camshaft only

15 Slide the crankshaft position sensor reluctor ring off the crankshaft **(see illustration)**.

16 Remove the timing chain tensioner pivot arm/chain guide **(see illustration)**.

17 Lift the timing chain off the camshaft sprockets and remove the timing chain and the crankshaft sprocket as an assembly from the engine. The crankshaft sprocket should slip off the crankshaft by hand. If not, use several flat bladed screwdrivers to evenly pry the sprocket off the crankshaft. **Note:** *If you intend to reuse the timing chain, use white paint or chalk to make a mark indicating the front of the chain. If a used timing chain is reinstalled with the wear pattern in the opposite direction noise and increased wear may occur.*

18 Remove the stationary timing chain guide **(see illustration 7.16)**.

19 To remove the camshaft sprockets, loosen the bolts while holding the lug on the camshaft with a wrench **(see illustration)**. Note the identification marks on the camshaft sprockets before removal, then remove the bolts. Pull on the sprockets by hand until they slip off the

dowels. If necessary, use a small puller, with the legs inserted in the relief holes, to pull the sprockets off. **Note:** *All models are equipped with variable valve timing, which consists of an actuator assembly attached to the intake camshaft sprocket. When removing the intake camshaft sprocket only loosen and remove the center bolt, which fastens the sprocket to the camshaft. Do not loosen the outer four bolts that secure the actuator to the sprocket.*

2009 and later models

20 Remove the timing chain tensioner mounting nuts and tensioner from the rear side of the timing chain cover.

21 Remove the oil filter housing mounting bolts and housing.

22 Once the housing is off, remove the O-rings.

23 Remove the engine mounting bracket from the front of the timing chain cover, then remove the timing chain cover fasteners and carefully pry the cover off the engine from several locations. **Note:** *The timing chain cover has several different size mounting bolts; take*

7.29a Wrap the chain around each of the timing sprockets and measure the diameter of the sprockets across the chain rollers - if the measurement exceeds the minimum sprocket diameter, the chain and the timing sprockets must be replaced

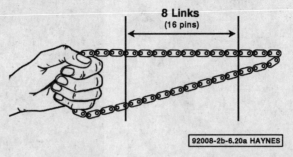

8 Links
(16 pins)

92008-2b-6.20a HAYNES

7.29b Timing chain stretch is measured by checking the length of the chain between 16 pins (2004 and earlier models) or 15 pins (2005 and later models) at 3 or more places (selected randomly) around the chain - if chain stretch exceeds the specifications, the chain must be replaced

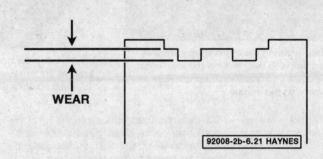

WEAR

92008-2b-6.21 HAYNES

7.30 Timing chain guide wear is measured from the top of the chain contact surface to the bottom of the wear grooves

note of each bolt's location so they can be returned to the same locations on reassembly.

24   Once the cover is off, remove the O-rings from the crankcase. **Note:** *The water pump is mounted to the timing chain cover; it is not necessary to remove the pump for the timing chain cover to be removed.*

25   Remove the top chain guide mounting bolts and guide.

26   Remove the timing chain tensioner pivot arm/chain guide and the stationary timing chain guide mounting bolts, then remove the guides from each side of the chain.

27   Place an adjustable wrench on the hex-shaped lug of the intake camshaft and turn the camshaft counterclockwise just enough to lift the timing chain off the camshaft sprockets and remove the timing chain from the engine. Then rotate the camshaft clockwise to its original position. **Note:** *If you intend to reuse the timing chain, use white paint or chalk to make a mark indicating the front of the chain. If a used timing chain is reinstalled with the wear pattern in the opposite direction, noise and increased wear may occur.*

28   To remove the camshaft sprockets, loosen the center bolt while holding the hex on the camshaft with a wrench **(see illustration 7.19).** Note the identification marks on the camshaft sprockets before removal, then remove the bolt. Pull on the sprockets by hand until they slip off the dowels. If necessary, use a small puller, with the legs inserted in the relief holes, to pull the sprocket off. **Note:** *These models are equipped with variable valve timing, which consists of an actuator assembly attached to the camshaft sprocket. When removing the sprocket, only loosen and remove the center bolt, which fastens the sprocket to the camshaft. Do not*

loosen the outer four bolts that secure the actuator to the sprocket.

Inspection

Refer to illustrations 7.29a, 7.29b and 7.30

29   Visually inspect all parts for wear and damage. Check the timing chain for loose pins, cracks, worn rollers and side plates. Check the sprockets for hook-shaped, chipped and broken teeth. Also check the timing chain for stretching and the diameter of the timing sprockets for wear with the chain assembled on the sprockets **(see illustration)**. Be sure to measure across the chain rollers when checking the sprocket diameter and to measure chain stretch at three or more places around the chain; if chain stretch exceeds the specifications, the chain must be replaced **(see illustration)**. Maximum chain elongation and minimum sprocket diameter (with chain) should not exceed the amount listed in this Chapter's Specifications. Replace the timing chain and sprockets as a set if the engine has high mileage or fails inspection.

30   Check the chain guides for excessive wear **(see illustration)**. Replace the chain guides if scoring or wear exceeds the amount listed in this Chapter's Specifications. Note that some scoring of the timing chain guide shoes is normal. If excessive wear is indicated, it will also be necessary to inspect the chain guide oil hole on the front of the oil pump for clogging (see Section 15).

Installation

Caution: *Before starting the engine, carefully rotate the crankshaft by hand through at least two full revolutions (use a socket and breaker*

bar on the crankshaft pulley center bolt). If you feel any resistance, STOP! There is something wrong - most likely, valves are contacting the pistons. You must find the problem before proceeding. Check your work and see if any updated repair information is available.

2008 and earlier 1.8L models

Refer to illustrations 7.36, 7.37, 7.38, 7.41, 7.43, 7.44 and 7.45

31   Remove all traces of old sealant from the timing chain cover and the mating surfaces of the engine block and cylinder head.

32   Make sure the camshafts are positioned with the dowel pins at the top in the 12 o'clock position, then install both camshaft sprockets in their original locations by aligning the dowel pin hole on the rear of the sprockets with dowel pin on the camshaft. Apply medium strength thread locking compound to the camshaft sprocket bolt threads and make sure the washers are in place. Hold the camshaft from turning as described in Step 19 and tighten the bolts to the torque listed in this Chapter's Specifications.

33   Rotate the camshafts as necessary to align the TDC marks on the camshaft sprockets **(see illustration 7.7a)**.

34   If the crankshaft has been rotated off TDC during this procedure, it will be necessary to rotate the crankshaft until the keyway is pointing straight up in the 12 o'clock position with the centerline of the cylinder bores.

35   Install the stationary timing chain guide **(see illustration 7.16)**.

36   Loop the timing chain around the crankshaft sprocket and align the No.1 colored link with the mark on the crankshaft sprocket. Install the chain and crankshaft sprocket as an assembly on the engine **(see illustration)**. **Note:** *There are three colored links on the*

7.36 Loop the timing chain around the crankshaft sprocket and align the No.1 colored link with the mark on the crankshaft sprocket, then install the chain and crankshaft sprocket as an assembly on the engine

7.37 Loop the timing chain up over the intake camshaft and around the exhaust camshaft, while aligning the remaining two colored links with the marks on the camshaft sprockets

timing chain. The No.1 colored link is the link farthest away from the two colored links that are closest together.

7.38 After the tensioner pivot arm is installed, make sure the tab (arrow) on the pivot arm can't move past the stopper on the cylinder head

37   Slip the timing chain into the lip of the stationary timing chain guide and over the intake camshaft sprocket, then around the exhaust camshaft sprocket making sure to align the remaining two colored links with the marks on the camshaft sprockets **(see illustration)**. Be sure to remove all slack from the right side of the chain when doing so.

38   Use one hand to remove the slack from the left side of the chain and install the timing chain tensioner pivot arm/chain guide. Tighten the pivot bolt to torque listed in this Chapter's Specifications. After installation, make sure the tab on the pivot arm can't move past the stopper on the cylinder head **(see illustration)**.

39   Reconfirm that the number one piston is still at TDC on the compression stroke and that the timing marks on the crankshaft and camshaft sprockets are aligned with the colored links on the chain.

40   Install the crankshaft position sensor reluctor ring with the "F" mark facing outward.

41   Apply a bead of RTV sealant to the timing chain cover sealing surfaces **(see illustra-**

tion). Place the timing chain cover in position on the engine and install the bolts in their original locations. Tighten the bolts evenly in several steps to the torque listed in this Chapter's Specifications **(see illustrations 7.14a and 7.14b)**. Be sure to follow the sealant manufacturer's recommendations for assembly and sealant curing times.

42   Install the water pump O-ring, the water pump and the engine mount bracket all within the sealant manufacturer's specified drying times. Before installing the engine mount bracket, apply a small amount of RTV sealant to the threads of the engine mount bracket bolts.

43   Reload and lock the timing chain tensioner to its zero position as follows:

a) *Raise the ratchet pawl and push the plunger inward until it bottoms out* **(see illustration)**.

b) *Engage the hook on the tensioner body with the pin on the tensioner plunger to lock the plunger in place.*

44   Lubricate the tensioner O-ring with a

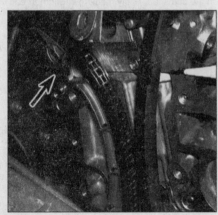

7.41 Apply a bead of sealant on each side of the parting line between the cylinder head and the engine block

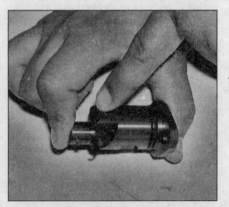

7.43 Raise the ratchet pawl and push the plunger inward until the hook on the tensioner body can be engaged with the pin on the plunger to lock the plunger in place

7.44 Apply a small amount of oil to the tensioner O-ring and insert the tensioner into the timing chain cover with the hook facing upward

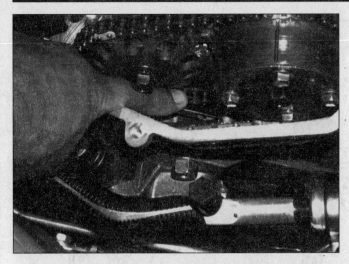

7.45 Depress the tensioner pivot arm and disengage the hook from the plunger pin to set tension on the timing chain

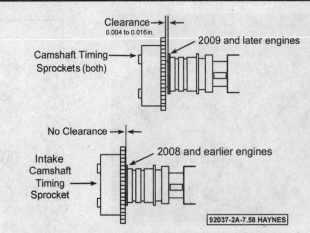

7.49 Camshaft sprocket installation details: on 2009 and later models, the clearance between the sprocket and flange should be between 0.004 to 0.016 inches; on 2008 and earlier engines there should be no clearance

small amount of oil and install the tensioner into the timing chain cover with the hook facing up (see illustration).

45 Install the crankshaft pulley/vibration damper (see Section 12). Rotate the engine clockwise slightly to set the chain tension. As the engine is rotated, the hook on the tensioner body should release itself from the pin on the plunger and allow the plunger to spring out and apply tension to the timing chain. If the plunger does not spring outward and apply tension to the timing chain, press downward on the pivot arm and release the hook with a screwdriver (see illustration).

46 Rotate the engine clockwise several turns and reposition the number one piston at TDC on the compression stroke (see Section 3). Visually confirm that the timing mark on the crankshaft pulley/vibration damper is aligned with the "0" mark on the timing chain cover and the camshaft sprocket marks are aligned and parallel with the top of the timing chain cover as shown in illustration 7.7a. Proceed to Step 68.

2009 and later models

Refer to illustrations 7.49, 7.60a and 7.60b, 7.61a, 7.61b and 7.65

Note: Remove all traces of old sealant from the timing chain cover and the mating surfaces of the engine block and cylinder head.

47 Make sure the camshafts are positioned with the dowel pins at the top in the 12 o'clock position, then carefully push the camshaft timing gear on to the camshaft with the dowel pin and key groove off-center. Turn the camshaft timing gear counterclockwise while pushing the gear on to the camshaft until the dowel drops in to the groove and then seat the camshaft gear to the camshaft. Caution: Do not turn the camshaft gear clockwise at this time, it may unseat the dowel pin.

48 Apply medium-strength thread locking compound to the camshaft sprocket bolt threads and make sure the washers are in place. Hold the camshaft from turning as

described in Step 19 and tighten the bolts to the torque listed in this Chapter's Specifications.

49 Make sure the clearance between the camshaft sprocket and camshaft flange is as specified (see illustration).

50 On intake camshafts, check to make sure the camshaft gear can be rotated clockwise and is locked in the furthest position clockwise.

51 Temporarily install the crankshaft pulley bolt and rotate the crankshaft counterclockwise until the keyway is pointing to the 12 o'clock position.

52 Rotate the camshafts as necessary to align the TDC marks on the camshaft sprockets (see illustration 7.7b).

53 Install the stationary timing chain guide mounting bolts and guide and tighten the bolts to the torque listed in this Chapter's Specifications.

54 Align the single orange link of the timing chain with the timing mark on the exhaust camshaft gear and install the chain on the sprocket. Slip the timing chain around the intake camshaft sprocket but not onto the teeth of the sprocket. Note: There are four colored links on the timing chain. The single orange link is for the exhaust camshaft, the two orange links are for the intake camshaft and the yellow colored link (farthest away) is for the crankshaft timing gear.

55 Guide the chain into the stationary chain guide and allow the chain to rest on the crankshaft at this time.

56 Using a wrench on the lug of the intake camshaft to prevent it from turning, rotate the camshaft timing gear counterclockwise to align the timing mark on the intake camshaft gear and the chain colored links. Once the intake camshaft gear and colored links are aligned, install the chain on to the teeth of the camshaft sprocket.

57 Again using a wrench on the lug of the intake camshaft to prevent it from turning, slowly rotate the intake camshaft timing gear

(only) clockwise, until yellow link of the chain is aligned with the timing mark on the crankshaft sprocket at the 3 o'clock position and the keyway is pointing to the 12 o'clock position.

58 Confirm that the number one piston is still at TDC on the compression stroke and that the timing marks on the crankshaft and camshaft sprockets are aligned with the colored links on the chain (see illustration 7.7b).

59 Install the top chain guide mounting bolts and guide and tighten the bolts to the torque listed in this Chapter's Specifications.

60 Apply a bead of RTV sealant to the timing chain cover sealing surfaces (see illustrations). Place the timing chain cover in posi-

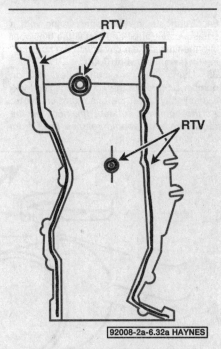

7.60a Timing chain cover sealant application details

7.60b Apply a bead of sealant on each side of the parting line between the cylinder head and engine block

tion on the engine and install the bolts in their original locations.

61 Tighten the bolts a little at time, in the proper sequence, to the torque listed in this Chapter's Specifications **(see illustrations)**. Be sure to follow the sealant manufacturer's recommendations for assembly and sealant curing times.

62 Install the chain tensioner pivot arm/chain guide mounting bolt, then tighten the bolt to the torque listed in this Chapter's Specifications.

63 Reload and lock the timing chain tensioner to its zero position as follows:

a) *Raise the ratchet pawl and push the plunger inward until it bottoms out* **(see illustration 7.43)**.

b) *Engage the hook on the tensioner body with the pin on the tensioner plunger to lock the plunger in place.*

64 Lubricate the tensioner O-ring with a small amount of oil and install the tensioner into the timing chain cover with the hook facing up **(see illustration 7.44)**.

65 Using the crankshaft pulley/vibration damper bolt, rotate the engine counterclockwise slightly to set the chain tension. **Note:** *As the engine is rotated, the hook on the tensioner body should release itself from*

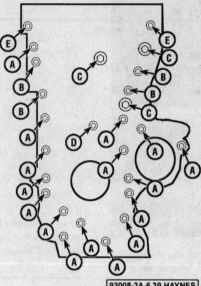

7.61a Timing chain cover bolt identification - 2009 and later models

the pin on the plunger and allow the plunger to spring out and apply tension to the timing chain **(see illustration)**. *If the plunger does not spring outward and apply tension to the timing chain, press downward on the pivot arm and release the hook with a screwdriver.*

66 Install the engine mounting bracket to the front of the timing chain cover and tighten the bolts in sequence to the torque listed in this Chapter's Specifications.

67 Install the crankshaft pulley/vibration damper (see Section 11).

All models

Caution: *Carefully and slowly rotate the crankshaft by hand through at least two full revolutions (use a socket and breaker bar on the crankshaft pulley center bolt). If you feel any resistance, STOP! There is something wrong - most likely, valves are contacting the pistons. You must find the problem before proceeding.*

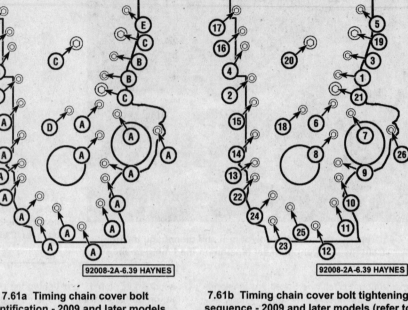

7.61b Timing chain cover bolt tightening sequence - 2009 and later models (refer to the Specifications for the torque settings)

68 Rotate the engine clockwise at least two revolutions and reposition the number one piston at TDC on the compression stroke (see Section 3). Visually confirm that the timing mark on the crankshaft pulley/vibration damper is aligned with the "0" mark on the timing chain cover and the camshaft sprocket marks are aligned and parallel with the top of the timing chain cover as shown in **illustrations 7.7a or 7.7b**.

69 The remainder of installation is the reverse of removal.

---

8 Camshafts and lifters - removal, inspection and installation

---

Note: *The camshafts should always be thoroughly inspected before installation and camshaft endplay should always be checked prior to camshaft removal (see Step 13).*

Removal

Refer to illustrations 8.4 and 8.7

1 Disconnect the cable from the negative terminal of the battery. Remove the valve cover (see Section 4).

2 On 2009 and later models, remove the cowl assembly (see Chapter 11) and the wiper motor and linkage (see Chapter 12).

3 Refer to Section 3 and place the engine on TDC for number 1 cylinder. Visually confirm the engine is at TDC on the compression stroke by verifying that the timing mark on the crankshaft pulley/vibration damper is aligned with the "0" mark on the timing chain cover and the camshaft sprocket TDC marks are aligned and parallel with the top of the timing chain cover **(see illustrations 3.8, 7.7a and 7.7b)**.

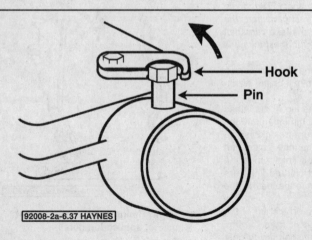

Hook

Pin

7.65 Rotate the engine counterclockwise to disengage the hook from the plunger pin on the tensioner. Rotate it clockwise and confirm that the plunger has extended outward against the pivot arm/chain guide

8.4 With the TDC marks aligned, apply a dab of paint to the timing chain links where they meet the upper timing marks on the camshaft sprockets

8.7 With the camshaft sprockets removed, hang the timing chain out of the way with a piece of wire and place a shop rag in the timing chain cover opening to prevent foreign objects from falling into the engine

4   With the TDC marks aligned, apply a dab of paint to the timing chain links where they meet the upper timing marks on the camshaft sprockets **(see illustration)**. **Note:** *There are two sets of marks on the camshaft sprockets. The marks that align at TDC are for TDC reference only, the other two marks are used to align the sprockets with the timing chain during installation.*

5   Using a wrench to hold the camshaft sprockets from turning, loosen the camshaft sprocket bolts several turns **(see illustration 7.19)**. If the camshaft sprockets have rotated during the bolt loosening process, rotate the engine clockwise until the "TDC" marks on the cam sprockets are realigned.

6   Remove the timing chain tensioner from the timing chain cover **(see illustration 7.13)** and the camshaft position sensor from the cylinder head (see Chapter 6).

7   Remove the camshaft sprocket retaining bolts. Disengage the timing chain from the sprockets and remove the camshaft sprockets from the engine. Make sure to note that the sprockets are marked "IN" for intake or "EX" for exhaust and cannot be interchanged. After removing the sprockets, hang the timing chain up with a piece of wire and attach it to an object on the firewall **(see illustration)**. This will prevent the timing chain from falling into the engine as the remaining steps in this procedure are performed. Also place a rag into the opening of the timing chain cover to prevent any foreign objects from falling into the engine.

2008 and earlier models

Refer to illustration 8.8

Caution: *Do not loosen the outer four bolts that secure the actuator to the camshaft timing gear.*

8   Verify the markings on the camshaft bearing caps. The caps should be marked from 1 to 5 with an "I" or an "E" mark on the cap indicating whether they're for the intake

8.8 The camshaft bearing caps are numbered and have an arrow that should face the timing chain end of the engine

or exhaust camshaft **(see illustration)**.

9   Loosen the camshaft bearing caps in two or three steps, in the reverse order of the tightening sequence **(see illustration 8.35)**. **Caution:** *Keep the caps in order. They must go back in the same location from which they were removed.*

10   Detach the bearing caps and remove the exhaust the camshaft sprocket retaining bolt. Disengage the exhaust sprocket from the camshaft and remove the exhaust camshaft from the cylinder head, then remove the intake camshaft and timing gear as an assembly. **Note:** *Mark the camshaft(s) "Intake" or "Exhaust" to avoid mixing them up.*

11   After removing the sprockets and camshafts, hang the timing chain up with a piece of wire and attach it to an object on the firewall. This will prevent the timing chain from falling into the engine as the remaining steps in this procedure are performed. Also place a rag into the opening of the timing chain cover to prevent any foreign objects from falling into the engine.

12   Inspect the camshafts and lifters as

described below. Also inspect the camshaft sprockets for wear on the teeth. Inspect the chains for cracks or excessive wear of the rollers, and for stretching (see Section 7). If any of the components show signs of excessive wear they must be replaced.

2009 and later models

Refer to illustrations 8.16a and 8.16b

Caution: *Do not loosen the outer four bolts that secure the actuator to the camshaft timing gear.*

Note: *The manufacturer recommends removing the engine and transaxle assembly (see Chapter 2B) to remove and install the camshaft housing, rockers and lifters.*

13   Using Toyota special tool #09961-00950 or equivalent, remove the top chain guide mounting bolts and chain guide.

14   Using a wrench on the lug of the exhaust camshaft to prevent it from turning, use Toyota special tool #09249-37010 or equivalent, on the exhaust camshaft timing gear bolt and loosen the bolt. **Note:** *The exhaust bolt can't*

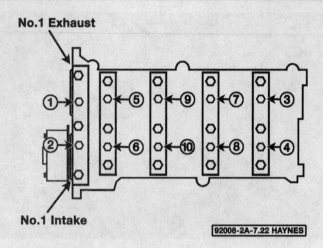

8.16a Remove the camshaft bearing cap-to-camshaft
housing bolts . . .

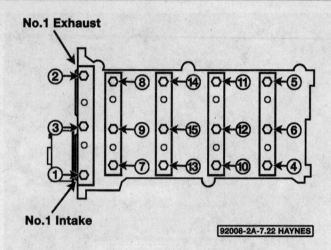

8.16b . . . then remove the camshaft bearing cap-to-cylinder head
bolts in sequence - 2009 and later models

be fully removed and must be removed along
with the camshaft timing gear.

15   Using a wrench on the lug of the intake
camshaft, rotate the intake camshaft counterclockwise just enough to release the chain
tension. Pull up on the chain, slide the exhaust
camshaft gear forward then up to remove it
and temporarily support the chain.

16   Loosen the camshaft bearing cap-to-
camshaft housing bolts in sequence **(see
illustration)** and remove them. Working with
one bearing cap at a time, remove the three
camshaft bearing cap-to-cylinder head bolts
(see illustration) in sequence. After removing the three bearing cap-to-cylinder head
bolts, lift the bearing cap off and immediately
install Toyota service special bolts and spacers in the camshaft bearing bolt locations
and tighten the bolts in sequence to 20 ft-lbs.
Note: *If the service bolts are not used, oil may
leak out between the camshaft housing and
cylinder head.*

17   Remove the exhaust camshaft and

the intake camshaft with timing gear as an
assembly. **Caution:** *Keep the caps in order.
They must go back in the same location they
were removed from.*

18   Hang the timing chain up with a piece of
wire and attach it to an object on the firewall
to prevent it from falling into the engine as the
remaining steps in this procedure are performed.

19   Inspect the camshafts and camshaft bearings as described below. Also inspect the camshaft sprockets for wear on the teeth. Inspect
the chains for cracks or excessive wear of the
rollers, and for stretching (see Section 7). If
any of the components show signs of excessive wear, they must be replaced.

Inspection

*Refer to illustrations 8.20, 8.22, 8.23, 8.25
and 8.26*

Note: *The camshaft endplay must be measured with the Variable Valve Timing (VVT)
actuator installed on the camshaft(s)*

20   Before the camshafts are removed from
the engine, check the camshaft endplay by
placing a dial indicator with the stem in line
with the camshaft and touching the snout **(see
illustration)**. Push the camshaft all the way
to the rear and zero the dial indicator. Next,
pry the camshaft to the front as far as possible and check the reading on the dial indicator. The distance it moves is the endplay. If it's
greater than the Specifications listed in this
Chapter, check the bearing caps for wear. If
the bearing caps are worn, the cylinder head
must be replaced.

21   With the camshafts removed, visually
check the camshaft bearing surfaces in the
cylinder head for pitting, score marks, galling
and abnormal wear. If the bearing surfaces
are damaged, the cylinder head may have to
be replaced.

22   Measure the outside diameter of each
camshaft bearing journal and record your
measurements **(see illustration)**. Compare
them to the journal outside diameter specified

8.20 Mount a dial indicator as shown to measure camshaft
endplay - with the dial zeroed, pry the camshaft forward and back
and read the endplay on the dial

8.22 Measure each journal diameter with a micrometer - if any
journal measures less than the specified limit, replace
the camshaft

8.23 Measure the lobe heights on each camshaft - if any lobe height is less than the specified allowable minimum, replace that camshaft

8.25 Wipe off the oil and inspect each lifter for wear and scuffing

in this Chapter, then measure the inside diameter of each corresponding camshaft bearing and record the measurements. Subtract each cam journal outside diameter from its respective cam bearing bore inside diameter to determine the oil clearance for each bearing. Compare the results to the specified journal-to-bearing clearance. If any of the measurements fall outside the standard specified wear limits in this Chapter, either the camshaft or the cylinder head, or both, must be replaced. **Note:** *If precision measuring tools are not available, Plastigage may be used to determine the bearing journal oil clearance (see Chapter 2B).*

23   Using a micrometer, measure the height of each camshaft lobe **(see illustration)**. Compare your measurements with this Chapter's Specifications. If the height for any one lobe is less than the specified minimum, replace the camshaft.

24   Check the camshaft runout by placing the camshaft back into the cylinder head and set up a dial indicator on the center journal. Zero the dial indicator. Turn the camshaft slowly and note the dial indicator readings. Runout should not exceed 0.0012 inch. If the measured runout exceeds the specified runout, replace the camshaft.

25   Inspect each lifter for scuffing and score marks **(see illustration)**.

26   Measure the outside diameter of each lifter **(see illustration)** and the corresponding lifter bore inside diameter. Subtract the lifter diameter from the lifter bore diameter to determine the oil clearance. Compare it to this Chapter's Specifications. If the oil clearance is excessive, a new cylinder head and/or new lifters will be required.

Installation

27   Clamp the intake camshaft in a vise using the flat spots on the camshaft, not the lobes, with the dowel pin at the top in the 12 o'clock position.

28   Carefully push the camshaft timing gear on to the camshaft with the dowel pin and key groove off-center.

29   Turn the camshaft timing gear coun-terclockwise while pushing the gear on to the camshaft until the dowel drops in to the groove. Once the dowel drops in to the groove, try to push it in a little more to make sure it has seated to the camshaft. **Caution:** *Do not turn the camshaft gear clockwise at this time, it may unseat the dowel pin.*

30   Apply medium-strength thread locking compound to the intake camshaft sprocket bolt threads, make sure the washer is in place and tighten the bolt to the torque listed in this Chapter's Specifications.

31   Make sure the clearance between the camshaft sprocket and camshaft flange is as specified **(see illustration 7.49)**.

32   Rotate the timing gear assembly clockwise until it locks into place, and remove the camshaft assembly from the vise.

2008 and earlier models

Refer to illustrations 8.33 and 8.35

33   Apply moly-based engine assembly lubricant to the camshaft lobes and journals and install the camshaft into the cylinder head

8.26 Measure the outside diameter of each lifter and the inside diameter of each lifter bore to determine the oil clearance measurement

8.33 Place the camshafts in the cylinder head with the No.1 cylinder lobes pointing inward at approximately a 30 degree angle

8.35 Camshaft bearing cap bolt TIGHTENING sequence (2008 and earlier models)

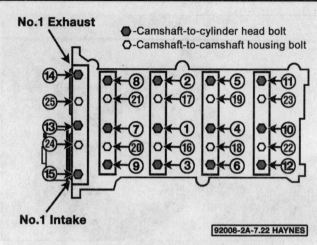

8.42 Camshaft bearing cap bolt TIGHTENING sequence (2009 and later models)

with the No.1 cylinder camshaft lobes pointing inward toward each other and the dowel pins facing upward **(see illustration)**. If the old camshafts are being used, make sure they're installed in the exact location from which they came.

34   Install the bearing caps and bolts and tighten them hand tight.

35   Tighten the bearing cap bolts in several equal steps, to the torque listed in this Chapter's Specifications, using the proper tightening sequence **(see illustration)**. Start with the front cap (with three bolts), then tighten the rest in sequence.

36   Engage the camshaft sprocket teeth with the timing chain links so that the match marks made during removal align with the upper timing marks on the sprockets, then position the sprockets over the dowels on the camshaft hubs and install the camshaft sprocket bolts finger tight. At this point the mark on the crankshaft pulley should be aligned with the "0" mark on the timing chain cover, the camshaft sprocket TDC marks should be aligned and parallel with the top of the timing chain cover and the timing chain match marks should be aligned with the upper timing sprocket marks with all of the slack in the chain positioned towards the tensioner side of the engine **(see illustration 8.4)**.

37   Double check that the timing sprockets are returned to the proper camshaft and tighten the camshaft sprocket bolts to the torque listed in this Chapter's Specifications.

38   Install the timing chain tensioner as described in Section 7, Steps 34 and 35.

39   The remainder of installation is the reverse of removal.

2009 and later models

Refer to illustration 8.42

40   Apply camshaft installation lubricant to the camshaft lobes and journals and place the exhaust camshaft, then the intake camshaft with the timing gear assembly (already installed) into the camshaft housing with both

dowel pins at the 12 o'clock position. **Note:** *Check the rocker arms and make sure none have moved out of position.*

41   Place the timing chain over the intake camshaft timing gear and align the marks made on the chain with the timing mark on the camshaft timing actuator **(see illustration 8.4)**.

42   Working with one bearing cap at a time, remove the Toyota service special bolts and spacers and immediately install the camshaft bearing cap to the camshaft housing and tighten the bearing cap-to-cylinder head bolts in several equal steps, to the torque listed in this Chapter's Specifications, using the proper tightening sequence. Once this is done, install the bearing cap-to-camshaft housing bolts and tighten the bolts in sequence, to the torque listed in this Chapter's Specifications **(see illustration)**.

43   Using a wrench on the lug of the intake camshaft, rotate the intake camshaft counterclockwise just enough to pull up on the chain. While holding the chain up, place the exhaust camshaft timing gear and sprocket bolt under the timing chain and align the marks made on the chain with the timing mark on the camshaft timing actuator.

44   Slide the timing chain gear down and onto the camshaft, carefully push the camshaft timing gear on to the camshaft with the dowel pin and key groove aligned.

45   If the dowel pin will not align with the groove, hold the camshaft and slightly turn the camshaft timing gear until the dowel drops in to the groove. Once the dowel is in the groove, push it in a little more to make sure it has seated to the camshaft. **Caution:** *Do not turn the camshaft gear clockwise at this time, it may unseat the dowel pin.*

46   Measure the clearance as shown in **illustration 7.49** and compare it to this Chapter's Specifications.

47   Make sure the camshaft sprocket teeth are engaged with the timing chain links so that the match marks made during removal align with the upper timing marks on the

sprockets. The mark on the crankshaft pulley should be aligned with the "0" mark on the timing chain cover, the camshaft sprocket TDC marks should be aligned, the timing chain match marks should be aligned with the upper timing sprocket marks and all of the slack in the chain positioned towards the tensioner side of the engine.

48   Using Toyota special tool #09249-37010 or equivalent, tighten the camshaft gear bolt to the torque listed in this Chapter's Specifications.

49   Install the top chain guide and guide mounting bolts, then tighten the bolt to the torque listed in this Chapter's Specifications using Toyota special tool #09961-00950 or equivalent.

50   Install the chain tensioner as described in Section 7, Steps 43 through 45.

51   The remainder of installation is the reverse of removal.

9   Intake manifold - removal and installation

Warning: *Wait until the engine is completely cool before beginning this procedure.*

Removal
2008 and earlier models

Refer to illustrations 9.4, 9.6a and 9.6b

1   Relieve the fuel system pressure (see Chapter 4).

2   Disconnect the negative cable from the battery.

3   Remove the engine cover (see Section 4), then release the two clamps and set aside the fuel-injection wiring harness.

4   Remove the fuel rail and injectors as an assembly (see Chapter 4). Also remove the throttle body from the intake manifold (see Chapter 4) **(see illustration)**. **Note:** *2005 and later models have a "drive-by-wire" electronic throttle control, which does not use a cable. Disconnect the electrical connector at the throttle motor on the throttle body.*

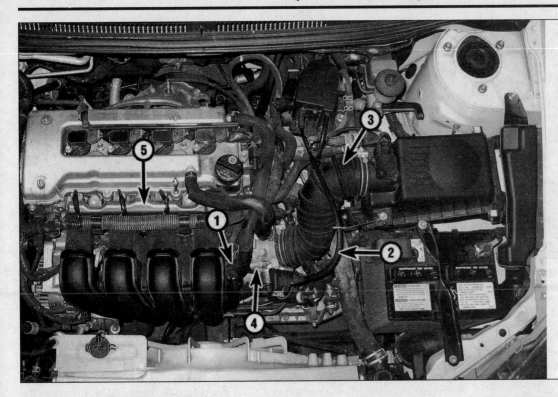

9.4 Label and disconnect the following components required for intake manifold removal

1 PCV hose
2 Accelerator cable
3 Air intake duct and air filter cover
4 Throttle body
5 Fuel rail and injectors

5 Label and detach the PCV and vacuum hoses connected to the rear of the intake manifold.

6 Remove the intake manifold mounting nuts, bolts and support bracket bolts and remove the manifold and the gasket from the engine **(see illustrations)**.

2009 and later models

7 Remove the engine cover (see Section 4).

8 Drain the engine coolant (see Chapter 1).

9 Remove the air cleaner assembly and throttle body (see Chapter 4).

10 Remove the wiring harness bracket mounting fastener and remove the bracket.

11 Remove the intake manifold mounting nuts and bolts. Remove the manifold and the gasket from the engine.

Installation

12 Clean the mating surfaces of the intake manifold and the cylinder head mounting surface with lacquer thinner or acetone. If the gasket shows signs of leaking, have the manifold checked for warpage at an automotive machine shop and resurfaced if necessary.

13 On 2008 and earlier models, install a new gasket over the manifold studs. Position the manifold on the cylinder head and install the nuts/bolts and bracket. On 2009 and later models, press a new gasket into the grooves on the intake manifold. Install the manifold

and gasket over the studs on the cylinder head then install the nuts/bolts.

14 Tighten the manifold-to-cylinder head nuts/bolts in three or four equal steps to the torque listed in this Chapter's Specifications. Work from the center out towards the ends to avoid warping the manifold. After the manifold-to-cylinder head bolts have been tightened to the proper torque, tighten the lower bracket bolts.

15 Install the remaining parts in the reverse order of removal. Check the coolant level, adding as necessary (see Chapter 1).

16 Before starting the engine, check the throttle linkage for smooth operation.

17 Run the engine and check for coolant and vacuum leaks.

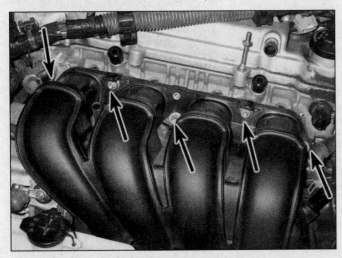

9.6a Intake manifold fastener locations . . .

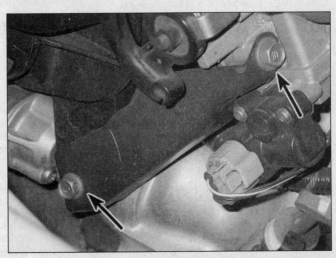

9.6b . . . and support bracket bolts

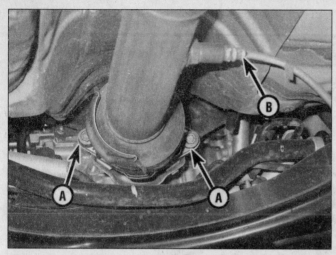

10.3 Working below the vehicle, remove the two spring-loaded exhaust pipe bolts (A). Be careful not to damage the oxygen sensor (B)

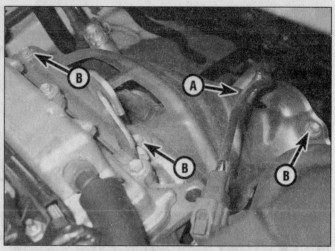

10.5 Working from the engine compartment, disconnect and remove the oxygen sensor (A), then remove the upper heat shield mounting bolts (B)

18   Road test the vehicle and check for proper operation of all accessories, including the cruise control system, if equipped.

10   Exhaust manifold - removal and installation

Warning: *The engine must be completely cool before beginning this procedure.*

Removal

Refer to illustrations 10.3 and 10.5

1   Disconnect the negative cable from the battery.
2   Raise the front of the vehicle and support it securely on jackstands.
3   Working below the vehicle, apply penetrating oil to the bolts and springs retaining the exhaust pipe to the manifold. After the bolts have soaked, remove the bolts retaining the exhaust pipe to the manifold. Separate the front exhaust pipe from the manifold, being careful not to damage the oxygen sensor **(see illustration)**. **Note:** *It may be necessary to remove the inner heat shield from above the right driveaxle to access one of the exhaust pipe-to-manifold bolts.*
4   Unbolt the lower exhaust manifold brace and remove it from the engine.
5   Working in the engine compartment, remove the heat shield from the manifold **(see illustration)**.
6   On 2009 and later models, remove the cowl assembly (see Chapter 11) and the wiper motor and linkage (see Chapter 12).

Installation

7   Use a scraper to remove all traces of old gasket material and carbon deposits from the manifold and cylinder head mating surfaces. If the gasket was leaking, have the manifold checked for warpage at an automo-

tive machine shop and resurfaced if necessary. **Note:** *If the manifold is being replaced with a new one it will be necessary to remove the lower heat shield and fasten it to the new manifold.*
8   Position a new gasket over the cylinder head studs noting any directional marks or arrows on the gasket if equipped.
9   Install the manifold and thread the mounting nuts into place.
10   Working from the center out, tighten the nuts/bolts to the torque listed in this Chapter's Specifications in three or four equal steps.
11   Reinstall the remaining parts in the reverse order of removal.
12   Run the engine and check for exhaust leaks.

11   Cylinder head - removal and installation

Warning: *The engine must be completely cool before beginning this procedure.*
Note: *If you're working on a 2009 and later model, the manufacturer recommends removing the engine and transaxle assembly to perform this procedure (see Chapter 2B).*

Removal

Refer to illustration 11.18

1   Relieve the fuel system pressure (see Chapter 4), then disconnect the cable from the negative terminal of the battery.
2   Drain the cooling system (see Chapter 1).
3   Remove the alternator (see Chapter 5).
4   Remove the valve cover (see Section 4).
5   Remove the throttle body, fuel injectors and fuel rail (see Chapter 4).
6   Remove the intake manifold (see Section 9).
7   Remove the exhaust manifold (see Section 10). **Note:** *The cylinder head can be*

removed with the exhaust manifold attached, but remember to disconnect the oxygen sensor first.
8   Remove the timing chain and camshaft sprockets (see Section 7).
9   Remove the camshafts and lifters (see Section 8).
10   On 2008 and earlier models, remove the camshafts and lifters (see Section 8).
11   On 2009 and later models, loosen the camshaft housing bearing cap bolts in two or three steps, in the reverse order of the tightening sequence **(see illustration 8.42)**.
12   Remove the bearing caps and camshafts from the camshaft housing. Carefully remove the camshaft housing by prying between the cylinder head and camshaft housing with a screwdriver.
13   Remove the rocker arms from the cylinder head. **Caution:** *Keep the rocker arms in order; they must go back in their original positions.*
14   Remove the lifters from the cylinder head. **Caution:** *Keep the lifters in order; they must go back in their original positions.*
15   Clean the camshaft housing mounting surface and the mating surface on the cylinder head. **Note:** *Be careful not to damage the cylinder head and camshaft housing.*
16   Inspect the camshafts, camshaft bearings, camshaft housing, rockers and lifters. Also inspect the camshaft sprockets for wear on the teeth. Inspect the chains for cracks or excessive wear of the rollers, and for stretching (see Section 7). If any of the components show signs of excessive wear, they must be replaced.
17   Refer to Section 5 and remove the variable valve timing control valve and filter.
18   Label and remove the coolant hoses, tubes and electrical connections from the cylinder head **(see illustration)**.
19   Loosen the cylinder head bolts in 1/4-turn increments until they can be removed by hand. Loosen the cylinder head bolts in the

11.18 Detach the ground straps (A), the ECT sensor connector (B), the coolant hoses (C) and the bracket retaining bolts (D)

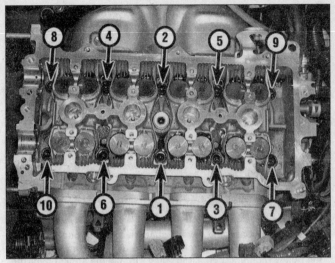

11.30a Cylinder head bolt TIGHTENING sequence - 2008 and earlier models

reverse order of the recommended tightening sequence **(see illustration 11.30a or 11.30b)** to avoid warping or cracking the cylinder head.

20   Lift the cylinder head off the engine block. If it's stuck, very carefully pry up at the transaxle end, beyond the gasket surface.

21   Remove any remaining external components from the cylinder head to allow for thorough cleaning and inspection.

Installation

Refer to illustrations 11.30a and 11.30b

22   The mating surfaces of the cylinder head and block must be perfectly clean when the cylinder head is installed.

23   Use a gasket scraper to remove all traces of carbon and old gasket material, then clean the mating surfaces with lacquer thinner or acetone. If there's oil on the mating surfaces when the cylinder head is installed, the gasket may not seal correctly and leaks could develop. When working on the block, stuff the cylinders with clean shop rags to keep out debris. Use a vacuum cleaner to remove material that falls into the cylinders.

24   Check the block and cylinder head mating surfaces for nicks, deep scratches and other damage. If damage is slight, it can be removed with a file; if it's excessive, machining may be the only alternative.

25   Use a tap of the correct size to chase the threads in the cylinder head bolt holes, then clean the holes with compressed air - make sure that nothing remains in the holes. **Warning:** *Wear eye protection when using compressed air!*

26   Using a wire brush, clean the threads on each bolt to remove corrosion and restore the threads. Dirt, corrosion, sealant and damaged threads will affect torque readings. Also check the cylinder head bolts for stretching. Measure the entire length of each bolt from the underside of the head to the tip of the threads. If the length of any bolt exceeds 5.846 inches,

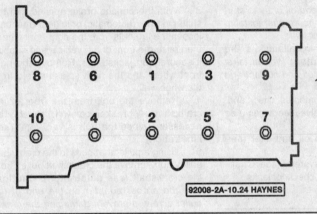

11.30b Cylinder head bolt TIGHTENING sequence - 2009 and later models

92008-2A-10.24 HAYNES

it must be replaced.

27   Install the components that were removed from the cylinder head.

28   Position the new gasket over the dowel pins in the block. Position the gasket with the "Lot #" mark facing up and near the timing chain end of the engine.

29   Carefully set the cylinder head on the block without disturbing the gasket.

30   Install the new cylinder head bolts and tighten them finger tight. Following the recommended sequence, tighten the bolts to the torque listed in this Chapter's Specifications **(see illustrations)**.

31   On 2009 and later models, coat the lifters with engine oil and install them into the cylinder head in the same locations from which they were removed.

32   Apply oil to the rocker arms and install them, making sure each rocker arm is seated to its lifter.

33   Install the camshaft bearings and oil control valve filter (if removed) into the camshaft housing.

34   Apply camshaft installation lubricant to the camshaft lobes and journals and install the camshaft into the camshaft housing.

35   Install the camshaft bearing caps to the camshaft housing and tighten the camshaft bearing cap-to-camshaft housing bolts in several equal steps, to the torque listed in this Chapter's Specifications, using the proper tightening sequence **(see illustration 8.42)**.

36   Check that the rocker arms are installed properly and have not moved.

37   Position the dowel pins facing upwards; the intake camshaft dowel pin should be at a 17-degree angle (1 o'clock position) and the exhaust pin should be straight up at the 12 o'clock position.

38   Apply a 1/4-inch wide bead of Toyota Genuine Seal Packing Black, Three Bond 1207B (or equivalent) to the camshaft housing-to-cylinder head contact surface. **Note:** *The camshaft housing must be installed within 3 minutes, and the bolts must be tightened within 15 minutes after applying seal packing.*

39   Install the camshaft housing to the cylinder head. Install the camshaft housing-to-cylinder head mounting bolts and tighten the bolts in several equal steps, to the torque listed in this Chapter's Specifications, using the proper tightening sequence **(see illustra-**

12.4 A puller base and several spacers can be mounted to the center hub of the pulley to keep the crankshaft from turning as the pulley retaining bolt is loosened - install the socket over the crankshaft bolt head before installing the puller, then insert the extension through the center hole of the puller

12.5 Reinstall the puller back onto the crankshaft pulley with the center bolt removed and remove the crankshaft pulley

tion 8.42). **Note:** *Do not add oil or try to start the engine for at least 4 hours after installation or the seal packing will leak.*

40   The remainder of installation is the reverse of removal. **Caution:** *Wait at least four hours before adding oil and coolant and starting the engine.*

41   On 2008 and earlier models, check and, if necessary, adjust the valve clearances (see Chapter 1).

42   Change the engine oil and filter (see Chapter 1).

43   Refill the cooling system (see Chapter 1), run the engine and check for leaks.

---

12 Crankshaft pulley/vibration damper - removal and installation

Refer to illustrations 12.4, 12.5 and 12.6

1   Detach the cable from the negative terminal of the battery.

2   Remove the drivebelt (see Chapter 1).

3   With the parking brake applied and the shifter in Park (automatic) or in gear (manual), loosen the lug nuts from the right front wheel, then raise the front of the vehicle and support it securely on jackstands. Remove the right front wheel and the right splash shield from the wheelwell.

4   Remove the bolt from the front of the crankshaft. A breaker bar will probably be necessary, since the bolt is very tight **(see illustration)**.

5   Using a puller that bolts to the crankshaft pulley hub, remove the crankshaft pulley from the crankshaft **(see illustration)**. **Caution:** *Use the proper adapter on the end of the puller screw to prevent damaging the crankshaft threads.* **Note:** *Depending on the type of puller you have it may be necessary to support the engine from above, remove the right side engine mount and lower to engine to gain sufficient clearance to use the puller.*

6   To install the crankshaft pulley, slide the pulley onto the crankshaft as far as it will slide on, then use a vibration damper installation tool to press the pulley onto the crankshaft. Note that the slot (keyway) in the hub must

be aligned with the Woodruff key in the end of the crankshaft **(see illustration)** and that the crankshaft bolt can also be used to press the crankshaft pulley into position.

7   Tighten the crankshaft bolt to the torque listed in this Chapter's Specifications.

8   The remaining installation steps are the reverse of removal.

---

13 Crankshaft front oil seal - replacement

Refer to illustrations 13.2, 13.3 and 13.4

1   Remove the crankshaft pulley (see Section 12).

2   Note how the seal is installed - the new one must be installed to the same depth and facing the same way. Carefully pry the oil seal out of the cover with a seal puller or a large screwdriver **(see illustration)**. Cut the lip of the seal with a utility knife to make removal easier. Be very careful not to distort the cover or scratch the crankshaft! Wrap electrician's tape around the tip of the screwdriver to avoid

12.6 Align the keyway in the crankshaft pulley hub with the Woodruff key in the crankshaft

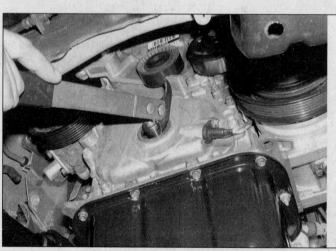

13.2 Carefully pry the old seal out of the timing chain cover - don't damage the crankshaft in the process

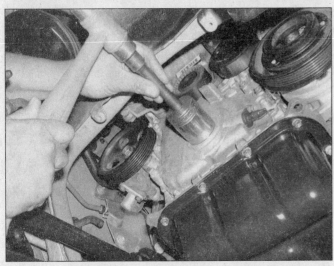

13.3 Drive the new seal into place with a large socket and hammer

13.4 If the sealing surface of the pulley hub has a wear groove from contact with the seal, repair sleeves are available at most auto parts stores

damage to the crankshaft.

3   Apply clean engine oil or multi-purpose grease to the outer edge of the new seal, then install it in the cover with the lip (spring side) facing IN. Drive the seal into place with a seal driver or a large socket and a hammer **(see illustration)**. Make sure the seal enters the bore squarely and stop when the front face is at the proper depth.

4   Check the surface on the pulley hub that the oil seal rides on. if the surface has been grooved from long-time contact with the seal, a press-on sleeve may be available to renew the sealing surface **(see illustration)**. This sleeve is pressed into place with a hammer and a block of wood and is commonly available at auto parts stores for various applications.

5   Lubricate the pulley hub with clean engine oil and reinstall the crankshaft pulley (see Section 12).

6   Install the crankshaft pulley retaining bolt and tighten it to the torque listed in this Chapter's Specifications.

7   The remainder of installation is the reverse of removal.

14   Oil pan - removal and installation

Note: *On 2009 and later models, the manufacturer recommends removing the engine and transaxle assembly to perform this procedure (see Chapter 2B).*

Removal

Refer to illustrations 14.4, 14.6a and 14.6b

1   Disconnect the cable from the negative terminal of the battery.

2   Set the parking brake and block the rear wheels.

3   Raise the front of the vehicle and support it securely on jackstands.

4   Remove the two plastic splash shields under the engine, if equipped. Support the engine from above with a hoist or engine support fixture and remove the front crossmember support **(see illustration)**.

5   Drain the engine oil and remove the oil filter (see Chapter 1). Remove the oil dipstick.

6   Remove the bolts and detach the oil pan. If it's stuck, pry it loose very carefully with a

14.4 With the engine supported from above, remove the front crossmember support

14.6a Oil pan mounting bolts

14.6b Pry the oil pan loose with a screwdriver or putty knife - be careful not to damage the mating surfaces of the pan and block or oil leaks may develop

small screwdriver or putty knife **(see illustrations)**. Don't damage the mating surfaces of the pan and block or oil leaks could develop.

Installation

7   Use a scraper to remove all traces of old sealant from the block and oil pan. Clean the mating surfaces with lacquer thinner or acetone.

8   Make sure the threaded bolt holes in the block are clean.

9   Check the oil pan flange for distortion, particularly around the bolt holes. Remove any nicks or burrs as necessary.

10   Inspect the oil pump pick-up tube assembly for cracks and a blocked strainer. If the pick-up was removed, clean it thoroughly and install it now, using a new gasket. Tighten the nuts/bolts to the torque listed in this Chapter's Specifications.

11   Apply a 3/16-inch wide bead of RTV sealant to the mating surface of the oil pan. **Note:** *Be sure to follow the sealant manufacturer's recommendations for assembly and sealant curing times.*

12   Carefully position the oil pan on the engine block and install the oil pan-to-engine

block bolts loosely.

13   Working from the center out, tighten the oil pan-to-engine block bolts to the torque listed in this Chapter's Specifications in three or four steps.

14   The remainder of installation is the reverse of removal. Be sure to wait at least one hour before adding oil to allow the sealant to properly cure.

15   Run the engine and check for oil pressure and leaks.

---

15   Oil pump - removal, inspection and installation

Note: *On 2009 and later models, the manufacturer recommends removing the engine and transaxle assembly to perform this procedure (see Chapter 2B).*

Removal

2008 and earlier models

Refer to illustrations 15.2 and 15.4

1   Refer to Section 7 and remove the timing

chain and the crankshaft sprocket.

2   Remove the five bolts and detach the oil pump body from the engine **(see illustration)**. You may have to pry carefully between the front of the block and the pump body with a screwdriver to remove it.

3   Use a scraper to remove all traces of sealant and old gasket material from the pump body and engine block, then clean the mating surfaces with lacquer thinner or acetone.

4   Remove the oil pressure relief valve from the pump body **(see illustration)**.

5   Remove the three screws and separate the pump cover from the body. Lift out the drive and driven rotors.

2009 and later models

Refer to illustrations 15.7a, 15.7b and 15.8

6   Remove the timing chain and crankshaft sprocket (see Section 7).

7   Remove the oil pump drive chain and sprockets **(see illustrations)**. Rotate the crankshaft clockwise 90-degrees to align the adjusting hole of oil pump drive shaft sprocket with the groove in the oil pump (which is at the 3 o'clock position).

8   Remove the three bolts and detach the

15.2 Oil pump mounting bolts

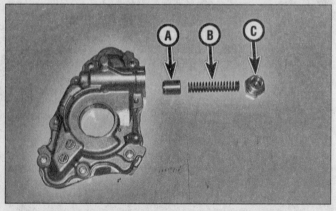

15.4 Oil pump pressure relief valve components

A   Pressure relief valve   C   Plug
B   Spring

15.7a Rotate the engine 90-degrees counterclockwise (from TDC) and set the crankshaft key to the left horizontal position (A), then remove the bolt (B) and the oil pump drive chain tensioner

15.7b Using a screwdriver to lock the lower sprocket in place, unscrew the retaining bolt and remove the drive chain and sprocket

oil pump body from the engine **(see illustration)**. You may have to pry carefully to remove it.

9   Use a scraper to remove all traces of sealant and old gasket material from the pump body and engine block, then clean the mating surfaces with brake system cleaner.

10   Remove the bolts and separate the pump cover from the pump body. Remove the drive and driven rotors.

Inspection

Refer to illustrations 15.13a, 15.13b, 15.13c, 15.14a and 15.14b

11   Clean all components with solvent, then inspect them for wear and damage.

12   Check the oil pressure relief valve piston sliding surface and valve spring. If either the spring or the valve is damaged, they must be replaced as a set.

13   Check the driven rotor-to-body clear-

15.8 Oil pump mounting bolts - 2009 and later models

ance, rotor-to-cover clearance and drive rotor tip clearance with a feeler gauge **(see illustrations)** and compare the results to this

Chapter's Specifications. If any clearance is excessive, replace the rotors as a set. If necessary, replace the oil pump body.

15.13a Measure the driven rotor-to-body clearance with a feeler gauge

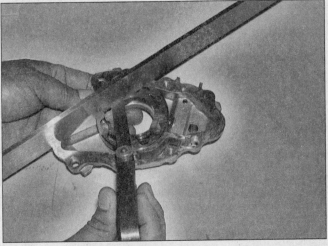

15.13b Using a straightedge and feeler gauge, measure the rotor-to-cover clearance

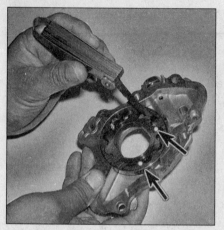

15.13c Measure the rotor tip clearance with a feeler gauge - install the rotors with the marks facing out, against the cover

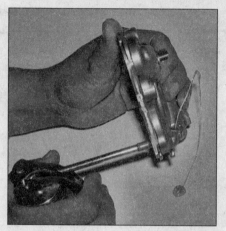

15.14a Check that the oil jet is free of debris (here, oil is being squirted into the port) - a blockage here will lead to an excessively worn timing chain and guides (2008 and earlier models)

15.14b Oil jet hole location (2009 and later models)

15.19 Place the gasket over the dowels (lower arrows) on the engine block - when installing the oil pump, align the flats in the pump rotor with the flats on the crankshaft (upper arrows)

15.27 Install the oil pump drive chain with the colored links aligned with the marks on the sprockets - 2009 and later models

14   Check the timing chain guide oil jet for blockage **(see illustration)**.

Installation

2008 and earlier models

Refer to illustration 15.19

15   Lubricate the drive and driven rotors with clean engine oil and place them in the pump body with the marks facing out **(see illustration 15.13c)**.

16   Pack the pump cavity with petroleum jelly and attach the pump cover, tighten the screws to the torque listed in this Chapter's Specifications.

17   Lubricate the oil pressure relief valve piston with clean engine oil and reinstall the valve components in the pump body.

18   Place a new oil pump gasket on the engine block.

19   Position the pump assembly against the block and install the mounting bolts. Make sure that the flats on the oil pump drive rotor align with the flats on the crankshaft **(see illustration)**.

20   Tighten the bolts to the torque listed in this Chapter's Specifications in three or four steps. Follow a criss-cross pattern to avoid warping the body.

21   Reinstall the remaining parts in the reverse order of removal.

22   Add oil if necessary, start the engine and check for oil pressure and leaks.

2009 and later models

Refer to illustration 15.27

23   Lubricate the pump cavity by pouring a small amount of clean engine oil into the inlet side of the oil pump and turning the drive gear shaft.

24   Position the oil pump and a new gasket against the block and install the mounting bolts.

25   Tighten the bolts to the torque listed in

this Chapter's Specifications in several steps. Follow a criss-cross pattern to avoid warping the body.

26   With the crankshaft key set at the 12 o'clock position and the flat on the oil pump driveshaft facing the 3 o'clock position, install the drive chain and sprockets so that the colored links on the chain align with the alignment marks on the drive gears. **Note:** *The oil pump drive gear timing mark should almost be at the 3 o'clock position and the oil pump driveshaft gear timing mark should almost be at the 9 o'clock position.*

27   Install the drive chain and sprockets so that the colored links on the chain align with the alignment marks on the drive gears **(see illustration)**.

28   Tighten the drive sprocket retaining fastener to the torque listed in this Chapter's Specifications.

29   Reinstall the remaining parts in the reverse order of removal.

16.3 Mark the flywheel/driveplate and the crankshaft so they can be reassembled in the same relative positions

16.5 On vehicles equipped with a spacer plate, note the position of the locating pin

16 Flywheel/driveplate - removal and installation

Note: *On 2009 and later models, the manufacturer recommends removing the engine and transaxle assembly to perform this procedure (see Chapter 2B).*

Removal

Refer to illustrations 16.3 and 16.5

1   Raise the vehicle and support it securely on jackstands, then refer to Chapter 7 and remove the transaxle.
2   Remove the pressure plate and clutch disc (see Chapter 8) (manual transaxle equipped vehicles).
3   Use a center punch or paint to make alignment marks on the flywheel/driveplate and crankshaft to ensure correct alignment during reinstallation **(see illustration)**.
4   Remove the bolts that secure the flywheel/driveplate to the crankshaft. If the crankshaft turns, have an assistant wedge a screwdriver in the ring gear teeth to jam the flywheel.
5   Remove the flywheel/driveplate from the crankshaft. Since the flywheel is fairly heavy, be sure to support it while removing the last bolt. Automatic transaxle equipped vehicles have spacers on both sides of the driveplate **(see illustration)**. Keep them with the driveplate. **Warning:** *The ring-gear teeth may be sharp; wear gloves to protect your hands.*

Installation

6   Clean the flywheel to remove grease and oil. Inspect the surface for cracks, rivet grooves, burned areas and score marks. Light scoring can be removed with emery cloth. Check for cracked and broken ring gear teeth. Lay the flywheel on a flat surface and use a straightedge to check for warpage.
7   Clean and inspect the mating surfaces of

the flywheel/driveplate and the crankshaft. If the crankshaft rear seal is leaking, replace it before reinstalling the flywheel/driveplate (see Section 17).
8   Position the flywheel/driveplate against the crankshaft. Be sure to align the marks made during removal. Note that some engines have an alignment dowel or staggered bolt holes to ensure correct installation. Before installing the bolts, apply thread-locking compound to the threads.
9   Wedge a screwdriver in the ring gear teeth to keep the flywheel/driveplate from turning and tighten the bolts to the torque listed in this Chapter's Specifications. Follow a criss-cross pattern and work up to the final torque in three or four steps.
10   The remainder of installation is the reverse of the removal procedure.

17 Rear main oil seal - replacement

Refer to illustration 17.3
Note: *On 2009 and later models, the manu-*

17.3 Carefully pry out the old seal with a screwdriver - it may be helpful to cut the seal lip with a razor blade first to make removal of the seal easier

facturer recommends removing the engine and transaxle assembly to perform this procedure (see Chapter 2B).
1   Remove the transaxle (see Chapter 7A or 7B).
2   Remove the flywheel/driveplate (see Section 16).
3   Pry the oil seal from the rear of the engine with a screwdriver **(see illustration)**. Be careful not to nick or scratch the crankshaft or the seal bore. Be sure to note how far it's recessed into the bore before removal so the new seal can be installed to the same depth. Thoroughly clean the seal bore in the block with a shop towel. Remove all traces of oil and dirt.
4   Lubricate the outside diameter of the seal and, using a seal installation tool, install the seal over the end of the crankshaft. Drive the new seal squarely into the seal bore and flush with the edge of tvhe seal retainer.
5   Install the flywheel/driveplate (see Section 16).
6   Install the transaxle (see Chapter 7A or 7B).

18.7 The preferred method to support the engine is with a support fixture like this that allows maximum working room around the engine top and bottom

18.8a To remove the passenger's side mount, detach the three mount-to-body bolts, the bolt at the engine . . .

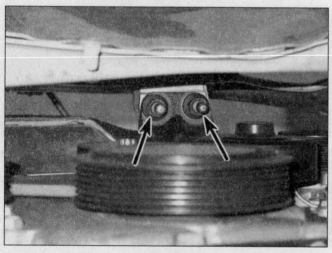

18.8b . . . and the mount bracket-to-engine mount bracket nuts (seen from below)

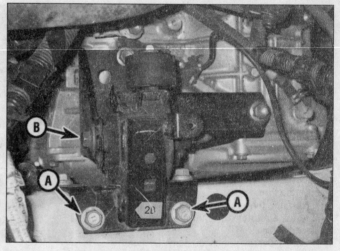

18.9 Driver's side engine mount details

A   *Mount-to-body bolts*   B   *Through-bolt*

18   Powertrain mounts - check and replacement

1   Engine mounts seldom require attention, but broken or deteriorated mounts should be replaced immediately or the added strain placed on the driveline components may cause damage or wear.

Check

Note: *During the check, the engine must be raised slightly to remove the weight from the mounts.*

2   Raise the vehicle and support it securely on jackstands, then position a jack under the engine oil pan. Place a large wood block between the jack head and the oil pan, then carefully raise the engine just enough to take the weight off the mounts. Do not position the wood block under the drain plug. **Warning:**

DO NOT place any part of your body under the engine **when** *it's supported only by a jack!*

3   Check the mounts to see if the rubber is cracked, hardened or separated from the metal casing, which would indicate the need for replacement.

4   Check for relative movement between the inner and outer portions of the mount (use a large screwdriver or pry bar to attempt to move the mounts). If movement is noted, replace the mount.

5   Check the mount fasteners to make sure they are tight.

6   Rubber preservative should be applied to the mounts to slow deterioration.

Replacement

Refer to illustrations 18.7, 18.8a, 18.8b, 18.9, 18.10a and 18.10b

7   Disconnect the cable from the negative

terminal of the battery, then raise the vehicle and support it securely on jackstands (if not already done). The engine should be supported from above, preferably with an engine support fixture available from tool rental yards **(see illustration)**.

8   To remove the right (passenger side) engine mount, remove the three bolts securing the mount to the body, then remove the three bolts and two nuts securing the mount bracket to the engine bracket **(see illustrations)**. If the vehicle is equipped with air conditioning, detach the refrigerant line bracket retaining nut and remove the mount from the engine compartment. Be sure to remove the mount bracket from the old mount and reinstall it on the new mount.

9   To remove the left (driver's side) engine mount, remove the four bolts securing the mount to the body, then remove the through-bolt securing the mount to the transaxle bracket **(see illustration)**. On manual trans-

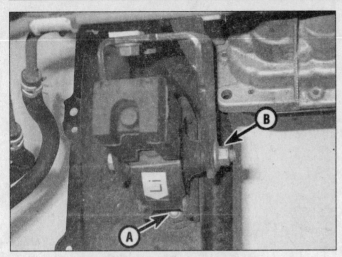

18.10a Front engine mount details

A   *Mount-to-lower frame (access from below, one shown)*
B   *Through-bolt (nut indicated)*

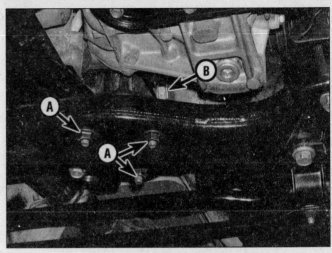

18.10b Rear engine mount details

A   *Mount-to-frame crossmember*
B   *Through-bolt*

axle equipped vehicles, it will be necessary to remove two bolts and an additional mount support bracket before removing the mount-to-body bolts and the mount through-bolt.

10   To remove the front and rear engine mounts, remove the bolts securing the mount to the lower frame crossmember, then remove the through-bolt securing the mount to the

engine bracket **(see illustrations)**.

11   Installation is the reverse of removal. Use thread locking compound on the mount bolts/ nuts and be sure to tighten them securely.

Notes

Chapter 2 Part B
General engine overhaul procedures

Contents

Specifications

General

Engine type	See Chapter 2A
Displacement	
2008 and earlier models (1ZZ-FE)	1.8 liters
2009 and later models (2ZR-FE)	1.8 liters
Bore and stroke	
2008 and earlier models (1ZZ-FE)	3.11 x 3.60 inches
2009 and later models (2ZR-FE)	3.17 x 3.48 inches
Cylinder compression pressure @ 250 rpm	
2008 and earlier models (1ZZ-FE)	
Standard	189 psi or more
Minimum	145 psi
Difference between cylinders	15 psi or less
2009 and later models (2ZR-FE)	
Standard	199 psi or more
Minimum	157 psi
Difference between cylinders	14.2 psi or less
Oil pressure (engine warm)	
2008 and earlier models (1ZZ-FE)	
At idle	4.3 psi minimum
At 3000 rpm	43 to 78 psi
2009 and later models (2ZR-FE)	
At idle	3.6 psi minimum
At 3000 rpm	22 to 58 psi

Torque specifications

Ft-lbs (unless otherwise indicated)

Connecting rod bearing cap nuts	
Step 1	15
Step 2	Tighten an additional 90-degrees (1/4 turn)
Main bearing cap bolts	
2008 and earlier models (inner bolts 1 through 10)	
Step 1	33
Step 2	Tighten an additional 90-degrees (1/4 turn)
2009 and later models	
Step 1	30
Step 2	Tighten an additional 90-degrees (1/4 turn)
Lower crankcase bolts (2009 and later models)	16
Block drain plug	18

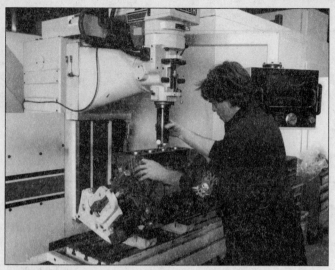

1.1 An engine block being bored - an engine rebuilder will use special machinery to recondition the cylinder bores

1.2 If the cylinders are bored, the machine shop will normally hone the engine on a machine like this

1 General information - engine overhaul

Refer to illustrations 1.1, 1.2, 1.3, 1.4, 1.5 and 1.6

Included in this portion of Chapter 2 are general information and diagnostic testing procedures for determining the overall mechanical condition of your engine.

The information ranges from advice concerning preparation for an overhaul and the purchase of replacement parts and/or components to detailed, step-by-step procedures covering removal and installation.

The following Sections have been written to help you determine whether your engine needs to be overhauled and how to remove and install it once you've determined it needs to be rebuilt. For information concerning in-vehicle engine repair, see Chapter 2A.

The Specifications included in this Part are general in nature and include only those necessary for testing the oil pressure and checking the engine compression. Refer to Chapter 2A for additional engine Specifications.

It's not always easy to determine when, or if, an engine should be completely overhauled, because a number of factors must be considered.

High mileage is not necessarily an indication that an overhaul is needed, while low mileage doesn't preclude the need for an overhaul. Frequency of servicing is probably the most important consideration. An engine that's had regular and frequent oil and filter changes, as well as other required maintenance, will most likely give many thousands of miles of reliable service. Conversely, a neglected engine may require an overhaul very early in its service life.

Excessive oil consumption is an indication that piston rings, valve seals and/or valve guides are in need of attention. Make sure that oil leaks aren't responsible before deciding that the rings and/or guides are bad. Per-

form a cylinder compression check to determine the extent of the work required (see Section 3). Also check the vacuum readings under various conditions (see Section 4).

Check the oil pressure with a gauge installed in place of the oil pressure sending unit and compare it to this Chapter's Specifications (see Section 2). If it's extremely low, the bearings and/or oil pump are probably worn out.

Loss of power, rough running, knocking or metallic engine noises, excessive valve train noise and high fuel consumption rates may also point to the need for an overhaul, especially if they're all present at the same time. If a complete tune-up doesn't remedy the situation, major mechanical work is the only solution.

An engine overhaul involves restoring the internal parts to the specifications of a new engine. During an overhaul, the piston rings are replaced and the cylinder walls are reconditioned (rebored and/or honed) **(see**

1.3 A crankshaft having a main bearing journal ground

1.4 A machinist checks for a bent connecting rod, using specialized equipment

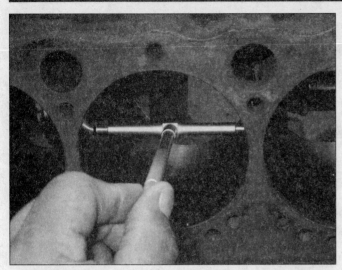

1.5 A bore gauge being used to check the main bearing bore

1.6 Uneven piston wear like this indicates a bent connecting rod

illustrations 1.1 and 1.2). If a rebore is done by an automotive machine shop, new oversize pistons will also be installed. The main bearings, connecting rod bearings and camshaft bearings are generally replaced with new ones and, if necessary, the crankshaft may be reground to restore the journals (see illustration 1.3). Generally, the valves are serviced as well, since they're usually in less-than-perfect condition at this point. While the engine is being overhauled, other components, such as the distributor, starter and alternator, can be rebuilt as well. The end result should be a like-new engine that will give many trouble-free miles. **Note:** *Critical cooling system components such as the hoses, drivebelts, thermostat and water pump should be replaced with new parts when an engine is overhauled. The radiator should be checked carefully to ensure that it isn't clogged or leaking* (see Chapter 3). *If you purchase a rebuilt engine or short block, some rebuilders will not warranty their engines unless the radiator has been professionally flushed. Also, we don't recommend overhauling the oil pump - always install a new one when an engine is rebuilt.*

Overhauling the internal components on today's engines is a difficult and time-consuming task which requires a significant amount of specialty tools and is best left to a professional engine rebuilder (see illustrations 1.4, 1.5 and 1.6). A competent engine rebuilder will handle the inspection of your old parts and offer advice concerning the reconditioning or replacement of the original engine. Never purchase parts or have machine work done on other components until the block has been thoroughly inspected by a professional machine shop. As a general rule, time is the primary cost of an overhaul, especially since the vehicle may be tied up for a minimum of two weeks or more. Be aware that some engine builders only have the capability to rebuild the engine you bring them while other rebuilders have a large inventory of rebuilt exchange engines in stock. Also be aware that many machine shops could take as much as two weeks time to completely rebuild your engine depending on shop workload. Sometimes it makes more sense to simply exchange your engine for another engine that's already rebuilt to save time.

2 Oil pressure check

Refer to illustration 2.2

1   Low engine oil pressure can be a sign of an engine in need of rebuilding. A 'low oil pressure' indicator (often called an 'idiot light') is not a test of the oiling system. Such indicators only come on when the oil pressure is dangerously low. Even a factory oil pressure gauge in the instrument panel is only a relative indication, although much better for driver information than a warning light. A better test is with a mechanical (not electrical) oil pressure gauge.
2   Locate the oil pressure indicator sending unit on the engine block (see illustration).
3   Unscrew and remove the oil pressure sending unit and then screw in the hose for your oil pressure gauge. If necessary, install an adapter fitting. Use Teflon tape or thread sealant on the threads of the adapter and/or the fitting on the end of your gauge's hose.
4   Connect an accurate tachometer to the engine, according to the tachometer manufacturer's instructions.
5   Check the oil pressure with the engine running (normal operating temperature) at the specified engine speed, and compare it to this Chapter's Specifications. If it's extremely low, the bearings and/or oil pump are probably worn out.

2.2 The oil-pressure sending unit is located at the front of the engine block, just above the oil filter

3 Cylinder compression check

Refer to illustration 3.6

1   A compression check will tell you what mechanical condition the upper end of your engine (pistons, rings, valves, head gaskets) is in. Specifically, it can tell you if the compression is down due to leakage caused by worn piston rings, defective valves and seats or a blown head gasket. **Note:** *The engine must be at normal operating temperature and the*

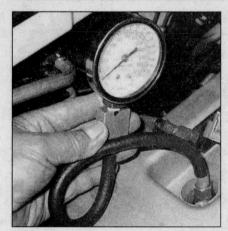

3.6 Use a compression gauge with a threaded fitting for the spark plug hole, not the type that requires hand pressure to maintain the seal - be sure to open the throttle valve as far as possible during the test

4.4 A simple vacuum gauge can be handy in diagnosing engine condition and performance

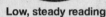

| Low, steady reading | Low, fluctuating needle | Regular drops |

Irregular drops   Rapid vibration

Large fluctuation   Slow fluctuation

STD-O-OBR HAYNES

4.6 Typical vacuum gauge readings

battery must be fully charged for this check.
2   Begin by cleaning the area around the spark plugs before you remove them (compressed air should be used, if available). The idea is to prevent dirt from getting into the cylinders as the compression check is being done.
3   Remove all of the spark plugs from the engine (see Chapter 1).
4   Block the throttle wide open.
5   Disable the fuel pump circuit by removing the circuit opening relay from the fuse/relay center in the engine compartment (see Chapter 4).
6   Install a compression gauge in the spark plug hole **(see illustration)**.
7   Crank the engine over at least seven compression strokes and watch the gauge. The compression should build up quickly in a healthy engine. Low compression on the first stroke, followed by gradually increasing pressure on successive strokes, indicates worn piston rings. A low compression reading on the first stroke, which doesn't build up during successive strokes, indicates leaking valves

or a blown head gasket (a cracked head could also be the cause). Deposits on the undersides of the valve heads can also cause low compression. Record the highest gauge reading obtained.
8   Repeat the procedure for the remaining cylinders and compare the results to this Chapter's Specifications.
9   Add some engine oil (about three squirts from a plunger-type oil can) to each cylinder, through the spark plug hole, and repeat the test.
10   If the compression increases after the oil is added, the piston rings are definitely worn. If the compression doesn't increase significantly, the leakage is occurring at the valves or head gasket. Leakage past the valves may be caused by burned valve seats and/or faces or warped, cracked or bent valves.
11   If two adjacent cylinders have equally low compression, there's a strong possibility that the head gasket between them is blown. The appearance of coolant in the combustion chambers or the crankcase would verify this condition.
12   If one cylinder is slightly lower than the others, and the engine has a slightly rough idle, a worn lobe on the camshaft could be the cause.

13   If the compression is unusually high, the combustion chambers are probably coated with carbon deposits. If that's the case, the cylinder head(s) should be removed and decarbonized.
14   If compression is way down or varies greatly between cylinders, it would be a good idea to have a leak-down test performed by an automotive repair shop. This test will pinpoint exactly where the leakage is occurring and how severe it is.

4   Vacuum gauge diagnostic checks

Refer to illustrations 4.4 and 4.6

A vacuum gauge provides inexpensive but valuable information about what is going on in the engine. You can check for worn rings or cylinder walls, leaking head or intake manifold gaskets, incorrect carburetor adjustments, restricted exhaust, stuck or burned valves, weak valve springs, improper ignition or valve timing and ignition problems.
Unfortunately, vacuum gauge readings are easy to misinterpret, so they should be used in conjunction with other tests to confirm the diagnosis.

Both the absolute readings and the rate of needle movement are important for accurate interpretation. Most gauges measure vacuum in inches of mercury (in-Hg). The following references to vacuum assume the diagnosis is being performed at sea level. As elevation increases (or atmospheric pressure decreases), the reading will decrease. For every 1,000 foot increase in elevation above approximately 2000 feet, the gauge readings will decrease about one inch of mercury.

Connect the vacuum gauge directly to the intake manifold vacuum, not to ported (throttle body) vacuum **(see illustration)**. Be sure no hoses are left disconnected during the test or false readings will result.

Before you begin the test, allow the engine to warm up completely. Block the wheels and set the parking brake. With the transmission in Park, start the engine and allow it to run at normal idle speed. **Warning:** *Keep your hands and the vacuum gauge clear of the fans.*

Read the vacuum gauge; an average, healthy engine should normally produce about 17 to 22 in-Hg with a fairly steady needle **(see illustration)**. Refer to the following vacuum gauge readings and what they indicate about the engine's condition:

1   A low steady reading usually indicates a leaking gasket between the intake manifold and cylinder head(s) or throttle body, a leaky vacuum hose, late ignition timing or incorrect camshaft timing.

2   If the reading is three to eight inches below normal and it fluctuates at that low reading, suspect an intake manifold gasket leak at an intake port or a faulty fuel injector.

3   If the needle has regular drops of about two-to-four inches at a steady rate, the valves are probably leaking. Perform a compression check or leak-down test to confirm this.

4   An irregular drop or down-flick of the needle can be caused by a sticking valve or an ignition misfire. Perform a compression check or leak-down test and read the spark plugs.

5   A rapid vibration of about four in-Hg vibration at idle combined with exhaust smoke indicates worn valve guides. Perform a leak-down test to confirm this. If the rapid vibration occurs with an increase in engine speed, check for a leaking intake manifold gasket or head gasket, weak valve springs, burned valves or ignition misfire.

6   A slight fluctuation, say one inch up and down, may mean ignition problems. Check all the usual tune-up items and, if necessary, run the engine on an ignition analyzer.

7   If there is a large fluctuation, perform a compression or leak-down test to look for a weak or dead cylinder or a blown head gasket.

8   If the needle moves slowly through a wide range, check for a clogged PCV system, incorrect idle fuel mixture, throttle body or intake manifold gasket leaks.

9   Check for a slow return after revving the engine by quickly snapping the throttle open until the engine reaches about 2,500 rpm and

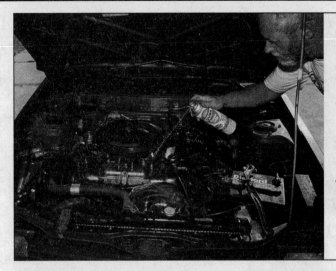

6.1 After tightly wrapping water-vulnerable components, use a spray cleaner on everything, with particular concentration on the greasiest areas, usually around the valve cover and lower edges of the block. If one section dries out, apply more cleaner

let it shut. Normally the reading should drop to near zero, rise above normal idle reading (about 5 in-Hg over) and then return to the previous idle reading. If the vacuum returns slowly and doesn't peak when the throttle is snapped shut, the rings may be worn. If there is a long delay, look for a restricted exhaust system (often the muffler or catalytic converter). An easy way to check this is to temporarily disconnect the exhaust ahead of the suspected part and redo the test.

5   Engine rebuilding alternatives

The do-it-yourselfer is faced with a number of options when purchasing a rebuilt engine. The major considerations are cost, warranty, parts availability and the time required for the rebuilder to complete the project. The decision to replace the engine block, piston/connecting rod assemblies and crankshaft depends on the final inspection results of your engine. Only then can you make a cost effective decision whether to have your engine overhauled or simply purchase an exchange engine for your vehicle.

Some of the rebuilding alternatives include:

Individual parts - If the inspection procedures reveal that the engine block and most engine components are in reusable condition, purchasing individual parts and having a rebuilder rebuild your engine may be the most economical alternative. The block, crankshaft and piston/connecting rod assemblies should all be inspected carefully by a machine shop first.

Short block - A short block consists of an engine block with a crankshaft and piston/connecting rod assemblies already installed. All new bearings are incorporated and all clearances will be correct. The existing camshafts, valve train components, cylinder head and external parts can be bolted to the short block with little or no machine shop work necessary.

Long block - A long block consists of a

short block plus an oil pump, oil pan, cylinder head, valve cover, camshaft and valve train components, timing sprockets and chain or gears and timing cover. All components are installed with new bearings, seals and gaskets incorporated throughout. The installation of manifolds and external parts is all that's necessary.

Low mileage used engines - Some companies now offer low mileage used engines which is a very cost effective way to get your vehicle up and running again. These engines often come from vehicles that have been in totaled in accidents or come from other countries that have a higher vehicle turn over rate. A low mileage used engine also usually has a similar warranty like the newly remanufactured engines.

Give careful thought to which alternative is best for you and discuss the situation with local automotive machine shops, auto parts dealers and experienced rebuilders before ordering or purchasing replacement parts.

6   Engine removal - methods and precautions

Refer to illustrations 6.1, 6.2, 6.3, 6.4 and 6.5

If you've decided that an engine must be removed for overhaul or major repair work, several preliminary steps should be taken. Read all removal and installation procedures carefully prior to committing this job. Some engines are removed by lowering to the floor and then raising the vehicle sufficiently to slide it out; this will require a vehicle hoist.

Locating a suitable place to work is extremely important. Adequate work space, along with storage space for the vehicle, will be needed. If a shop or garage isn't available, at the very least a flat, level, clean work surface made of concrete or asphalt is required. Cleaning the engine compartment and engine before beginning the removal procedure will help keep tools clean and organized **(see illustrations 6.1 and 6.2)**.

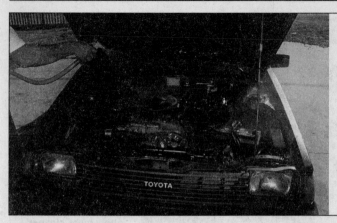

6.2 Depending on how dirty the engine is, let the cleaner soak in according to the directions and then hose off the grime and cleaner. Get the rinse water down into every area you can get at; then dry important components with a hair dryer or paper towels

An engine hoist or A-frame will also be necessary. Make sure the equipment is rated in excess of the combined weight of the engine and transaxle. Safety is of primary importance, considering the potential hazards involved in lifting the engine out of the vehicle.

If you're a novice at engine removal, get at least one helper. One person cannot easily do all the things you need to do to lift a big heavy engine out of the engine compartment. Also helpful is to seek advice and assistance from someone who's experienced in engine removal.

Plan the operation ahead of time. Arrange for or obtain all of the tools and equipment you'll need prior to beginning the job **(see illustrations 6.3, 6.4 and 6.5)**. Some of the equipment necessary to perform engine removal and installation safely and with relative ease are (in addition to an engine hoist) a heavy duty floor jack, complete sets of wrenches and sockets as described in the front of this manual, wooden blocks, plenty of rags and cleaning solvent for mopping up spilled oil, coolant and gasoline. If the hoist must be rented, make sure that you arrange for it in advance and have everything

disconnected and/or removed before bringing the hoist home. This will save you money and time.

Plan for the vehicle to be out of use for quite a while. A machine shop can do the work that is beyond the scope of the home mechanic. Machine shops often have a busy schedule, so before removing the engine, consult the shop for an estimate of how long it will take to rebuild or repair the components that may need work.

---

7   Engine - removal and installation

Refer to illustrations 7.17a, 7.17b, 7.27 and 7.30

Warning 1: *The models covered by this manual are equipped with Supplemental Restraint systems (SRS), more commonly known as airbags. Always disable the airbag system before working in the vicinity of the impact sensors, steering column or instrument panel to avoid the possibility of accidental deployment of the airbag, which could cause personal injury (see Chapter 12).*

6.3 Get an engine hoist that's strong enough to easily lift your engine in and out of the engine compartment; an adapter, like the one shown here, can be used to change the angle of the engine as it's being removed or installed

Warning 2: *Gasoline is extremely flammable, so take extra precautions when you work on any part of the fuel system. Don't smoke or allow open flames or bare light bulbs near the work area, and don't work in a garage where a gas-type appliance (such as a water heater or a clothes dryer) is present. Since gasoline is carcinogenic, wear latex gloves when there's a possibility of being exposed to fuel, and, if you spill any fuel on your skin, rinse it off immediately with soap and water. Mop up any spills immediately and do not store fuel-soaked rags where they could ignite. The fuel system is under constant pressure, so, if any fuel lines are to be disconnected, the fuel pressure in the system must be relieved first (see Chapter 4 for more information). When you perform any kind of work on the fuel system, wear safety glasses and have a Class B type fire extinguisher on hand.*

Warning 3: *Wait until the engine is completely cool before beginning this procedure*

Note 1: *Engine removal on these vehicles is a difficult job, especially for the do-it-yourself mechanic working at home. Because of the vehicle's design, the manufacturer states that the engine and transaxle have to be removed as a unit from the bottom of the vehicle, not the top. With a floor jack and jackstands, the vehicle can't be raised high enough or supported safely enough for the engine/transaxle assembly to slide out from underneath. The manufacturer recommends that removal of the engine/transaxle assembly only be performed with the use of a frame-contact type vehicle hoist.*

6.4 Get an engine stand sturdy enough to firmly support the engine while you're working on it. Stay away from three-wheeled models; they have a tendency to tip over more easily, so get a four-wheeled unit

6.5 A clutch alignment tool is necessary if you plan to install a rebuilt engine mated to a manual transaxle

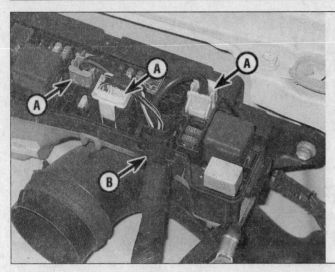

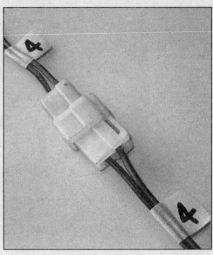

7.17a Unplug these electrical connectors (A) from the underhood fuse/relay box, then slide the harness up and out of the slot in the side of the box (B)

7.17b Label both ends of each wire and hose before disconnecting it - do the same for vacuum hoses

Note 2: *Keep in mind that during this procedure you'll have to adjust the height of the vehicle with the vehicle hoist to perform certain operations.*

Removal

1   Park the vehicle on a frame-contact type vehicle hoist, then engage the arms of the hoist with the jacking points of the vehicle. Raise the hoist arms until they contact the vehicle, but not so much that the wheels come off the ground.

2   Loosen the wheel lug nuts and the driveaxle/hub nuts (see Chapter 8).

3   Relieve the fuel system pressure (see Chapter 4).

4   Remove the battery and battery tray (see Chapter 5).

5   Remove the air filter housing and air intake duct (see Chapter 4).

6   Drain the engine coolant (see Chapter 1).

7   Drain the engine oil (see Chapter 1).

8   Drain the transaxle lubricant or fluid (see Chapter 1).

9   Remove the engine cooling fan. Also remove the radiator (see Chapter 3).

10   If equipped with an automatic transaxle, disconnect the fluid cooler lines from the transaxle.

11   Disconnect the fuel feed hose from the rigid line on the left (driver's) side of the engine compartment (see Chapter 4). Plug the line and fitting.

12   If equipped with cruise control, detach the cable from the throttle body, then remove the cruise control actuator.

13   Detach the heater hoses from the heater core tubes at the firewall (see Chapter 3).

14   Detach the shift cable(s) from the transaxle (see Chapter 7A or 7B).

15   If equipped with a manual transaxle, remove the clutch release cylinder (see Chapter 8).

16   Remove the air conditioning compressor without disconnecting the refrigerant lines (see Chapter 3). Tie the compressor out of the way.

17   Disconnect the engine wiring harness from the underhood fuse/relay box **(see illus-**

tration). Also label and detach any other electrical connectors/wiring harnesses and vacuum hoses between the engine and the vehicle **(see illustration)**.

18   Remove the glove box door, then disconnect the electrical connectors from the PCM (see Chapter 6) and the junction block. Dislodge the grommet from the firewall and pull the harness into the engine compartment.

19   Using a suction gun, remove as much fluid as possible from the power steering fluid reservoir. Unscrew the nut securing the power steering gear pressure line to the right side of the engine compartment (near the strut tower), then disconnect the hose from the line. Also, disconnect the supply (large diameter) hose from the power steering fluid reservoir.

20   Disconnect the steering column intermediate shaft from the steering gear (see Chapter 10).

21   Raise the vehicle on the hoist, the remove the front wheels. Detach the tie-rod ends from the steering knuckles (see Chapter 10).

22   Unbolt the exhaust pipe from the exhaust manifold (see Chapter 2A, Section 10).

23   Remove the driveaxle/hub nuts.

24   Unscrew the fasteners and separate the balljoints from the control arms (see Chapter 10).

25   Remove the driveaxles (see Chapter 8).

26   Disconnect the stabilizer bar links from the stabilizer bar (see Chapter 10).

27   Support the engine/transaxle assembly from above with an engine hoist. Attach the hoist chain to the lifting brackets. If no lifting brackets or hooks are present, lifting hooks may be available from your local auto parts store or dealer parts department. If not, you will have to fasten the chains to some substantial parts of the engine - ones that are strong enough to take the weight, but in locations that will provide good balance. If you're attaching a chain to a stud on the engine, or are using a bolt passing through the chain and into a threaded hole, place a washer between the nut or bolt head and the chain and tighten the nut or bolt securely **(see illustration)**. **Warning:** *Do not place any part of your body*

7.27 This engine was equipped with one lifting hook, at the back of the cylinder head near the transaxle. At the other end of the head there was no hook, but there was a large threaded hole that we used for connecting the lifting chain

under the engine/transaxle when it's supported only by a hoist or other lifting device.

28   Take up the slack until there is slight tension on the engine hoist. Position the chain on the hoist so it balances the engine and the transaxle level with the vehicle. **Note 1:** *Depending on the design of the engine hoist, it may be helpful to position the hoist from the side of the vehicle, so that when the engine/transaxle assembly is lowered, it will fit between the legs of the hoist.* **Note 2:** *The sling or chain must be long enough to allow the engine hoist to lower the engine/transaxle assembly to the ground, without letting the hoist arm contact the vehicle.*

29   Support the front suspension crossmember with a pair of floor jacks. Recheck to be sure that there aren't any hoses or wiring harnesses between the engine, crossmember and the vehicle.

30   Remove the bolts securing the front sus-

7.30 Locations of the front suspension crossmember and longitudinal crossmember-to-vehicle bolts

9.1 Before you try to remove the pistons, use a ridge reamer to remove the raised material (ridge) from the top of the cylinders

pension crossmember and the longitudinal crossmember to the vehicle **(see illustration)**.

31   Remove the through-bolt from the powertrain mount securing the transaxle to the left (driver's) side of the engine compartment, and the mount-to-engine bracket fasteners on the right-side mount (see Chapter 2A).

32   Recheck to be sure nothing is still connecting the engine or transaxle to the vehicle. Disconnect and label anything still remaining.

33   Lower the engine/transaxle/crossmember assembly. Once the assembly is on the floor, disconnect the engine lifting hoist and raise the vehicle until it clears the engine/transaxle assembly.

34   Reconnect the chain or sling to support the engine and transaxle.

35   Raise the engine/transaxle assembly, remove the fasteners connecting the remaining powertrain mounts to the crossmember, then move the crossmember out of the way. Support the engine with blocks of wood or another floor jack, while leaving the sling or chain attached. Support the transaxle with another floor jack, preferably one with a transaxle jack head adapter. At this point the transaxle can be unbolted and removed from the engine. Be very careful to ensure that the components are supported securely so they won't topple off their supports during disconnection.

36   Reconnect the lifting chain to the engine, then raise the engine and attach it to an engine stand.

Installation

37   Installation is the reverse of removal, noting the following points:

a) *Check the powertrain mounts. If they're worn or damaged, replace them.*

b) *Attach the transaxle to the engine following the procedure described in Chapter 7.*

c) *When installing the crossmember, tighten the mounting bolts to the torque listed in the Chapter 10 Specifications.*

d) *Tighten the driveaxle/hub nuts to the torque listed in the Chapter 8 Specifications. Tighten all steering and suspension fasteners to the torque listed in the Chapter 10 Specifications. Tighten the wheel lug nuts to the torque listed in the Chapter 1 Specifications.*

e) *Refill the engine coolant, oil, power steering and transaxle fluids (see Chapter 1).*

f) *Run the engine and check for proper operation and leaks. Shut off the engine and recheck fluid levels.*

---

8   Engine overhaul - disassembly sequence

---

1   It's much easier to remove the external components if it's mounted on a portable engine stand. A stand can often be rented quite cheaply from an equipment rental yard. Before the engine is mounted on a stand, the flywheel/driveplate should be removed from the engine.

2   If a stand isn't available, it's possible to remove the external engine components with it blocked up on the floor. Be extra careful not to tip or drop the engine when working without a stand.

3   If you're going to obtain a rebuilt engine, all external components must come off first, to be transferred to the replacement engine. These components include:

Clutch and flywheel (models with manual transaxle)
Driveplate (models with automatic transaxle)
Ignition system components
Emissions-related components
Engine mounts and mount brackets
Fuel injection components
Intake/exhaust manifolds
Oil filter
Thermostat and housing assembly
Water pump

Note: *When removing the external compo-*

nents from the engine, pay close attention to details that may be helpful or important during installation. Note the installed position of gaskets, seals, spacers, pins, brackets, washers, bolts and other small items.

4   If you're going to obtain a short block (assembled engine block, crankshaft, pistons and connecting rods), then you should remove the timing belt, cylinder head, oil pan, oil pump pick-up tube, oil pump and water pump from your engine so that you can turn in your old short block to the rebuilder as a core. See *Engine rebuilding alternatives* for additional information regarding the different possibilities to be considered. **Caution:** *2009 and later models have a removable cylinder block water jacket and should not be machined.*

---

9   Pistons and connecting rods - removal and installation

Removal

Refer to illustrations 9.1, 9.3 and 9.4

Note: *Prior to removing the piston/connecting rod assemblies, remove the cylinder head, upper (aluminum) oil pan section and oil pan (see Chapter 2A or 2A).*

1   Use your fingernail to feel if a ridge has formed at the upper limit of ring travel (about 1/4-inch down from the top of each cylinder). If carbon deposits or cylinder wear have produced ridges, they must be completely removed with a special tool **(see illustration)**. Follow the manufacturer's instructions provided with the tool. Failure to remove the ridges before attempting to remove the piston/connecting rod assemblies may result in piston breakage.

2   After the cylinder ridges have been removed, turn the engine so the crankshaft is facing up.

3   Before the main bearing cap assembly and connecting rods are removed, check the connecting rod endplay with feeler gauges.

9.3 Checking the connecting rod endplay (side clearance)

9.4 If the connecting rods and caps are not marked, use a center punch or numbered impression stamps to mark the caps to the rods by cylinder number - do not confuse the markings shown here with rod numbers, these are bearing size identifications

9.13 Install the piston ring into the cylinder then push it down into position using a piston so the ring will be square in the cylinder

Slide them between the first connecting rod and the crankshaft throw until the play is removed **(see illustration)**. Repeat this procedure for each connecting rod. The endplay is equal to the thickness of the feeler gauge(s). Check with an automotive machine shop for the endplay service limit. If the play exceeds the service limit, new connecting rods will be required. If new rods (or a new crankshaft) are installed, the endplay may fall under the minimum allowable clearance. If it does, the rods will have to be machined to restore it. If necessary, consult an automotive machine shop for advice.

4   Check the connecting rods and caps for identification marks **(see illustration)**. If they aren't plainly marked, use a small center-punch to make the appropriate number of indentations on each rod and cap (1, 2, 3, etc., depending on the cylinder they're associated with).

5   Loosen each of the connecting rod cap bolts 1/2-turn at a time until they can be removed by hand. Remove the number one connecting rod cap and bearing insert. Don't drop the bearing insert out of the cap. **Note:** *Use new bolts when reassembling the engine,*

but save the old ones for use when checking the bearing oil clearance.

6   Remove the bearing insert and push the connecting rod/piston assembly out through the top of the engine. Use a wooden or plastic hammer handle to push on the upper bearing surface in the connecting rod. If resistance is felt, double-check to make sure that all of the ridge was removed from the cylinder.

7   Repeat the procedure for the remaining cylinders.

8   After removal, reassemble the connecting rod caps and bearing inserts in their respective connecting rods and install the cap bolts finger tight.

9   Leaving the old bearing inserts in place until reassembly will help prevent the connecting rod bearing surfaces from being accidentally nicked or gouged.

10   The pistons and connecting rods are now ready for inspection and overhaul at an automotive machine shop.

Piston ring installation

Refer to illustrations 9.13, 9.14, 9.15, 9.19a, 9.19b and 9.22

11   Before installing the new piston rings, the ring end gaps must be checked. It's assumed that the piston ring side clearance has been checked and verified correct. **Note:** *Pistons and rods can only be installed after the crankshaft has been installed* (see Section 10).

12   Lay out the piston/connecting rod assemblies and the new ring sets so the ring sets will be matched with the same piston and cylinder during the end gap measurement and engine assembly.

13   Insert the top (number one) ring into the first cylinder and square it up with the cylinder walls by pushing it in with the top of the piston **(see illustration)**. The ring should be near the bottom of the cylinder, at the lower limit of ring travel.

14   To measure the end gap, slip feeler gauges between the ends of the ring until a gauge equal to the gap width is found **(see illustration)**. The feeler gauge should slide between the ring ends with a slight amount of drag. Check with an automotive machine shop for the correct end gap for your engine. If the gap is larger or smaller than specified, double-check to make sure you have the correct rings before proceeding.

15   If the gap is too small, it must be enlarged or the ring ends may come in contact with each other during engine operation, which can cause serious damage to the engine. The end gap can be increased by filing the ring ends very carefully with a fine file. Mount the file in a vise equipped with soft jaws, slip the ring over the file with the ends contacting the file face and slowly move the ring to remove material from the ends. When performing this operation, file only by pushing the ring from the outside end of the file towards the vise **(see illustration)**.

16   Excess end gap isn't critical unless it's greater than approximately 0.040-inch. Again, double-check to make sure you have the cor-

9.14 With the ring square in the cylinder, measure the ring end gap with a feeler gauge

9.15 If the ring end gap is too small, clamp a file in a vise as shown and file the piston ring ends - be sure to file the ends squarely and finish by removing all raised material or burrs with a fine stone

ENGINE BEARING ANALYSIS

Debris

Babbitt bearing embedded with debris from machinings

Microscopic detail of debris

Microscopic detail of gouges

Overplated copper alloy bearing gouged by cast iron debris

Aluminum bearing embedded with glass beads

Microscopic detail of glass beads

Damaged lining caused by dirt left on the bearing back

Misassembly

Result of a lower half assembled as an upper - blocking the oil flow

Excessive oil clearance is indicated by a short contact arc

Polished and oil-stained backs are a result of a poor fit in the housing bore

Result of a wrong, reversed, or shifted cap

Overloading

Damage from excessive idling which resulted in an oil film unable to support the load imposed

Damaged upper connecting rod bearings caused by engine lugging; the lower main bearings (not shown) were similarly affected

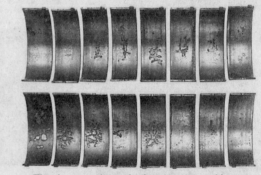

The damage shown in these upper and lower connecting rod bearings was caused by engine operation at a higher-than-rated speed under load

Misalignment

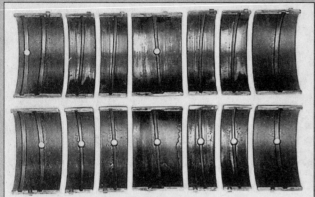

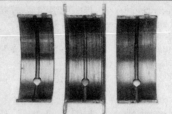

A poorly finished crankshaft caused the equally spaced scoring shown

A tapered housing bore caused the damage along one edge of this pair

A bent connecting rod led to the damage in the "V" pattern

A warped crankshaft caused this pattern of severe wear in the center, diminishing toward the ends

Lubrication

Result of dry start: The bearings on the left, farthest from the oil pump, show more damage

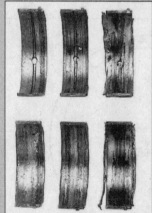

Result of a low oil supply or oil starvation

Severe wear as a result of inadequate oil clearance

Corrosion

Microscopic detail of corrosion

Corrosion is an acid attack on the bearing lining generally caused by inadequate maintenance, extremely hot or cold operation, or inferior oils or fuels

Microscopic detail of cavitation

Example of cavitation - a surface erosion caused by pressure changes in the oil film

Damage from excessive thrust or insufficient axial clearance

Bearing affected by oil dilution caused by excessive blow-by or a rich mixture

rect ring type and that you are referencing the correct section and category of specifications.

17   Repeat the procedure for each ring that will be installed in the first cylinder and for each ring in the remaining cylinders. Remember to keep rings, pistons and cylinders matched up.

18   Once the ring end gaps have been checked/corrected, the rings can be installed on the pistons.

19   The oil control ring (lowest one on the piston) is usually installed first. It's composed of three separate components. Slip the spacer/expander into the groove **(see illustration)**. If an anti-rotation tang is used, make sure it's inserted into the drilled hole in the ring groove. Next, install the upper side rail in the same manner **(see illustration)**. Don't use a piston ring installation tool on the oil ring side rails, as they may be damaged. Instead, place one end of the side rail into the groove between the spacer/expander and the ring land, hold it firmly in place and slide a finger around the piston while pushing the rail into the groove. Finally, install the lower side rail.

20   After the three oil ring components have been installed, check to make sure that both the upper and lower side rails can be rotated smoothly inside the ring grooves.

21   The number two (middle) ring is installed next. It's usually stamped with a mark that must face up, toward the top of the piston. Do not mix up the top and middle rings, as they have different cross-sections. **Note:** *Always follow the instructions printed on the ring package or box - different manufacturers may require different approaches.*

22   Use a piston ring installation tool and make sure the identification mark is facing the top of the piston, then slip the ring into the middle groove on the piston **(see illustration)**. Don't expand the ring any more than necessary to slide it over the piston.

23   Install the number one (top) ring in the same manner. Make sure the mark is facing up. Be careful not to confuse the number one

9.19a Installing the spacer/expander in the oil ring groove

9.19b DO NOT use a piston ring installation tool when installing the oil control side rails

and number two rings.

24   Repeat the procedure for the remaining pistons and rings.

Installation

25   Before installing the piston/connecting rod assemblies, the cylinder walls must be perfectly clean, the top edge of each cylinder bore must be chamfered, and the crankshaft must be in place.

26   Remove the cap from the end of the number one connecting rod (refer to the marks made during removal). Remove the original bearing inserts and wipe the bearing surfaces of the connecting rod and cap with a clean, lint-free cloth. They must be kept spotlessly clean.

Connecting rod bearing oil clearance check

Refer to illustrations 9.29, 9.34, 9.36 and 9.40

27   Clean the back side of the new upper bearing insert, then lay it in place in the connecting rod. Make sure the tab on the bearing

fits into the recess in the rod. Don't hammer the bearing insert into place and be very careful not to nick or gouge the bearing face. Don't lubricate the bearing at this time.

28   Clean the back side of the other bearing insert and install it in the rod cap. Again, make sure the tab on the bearing fits into the recess in the cap, and don't apply any lubricant. It's critically important that the mating surfaces of the bearing and connecting rod are perfectly clean and oil free when they're assembled.

29   Position the piston ring gaps at 90-degree intervals around the piston as shown **(see illustration)**.

30   Lubricate the piston and rings with clean engine oil and attach a piston ring compressor to the piston. Leave the skirt protruding about 1/4-inch to guide the piston into the cylinder. The rings must be compressed until they're flush with the piston.

31   Rotate the crankshaft until the number one connecting rod journal is at BDC (bottom dead center) and apply a liberal coat of engine oil to the cylinder walls.

32   With the mark (dot, arrow or letter R or

9.22 Use a piston ring installation tool to install the number 2 and the number 1 (top) rings - be sure the directional mark on the piston ring(s) is facing toward the top of the piston

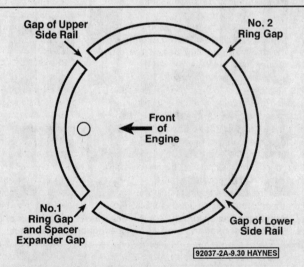

9.29 Position the piston ring end gaps as shown

9.34 Use a plastic or wooden hammer handle to push the piston into the cylinder

9.36 Place Plastigage on each connecting rod bearing journal parallel to the crankshaft centerline

9.40 Use the scale on the Plastigage package to determine the bearing oil clearance - be sure to measure the widest part of the Plastigage and use the correct scale; it comes with both standard and metric scales

L) on top of the piston facing the front (timing chain end) of the engine, gently insert the piston/connecting rod assembly into the number one cylinder bore and rest the bottom edge of the ring compressor on the engine block. **Note:** *The connecting rod also has a mark on it that must face the correct direction. On all models, the marks on the connecting rods face the front (timing chain) of the engine.*

33   Tap the top edge of the ring compressor to make sure it's contacting the block around its entire circumference.

34   Gently tap on the top of the piston with the end of a wooden or plastic hammer handle **(see illustration)** while guiding the end of the connecting rod into place on the crankshaft journal. The piston rings may try to pop out of the ring compressor just before entering the cylinder bore, so keep some downward pressure on the ring compressor. Work slowly, and if any resistance is felt as the piston enters the cylinder, stop immediately. Find out what's hanging up and fix it before proceeding. Do not, for any reason, force the piston into the cylinder - you might break a ring and/or the piston.

35   Once the piston/connecting rod assembly is installed, the connecting rod bearing oil clearance must be checked before the rod cap is permanently installed.

36   Cut a piece of the appropriate size Plastigage slightly shorter than the width of the connecting rod bearing and lay it in place on the number one connecting rod journal, parallel with the journal axis **(see illustration)**.

37   Clean the connecting rod cap bearing face and install the rod cap. Make sure the mating mark on the cap is on the same side as the mark on the connecting rod.

38   Install the old rod bolts, at this time, and tighten them to the torque listed in this Chapter's Specifications, working up to it in three steps. **Note:** *Use a thin-wall socket to avoid erroneous torque readings that can result if the socket is wedged between the rod cap and the bolt. If the socket tends to wedge itself between the fastener and the cap, lift up on it*

slightly until it no longer contacts the cap. DO NOT rotate the crankshaft at any time during this operation.

39   Remove the fasteners and detach the rod cap, being very careful not to disturb the Plastigage. Discard the cap bolts at this time as they should not be reused.

40   Compare the width of the crushed Plastigage to the scale printed on the Plastigage envelope to obtain the oil clearance **(see illustration)**. The connecting rod oil clearance is usually about 0.001 to 0.002 inch. Consult an automotive machine shop for the clearance specified for the rod bearings on your engine.

41   If the clearance is not as specified, the bearing inserts may be the wrong size (which means different ones will be required). Before deciding that different inserts are needed, make sure that no dirt or oil was between the bearing inserts and the connecting rod or cap when the clearance was measured. Also, recheck the journal diameter. If the Plastigage was wider at one end than the other, the journal may be tapered. If the clearance still exceeds the limit specified, the bearing will have to be replaced with an undersize bearing. **Caution:** *When installing a new crankshaft always use a standard size bearing.*

Final installation

42   Carefully scrape all traces of the Plastigage material off the rod journal and/or bearing face. Be very careful not to scratch the bearing - use your fingernail or the edge of a plastic card.

43   Make sure the bearing faces are perfectly clean, then apply a uniform layer of clean moly-base grease or engine assembly lube to both of them. You'll have to push the piston into the cylinder to expose the face of the bearing insert in the connecting rod.

44   Slide the connecting rod back into place on the journal, install the rod cap, install the nuts or bolts and tighten them to the torque listed in this Chapter's Specifications. Again, work up to the torque in three steps.

45   Repeat the entire procedure for the

remaining pistons/connecting rods.

46   The important points to remember are:

a) *Keep the back sides of the bearing inserts and the insides of the connecting rods and caps perfectly clean when assembling them.*

b) *Make sure you have the correct piston/rod assembly for each cylinder.*

c) *The mark on the piston must face the front (timing chain end) of the engine.*

d) *Lubricate the cylinder walls liberally with clean oil.*

e) *Lubricate the bearing faces when installing the rod caps after the oil clearance has been checked.*

47   After all the piston/connecting rod assemblies have been correctly installed, rotate the crankshaft a number of times by hand to check for any obvious binding.

48   As a final step, check the connecting rod endplay again. If it was correct before disassembly and the original crankshaft and rods were reinstalled, it should still be correct. If new rods or a new crankshaft were installed, the endplay may be inadequate. If so, the rods will have to be removed and taken to an automotive machine shop for resizing.

10 Crankshaft - removal and installation

Removal

Refer to illustrations 10.1 and 10.3

Note: *The crankshaft can be removed only after the engine has been removed from the vehicle. It's assumed that the flywheel or driveplate, crankshaft pulley, timing chain, oil pan, oil pump body, oil filter and piston/connecting rod assemblies have already been removed.*

1   Before the crankshaft is removed, measure the endplay. Mount a dial indicator with

COMMON ENGINE OVERHAUL TERMS

B

Backlash - The amount of play between two parts. Usually refers to how much one gear can be moved back and forth without moving gear with which it's meshed.

Bearing Caps - The caps held in place by nuts or bolts which, in turn, hold the bearing surface. This space is for lubricating oil to enter.

Bearing clearance - The amount of space left between shaft and bearing surface. This space is for lubricating oil to enter.

Bearing crush - The additional height which is purposely manufactured into each bearing half to ensure complete contact of the bearing back with the housing bore when the engine is assembled.

Bearing knock - The noise created by movement of a part in a loose or worn bearing.

Blueprinting - Dismantling an engine and reassembling it to EXACT specifications.

Bore - An engine cylinder, or any cylindrical hole; also used to describe the process of enlarging or accurately refinishing a hole with a cutting tool, as to bore an engine cylinder. The bore size is the diameter of the hole.

Boring - Renewing the cylinders by cutting them out to a specified size. A boring bar is used to make the cut.

Bottom end - A term which refers collectively to the engine block, crankshaft, main bearings and the big ends of the connecting rods.

Break-in - The period of operation between installation of new or rebuilt parts and time in which parts are worn to the correct fit. Driving at reduced and varying speed for a specified mileage to permit parts to wear to the correct fit.

Bushing - A one-piece sleeve placed in a bore to serve as a bearing surface for shaft, piston pin, etc. Usually replaceable.

C

Camshaft - The shaft in the engine, on which a series of lobes are located for operating the valve mechanisms. The camshaft is driven by gears or sprockets and a timing chain. Usually referred to simply as the cam.

Carbon - Hard, or soft, black deposits found in combustion chamber, on plugs, under rings, on and under valve heads.

Cast iron - An alloy of iron and more than two percent carbon, used for engine blocks and heads because it's relatively inexpensive and easy to mold into complex shapes.

Chamfer - To bevel across (or a bevel on) the sharp edge of an object.

Chase - To repair damaged threads with a tap or die.

Combustion chamber - The space between the piston and the cylinder head, with the piston at top dead center, in which air-fuel mixture is burned.

Compression ratio - The relationship between cylinder volume (clearance volume) when the piston is at top dead center and cylinder volume when the piston is at bottom dead center.

Connecting rod - The rod that connects the crank on the crankshaft with the piston. Sometimes called a con rod.

Connecting rod cap - The part of the connecting rod assembly that attaches the rod to the crankpin.

Core plug - Soft metal plug used to plug the casting holes for the coolant passages in the block.

Crankcase - The lower part of the engine in which the crankshaft rotates; includes the lower section of the cylinder block and the oil pan.

Crank kit - A reground or reconditioned crankshaft and new main and connecting rod bearings.

Crankpin - The part of a crankshaft to which a connecting rod is attached.

Crankshaft - The main rotating member, or shaft, running the length of the crankcase, with offset throws to which the connecting rods are attached; changes the reciprocating motion of the pistons into rotating motion.

Cylinder sleeve - A replaceable sleeve, or liner, pressed into the cylinder block to form the cylinder bore.

D

Deburring - Removing the burrs (rough edges or areas) from a bearing.

Deglazer - A tool, rotated by an electric motor, used to remove glaze from cylinder walls so a new set of rings will seat.

E

Endplay - The amount of lengthwise movement between two parts. As applied to a crankshaft, the distance that the crankshaft can move forward and back in the cylinder block.

F

Face - A machinist's term that refers to removing metal from the end of a shaft or the face of a larger part, such as a flywheel.

Fatigue - A breakdown of material through a large number of loading and unloading cycles. The first signs are cracks followed shortly by breaks.

Feeler gauge - A thin strip of hardened steel, ground to an exact thickness, used to check clearances between parts.

Free height - The unloaded length or height of a spring.

Freeplay - The looseness in a linkage, or an assembly of parts, between the initial application of force and actual movement. Usually perceived as slop or slight delay.

Freeze plug - See Core plug.

G

Gallery - A large passage in the block that forms a reservoir for engine oil pressure.

Glaze - The very smooth, glassy finish that develops on cylinder walls while an engine is in service.

H

Heli-Coil - A rethreading device used when threads are worn or damaged. The device is installed in a retapped hole to reduce the thread size to the original size.

I

Installed height - The spring's measured length or height, as installed on the cylinder head. Installed height is measured from the spring seat to the underside of the spring retainer.

J

Journal - The surface of a rotating shaft which turns in a bearing.

K

Keeper - The split lock that holds the valve spring retainer in position on the valve stem.

Key - A small piece of metal inserted into matching grooves machined into two parts fitted together - such as a gear pressed onto a shaft - which prevents slippage between the two parts.

Knock - The heavy metallic engine sound, produced in the combustion chamber as a result of abnormal combustion - usually detonation. Knock is usually caused by a loose or worn bearing. Also referred to as detonation, pinging and spark knock. Connecting rod or main bearing knocks are created by too much oil clearance or insufficient lubrication.

L

Lands - The portions of metal between the piston ring grooves.

Lapping the valves - Grinding a valve face and its seat together with lapping compound.

Lash - The amount of free motion in a gear train, between gears, or in a mechanical assembly, that occurs before movement can begin. Usually refers to the lash in a valve train.

Lifter - The part that rides against the cam to transfer motion to the rest of the valve train.

M

Machining - The process of using a machine to remove metal from a metal part.

Main bearings - The plain, or babbit, bearings that support the crankshaft.

Main bearing caps - The cast iron caps, bolted to the bottom of the block, that support the main bearings.

O

O.D. - Outside diameter.

Oil gallery - A pipe or drilled passageway in the engine used to carry engine oil from one area to another.

Oil ring - The lower ring, or rings, of a piston; designed to prevent excessive amounts of oil from working up the cylinder walls and into the combustion chamber. Also called an oil-control ring.

Oil seal - A seal which keeps oil from leaking out of a compartment. Usually refers to a dynamic seal around a rotating shaft or other moving part.

O-ring - A type of sealing ring made of a special rubberlike material; in use, the O-ring is compressed into a groove to provide the sealing action.

Overhaul - To completely disassemble a unit, clean and inspect all parts, reassemble it with the original or new parts and make all adjustments necessary for proper operation.

P

Pilot bearing - A small bearing installed in the center of the flywheel (or the rear end of the crankshaft) to support the front end of the input shaft of the transmission.

Pip mark - A little dot or indentation which indicates the top side of a compression ring.

Piston - The cylindrical part, attached to the connecting rod, that moves up and down in the cylinder as the crankshaft rotates. When the fuel charge is fired, the piston transfers the force of the explosion to the connecting rod, then to the crankshaft.

Piston pin (or wrist pin) - The cylindrical and usually hollow steel pin that passes through the piston. The piston pin fastens the piston to the upper end of the connecting rod.

Piston ring - The split ring fitted to the groove in a piston. The ring contacts the sides of the ring groove and also rubs against the cylinder wall, thus sealing space between piston and wall. There are two types of rings: Compression rings seal the compression pressure in the combustion chamber; oil rings scrape excessive oil off the cylinder wall.

Piston ring groove - The slots or grooves cut in piston heads to hold piston rings in position.

Piston skirt - The portion of the piston below the rings and the piston pin hole.

Plastigage - A thin strip of plastic thread, available in different sizes, used for measuring clearances. For example, a strip of plastigage is laid across a bearing journal and mashed as parts are assembled. Then parts are disassembled and the width of the strip is measured to determine clearance between journal and bearing. Commonly used to measure crankshaft main-bearing and connecting rod bearing clearances.

Press-fit - A tight fit between two parts that requires pressure to force the parts together. Also referred to as drive, or force, fit.

Prussian blue - A blue pigment; in solution, useful in determining the area of contact between two surfaces. Prussian blue is commonly used to determine the width and location of the contact area between the valve face and the valve seat.

R

Race (bearing) - The inner or outer ring that provides a contact surface for balls or rollers in bearing.

Ream - To size, enlarge or smooth a hole by using a round cutting tool with fluted edges.

Ring job - The process of reconditioning the cylinders and installing new rings.

Runout - Wobble. The amount a shaft rotates out-of-true.

S

Saddle - The upper main bearing seat.

Scored - Scratched or grooved, as a cylinder wall may be scored by abrasive particles moved up and down by the piston rings.

Scuffing - A type of wear in which there's a transfer of material between parts moving against each other; shows up as pits or grooves in the mating surfaces.

Seat - The surface upon which another part rests or seats. For example, the valve seat is the matched surface upon which the valve face rests. Also used to refer to wearing into a good fit; for example, piston rings seat after a few miles of driving.

Short block - An engine block complete with crankshaft and piston and, usually, camshaft assemblies.

Static balance - The balance of an object while it's stationary.

Step - The wear on the lower portion of a ring land caused by excessive side and back-clearance. The height of the step indicates the ring's extra side clearance and the length of the step projecting from the back wall of the groove represents the ring's back clearance.

Stroke - The distance the piston moves when traveling from top dead center to bottom dead center, or from bottom dead center to top dead center.

Stud - A metal rod with threads on both ends.

T

Tang - A lip on the end of a plain bearing used to align the bearing during assembly.

Tap - To cut threads in a hole. Also refers to the fluted tool used to cut threads.

Taper - A gradual reduction in the width of a shaft or hole; in an engine cylinder, taper usually takes the form of uneven wear, more pronounced at the top than at the bottom.

Throws - The offset portions of the crankshaft to which the connecting rods are affixed.

Thrust bearing - The main bearing that has thrust faces to prevent excessive endplay, or forward and backward movement of the crankshaft.

Thrust washer - A bronze or hardened steel washer placed between two moving parts. The washer prevents longitudinal movement and provides a bearing surface for thrust surfaces of parts.

Tolerance - The amount of variation permitted from an exact size of measurement. Actual amount from smallest acceptable dimension to largest acceptable dimension.

U

Umbrella - An oil deflector placed near the valve tip to throw oil from the valve stem area.

Undercut - A machined groove below the normal surface.

Undersize bearings - Smaller diameter bearings used with re-ground crankshaft journals.

V

Valve grinding - Refacing a valve in a valve-refacing machine.

Valve train - The valve-operating mechanism of an engine; includes all components from the camshaft to the valve.

Vibration damper - A cylindrical weight attached to the front of the crankshaft to minimize torsional vibration (the twist-untwist actions of the crankshaft caused by the cylinder firing impulses). Also called a harmonic balancer.

W

Water jacket - The spaces around the cylinders, between the inner and outer shells of the cylinder block or head, through which coolant circulates.

Web - A supporting structure across a cavity.

Woodruff key - A key with a radiused backside (viewed from the side).

10.1 Checking crankshaft endplay with a dial indicator

10.3 Checking crankshaft endplay with feeler gauges at the thrust bearing journal

10.17 Place the Plastigage onto the crankshaft bearing journal as shown

the indicator in line with the crankshaft and touching the end of the crankshaft **(see illustration)**.

2 Pry the crankshaft all the way to the rear and zero the dial indicator. Next, pry the crankshaft to the front as far as possible and check the reading on the dial indicator. The distance traveled is the endplay. A typical crankshaft endplay will fall between 0.003 to 0.010-inch. If it's greater than that, check the crankshaft thrust surfaces for wear after its removed. If no wear is evident, new main bearings should correct the endplay.

3 If a dial indicator isn't available, feeler gauges can be used. Gently pry the crankshaft all the way to the front of the engine. Slip feeler gauges between the crankshaft and the front face of the thrust bearing or washer to determine the clearance **(see illustration)**.

4 Loosen the main bearing cap bolts 1/4-turn at a time each, until they can be removed by hand. Loosen the bolts in a sequence *opposite* of the tightening sequence **(see illustration 10.19)**.

5 Gently tap the main bearing cap assembly with a soft-face hammer. Pull the main bearing cap straight up and off the cylinder block. Try not to drop the bearing inserts if they come out with the assembly. If the assembly is stuck to the engine block, pry carefully at the small slotted areas around the perimeter of the assembly (they're provided for this purpose).

6 Carefully lift the crankshaft out of the engine. It may be a good idea to have an assistant available, since the crankshaft is quite heavy and awkward to handle.

Installation

7 Crankshaft installation is the first step in engine reassembly. It's assumed at this point that the engine block and crankshaft have been cleaned, inspected and repaired or reconditioned.

8 Position the engine block with the bottom facing up.

9 If they're still in place, remove the original bearing inserts from the block and from the main bearing cap assembly.

10 Wipe the bearing surfaces of the block and main bearing cap assembly with a clean, lint-free cloth. They must be kept spotlessly clean. This is critical for determining the correct bearing oil clearance.

Main bearing oil clearance check

Refer to illustrations 10.17, 10.19 and 10.21

11 Without mixing them up, clean the back sides of the new upper main bearing inserts (with grooves and oil holes) and lay one in each main bearing saddle in the block. Each upper bearing has an oil groove and oil hole in it. **Caution:** *The oil holes in the block must line up with the oil holes in the upper bearing inserts.* The thrust bearings (washers) must be installed in the number three (center) cap. Install the thrust bearings with the oil grooves facing out. Install the thrust washers with the grooved side facing out. Install the thrust washers so that one set is located in the block and the other set is with the main bearing cap assembly. Clean the back sides of the lower main bearing inserts (without grooves) and lay them in the corresponding location in the main bearing cap assembly. Make sure the tab on the bearing insert fits into the recess in the block or main bearing cap assembly.

Caution: *Do not hammer the bearing insert into place and don't nick or gouge the bearing faces. DO NOT apply any lubrication at this time.*

12 Clean the faces of the bearing inserts in the block and the crankshaft main bearing journals with a clean, lint-free cloth.

13 Check or clean the oil holes in the crankshaft, as any dirt here can go only one way - straight through the new bearings.

14 Once you're certain the crankshaft is clean, carefully lay it in position in the cylinder block.

15 Before the crankshaft can be permanently installed, the main bearing oil clearance must be checked.

16 Cut several strips of the appropriate size of Plastigage (they must be slightly shorter than the width of the main bearing journal).

17 Place one piece on each crankshaft main bearing journal, parallel with the journal axis **(see illustration)**.

18 Clean the faces of the bearing inserts in the main bearing cap assembly. Install the assembly onto the crankshaft and cylinder block. DO NOT disturb the Plastigage.

19 Apply clean engine oil to all bolt threads prior to installation, then install all bolts finger-tight. Tighten main bearing cap assembly bolts in the sequence shown **(see illustration)** pro-

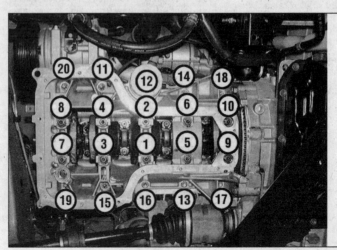

10.19 Main bearing cap bolt tightening sequence

10.21 Use the scale on the Plastigage package to determine the bearing oil clearance - be sure to measure the widest part of the Plastigage and use the correct scale; it comes with both standard and metric scales

gressing in two steps, to the torque listed in this Chapter's Specifications. DO NOT rotate the crankshaft at any time during this operation. **Note:** *At this stage it is only necessary to tighten bolts 1 through 10, and don't apply any sealant to the surfaces until final installation.*

20   Remove the bolts in the *reverse* order of the tightening sequence and carefully lift the main bearing cap assembly straight up and off the block. Do not disturb the Plastigage or rotate the crankshaft. If the main bearing cap assembly is difficult to remove, tap it gently from side-to-side with a soft-face hammer to loosen it.

21   Compare the width of the crushed Plastigage on each journal to the scale printed on the Plastigage envelope to determine the main bearing oil clearance **(see illustration)**. A typical main bearing oil clearance should fall between 0.0015 to 0.0023-inch. Check with an automotive machine shop for the clearance specified for your engine.

22   If the clearance is not as specified, the bearing inserts may be the wrong size (which means different ones will be required). Before deciding if different inserts are needed, make sure that no dirt or oil was between the bearing inserts and the cap assembly or block when the clearance was measured. If the Plastigage was wider at one end than the other, the crankshaft journal may be tapered. If the clearance still exceeds the limit specified, the bearing insert(s) will have to be replaced with an undersize bearing insert(s). **Caution:** *When installing a new crankshaft always install a standard bearing insert set.*

23   Carefully scrape all traces of the Plastigage material off the main bearing journals and/or the bearing insert faces. Be sure to remove all residue from the oil holes. Use your fingernail or the edge of a plastic card - don't nick or scratch the bearing faces.

Final installation

24   Carefully lift the crankshaft out of the cylinder block.

25   Clean the bearing insert faces in the cylinder block, then apply a thin, uniform layer of moly-base grease or engine assembly lube to each of the bearing surfaces. Be sure to coat the thrust faces as well as the journal face of the thrust bearing.

26   Make sure the crankshaft journals are clean, then lay the crankshaft back in place in the cylinder block.

27   Clean the bearing insert faces and then apply the same lubricant to them.

28   Apply a 1/8-inch diameter bead of RTV sealant to the main bearing cap mating surface on the engine block, then place the main bearing cap assembly over the crankshaft and carefully tap it down into position on the engine block.

29   Apply clean engine oil to the bolt threads, wipe off any excess oil and then install the bolts finger-tight.

30   Tighten the main bearing cap bolts in the indicated sequence **(see illustration 10.19)**, to 10 or 12 foot-pounds.

31   Gently tap the crankshaft back-and-forth with a soft face mallet to seat the thrust bearing.

32   Tighten the inner main bearing cap bolts (bolts 1 through 10) in two steps in the indicated sequence **(see illustration 10.19)** and to the torque and angle of rotation listed in this Chapter's Specifications. Then tighten the outer bolts (bolts 11 through 20) to the torque listed in this Chapter's Specifications, in sequence.

33   Recheck crankshaft endplay with a feeler gauge or a dial indicator. The endplay should be correct if the crankshaft thrust faces aren't worn or damaged and if new bearings have been installed.

34   Rotate the crankshaft a number of times by hand to check for any obvious binding. It should rotate with a running torque of 50 in-lbs or less. If the running torque is too high, correct the problem at this time.

35   Install the new rear main oil seal (see Chapter 2A).

11   Engine overhaul - reassembly sequence

1   Before beginning engine reassembly, make sure you have all the necessary new parts, gaskets and seals as well as the following items on hand:

   Common hand tools
   A 1/2-inch drive torque wrench
   New engine oil
   Gasket sealant
   Thread locking compound

2   If you obtained a short block it will be necessary to install the cylinder head, the oil pump and pick-up tube, the oil pan, the water

pump, the timing chain and cover, and the valve cover (see Chapter 2A). In order to save time and avoid problems, the external components must be installed in the following general order:

   Thermostat and housing cover
   Water pump
   Intake and exhaust manifolds
   Fuel injection components
   Emission control components
   Spark plugs
   Ignition coils
   Oil filter
   Engine mounts and mount brackets
   Flywheel and clutch (manual transaxle)
   Driveplate (automatic transaxle)

12   Initial start-up and break-in after overhaul

Warning: *Have a fire extinguisher handy when starting the engine for the first time.*

1   Once the engine has been installed in the vehicle, double-check the engine oil and coolant levels.

2   With the spark plugs out of the engine and the ignition system and fuel pump disabled, crank the engine until oil pressure registers on the gauge or the light goes out.

3   Install the spark plugs, hook up the plug wires and/or ignition coils and restore the ignition system and fuel pump functions.

4   Start the engine. It may take a few moments for the fuel system to build up pressure, but the engine should start without a great deal of effort.

5   After the engine starts, it should be allowed to warm up to normal operating temperature. While the engine is warming up, make a thorough check for fuel, oil and coolant leaks.

6   Shut the engine off and recheck the engine oil and coolant levels.

7   Drive the vehicle to an area with minimum traffic, accelerate from 30 to 50 mph, then allow the vehicle to slow to 30 mph with the throttle closed. Repeat the procedure 10 or 12 times. This will load the piston rings and cause them to seat properly against the cylinder walls. Check again for oil and coolant leaks.

8   Drive the vehicle gently for the first 500 miles (no sustained high speeds) and keep a constant check on the oil level. It is not unusual for an engine to use oil during the break-in period.

9   At approximately 500 to 600 miles, change the oil and filter.

10   For the next few hundred miles, drive the vehicle normally. Do not pamper it or abuse it.

11   After 2000 miles, change the oil and filter again and consider the engine broken in.

Notes

Chapter 3
Cooling, heating and air conditioning systems

Contents

Specifications

General

Radiator cap pressure rating	10.7 to 14.9 psi
Thermostat rating	176 to 183 degrees F
Refrigerant type	R-134a
Refrigerant capacity	17 ounces

Torque specifications   Ft-lbs (unless otherwise indicated)

Note: *One foot-pound (ft-lb) of torque is equivalent to 12 inch-pounds (in-lbs) of torque. Torque values below approximately 15 foot-pounds are expressed in inch-pounds, because most foot-pound torque wrenches are not accurate at these smaller values.*

Thermostat housing bolts	96 in-lbs
Water pump-to-block bolts	
2008 and earlier models	
Smaller bolts	80 in-lbs
Larger bolts	96 in-lbs
2009 and later models	
Shorter bolts (3 bolts)	18
Longer bolts (2 bolts)	19

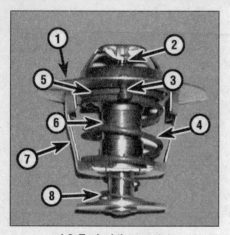

1.2 Typical thermostat

1	Flange	5	Valve seat
2	Piston	6	Valve
3	Jiggle valve	7	Frame
4	Main coil	8	Secondary
	spring		coil spring

1 General information

Engine cooling system

Refer to illustration 1.2

All vehicles covered by this manual employ a pressurized engine cooling system with thermostatically-controlled coolant circulation. An impeller type water pump mounted on the front of the block pumps coolant through the engine. The coolant flows around each cylinder and toward the rear of the engine. Cast-in coolant passages direct coolant around the intake and exhaust ports, near the spark plug areas and in proximity to the exhaust valve guides.

A wax-pellet type thermostat is located in the thermostat housing at the timing chain end of the engine **(see illustration)**. During warm up, the closed thermostat prevents coolant from circulating through the radiator. When

the engine reaches normal operating temperature, the thermostat opens and allows hot coolant to travel through the radiator, where it is cooled before returning to the engine.

The cooling system is sealed by a pressure-type radiator cap. This raises the boiling point of the coolant, and the higher boiling point of the coolant increases the cooling efficiency of the radiator. If the system pressure exceeds the cap pressure-relief value, the excess pressure in the system forces the spring-loaded valve inside the cap off its seat and allows the coolant to escape through the overflow tube into a coolant reservoir. When the system cools, the excess coolant is automatically drawn from the reservoir back into the radiator.

The coolant reservoir serves as both the point at which fresh coolant is added to the cooling system to maintain the proper fluid level and as a holding tank for overheated coolant.

This type of cooling system is known as a closed design because coolant that escapes past the pressure cap is saved and reused.

Heating system

Refer to illustration 1.6

The heating system consists of a blower fan and heater core located within the heater box under the right end of the dashboard, the inlet and outlet hoses connecting the heater core to the engine cooling system and the heater/air conditioning control head on the dashboard **(see illustration)**. Hot engine coolant is circulated through the heater core. When the heater mode is activated, a flap door opens to expose the heater box to the passenger compartment. A fan switch on the control head activates the blower motor, which forces air through the core, heating the air.

Air conditioning system

The air conditioning system consists of a condenser mounted in front of the radiator, an evaporator mounted adjacent to the heater core, a compressor mounted on the engine,

a filter-drier which contains a high pressure relief valve and the plumbing connecting all of the above.

A blower fan forces the warmer air of the passenger compartment through the evaporator core (sort of a radiator-in-reverse), transferring the heat from the air to the refrigerant. The liquid refrigerant boils off into low pressure vapor, taking the heat with it when it leaves the evaporator. The compressor keeps refrigerant circulating through the system, pumping the warmed coolant through the condenser where it is cooled and then circulated back to the evaporator.

2 Antifreeze - general information

Refer to illustration 2.4

Warning: *Do not allow antifreeze to come in contact with your skin or painted surfaces of the vehicle. Rinse off spills immediately with plenty of water. Antifreeze is highly toxic if ingested. Never leave antifreeze lying around in an open container or in puddles on the floor; children and pets are attracted by its sweet smell and may drink it. Check with local authorities about disposing of used antifreeze. Many communities have collection centers that will see that antifreeze is disposed of safely. Never dump used antifreeze on the ground or into drains.*

Note: *Non-toxic antifreeze is now manufactured and available at local auto parts stores, but even these types should be disposed of properly.*

The cooling system should be filled with a water/ethylene-glycol based antifreeze solution, which will prevent freezing down to at least -20 degrees F, or lower if local climate requires it. It also provides protection against corrosion and increases the coolant boiling point.

The cooling system should be drained, flushed and refilled every 30,000 miles or every two years (see Chapter 1). The use of antifreeze solutions for periods of longer

1.6 Under-dash arrangement of the blower unit (A) and evaporator/heater core housing (B)

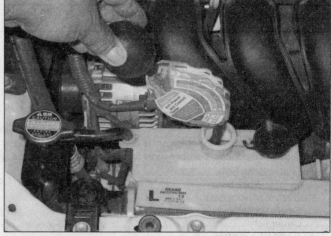

2.4 An inexpensive hydrometer can be used to test the condition of your coolant

3.8 Thermostat housing mounting nuts

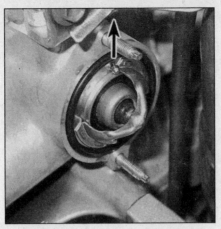

3.9 The thermostat is installed with the spring end towards the engine, and the jiggle pin in the 12 o'clock position

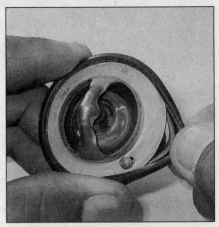

3.10 The thermostat gasket, which is actually a grooved sealing ring, fits around the edge of the thermostat

than two years is likely to cause damage and encourage the formation of rust and scale in the system. If your tap water is hard, i.e. contains a lot of dissolved minerals, use distilled water with the antifreeze.

Before adding antifreeze to the system, check all hose connections, because antifreeze tends to leak through very minute openings. Engines do not normally consume coolant. Therefore, if the level goes down, find the cause and correct it.

The exact mixture of antifreeze-to-water you should use depends on the relative weather conditions. The mixture should contain at least 50 percent antifreeze, but should never contain more than 70 percent antifreeze. Consult the mixture ratio chart on the antifreeze container before adding coolant. Hydrometers are available at most auto parts stores to test the ratio of antifreeze to water **(see illustration)**. Use antifreeze that meets the vehicle manufacturer's specifications.

3 Thermostat - check and replacement

Warning: *Do not attempt to remove the radiator cap, coolant or thermostat until the engine has cooled completely.*

Check

1   Before assuming the thermostat is responsible for a cooling system problem, check the coolant level (see Chapter 1), drivebelt tension (see Chapter 1) and temperature gauge (or light) operation.
2   If the engine takes a long time to warm up (as indicated by the temperature gauge or heater operation), the thermostat is probably stuck open. Replace the thermostat with a new one.
3   If the engine runs hot, use your hand to check the temperature of the lower radiator hose. If the hose is not hot, but the engine is, the thermostat is probably stuck in the closed position, preventing the coolant inside

the engine from traveling through the radiator. Replace the thermostat. **Caution:** *Do not drive the vehicle without a thermostat. The computer may stay in open loop and emissions and fuel economy will suffer.*
4   If the lower radiator hose is hot, it means that the coolant is flowing and the thermostat is open. Consult the *Troubleshooting* Section at the front of this manual for further diagnosis.

Replacement

Refer to illustrations 3.8, 3.9 and 3.10
5   Disconnect the negative cable from the battery.
6   Drain the coolant from the radiator (see Chapter 1).
7   Remove the engine drivebelt (see Chapter 1) and the alternator (see Chapter 5).
8   Detach the thermostat housing from the engine **(see illustration)**. Be prepared for some coolant to spill as the gasket seal is broken. The radiator hose can be left attached to the housing, unless the housing itself is to be replaced.
9   Remove the thermostat, noting the direc-

4.2 Disconnect the fan wiring connector and connect jumper wires directly to the positive and negative terminals of the battery - this view is from the driver's side

tion in which it was installed in the housing, and thoroughly clean the sealing surfaces **(see illustration)**.
10   Fit a new gasket onto the thermostat **(see illustration)**. Make sure it is evenly fitted all the way around.
11   Install the thermostat and housing, positioning the jiggle pin at the highest point.
12   Tighten the housing fasteners to the torque listed in this Chapter's Specifications and reinstall the remaining components in the reverse order of removal.
13   Refill the cooling system (see Chapter 1), run the engine and check for leaks and proper operation.

4 Engine cooling fan and relay - check and replacement

Warning: *To avoid possible injury, keep clear of the fan blades, as they may start turning at any time!*

Check

Refer to illustration 4.2
1   On these models the engine cooling fan is controlled by the Powertrain Control Module (PCM) through the inputs it receives from the coolant temperature sensor. Refer to Chapter 6 for coolant temperature sensor information. The following fan motor and relay checks still apply to these models.
2   To test an inoperative fan motor (one that doesn't come on when the engine gets hot or when the air conditioner is on), first check the fuses and/or fusible links (see Chapter 12). Then disconnect the electrical connector at the motor and use fused jumper wires to connect the fan directly to the battery **(see illustration)**. If the fan still does not work, replace the fan motor. **Warning:** *Do not allow the test clips to contact each other or any metallic part of the vehicle.*
3   If the motor tested OK in the previous test but is still inoperative, then the fault lies in the relays, fuse, wiring or PCM.

4.7a Remove the left-side mounting bolt for the fan assembly . . .

4.7b . . . and the right-side fan assembly bolt

4.8 Remove this nut to detach the fan blades from the motor

Replacement

4   Disconnect the negative battery cable.

5   Disconnect the wiring connector at the fan motor.

6   Disconnect the coolant overflow hose from the top of the radiator.

2008 and earlier models

Refer to illustrations 4.7a, 4.7b, 4.8 and 4.9

7   Unbolt the fan shroud from the radia-

4.9 Remove the motor from the shroud

tor and lift the fan/shroud/coolant reservoir assembly from the vehicle **(see illustrations)**.

8   Hold the fan blades and remove the fan retaining nut (and spacer, if equipped) **(see illustration)**.

9   Unbolt the fan motor from the shroud **(see illustration)**.

10   Installation is the reverse of removal.

2009 and later models

Warning: *Wait until the engine is completely cool before performing this procedure.*

11   Drain the cooling system (see Chapter 1) and remove cooling fans and the radiator (see Section 5) as an assembly

12   Remove the fan shroud mounting bolts and separate the fan assembly from the radiator.

13   Installation is the reverse of removal.

---

5   Radiator - removal and installation

Refer to illustrations 5.6, 5.7 and 5.8

Warning: *Do not start this procedure until the*

engine is completely cool.

1   Disconnect the negative battery cable.

2   Drain the engine coolant (see Chapter 1).

3   Detach the upper and lower radiator hoses from the radiator.

4   Disconnect the reservoir hose from the radiator filler neck.

5   Remove the cooling fan (see Section 4).

6   If equipped with an automatic transaxle, disconnect the cooler lines from the radiator **(see illustration)**. Place a drip pan to catch the fluid and cap the fittings.

7   Remove the two upper radiator mounting brackets **(see illustration)**. **Note:** *The bottom of the radiator is retained by grommeted projections that fit into holes in the body.*

8   Lift out the radiator **(see illustration)**. Be aware of dripping fluids and the sharp fins.

2009 and later models

9   Remove the battery (see Chapter 5).

10   Remove the front grille and bumper cover (see Chapter 11).

11   Remove the upper radiator support bracket mounting bolts, brackets and rubber mounts.

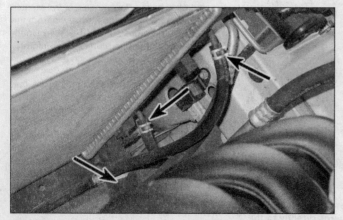

5.6 Remove the automatic transaxle cooler lines and the lower radiator hose from the left side of the radiator

5.7 Remove the upper hold-down clamps (A) from each end of the radiator support - the other bolts (B) are for the air conditioning condenser

5.8 Remove the radiator carefully, and do not lose the rubber mounts - they must be in place on the bottom projections when the radiator is reinstalled

7.5 Water pump bolt locations (rear and lower bolts not visible in this photo)

12   Remove the hood latch assembly (see Chapter 11), support bracket mounting bolts and bracket.

13   Disconnect the coolant bypass hose from the radiator.

14   Disconnect the horn electrical connector (see Chapter 12).

15   Remove the radiator support mounting bolts and remove the support.

16   Remove the fan shroud top support mounting bolts, disengage the plastic clips and remove the support.

17   Disconnect the cooling fan motor electrical connectors.

18   Remove the radiator and cooling fan shroud as an assembly.

19   Remove the cooling fan shroud mounting bolts from the bottom of the radiator and separate the fan shroud from the radiator.

All models

20   With the radiator removed, it can be inspected for leaks, damage and internal blockage. If in need of repairs, have a professional radiator shop or dealer service department perform the work as special techniques are required.

21   Bugs and dirt can be cleaned from the radiator with compressed air and a soft brush. Don't bend the cooling fins as this is done. **Warning:** *Wear eye protection when using compressed air.*

22   Installation is the reverse of the removal procedure. Be sure the rubber mounts are in place on the bottom of the radiator.

23   After installation, fill the cooling system with the proper mixture of antifreeze and water. Refer to Chapter 1 if necessary.

24   Start the engine and check for leaks. Allow the engine to reach normal operating temperature, indicated by both radiator hoses becoming hot. Recheck the coolant level and add more if required.

25   On automatic transmission equipped models, check and add fluid as needed.

6   Water pump - check

1   A failure in the water pump can cause serious engine damage due to overheating.

2   With the engine running and warmed to normal operating temperature, squeeze the upper radiator hose. If the water pump is working properly, a pressure surge should be felt as the hose is released. **Warning:** *Keep hands away from fan blades!*

3   Water pumps are equipped with weep or vent holes. If a failure occurs in the pump seal, coolant will leak from this hole. In most cases it will be necessary to use a flashlight to find the hole on the water pump by looking through the space behind the pulley just below the water pump shaft.

4   If the water pump shaft bearings fail there may be a howling sound at the front of the engine while it is running. Bearing wear can be felt if the water pump pulley is rocked up and down. Do not mistake drivebelt slippage, which causes a squealing sound, for water pump failure. Spray automotive drivebelt dressing on the belt to eliminate the belt as a possible cause of the noise.

7   Water pump - removal and installation

Refer to illustration 7.5

Warning: *Do not start this procedure until the engine is completely cool.*

1   Disconnect the cable from the negative terminal of the battery. (see Chapter 1).

2   Referring to Chapter 1, drain the cooling system and remove the engine drivebelt (see Chapter 1).

3   Remove the right side splash shield.

4   Remove the alternator (see Chapter 5).

5   Remove the bolts retaining the water pump to the engine block and remove the water pump **(see illustration)**. Note the length and the position of the bolts as they were orig-

inally installed before removing them.

6   Thoroughly clean all sealing surfaces, removing the O-ring from the groove in the timing chain cover.

7   Install a new O-ring in the timing chain cover and place the water pump in position. Install the bolts in their original positions and tighten them to the torque listed in this Chapter's Specifications.

8   Install the remaining parts in the reverse order of removal. Refill the cooling system (see Chapter 1), run the engine and check for leaks and proper operation.

8   Coolant temperature sensor - replacement

On these vehicles there is only one coolant temperature sensor - the Engine Coolant Temperature (ECT) sensor, which provides information to the PCM for engine management and also for the temperature gauge on the instrument panel. Refer to Chapter 6 for the ECT sensor replacement procedure.

9   Blower motor - removal and installation

Refer to illustrations 9.2 and 9.3

Warning: *These models are equipped with a Supplemental Restraint System (SRS), more commonly known as airbags. Always disable the airbag system before working in the vicinity of any airbag system component to avoid the possibility of accidental deployment of the airbag(s), which could cause personal injury (see Chapter 12).*

1   The blower unit is located in the passenger compartment under the glove box area. If the blower doesn't work, check the fuse and all connections in the circuit for looseness and corrosion. Make sure the battery is fully charged.

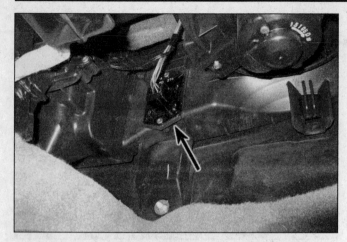

**9.2 Blower motor resistor location - the resistor is retained
by two screws**

**9.3 Disconnect the electrical connector (A) then remove the three
screws (B) and lower the blower motor from the housing**

2   If the blower motor operates at High speed, but not at one or more of the lower speeds, check the blower motor resistor, located under the instrument panel on the passenger side **(see illustration)**. Note: *On 2009 and later models, it will be necessary to remove the instrument panel under cover by releasing the three clips and letting the cover swing forward, exposing the blower motor.*

3   If the blower motor must be replaced, disconnect the wiring connector to the blower, then remove the three mounting screws and lower the blower assembly from the housing **(see illustration)**. The fan can be removed and reused on the new blower motor.

4   Installation is the reverse of removal.

10 Heater core - removal and installation

Refer to illustrations 10.3, 10.6, 10.8a, 10.8b, 10.8c, 10.9, 10.10, 10.11, 10.12a, 10.12b and 10.13

Warning 1: *These models are equipped with a Supplemental Restraint System (SRS), more commonly known as airbags. Always*

disable the airbag system before working in the vicinity of any airbag system component to avoid the possibility of accidental deployment of the airbag(s), which could cause personal injury (see Chapter 12).

Warning 2: *Wait until the engine is completely cool before beginning this procedure.*

Note: *This procedure requires the removal of the instrument panel, and the cross-cowl support tube and steering column. This involves disconnecting numerous electrical connectors and there is the potential for breakage of delicate plastic tabs on various components. This is a difficult job for the average home mechanic.*

1   Disconnect the negative cable from the battery.

2   Drain the cooling system (see Chapter 1). It's not necessary to have the refrigerant recovered because, for heater core removal, the two refrigerant connections at the firewall do not have to be disconnected. However, moving the heat/AC unit away from the firewall for heater core removal is made easier by removing the screw securing the two refrigerant lines to the right fenderwell in the engine compartment.

3   Working in the engine compartment, dis-

connect the heater hoses at the firewall **(see illustration)**.

4   Refer to Chapters 11 and 12 and remove the center console, glove compartment, glove compartment liner, ashtray, radio and center dash bezels.

5   Refer to Section 11 to remove the heater/ air conditioning controls and the instrument panel.

6   Remove the steering column pinch-bolt at the joint near the firewall **(see illustration)**.

7   Major electrical harnesses are attached to the body and the cross-cowl support tube. Disconnect the main electrical connectors at either end of the instrument panel (near the kick panels), and at the center area below the instrument panel. Disconnect all harness connectors from the body side, but leave all harnesses attached to the cross-cowl tube. Use tape to tag and identify all connectors before separating them and take photos for later reference.

8   Remove all the fasteners securing the cross-cowl support tube to the cowl and the tube-to-floor brace **(see illustrations)**. When the tube is loose, you can drop the cowl tube down to the floor with the steering column still attached.

9   The heating/air-conditioning compo-

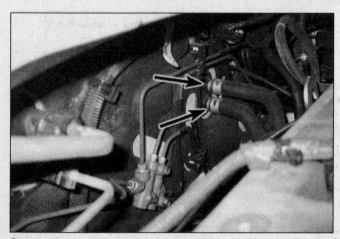

**10.3 Disconnect the heater hoses
at the firewall**

10.6 Remove the pinch bolt at the bottom of the steering column

10.8a Remove the fasteners and the cowl-tube-to-floor brace(s)

10.8b The cross-cowl support tube is secured to the vehicle at each side - remove the bolts and clamp at each end (right side shown)

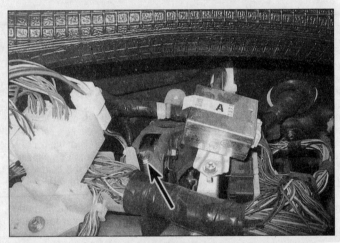

10.8c Remove this screw in the center of the cross-cowl tube

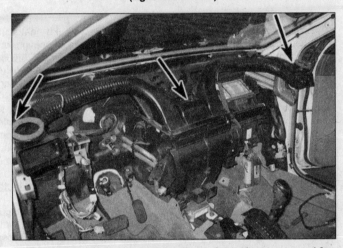

10.9 Shown with the cowl tube and steering column removed for clarity, remove the fasteners/clips and the number 1 duct

nents are in several large plastic housings connected together and secured to the interior side of the firewall. To service the heater core, the entire assembly does not have to be removed from the vehicle, but the assembly must be unbolted and pulled out far enough for the heater core tubes to come through the firewall into the interior. Remove the number 1 air duct **(see illustration)**. **Note:** *On 2009 and later models, disconnect the electrical connectors to the power steering ECU. Remove the ECU assembly mounting fasteners and the ECU for access to the top of the HVAC unit.*

10   Remove the defroster duct above the heat/air housing **(see illustration)**.

11   Remove the fasteners securing the complete HVAC housing unit to the firewall **(see illustration)**.

10.10 Remove the defroster duct from the top of the heat/AC housing

10.11 Remove the four nuts and one bolt securing the HVAC assembly to the firewall

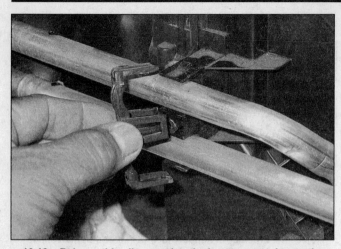

10.12a Release this clip securing the heater core tubes to the side of the case

10.12b Remove the plastic cover over the left end of the heater core

12   Disconnect the clips securing the tubes to the housing **(see illustrations)**. **Note:** *On 2009 and later models, a second heater is used. It's an electric Quick Heater Assembly and is mounted with two fasteners to the HVAC assembly. Once the HVAC unit is exposed the quick heater unit can be unbolted from the HVAC unit for replacement.*

10.13 Slide the heater core out of the left side of the housing, making sure the pipes clear obstructions on the firewall

13   Pull the heater unit out away from the firewall just enough for the heater core tubes to come through the firewall all the way, then remove the heater core from the housing **(see illustration)**. Keep plenty of towels or rags on the carpeting to catch any coolant that may drip. **Caution:** *Work slowly and carefully to avoid breaking any plastic components during removal. The assembly must be pulled out (toward the rear of the vehicle) far enough for the tubes to clear the brake assembly at the firewall.*

14   Installation is the reverse order of removal.

15   Refill the cooling system, reconnect the battery and run the engine. Check for leaks and proper system operation.

11   Heater and air conditioning control assembly - removal and installation

Refer to illustrations 11.2, 11.3, 11.4a and 11.4b

Warning: *These models are equipped with a*

Supplemental Restraint System (SRS), more commonly known as airbags. Always disable the airbag system before working in the vicinity of any airbag system component to avoid the possibility of accidental deployment of the airbag(s), which could cause personal injury (see Chapter 12).

1   Disconnect the negative cable from the battery.

2   Pull off the center knob from the heat/AC control unit **(see illustration)**. This exposes a screw securing the top of the center trim panel, the rest of the panel is retained by clips.

3   Remove the center cluster trim panel (see Chapter 11). Pull the center trim panel out far enough to mark the electrical connectors, then disconnect them **(see illustration)**. On 2009 and later models, disengage the clips and remove the center instrument cluster panel hole cover below the control assembly. Turn the shift lever knob counterclockwise and remove the shift lever knob, then disengage the claws and clips and remove the shifter trim cover.

4   Pull the control unit out enough to dis-

11.2 Remove the center knob from the heat/AC control panel and remove the screw holding the trim panel

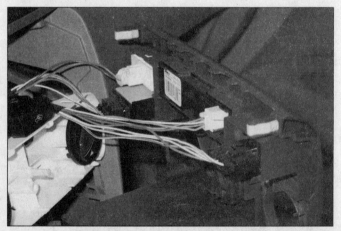

11.3 Pry the center instrument panel trim panel out, then disconnect the electrical connectors

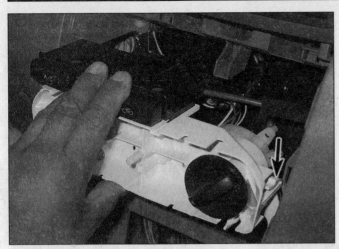

11.4a Release the control panel from two claw-clips by pulling it straight out

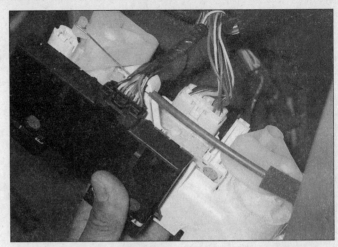

11.4b Behind the control panel, disconnect the electrical connectors and use a screwdriver the open the clips holding the two control cables

connect the heater control cables from the rear of the control unit. Disconnect the electrical connectors from the blower speed switch and the A/C switch **(see illustrations)**.

5   Installation is the reverse of the removal procedure.

6   Run the engine and check for proper functioning of the heater (and air conditioning, if equipped).

12 Air conditioning and heating system - check and maintenance

Air conditioning system

Warning: *The air conditioning system is under high pressure. Do not loosen any hose fittings or remove any components until the system has been discharged. Air conditioning refrigerant should be properly discharged into an EPA-approved recovery/recycling unit by a dealer service department or an automotive air conditioning repair facility. Always wear eye protection when disconnecting air conditioning system fittings.*

1   The following maintenance checks should be performed on a regular basis to ensure that the air conditioner continues to operate at peak efficiency **(see illustration)**:

a) *Inspect the condition of the drivebelt. If it is worn or deteriorated, replace it (see Chapter 1).*

b) *Inspect the system hoses. Look for cracks, bubbles, hardening and deterioration. Inspect the hoses and all fittings for oil bubbles or seepage. If there is any evidence of wear, damage or leakage, replace the hose(s).*

c) *Inspect the condenser fins for leaves, bugs and any other foreign material that may have embedded itself in the fins. Use a "fin comb" or compressed air to remove debris from the condenser.*

d) *Make sure the system has the correct refrigerant charge.*

2   It's a good idea to operate the system for about ten minutes at least once a month. This is particularly important during the winter months because long term non-use can cause hardening, and subsequent failure, of the seals.

3   Leaks in the air conditioning system are best spotted when the system is brought up to operating temperature and pressure, by running the engine with the air conditioning ON for five minutes. Shut the engine off and inspect the air conditioning hoses and connections. Traces of oil usually indicate refrigerant leaks.

4   Because of the complexity of the air conditioning system and the special equipment required to effectively work on it, accurate troubleshooting of the system should be left to a professional technician.

5   If the air conditioning system doesn't operate at all, check the fuse panel and the air conditioning relay, located in the fuse/relay box in the engine compartment.

6   The most common cause of poor cooling is simply a low system refrigerant charge. If a

noticeable drop in cool air output occurs, the following quick check will help you determine if the refrigerant level is low. For more complete information on the air conditioning system, refer to the *Haynes Automotive Heating and Air Conditioning Manual.*

Checking the refrigerant charge

Refer to illustrations 12.9 and 12.10

7   Warm the engine up to normal operating temperature.

8   Place the air conditioning temperature selector at the coldest setting and put the blower at the highest setting. Open the doors (to make sure the air conditioning system doesn't cycle off as soon as it cools the passenger compartment).

9   With the compressor engaged - the clutch will make an audible click and the center of the clutch will rotate - feel the large pipe exiting from the evaporator at the firewall **(see illustration)**.

10   The large evaporator outlet pipe should feel cold. If the evaporator outlet is warm or moderately warm, the system needs a charge.

12.9 With the system operating, the evaporator outlet line (large tubing) should feel colder than the smaller line

12.10 Check the temperature of the output air in the center register with a thermometer - it should be 35-40 degrees below the ambient air temperature

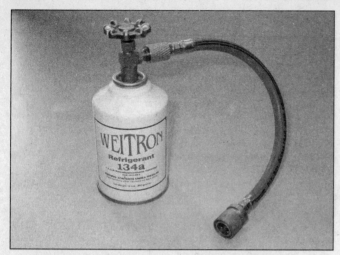

12.12 A basic charging kit is available at most auto parts stores - it must say R-134a and so must the cans of refrigerant you buy

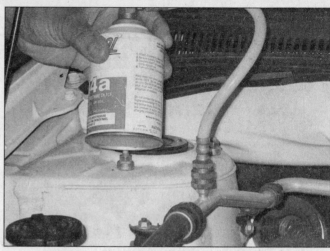

12.15 Add R-134a refrigerant to the low-side port only - the procedure will go faster if you wrap the can with a warm wet towel to prevent icing

Insert a thermometer in the center air distribution duct while operating the air conditioning system **(see illustration)** - the temperature of the output air should be 35 to 40 degrees F below the ambient air temperature (down to approximately 40 degrees F). If the ambient (outside) air temperature is very high, say 110 degrees F, the duct air temperature may be as high as 60 degrees F, but generally the air conditioning is 35 to 40 degrees F cooler than the ambient air. If the air isn't as cold as it used to be, the system probably needs a charge. Further inspection or testing of the system is beyond the scope of the home mechanic and should be left to a professional.

11   Before any components are replaced, the refrigerant should be discharged and recovered by a licensed air conditioning technician first. After your repairs, the shop can recharge your system, giving you credit for the amount they removed originally.

Adding refrigerant

Refer to illustrations 12.12 and 12.15

Caution: *All models covered by this manual use environmentally-friendly R-134a refrigerant. When replacing entire components, additional refrigerant oil should be added equal to the amount that is removed with the component being replaced. Be sure to read the can before adding any oil to the system, to make sure it is compatible with an R-134a system.*

12   Buy an automotive charging kit at an auto parts store. A charging kit includes a can of R-134a refrigerant, a tap valve and a short section of hose that can be attached between the tap valve and the system low side service valve **(see illustration)**.

13   Connect the charging kit by following the manufacturer's instructions.

14   Back off the valve handle on the charging kit and screw the kit onto the refrigerant can, making sure first that the O-ring or rubber seal inside the threaded portion of the kit is in place. **Warning:** *Wear protective eye-*

wear when dealing with pressurized refrigerant cans.

15   Remove the dust cap from the low-side charging port and attach the quick-connect fitting on the kit hose **(see illustration)**. **Warning:** *DO NOT hook the charging kit hose to the system high side! The fittings on the charging kit are designed to fit only on the low side of the system.*

16   Warm the engine to normal operating temperature and turn on the air conditioner. Keep the charging kit hose away from the fan and other moving parts.

17   Turn the valve handle on the kit until the stem pierces the can, then back the handle out to release the refrigerant. You should be able to hear the rush of gas. Add refrigerant to the low side of the system until both the outlet and the evaporator inlet pipe feel about the same temperature. Allow stabilization time between each addition. **Warning:** *Never add more than two cans of refrigerant to the system. The can may tend to frost up, slowing the procedure. Wrap a shop towel wet with hot water around the bottom of the can to keep it from frosting.*

18   If you have an accurate thermometer, you can place it in the center air conditioning duct inside the vehicle to monitor the air temperature. A charged system that is working properly, should output air down to approximately 40 degrees F.

19   When the can is empty, turn the valve handle to the closed position and release the connection from the low-side port. Replace the dust cap.

20   Remove the charging kit from the can and store the kit for future use with the piercing valve in the UP position, to prevent inadvertently piercing the can on the next use.

Heating systems

Refer to illustration 12.25

21   If the air coming out of the heater vents isn't hot, the problem could stem from any of

the following causes:

a) *The thermostat is stuck open, preventing the engine coolant from warming up enough to carry heat to the heater core. Replace the thermostat (see Section 3).*

b) *A heater hose is blocked, preventing the flow of coolant through the heater core. Feel both heater hoses at the firewall. They should be hot. If one of them is cold, there is an obstruction in one of the hoses or in the heater core, or the heater control valve is shut. Detach the hoses and back flush the heater core with a water hose. If the heater core is clear but circulation is impeded, remove the two hoses and flush them out with a water hose.*

c) *If flushing fails to remove the blockage from the heater core, the core must be replaced. (see Section 10).*

22   If the blower motor speed does not correspond to the setting selected on the blower switch, the problem could be a bad fuse, circuit, switch, blower motor resistor or motor (see Sections 9 and 11).

23   If there isn't any air coming out of the vents:

a) *Turn the ignition ON and activate the fan control. Place your ear at the heating/air conditioning register (vent) and listen. Most motors are audible. Can you hear the motor running?*

b) *If you can't (and have already verified that the blower switch and the blower motor resistor are good), the blower motor itself is probably bad (see Section 9).*

24   If the carpet under the heater core is damp, or if antifreeze vapor or steam is coming through the vents, the heater core is leaking. Remove it (see Section 10) and install a new unit (most radiator shops will not repair a leaking heater core).

25   Inspect the drain hose from the heater/air conditioning assembly at the right side of

12.25 The drain hose from the heater/air-conditioning unit (arrow) should be kept clear to allow drainage of condensation - shown here from underneath, the hose is on the right side, below the power steering pump

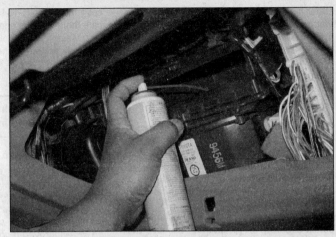

12.29 Remove the cabin air filter, then insert the disinfectant spray nozzle - be sure to support the nozzle so it doesn't get tangles in the blower fan

the firewall, making sure it is not clogged **(see illustration)**.

Eliminating air-conditioning odors

Refer to illustration 12.29

26   Unpleasant odors that often develop in air-conditioning systems are caused by the growth of a fungus, usually on the surface of the evaporator core. The warm, humid environment there is a perfect breeding ground for mildew to develop. The evaporator core in your Corolla has been factory-treated with an anti-bacterial coating to reduce this, but climactic conditions can still cause odors to develop.

27   Dealerships have a lengthy and often expensive process for eliminating the fungus by opening up the evaporator case and using a powerful disinfectant and rinse on the core until the fungus is gone. You can service your own system at home, but it takes something much stronger than basic household germ-killers or deodorizers.

28   Aerosol disinfectants for automotive air-conditioning systems are available in most auto parts stores, but remember when shopping for them that the most effective treatments are also the most expensive. The basic procedure for using these sprays is to start by running the system in the RECIRC mode for ten minutes with the blower on its highest speed. Use the highest heat mode to dry out the system and keep the compressor from engaging by disconnecting the wiring connector at the compressor (see Section 14).

29   The disinfectant can usually comes with a long spray hose. Remove the cabin air filter, point the nozzle inside the hole and to the left towards the evaporator core, and spray according to the manufacturer's recommendations **(see illustration)**. Follow the manufacturer's recommendations for the length of spray and waiting time between applications.

30   Once the evaporator has been cleaned,

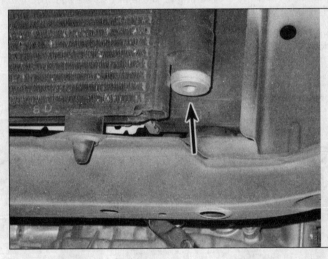

13.3 After the system has been discharged, remove the Allen plug at the bottom of the receiver-drier

the best way to prevent the mildew from coming back again is to make sure your evaporator housing drain tube is clear **(see illustration 12.25)** and to run the defrost cycle briefly to dry the evaporator out after a long drive with the air conditioning on.

13 Air conditioning receiver-drier - removal and installation

Refer to illustration 13.3

Warning: *The air conditioning system is under high pressure. Do not loosen any hose fittings or remove any components until the system has been discharged. Air conditioning refrigerant should be properly discharged into an EPA-approved recovery/recycling unit by a dealer service department or an automotive air conditioning repair facility. Always wear eye protection when disconnecting air conditioning system fittings.*

Note: *On 2009 and later models, the condenser must be removed for access to the receiver-drier plug (see Section 15).*

1   Have the refrigerant discharged and

recovered by an air conditioning technician.

2   The receiver-drier is mounted on the passenger's side of the vehicle, at the end of the condenser.

3   Using a Allen wrench, remove the large plug at the bottom of the receiver-drier **(see illustration)**. Use needle-nose pliers to grip and remove the filter-drier element inside the receiver.

4   Installation is the reverse of removal. Install a new filter-drier element and lubricate the plug's O-ring with a touch of refrigerant oil.

5   Have the system evacuated, charged and leak tested by the shop that discharged it. If the receiver-drier or condenser was replaced, have them add new refrigeration oil to the system. Use only refrigerant oil compatible with R-134a refrigerant.

14 Air conditioning compressor - removal and installation

Refer to illustration 14.4

Warning: *The air conditioning system is*

under high pressure. Do not loosen any hose fittings or remove any components until the system has been discharged. Air conditioning refrigerant should be properly discharged into an EPA-approved recovery/recycling unit by a dealer service department or an automotive air conditioning repair facility. Always wear eye protection when disconnecting air conditioning system fittings.

Caution: *The receiver-drier element should be replaced whenever a new compressor is installed (see Section 13).*

1   Have the refrigerant discharged by an automotive air conditioning technician.

2   Disconnect the negative cable from the battery.

3   Raise the front of the vehicle and support it securely on jackstands. Remove the engine under cover (if equipped). Remove the drivebelt from the compressor (see Chapter 1).

4   Detach the wiring connector and disconnect the refrigerant lines **(see illustration)**.

5   Unbolt the compressor and lift it from the vehicle.

6   If a new or rebuilt compressor is being installed, follow the directions supplied with the compressor regarding the proper level of oil prior to installation.

7   Installation is the reverse of removal. Replace any O-rings with new ones specifi-

cally made for R-134a refrigerant and lubricate them with the same oil.

8   Have the system evacuated, recharged and leak tested by the shop that discharged it.

---

15   Air conditioning condenser - removal and installation

Refer to illustration 15.3

Warning 1: *The air conditioning system is under high pressure. Do not loosen any hose fittings or remove any components until the system has been discharged. Air conditioning refrigerant should be properly discharged into an EPA-approved recovery/recycling unit by a dealer service department or an automotive air conditioning repair facility. Always wear eye protection when disconnecting air conditioning system fittings.*

Warning 2: *These models are equipped with a Supplemental Restraint System (SRS), more commonly known as airbags. Always disable the airbag system before working in the vicinity of any airbag system component to avoid the possibility of accidental deployment of the airbag(s), which could cause personal injury (see Chapter 12).*

Warning 3: *Wait until the engine is completely cool before beginning this procedure.*

Caution: *The receiver-drier element should be replaced if the condenser is being replaced due to leakage (see Section 13).*

1   Have the refrigerant discharged and recovered by an air conditioning technician.

2   Remove the radiator as described in Section 5.

3   Disconnect the condenser inlet and outlet fittings **(see illustration)**. Cap the open fittings immediately to keep moisture and contamination out of the system.

4   Remove the condenser mounting bolts **(see illustration 5.7)**, angle the condenser back and lift it out.

5   Install the condenser, brackets and bolts, making sure the rubber cushions fit on the mounting points properly.

6   Reconnect the refrigerant lines, using new O-rings where needed. If a new condenser has been installed, add approximately 1.5 to 2.0 fluid ounces of new, R-134a-compatible refrigerant oil.

7   Reinstall the remaining parts in the reverse order of removal.

8   Refill the cooling system (see Chapter 1).

9   Have the system evacuated, charged and leak tested by the shop that discharged it.

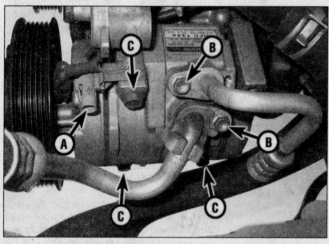

14.4 Air conditioning compressor mounting details

A   Electrical connector (unplugged)
B   Refrigerant line flange bolts
C   Compressor mounting bolts

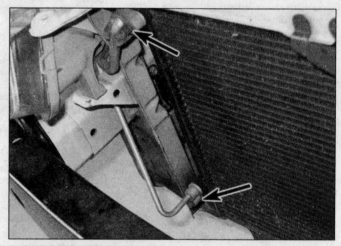

15.3 Disconnect the refrigerant connections on the right (passenger's) side of the condenser by removing the flange bolts

Notes

Notes

Chapter 4
Fuel and exhaust systems

Contents

Specifications

Fuel system

Fuel pressure (key On, engine Off)	44 to 50 psi
Fuel injector resistance (at 68-degrees F)	
2003 and 2004 models	13.4 to 14.2 ohms
2005 and later models	11.6 to 12.4 ohms

Torque specifications

Ft-lbs (unless otherwise indicated)

Note: *One foot-pound (ft-lb) of torque is equivalent to 12 inch-pounds (in-lbs) of torque. Torque values below approximately 15 ft-lbs are expressed in inch-pounds, since most foot-pound torque wrenches are not accurate at these smaller values.*

Intake manifold mounting bolts	22
Fuel rail mounting bolts	
2003 and 2004 models	168 in-lbs
2005 and later models	21
Throttle body mounting bolts/nuts	
2003 and 2004	22
2005 through 2008 models	80 in-lbs
2009 and later models	84 in-lbs
Throttle body upper bracket bolts (2003 and 2004 models with manual transaxle only)	115 in-lbs

1   General information

The fuel system consists of a fuel tank, an electric fuel pump (located in the fuel tank), an EFI/fuel pump relay, fuel injectors, a fuel pressure regulator, an air filter assembly and a throttle body unit. All models covered by this manual are equipped with a multi port fuel injection system.

Multi port fuel injection system

Multi port fuel injection uses timed impulses to sequentially inject the fuel directly into the intake port of each cylinder. The injectors are controlled by the Powertrain Control Module (PCM). The PCM monitors various engine parameters and delivers the exact amount of fuel, in the correct sequence, into the intake ports. The throttle body serves only to control the amount of air passing into the system. Because each cylinder is equipped with an injector mounted immediately adjacent to the intake valve, much better control of the fuel/air mixture ratio is possible.

Fuel pump and lines

Fuel is delivered from the fuel tank to the fuel injection system through a metal line running along the underside of the vehicle by an electric fuel pump inside the fuel tank. The fuel pressure regulator is located in the fuel tank with the fuel pump, and excessive fuel pressure is bled-off directly into the fuel tank.

The fuel pump will operate as long as the engine is cranking or running and the PCM is receiving ignition reference pulses from the electronic ignition system (see Chapter 5). If there are no reference pulses, the fuel pump will shut off after 2 or 3 seconds.

Exhaust system

The exhaust system includes an exhaust manifolds, a catalytic converter, an exhaust pipe, and a muffler.

The catalytic converter is an emission control device added to the exhaust system to reduce pollutants. A three-way (reduction) catalyst is used to reduce hydrocarbons (HC), carbon monoxide (CO) and oxides of nitrogen (NOx). Refer to Chapter 6 for more information regarding the catalytic converter.

2   Fuel pressure relief procedure

Warning: *Gasoline is extremely flammable, so take extra precautions when you work on any part of the fuel system. Don't smoke or allow open flames or bare light bulbs near the work area, and don't work in a garage where a gas-type appliance (such as a water heater or a clothes dryer) is present. Since gasoline is carcinogenic, wear fuel-resistant gloves when there's a possibility of being exposed to fuel, and, if you spill any fuel on your skin, rinse it off immediately with soap and water. Mop up any spills immediately and do not store fuel-soaked rags where they could ignite. The*

fuel system is under constant pressure, so, if any fuel lines are to be disconnected, the fuel pressure in the system must be relieved first. When you perform any kind of work on the fuel system, wear safety glasses and have a Class B type fire extinguisher on hand.

1   Before servicing any fuel system component, you must relieve the fuel pressure to minimize the risk of fire or personal injury.
2   Remove the fuel filler cap - this will relieve any pressure built up in the tank.
3   Remove the rear seat cushion (see Chapter 11), then remove the cover and unplug the fuel pump electrical connector **(see illustrations 5.4 and 5.5a)**.
4   Attempt to start the engine - the engine will stall. Crank the engine for 3 or 4 seconds, then turn the ignition key to Off.
5   The fuel system is now depressurized.
Note: *Place a rag around the fuel line before removing any hose clamp or fitting to prevent any residual fuel from spilling onto the engine.*
6   Before working on the fuel system, disconnect the cable from the negative terminal of the battery.

3   Fuel pump/fuel pressure - check

Warning: *Gasoline is extremely flammable, so take extra precautions when you work on any part of the fuel system. See the* **Warning** *in Section 2.*

General checks

1   Check that there is adequate fuel in the fuel tank.
2   Verify the fuel pump actually runs. Have an assistant turn the ignition switch to ON - you should hear a brief whirring noise (for approximately two seconds) as the pump comes on and pressurizes the system. **Note:** *The fuel pump is easily heard through the gas tank filler neck.* If there is no response from the fuel pump (makes no sound) proceed to

Step 8 and check the fuel pump electrical circuit. If the fuel pump runs, but a fuel system problem is suspected, continue with the fuel pump pressure check.

Fuel pump pressure check

Refer to illustration 3.3a and 3.3b
Note: *In order to perform the fuel pressure test, you will need to obtain a fuel pressure gauge capable of measuring high fuel pressure and the proper adapter set for the specific fuel injection system.*
3   Relieve the fuel system pressure (see Section 2). Remove the fuel line from the fuel rail and where this line attaches to a steel line near the master cylinder. A simple special tool is used to separate the quick-connect fittings (see Section 4). The fuel pressure test hose temporarily replaces this factory hose **(see illustrations)**. Make sure the clamps are tight on the hoses.
4   Turn all the accessories Off and switch the ignition key On. The fuel pump should run for about two seconds; note the reading on the gauge. After the pump stops running, the pressure should hold steady. After five minutes it should not drop below the minimum listed in this Chapter's Specifications.
5   Start the engine and let it idle at normal operating temperature. The pressure should remain the same. If all the pressure readings are within the limits listed in this Chapter's Specifications, the system is operating properly.
6   If the fuel pressure is not within specifications, check the following:

a)   If the pressure is higher than specified, replace the fuel pressure regulator (see Section 6).
b)   If the pressure is lower than specified, the fuel filter could be clogged, the fuel line from the fuel rail to the fuel tank could be restricted, the fuel injectors could be leaking, or the fuel pressure regulator and/or the fuel pump could be defective (this is probably the most likely cause).

3.3a A fuel pressure testing kit like this should contain all the necessary fittings and adapters, along with the fuel pressure gauge, to test most automotive systems

3.3b Attach the fuel pressure gauge with fuel hose and clamps between the fuel rail and the fuel feed line - turn the ignition key ON and check the fuel pressure

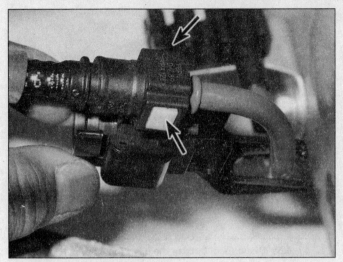

4.12a To disconnect a plastic type fitting, squeeze the retaining tabs in and pull the lines apart

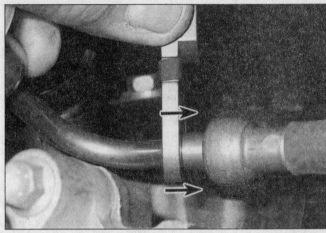

4.12b To disconnect a metal collar type quick-connect fitting, remove the safety tether and place the tool squarely over the fuel line; push the tool into the fitting and pull the lines apart (the tool is not required to connect the fitting)

In this situation, it is recommended that both the fuel pressure regulator and fuel pump be replaced to prevent any future fuel pressure problems. **Note:** *The fuel filter is part of the fuel pump assembly. Check with your local auto parts store or dealer parts department regarding parts availability.*

7   After the testing is done, relieve the fuel pressure (see Section 2) and remove the fuel pressure gauge.

Fuel pump electrical circuit check

8   If the pump does not turn on (makes no sound) with the ignition switch in the ON position, check the EFI fuse located in the engine compartment fuse center. If the fuse is blown, replace the fuse and see if the pump works. If the pump now works, check for a short in the circuit between the fuel pump relay (circuit opening relay) and the fuel pump. Also check the EFI relay and the circuit opening relay (C/OPN).

9   If the relays are good and the fuel pump does not operate, check the wiring from the underhood fuse/relay box to the fuel pump.

---

4   Fuel lines and fittings - general information and replacement

Warning: *Gasoline is extremely flammable, so take extra precautions when you work on any part of the fuel system. See the* **Warning** *in Section 2.*

1   Always relieve the fuel pressure before servicing fuel lines or fittings (see Section 2).

2   The fuel line extends from the fuel tank to the engine compartment. The line is secured to the underbody with clip and screw assemblies. This line must be occasionally inspected for leaks, kinks and dents.

3   If evidence of dirt is found in the system or fuel filter during disassembly, the line should be disconnected and blown out. Check the fuel strainer on the fuel gauge sending unit (see Section 5) for damage and deterioration.

Steel tubing

4   If replacement of a fuel line or emission line is called for, use welded steel tubing meeting the manufacturer's specifications or its equivalent.

5   Don't use copper or aluminum tubing to replace steel tubing. These materials cannot withstand normal vehicle vibration.

6   Because fuel lines used on fuel-injected vehicles are under high pressure, they require special consideration.

7   Some fuel lines have threaded fittings with O-rings. Any time the fittings are loosened to service or replace components:

a) *Use a backup wrench while loosening and tightening the fittings.*

b) *Check all O-rings for cuts, cracks and deterioration. Replace any that appear hardened, worn or damaged.*

c) *If the lines are replaced, always use original equipment parts, or parts that meet the original equipment standards specified in this Section.*

Flexible hose

Warning: *Use only original equipment replacement hoses or their equivalent. Others may fail from the high pressures of this system.*

8   Don't route fuel hose within four inches of any part of the exhaust system or within ten inches of the catalytic converter. Metal lines and rubber hoses must never be allowed to chafe against the frame. A minimum of 1/4-inch clearance must be maintained around a line or hose to prevent contact with the frame.

9   Some models may be equipped with nylon fuel line and quick-connect fittings at the fuel filter and/or fuel pump. The quick-connect fittings cannot be serviced separately.

Do not attempt to service these types of fuel lines in the event the retainer tabs or the line becomes damaged. Replace the entire fuel line as an assembly.

Replacement

Refer to illustrations 4.12a and 4.12b

10   In the event of any fuel line damage (metal or flexible lines) it is necessary to replace the damaged lines with factory replacement parts. Others may fail from the high pressures of this system.

11   Relieve the fuel pressure.

12   Remove all fasteners attaching the lines to the vehicle body. On fuel lines so equipped, detach the clamp(s) that attach the fuel hoses to the metal lines, then pull the hose off the fitting. Twisting the hoses back and forth will allow them to separate more easily. To separate quick-connect fittings, hold the connector with one hand and depress the retaining tabs with the other hand, then separate the connector from the pipe **(see illustrations)**. Some fittings require the use of a dedicated, yet simple tool.

13   Installation is the reverse of removal, making sure to use new O-rings. On plastic quick-connect fittings, align the retainer locking pawls with the connector grooves. Push the connector onto the pipe until both retaining pawls lock with a clicking sound, then reinstall the covers.

---

5   Fuel pump - removal and installation

Refer to illustrations 5.4, 5.5a, 5.5b, 5.5c, 5.6, 5.7, 5.8, 5.9a and 5.9b

Warning: *Gasoline is extremely flammable, so take extra precautions when you work on any part of the fuel system. See the* **Warning** *in Section 2.*

1   Relieve the fuel system pressure (see

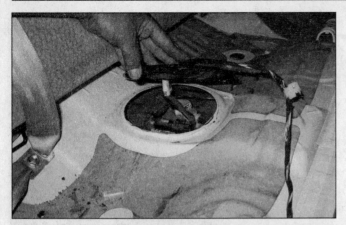

5.4 On 2003 and 2004 models, pry the fuel pump access cover off (it's secured by butyl tape). On 2005 models it's secured by four screws

5.5a Disconnect both of the electrical connectors

Section 2), then disconnect the cable from the negative terminal of the battery. Remove the fuel tank cap.

2   Disconnect the cable from the negative terminal of the battery.

3   Remove the rear seat from inside the passenger compartment (see Chapter 11).

4   Remove the fuel pump/sending unit access cover **(see illustration)**.

5   Unplug the electrical connectors **(see illustration)**, then disconnect the fuel lines **(see illustrations)**. **Note:** *On 2005 and later models, the quick-release fitting on the pressure line can be squeezed by hand, without pliers.*

6   On 2003 and 2004 models, remove the fuel pump/sending unit retaining screws and remove the mounting flange **(see illustration)**. On 2005 and later models, the fuel pump assembly is retained to the tank by a large screw-on ring. A special tool (available at most auto parts stores) is available which makes loosening and tightening this ring very easy, but a large pair of water pump pliers will work.

7   Carefully withdraw the fuel pump/fuel level sending unit assembly from the fuel tank

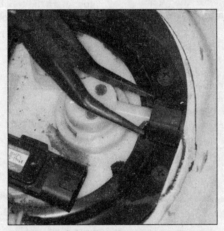

5.5b Use needle-nose pliers to release the quick-release fitting securing the fuel return line

(see illustration).

8   The components of the fuel pump assembly are modular and all attach to the main housing **(see illustration)**.

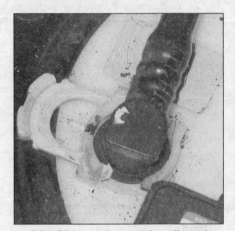

5.5c Slide out the retaining clip and remove the fuel pressure hose from the assembly

9   Remove the plastic support on the bottom of the pump by releasing the clips with a screwdriver, the pull off the rubber isolator, the fuel sock filter clip, then the electrical connec-

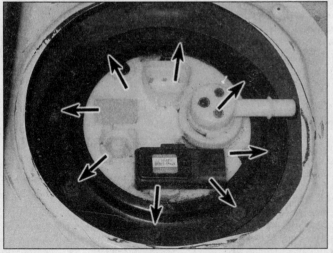

5.6 Remove the fuel pump/sending unit assembly mounting screws (2003 and 2004 models)

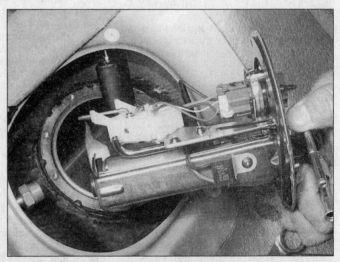

5.7 Lift the fuel pump/sending unit assembly from the fuel tank at an angle so as not to damage the inlet screen or float arm

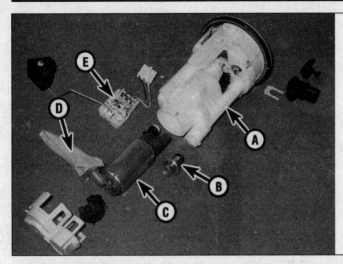

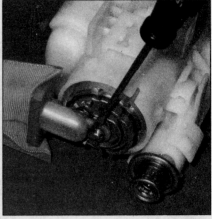

5.8 Exploded view of the fuel pump assembly

A Fuel filter
B Fuel pressure regulator
C Fuel pump
D Sock (inlet) filter
E Fuel level sending unit

5.9a After removing the plastic support, carefully use a screwdriver to remove the clip securing the sock filter to the pump

tor **(see illustrations)**.

10 Withdraw the pump from the housing.

11 Inspect the strainer for contamination. If it is dirty, replace it.

12 Reassemble the fuel pump/sending unit in the reverse order of disassembly.

13 Install the fuel pump/sending unit assembly in the fuel tank. Connect the fuel line and electrical connectors.

14 The remainder of installation is the reverse of removal.

6 Fuel pressure regulator - removal and installation

Refer to illustration 6.3

Warning: *Gasoline is extremely flammable, so take extra precautions when you work on any part of the fuel system. See the* **Warning** *in Section 2.*

1 Relieve the fuel system pressure (see Section 2), then disconnect the cable from the negative terminal of the battery. Remove the fuel tank cap.

2 Remove the fuel pump assembly (see Section 5).

3 Twist the fuel pressure regulator from the assembly **(see illustration)**.

4 Installation is the reverse of removal. Be sure to install a new O-ring on the fuel pressure regulator.

7 Fuel level sending unit - replacement

Refer to illustration 7.4

Warning: *Gasoline is extremely flammable, so take extra precautions when you work on any part of the fuel system. See the* **Warning** *in Section 2.*

1 Remove the fuel pump/fuel level sending unit assembly from the fuel tank (see Section 5).

2 Carefully angle the sending unit out of the opening without damaging the fuel level float located at the bottom of the assembly.

3 Disconnect the electrical connector from the sending unit.

4 Pry the sending unit from the retaining clips **(see illustration)** and separate it from the assembly.

5 Installation is the reverse of removal.

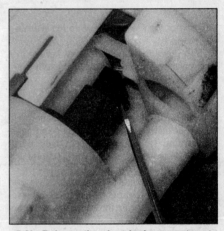

5.9b Release the electrical connector at the top of the fuel pump assembly

8 Fuel tank - removal and installation

Refer to illustrations 8.8 and 8.9

Warning: *Gasoline is extremely flammable, so take extra precautions when you work on*

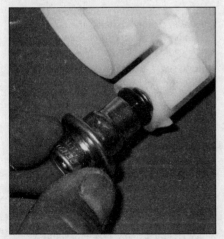

6.3 The fuel pressure regulator is a push-fit in the fuel pump/sending unit assembly; make sure the old O-ring comes out with it

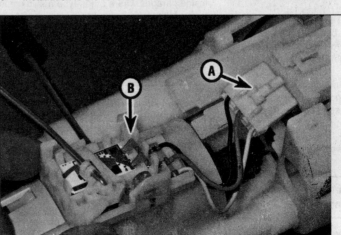

7.4 Disconnect the electrical connector (A) and pry the fuel-level sending unit from the clips (B)

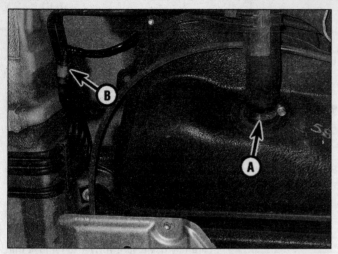

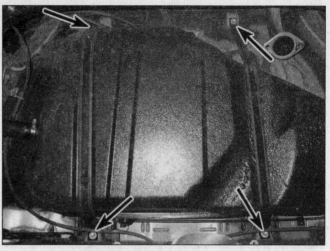

8.8 Remove the clamp that retains the fuel filler hose (A) and separate the fuel hose disconnects (B)

8.9 Remove the tank strap bolts (shown for clarity without supports required for tank removal)

any part of the fuel system. See the **Warning** *in Section 2.*

1   Remove the fuel filler cap to relieve fuel tank pressure. Relieve the fuel system pressure (see Section 2).

2   Detach the cable from the negative terminal of the battery.

3   Siphon or pump the fuel into an approved container using a siphoning kit or hand operated pump (available at most auto parts stores). **Warning:** *Do not start the siphoning action by mouth!*

4   Remove the fuel pump access cover and disconnect the fuel pump electrical connector and fuel lines from the fuel pump unit (see Section 5).

5   Raise the vehicle and support it securely on jackstands.

6   Remove the center exhaust pipe and the heat insulator from the vehicle (see Section 16).

7   Detach the parking brake cables from the underbody and position them aside.

8   Disconnect the fuel lines, the vapor return line and the fuel filler hose **(see illustration)**. **Note:** *Be sure to plug the hoses to prevent leakage and contamination of the fuel system.*

9   Support the fuel tank with a floor jack. Place a sturdy plank between the jack head and the fuel tank to protect the tank. Remove the bolts from the fuel tank retaining straps **(see illustration)**.

10   Lower the tank enough to disconnect the electrical connector and ground strap from the fuel pump/fuel gauge sending unit, if you have not already done so.

11   Remove the tank from the vehicle.

12   Installation is the reverse of removal.

9 Fuel tank cleaning and repair - general information

1   Any repairs to the fuel tank or filler neck should be carried out by a professional who

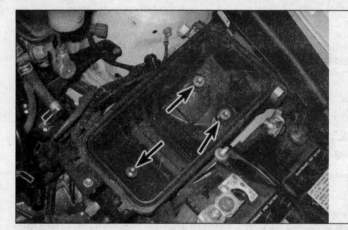

has experience in this critical and potentially dangerous work. Even after cleaning and flushing of the fuel system, explosive fumes can remain and ignite during repair of the tank.

2   If the fuel tank is removed from the vehicle, it should not be placed in an area where sparks or open flames could ignite the fumes coming out of the tank. Be especially careful inside garages where a gas-type appliance is located, because it could cause an explosion.

10 Air filter housing - removal and installation

Refer to illustration 10.3

1   Disconnect the air intake hose and breather hose from the housing cover. Disconnect the electrical connector from the intake air temperature sensor.

2   Detach the clips and remove the air filter housing cover and the air filter element (see Chapter 1).

3 .   Remove the three bolts and remove the air filter housing from the engine compartment **(see illustration)**.

4   Installation is the reverse of removal.

10.3 Remove the bolts that retain the air filter housing to the engine compartment

11 Accelerator cable - removal, installation and adjustment

Refer to illustrations 11.2, 11.3a, 11.3b and 11.4

Note 1: *2005 and later models do not have an accelerator cable. Instead, the throttle body has an electric motor that operates the throttle and is controlled by the PCM.*

Note 2: *2004 and earlier models with cruise control have two accelerator cables - one from the accelerator pedal to the cruise control actuator and one from the cruise control actuator to the throttle body.*

Removal

1   Detach the cable from the negative terminal of the battery. On models with cruise control, remove the cover from the cruise control actuator.

2   Loosen the locknut on the threaded portion of the throttle cable at the throttle body or cruise control actuator **(see illustration)**.

3   Rotate the throttle lever or cruise control actuator and slip the throttle cable end out of the slot in the lever **(see illustration)**.

4   Detach the throttle cable from the accel-

11.2 Loosen the locknuts on the accelerator cable

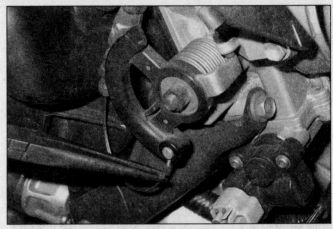

11.3a Rotate the throttle lever and remove the cable end from the slot in the throttle lever . . .

erator pedal **(see illustration)**. Remove the two bolts securing the cable retainer to the firewall.

5   From inside the vehicle, pull the cable through the firewall.

Installation and adjustment

6   Installation is the reverse of removal. Make sure the cable casing grommet seats properly in the firewall.

7   To adjust the cable, fully depress the accelerator pedal and check that the throttle is fully opened.

8   If not fully opened, loosen the locknuts, depress accelerator pedal and adjust the cable until the throttle is fully open.

9   Tighten the locknuts and recheck the adjustment. Make sure the throttle closes fully when the pedal is released.

---

12 Fuel injection system - general information

1   All models are equipped with a multi port fuel injection system. The fuel injection system is composed of three basic subsystems: fuel system, air induction system and electronic engine control system.

Fuel system

2   An electric fuel pump located inside the fuel tank supplies fuel under constant pressure to the fuel rail, which distributes fuel evenly to all injectors. From the fuel rail, fuel is injected into the intake ports, just above the intake valves, by electronic fuel injectors. The amount of fuel supplied by the injectors is precisely controlled by an electronic Powertrain Control Module (PCM). The fuel pressure regulator maintains a constant pressure to the fuel rail regardless of engine load. The fuel pressure regulator and fuel filter are located in the fuel tank along with the fuel pump.

Air induction system

3   The air induction system consists of an air filter housing, the throttle body and the

duct connecting the two. The throttle plate inside the throttle body is controlled by the driver. As the throttle plate opens, additional air is drawn into the cylinders. The information provided by the various sensors allows the PCM to determine the exact amount of fuel to be injected by the injectors during the various operating conditions.

Electronic engine control system

4   The electronic engine control system controls the fuel injection, ignition and emissions systems by means of a Powertrain Control Module (PCM), which employs a microprocessor. The PCM receives signals from a number of information sensors, which monitor such variables as intake air temperature, throttle angle, coolant temperature, engine rpm, engine load, vehicle speed and exhaust oxygen content. These signals help the PCM determine the injection duration necessary for the optimum air/fuel ratio. The sensors and their corresponding PCM-controlled relays, are located throughout the engine compartment. For further information regarding the PCM and its relationship to the fuel injection and ignition systems, see Chapter 6.

13 Fuel injection system - check

Refer to illustrations 13.7, 13.8 and 13.9
Note: *The following procedure is based on the assumption that the fuel pump is working and the fuel pressure is adequate (see Section 3).*

1   Check the ground wire connections for tightness. Check all wiring and electrical connectors that are related to the system. Loose electrical connectors and poor grounds can cause many problems that resemble more serious malfunctions.

2   Check to see that the battery is fully charged, as the control unit and sensors depend on an accurate supply voltage in order to properly meter the fuel.

3   Check the air filter element - a dirty or

partially blocked filter will severely impede performance and economy (see Chapter 1).

4   Check the fuses. If a blown fuse is found, replace it and see if it blows again. If it does, search for a grounded wire in the fuel injection system wiring harness.

5   Check the air intake duct from the air

11.3b . . . or the cruise control actuator

11.4 Separate the cable from the accelerator pedal arm and slide the cable end out of the slot in the arm

13.7 Use a stethoscope or a screwdriver to determine if the injectors are working properly - they should make a steady clicking sound that rises and falls with engine speed changes

13.8 Install the "noid" light into the fuel injector electrical connector and check to see that it flashes with the engine running

cleaner housing to the intake manifold for leaks, which will result in an excessively lean mixture. Also check the condition of the vacuum hoses connected to the intake manifold.

6   Remove the air intake duct from the throttle body and check for dirt, carbon, varnish, or other residue in the throttle body, particularly around the throttle plate. If it's dirty, refer to Chapter 6 and troubleshoot the PCV system for the cause of excessive varnish buildup.

7   With the engine running, place a stethoscope against each injector, one at a time, and listen for a clicking sound, indicating operation **(see illustration)**. If you don't have an automotive stethoscope you can use a long screwdriver; just place the tip of the screwdriver against the injector body and press your ear against the handle.

8   If there is a problem with an injector, purchase a special injector test light (noid light) and install it into the injector electrical connector **(see illustration)**. Start the engine and make sure that each injector connector flashes the noid light. This will test for the proper voltage signal to the injector.

9   With the engine OFF and the fuel injector electrical connectors disconnected, measure the resistance of each injector **(see illustration)**. Compare your measurement with the value listed in this Chapter's Specifications. If the injector resistance is excessive or an open or short circuit is indicated, replace the injector (see Section 15).

10   Additional fuel injection control system component checks can be found in Chapter 6.

---

14   Throttle body - removal and installation

Refer to illustration 14.7

Warning: *Wait until the engine is completely cool before beginning this procedure.*

1   Detach the cable from the negative terminal of the battery.

2   Loosen the hose clamps and remove the air intake duct.

3   On 2003 and 2004 models, detach the accelerator cable from the throttle lever

(see Section 11).

4   Detach the throttle cable bracket and set it aside (it's not necessary to detach the throttle cable from the bracket).

5   Clearly label, then detach, all vacuum and coolant hoses from the throttle body. Plug the coolant hoses to prevent coolant loss.

6   Disconnect the electrical connectors from the throttle position sensor, idle air control valve, manifold absolute pressure sensor and/or mass airflow sensor, as required. On 2005 and later models, disconnect the electrical connector at the throttle body motor.

7   Remove the throttle body mounting bolts/nuts **(see illustration)**.

8   Detach the throttle body and gasket from the intake manifold.

9   Using a soft brush and carburetor cleaner, thoroughly clean the throttle body casting, then blow out all passages with compressed air. **Caution:** *Do not clean the throttle position sensor with anything. Just wipe it off carefully with a clean, soft cloth.*

13.9 Using an ohmmeter, measure the resistance across the terminals of the injector

14.7 Throttle-body mounting details - disconnect the electrical connectors and hoses, then remove the two mounting nuts and two bolts

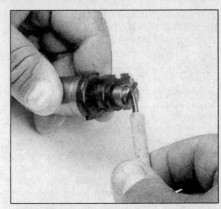

15.5 Remove the two mounting bolts and pull up the fuel rail from the cylinder head

15.6a Remove the O-ring from the injector

10   Installation of the throttle body is the reverse of removal.
11   Tighten the throttle body mounting bolts/nuts to the torque listed in this Chapter's Specifications.
12   Check the coolant level, adding as necessary (see Chapter 1).

15   Fuel rail and injectors - removal and installation

Refer to illustrations 15.5, 15.6a, 15.6b and 15.7

Warning: *Gasoline is extremely flammable, so take extra precautions when you work on any part of the fuel system. See the* **Warning** *in Section 2.*

1   Relieve the fuel pressure (see Section 2) and detach the cable from the negative terminal of the battery.
2   Detach the PCV hose from the valve cover and remove the engine cover (over the valve cover).
3   Disconnect the electrical connectors from the fuel injectors. Open the wiring harness clamps and position the wiring harness aside.

4   Disconnect the fuel line leading to the fuel rail (see Section 4 for fuel line disconnect procedures).
5   Remove the fuel rail mounting bolts and carefully withdraw the fuel rail and injectors from the cylinder head **(see illustration)**.
6   Replace the O-ring and grommet on each injector **(see illustrations)**.
7   Remove the insulators in the cylinder head and replace them with new ones **(see illustration)**.
8   Lubricate the O-rings with clean engine oil and install the fuel injectors onto the fuel rail. Make sure the spacers are in place and install the fuel rail/injector assembly onto the cylinder head. Install the fuel rail mounting bolts and tighten the bolts to the torque listed in this Chapter's Specifications.
9   The remainder of installation is the reverse of removal.

16   Exhaust system servicing - general information

Refer to illustration 16.1

Warning: *Inspection and repair of exhaust system components should be done only after*

15.6b Remove the grommet from the injector

the system components have cooled completely.

1   The exhaust system consists of the exhaust manifold, catalytic converter, the muffler, the tailpipe and all connecting pipes, brackets, hangers and clamps. The exhaust system is attached to the body with mounting brackets and rubber hangers **(see illustration)**. If any of these parts are damaged or deteriorated, excessive noise and vibration will be transmitted to the body.

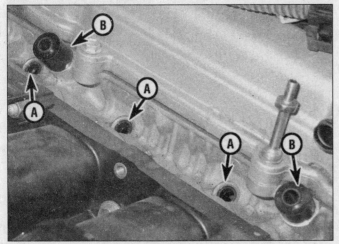

15.7 Install new insulators in the cylinder head holes (A), and position the two spacers (B) before installing the fuel rail

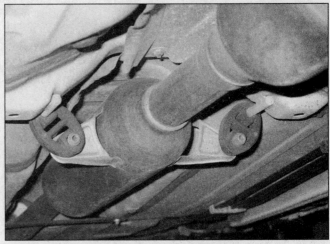

16.1 Check all of the exhaust system rubber hangers for cracking, replacing them as necessary

2   Conducting regular inspections of the exhaust system will keep it safe and quiet. Look for any damaged or bent parts, open seams, holes, loose connections, excessive corrosion or other defects which could allow exhaust fumes to enter the vehicle. Deteriorated exhaust system components should not be repaired - they should be replaced with new parts.

3   If the exhaust system components are extremely corroded or rusted together, they will probably have to be cut from the exhaust system. The convenient way to accomplish this is to have a muffler repair shop remove the corroded sections with a cutting torch. If, however, you want to save money by doing it yourself and you don't have an oxy/acetylene welding outfit with a cutting torch, simply cut off the old components with a hack-saw. If you have compressed air, special pneumatic cutting chisels can also be used. If you do decide to tackle the job at home, be sure to wear eye protection to protect your eyes from metal chips and work gloves to protect your hands.

4   Here are some simple guidelines to apply when repairing the exhaust system:

a) *Work from the back to the front when removing exhaust system components.*

b) *Apply penetrating oil to the exhaust system component fasteners to make them easier to remove.*

c) *Use new gaskets, hangers and clamps when installing exhaust system components.*

d) *Apply anti-seize compound to the threads of all exhaust system fasteners during reassembly.*

e) *Be sure to allow sufficient clearance between newly installed parts and all points on the underbody to avoid overheating the floor pan and possibly damaging the interior carpet and insulation. Pay particularly close attention to the catalytic converter and its heat shield.* **Warning:** *The catalytic converter operates at very high temperatures and takes a long time to cool. Wait until it's completely cool before attempting to remove the converter. Failure to do so could result in serious burns.*

Chapter 5
Engine electrical systems

Contents

Specifications

Charging system

Charging voltage	12.9 to 14.9 volts
Standard amperage	
All lights and accessories turned off	Less than 10 amps
Headlights (hi-beam) and heater blower motor turned on	30 amps or more

1 General information

The engine electrical systems include all ignition, charging and starting components. Because of their engine-related functions, these components are discussed separately from chassis electrical devices such as the lights, the instruments, etc. (which are included in Chapter 12).

Always observe the following precautions when working on the electrical systems:

a) *Be extremely careful when servicing engine electrical components. They are easily damaged if checked, connected or handled improperly.*

b) *Never leave the ignition switch on for long periods of time (10 minutes maximum) with the engine off.*

c) *Don't disconnect the battery cables while the engine is running.*

d) *Maintain correct polarity when connecting a battery cable from another vehicle during jump-starting.*

e) *Always disconnect the negative cable first and hook it up last or the battery may be shorted by the tool being used to loosen the cable clamps.*

It's also a good idea to review the safety-related information regarding the engine electrical systems located in the *Safety first* section near the front of this manual before beginning any operation included in this Chapter.

2 Battery - emergency jump starting

Refer to the *Booster battery (jump) starting* procedure at the front of this manual.

3 Battery - check and replacement

Warning: *Hydrogen gas is produced by the battery, so keep open flames and lighted cigarettes away from it at all times. Always wear eye protection when working around a battery. Rinse off spilled electrolyte immediately with large amounts of water.*

Check

Refer to illustrations 3.2 and 3.3

1   The battery's surface charge must be removed before accurate voltage measurements can be made. Turn On the high beams for ten seconds, then turn them Off, and let the vehicle stand for two minutes. Remove the battery from the vehicle (see Steps 4 through 10).

2   Check the battery state of charge. Visually inspect the indicator eye on the top of the

3.2 To test the open circuit voltage of the battery, connect a voltmeter to the battery - a fully charged battery should measure at least 12.4 volts (depending on outside air temperature)

3.3 Connect a battery load tester to the battery and check the battery condition under load, following the tool manufacturer's instructions

battery, if the indicator eye is clear, charge the battery as described in Chapter 1. Next perform an open voltage circuit test using a digital voltmeter **(see illustration)**. With the engine and all accessories Off, connect the negative probe of the voltmeter to the negative terminal of the battery and the positive probe to the positive terminal of the battery. The battery voltage should be 12.4 volts or more. If the battery is less than the specified voltage, charge the battery before proceeding to the next test. Do not proceed with the battery load test unless the battery charge is correct.

3   Perform a battery load test. An accurate check of the battery condition can only be performed with a load tester (available at most auto parts stores). This test evaluates the ability of the battery to operate the starter and other accessories during periods of heavy amperage draw (load). Install a special battery load-testing tool onto the terminals **(see illustration)**. Load test the battery according to the tool manufacturer's instructions. This tool utilizes a carbon pile to increase the load demand (amperage draw) on the battery. Maintain the load on the battery for 15 seconds or less and observe that the battery voltage does not drop below 9.6 volts. If the battery condition is weak or defective,

the tool will indicate this condition immediately. **Note:** *Cold temperatures will cause the minimum voltage requirements to drop slightly. Follow the chart given in the tool manufacturer's instructions to compensate for cold climates. Minimum load voltage for freezing temperatures (32-degrees F) should be approximately 9.1 volts.*

Replacement

Refer to illustration 3.6

4   Disconnect the cable from the negative battery terminal.

5   Disconnect the positive battery cable.

6   Remove the battery hold-down clamp **(see illustration)**.

7   Remove the battery and place it on a workbench. **Note:** *Battery handling tools are available at most auto parts stores for a reasonable price. They make it easier to remove and carry the battery.*

8   While the battery is removed, inspect the tray, retainer brackets and related fasteners for corrosion or damage.

9   If corrosion is evident, remove the battery tray and use a baking soda/water solution to clean the corroded area to prevent further oxidation. Repaint the area as necessary using rust resistant paint.

10   Clean and service the battery and cables (see Chapter 1).

11   If you are replacing the battery, make sure you purchase one that is identical to yours, with the same dimensions, amperage rating, cold cranking amps rating, etc. Make sure it is fully charged prior to installation in the vehicle.

12   Installation is the reverse of removal. Connect the positive cable first and the negative cable last.

13   After connecting the cables to the battery, apply a light coating of battery terminal corrosion inhibitor to the connections to help prevent corrosion.

4   Battery cables - replacement

1   Periodically inspect the entire length of each battery cable for damage, cracked or burned insulation and corrosion. Poor battery cable connections can cause starting problems and decreased engine performance.

2   Check the cable-to-terminal connections at the ends of the cables for cracks, loose wire strands and corrosion. The presence of white, fluffy deposits under the insulation at the cable terminal connection is a sign that the cable is corroded and should be replaced. Check the terminals for distortion, missing mounting bolts and corrosion.

3   When removing the cables, always disconnect the negative cable first and hook it up last or the battery may be shorted by the tool used to loosen the cable clamps. Even if only the positive cable is being replaced, be sure to disconnect the negative cable from the battery first (see Chapter 1 for further information regarding battery cable removal).

4   Disconnect the old cables from the battery, then trace each of them to their opposite ends and detach them from the starter solenoid and ground terminals. Note the routing of each cable to ensure correct installation.

5   If you are replacing either or both of the old cables, take them with you when buying

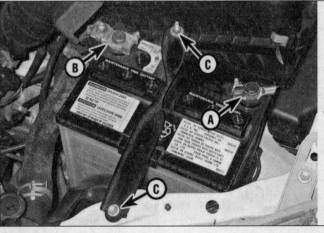

3.6 To remove the battery, detach the negative battery cable first (A), then the positive cable (B), then remove the hold-down clamp nut and bolt (C) and remove the hold-down clamp

new cables. It is vitally important that you replace the cables with identical parts. Cables have characteristics that make them easy to identify: positive cables are usually red, larger in cross-section and have a larger diameter battery post clamp; ground cables are usually black, smaller in cross-section and have a slightly smaller diameter clamp for the negative post.

6   Clean the threads of the solenoid or ground connection with a wire brush to remove rust and corrosion. Apply a light coat of battery terminal corrosion inhibitor, or petroleum jelly, to the threads to prevent future corrosion.

7   Attach the cable to the solenoid or ground connection and tighten the mounting nut/bolt securely.

8   Before connecting a new cable to the battery, make sure that it reaches the battery post without having to be stretched.

9   Connect the positive cable first, followed by the negative cable.

5   Ignition system - general information and precautions

1   All models are equipped with a distributorless ignition system. The ignition system consists of the battery, ignition coils, spark plugs, camshaft position sensor, crankshaft position sensor and the Powertrain Control Module (PCM). The PCM controls the ignition timing and spark advance characteristics for the engine. The ignition timing is not adjustable.

2   The crankshaft position sensor and camshaft position sensor generate pulses that are input to the Powertrain Control Module. The PCM determines piston position and engine speed from these two sensors. The PCM calculates injector sequence and ignition timing from the piston position. Refer to Chapter 6 for testing and replacement procedures for the crankshaft position sensor and camshaft position sensor.

3   These models utilize an individual ignition coil for each cylinder. The unit is positioned directly over each spark plug. The PCM fires each coil sequentially in the firing order sequence.

4   The PCM controls the ignition system by opening and closing the primary ignition coil control circuit. The computerized ignition system provides complete control of the ignition timing by determining the optimum timing in response to engine speed, coolant temperature, throttle position and engine load. These parameters are relayed to the PCM by the camshaft position sensor, crankshaft position sensor, throttle position sensor, coolant temperature sensor or manifold absolute pressure sensor or mass airflow sensor. Refer to Chapter 6 for additional information on the various sensors.

5   The ignition system is also integrated with a knock sensor. The system uses a knock sensor in conjunction with the PCM to

6.2 To use a calibrated ignition tester (available at most auto parts stores), remove one coil and plug the tester into the boot, clip the tester to a good ground, then crank the engine over - if there is enough voltage to fire the test plug, bright blue spark will be clearly visible between the electrode tip and the tester body

control spark timing. The knock sensor system allows the engine to use maximum spark advance without spark knock, which improves driveability and fuel economy.

6   When working on the ignition system, take the following precautions:

a) *Do not keep the ignition switch on for more than 10 seconds if the engine will not start.*

b) *Always connect a tachometer in accordance with the manufacturer's instructions. Some tachometers may be incompatible with this ignition system. Consult the tachometer manufacturer's consultant before buying a tachometer for use with this vehicle.*

c) *Never allow the ignition coil terminals to touch ground. Grounding the coil could result in damage to the igniter and/or the ignition coil.*

d) *Do not disconnect the battery when the engine is running.*

e) *Make sure the igniter is properly grounded.*

6   Ignition system - check

Refer to illustrations 6.2 and 6.5

Warning: *Because of the high voltage generated by the ignition system, extreme care should be taken whenever an operation is performed involving ignition components.*

1   If a malfunction occurs and the vehicle won't start, do not immediately assume that the ignition system is causing the problem. First, check the following items:

a) *Make sure the battery cable clamps, where they connect to the battery, are clean and tight.*

b) *Test the condition of the battery (see Section 3). If it does not pass all the tests, replace it with a new battery.*

c) *Check the ignition system wiring and connections.*

d) *Check the related fuses inside the fuse box (see Chapter 12). If they're burned, determine the cause and repair the circuit.*

2   If the engine turns over but won't start,

make sure there is sufficient secondary ignition voltage to fire the spark plug. Obtain a calibrated ignition system tester (available at most auto parts stores). Connect the clip on the tester to a bolt or metal bracket on the engine **(see illustration)**. Remove an ignition coil (see Section 7) and attach the calibrated ignition system tester to the spark plug boot. Reconnect the electrical connector to the coil and clip the tester to a good ground. Crank the engine and watch the end of the tester to see if a bright blue, well-defined spark occurs (weak spark or intermittent spark is the same as no spark).

3   If spark occurs, sufficient voltage is reaching the plug to fire it (repeat the check at the remaining ignition coils to verify that the coils are good). If the ignition system is operating properly the problem lies elsewhere; i.e. a mechanical or fuel system problem. However, the plugs themselves may be fouled, so remove and check them as described in Chapter 1.

4   If no spark occurs, remove the electrical connector from the suspected ignition coil and check the terminals for damage.

5   If no sparks or intermittent sparks occur, check for battery voltage to the ignition coils **(see illustration)**.

6.5 Disconnect the electrical connector from the ignition coil and check for battery voltage at terminal no. 1 with the ignition key On - also check for continuity to a good engine ground point at terminal no. 4

6   Refer to Chapter 6 and use a code-reading tool to check for Diagnostic Trouble Codes relating to the ignition system, the PCM, or the camshaft and crankshaft position sensors

7   Ignition coils - replacement

Refer to illustration 7.2

Note: *Toyota does not publish primary or secondary resistance specifications for the ignition coils units used on these models. The only way to check them is to substitute a known good unit. But this option isn't feasible for a home mechanic because you can't return electrical components to a parts department once you have purchased them. If you have already eliminated all other possible causes of an ignition malfunction, a defective ignition coil/igniter unit is the likely cause of the problem, but the only way to verify this is to substitute a known good unit.*

1   Remove the engine cover. Disconnect the negative cable from the battery (see Chapter 1).

2   Disconnect the electrical connector(s) from the coil(s), then remove the mounting bolt(s) **(see illustration)**.

3   Carefully withdraw each coil from the cylinder head.

4   Installation is the reverse of removal.

8   Charging system - general information and precautions

The charging system includes the alternator, an internal voltage regulator, a charge indicator, the battery, a fusible link and the wiring between all the components. The charging system supplies electrical power for the ignition system, the lights, the radio, etc. The alternator is driven by a drivebelt at the front of the engine.

The purpose of the voltage regulator is to limit the alternator's voltage to a preset value. This prevents power surges, circuit overloads, etc., during peak voltage output.

The fusible link is a short length of insulated wire integral with the engine compartment wiring harness. The link is several wire gauges smaller in diameter than the circuit it protects. See Chapter 12 for additional information regarding fusible links.

The charging system doesn't ordinarily require periodic maintenance. However, the drivebelt, battery and wires and connections should be inspected at the intervals outlined in Chapter 1.

The dashboard warning light should come on when the ignition key is turned to Start, then should go off immediately. If it remains on, there is a malfunction in the charging system. Some vehicles are also equipped with a voltage gauge. If the voltage gauge indicates abnormally high or low voltage, check the charging system (see Section 9).

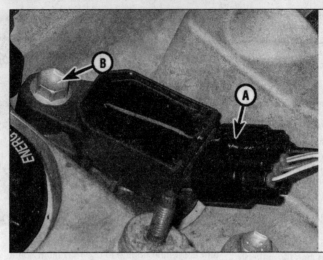

7.2 Disconnect the electrical connectors (A) at each coil, then remove the mounting bolt (B)

Be very careful when making electrical circuit connections to a vehicle equipped with an alternator and note the following:

a) *When reconnecting wires to the alternator from the battery, be sure to note the polarity.*

b) *Before using welding equipment to repair any part of the vehicle, disconnect the wires from the alternator and the battery terminals.*

c) *Never start the engine with a battery charger connected.*

d) *Always disconnect both battery leads before using a battery charger.*

e) *The alternator is driven by an engine drivebelt that could cause serious injury if your hand, hair or clothes become entangled in it with the engine running.*

f) *Because the alternator is connected directly to the battery, it could arc or cause a fire if overloaded or shorted out.*

g) *Wrap a plastic bag over the alternator and secure it with rubber bands before steam cleaning the engine.*

9   Charging system - check

Refer to illustration 9.3

1   If a malfunction occurs in the charging circuit, don't automatically assume that the alternator is causing the problem. First check the following items:

a) *Check the drivebelt tension and its condition. Replace it if worn or deteriorated.*

b) *Make sure the alternator mounting bolts are tight.*

c) *Inspect the alternator wiring harness and the electrical connectors at the alternator and voltage regulator. They must be in good condition and tight.*

d) *Check the fusible link located at the positive battery cable or the large main fuses in the engine compartment. If it's burned, determine the cause, repair the circuit and replace the link or fuse (the vehicle won't start and/or the accessories won't work if the fusible link or fuse blows).*

e) *Check all the fuses that are in series with the charging system circuit. The location of these fuses and fusible links may vary from year and model but the designations are the same; main fusible link 2.0L, Alt fuse (100 amp), AM1 (25 amp), AM2 (15 amp), Main fuse (30A), Gauge (10A), and ALT-S (5 amp).*

f) *Start the engine and check the alternator for abnormal noises (a shrieking or squealing sound indicates a bad bushing).*

g) *Check the specific gravity of the battery electrolyte. If it's low, charge the battery (doesn't apply to maintenance free batteries).*

h) *Make sure that the battery is fully charged (one bad cell in a battery can cause overcharging by the alternator).*

i) *Disconnect the battery cables (negative first, then positive). Inspect the battery posts and the cable clamps for corrosion. Clean them thoroughly if necessary (see Section 4 and Chapter 1). Reconnect the positive cable, then the negative cable.*

2   With the ignition key off, check the battery voltage with no accessories operating. It should be approximately 12.5 volts. It may be slightly higher if the engine had been operating within the last hour.

3   Connect a multimeter to the charging system following the tool manufacturer's instructions. Start the engine, and check the battery voltage and amperage. It should now be approximately 13.2 to 15.0 volts at 10 amps or less **(see illustration)**.

4   Load the battery by turning on the high beam headlights and the air conditioning (if equipped and place the blower fan on HIGH. Raise the engine speed to 2,000 rpm and check the voltage and amperage. If the charging system is working properly the voltage should stay above 13.5 volts and the amperage should be 30 amps or more (depending on the condition of the battery - it could be less than 30 amps).

5   If the voltage rises above 15.0 volts in either test, the regulator is defective.

6   If the indicated voltage reading is less

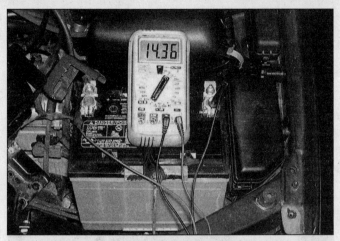

9.3 Connect a voltmeter to the battery terminals and check the battery voltage with the engine Off, and then again with the engine running

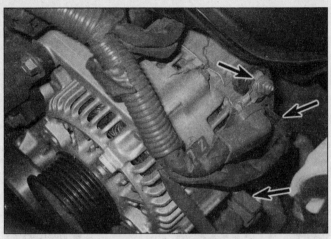

10.2 Disconnect the electrical connections from the alternator

than the specified charge voltage, the alternator is probably defective. Have the charging system checked at a dealer service department or other properly equipped repair facility. **Note:** *Many auto parts stores will bench test an alternator off the vehicle. Refer to your local auto parts store regarding their policy (many stores will perform this service free of charge).*

10 Alternator - removal and installation

Refer to illustrations 10.2 and 10.3

1   Detach the cable from the negative terminal of the battery. Remove the drivebelt (see Chapter 1).

2   Disconnect the electrical connectors from the alternator **(see illustration).**

3   Remove the alternator mounting bolts **(see illustration).**

4   Remove the alternator from the engine.

5   If you are replacing the alternator, take the old alternator with you when purchasing a replacement unit. Make sure that the new/rebuilt unit is identical to the old alternator.

10.3 Alternator mounting bolts

Look at the terminals - they should be the same in number, size and locations as the terminals on the old alternator. Finally, look at the identification markings - they will be stamped in the housing or printed on a tag or plaque affixed to the housing. Make sure that these numbers are the same on both alternators.

6   Many new/rebuilt alternators do not have a pulley installed, so you may have to switch the pulley from the old unit to the new/rebuilt one. When buying an alternator, find out the shop's policy regarding installation of pulleys - some shops will perform this service free of charge.

7   Installation is the reverse of removal.

8   After the alternator is installed, install the drivebelt.

9   Check the charging voltage to verify proper operation of the alternator (see Section 9).

11 Starting system - general information and precautions

The starting system consists of the battery, the starter motor, the starter solenoid and the electrical circuit connecting the components. The solenoid is mounted directly on the starter motor.

The starter motor assembly is installed on the front (radiator) side of the engine on the lower section of transaxle bellhousing.

When the ignition key is turned to the START position, the starter solenoid is actuated through the starter control circuit. The starter solenoid then connects the battery to the starter. The battery supplies the electrical energy to the starter motor, which does the actual work of cranking the engine.

The starter motor on a vehicle equipped with a manual transaxle can be operated only when the clutch pedal is depressed; the starter on a vehicle equipped with an automatic transaxle can be operated only when the transaxle selector lever is in Park or Neutral.

Always observe the following precautions when working on the starting system:

a) *Excessive cranking of the starter motor can overheat it and cause serious damage. Never operate the starter motor for more than 15 seconds at a time without pausing to allow it to cool for at least two minutes.*

b) *The starter is connected directly to the battery and could arc or cause a fire if mishandled, overloaded or short-circuited.*

c) *Always detach the cable from the negative terminal of the battery before working on the starting system.*

12 Starter motor and circuit - check

Refer to illustration 12.3

Note: *Before diagnosing starter problems, make sure the battery is fully charged.*

1   If a malfunction occurs in the starting circuit, do not immediately assume that the starter is causing the problem. First, check the following items:

a) *Make sure the battery cable clamps, where they connect to the battery, are clean and tight.*

b) *Check the condition of the battery cables (see Section 4). Replace any defective battery cables with new parts.*

c) *Test the condition of the battery (see Section 3). If it does not pass all the tests, replace it with a new battery.*

d) *Check the starter solenoid wiring and connections. Refer to the wiring diagrams at the end of Chapter 12.*

e) *Check the starter mounting bolts for tightness.*

f) *Check the fusible links near the positive battery terminal. If they're burned, determine the cause and repair the circuit. Also, check the ignition switch circuit for correct operation (see Chapter 12).*

12.3 To use an inductive ammeter, simply hold the ammeter over the positive or negative cable (whichever is more accessible)

13.4 Disconnect the electrical connector (A), then remove the nut securing the starter cable (B)

g) *Check the operation of the transmission range sensor (automatic transaxle) or clutch start switch (manual transaxle). Make sure the shift lever is in PARK or NEUTRAL (automatic transaxle) or the clutch pedal is pressed (manual transaxle). Refer to Chapter 7 for the transmission range sensor check and adjustment procedure. Refer to Chapter 12 wiring diagrams, if necessary, when performing circuit checks. These systems must operate correctly to provide battery voltage to the ignition solenoid.*

2   If the starter does not actuate when the ignition switch is turned to the start position, check for battery voltage to the solenoid. This will determine if the solenoid is receiving the correct voltage signal from the ignition switch. Connect a test light or voltmeter to the starter solenoid positive terminal and while an assistant turns the ignition switch to the start position. If voltage is not available, refer to the wiring diagrams in Chapter 12 and check all the fuses and relays in series with the starting system. If voltage is available but the starter motor does not operate, remove the starter from the engine compartment (see Section 13) and bench test the starter (see Step 4).

3   If the starter turns over slowly, check the starter cranking voltage and the current draw from the battery. This test must be performed with the starter assembly on the engine. Crank the engine over (for 10 seconds or less) and observe the battery voltage. It should not drop below 8.0 volts on manual transaxle models or 8.5 volts on automatic transaxle models. Also, observe the current draw using an ammeter **(see illustration)**. It should not exceed 400 amps or drop below 250 amps. If the starter motor cranking amp values are not within the correct range, replace it with a new unit. There are several conditions that may affect the starter cranking potential. The battery must be in good condition and the battery cold-cranking

rating must not be under-rated for the particular application. Be sure to check the battery specifications carefully. The battery terminals and cables must be clean and not corroded. Also, in cases of extreme cold temperatures, make sure the battery and/or engine block is warmed before performing the tests.

4   If the starter is receiving voltage but does not activate, remove and check the starter/solenoid assembly on the bench. Most likely the solenoid is defective. In some rare cases, the engine may be seized so be sure to try and rotate the crankshaft pulley (see Chapter 2A) before proceeding. With the starter/solenoid assembly mounted in a vise on the bench, install one jumper cable from the negative battery terminal to the body of the solenoid. Install the other jumper cable from the positive battery terminal to the B+ terminal on the solenoid. Install a starter switch and apply battery voltage to the solenoid S terminal (for 10 seconds or less) and see if the solenoid plunger, shift lever and overrunning clutch extends and rotates the pinion drive. If the pinion drive extends but does not rotate, the solenoid is operating but the starter motor

13.5 Remove the starter mounting bolts (lower bolt shown)

is defective. If there is no movement but the solenoid clicks, the solenoid and/or the starter motor is defective. If the solenoid plunger extends and rotates the pinion drive, the starter/solenoid assembly is working properly.

13   Starter motor - removal and installation

2008 and earlier models

Refer to illustrations 13.4 and 13.5

Note: *The starter motor and solenoid assembly cannot be repaired using separate components. In the event of failure, exchange the starter/solenoid assembly for a new or rebuilt complete unit.*

1   Detach the cable from the negative terminal of the battery (see Chapter 1).
2   Raise the vehicle and support it securely on jackstands.
3   Remove the splash shield from under the engine.
4   Disconnect the electrical connector from the starter solenoid, then remove the nut and disconnect the battery cable from the solenoid, too **(see illustration)**.
5   Remove the starter motor mounting bolts and remove the starter from the vehicle **(see illustration)**.
6   Installation is the reverse of removal.

2009 and later models

7   Remove the transaxle fluid dipstick tube bracket mounting bolt and carefully pull the dipstick tube from the transaxle. **Note:** *The O-ring should be replaced on the bottom of the dipstick tube.*
8   Disconnect the electrical connectors from the starter solenoid.
9   Remove the starter mounting bolts and starter.
10   Installation is the reverse of removal

Chapter 6
Emissions and engine control systems

Contents

1 General information

Refer to illustrations 1.6a and 1.6b

To prevent pollution of the atmosphere from incompletely burned and evaporating gases, and to maintain good driveability and fuel economy, a number of emission control systems are incorporated. They include the:

On-Board Diagnostic (OBD) II system
Electronic Fuel Injection (EFI) system
Evaporative Emissions Control (EVAP)
  system
Positive Crankcase Ventilation (PCV)
  system
Catalytic converter

The Sections in this Chapter include general descriptions, checking procedures within the scope of the home mechanic and component replacement procedures (when possible) for each of the systems listed above.

Before assuming that an emissions control system is malfunctioning, check the fuel and ignition systems carefully. The diagnosis of some emission control devices requires specialized tools, equipment and training. If checking and servicing become too difficult or if a procedure is beyond your ability, consult a dealer service department or other repair shop. Remember, the most frequent cause of emissions problems is simply a loose or bro-ken wire or vacuum hose, so always check the hose and wiring connections first.

This doesn't mean, however, that emissions control systems are particularly difficult to maintain and repair. You can quickly and easily perform many checks and do most of the regular maintenance at home with common tune-up and hand tools. **Note:** *Because of a Federally mandated warranty which covers the emissions control system components, check with your dealer about warranty coverage before working on any emissions-related systems. Once the warranty has expired, you may wish to perform some of the component checks and/or replacement procedures in this Chapter to save money.*

Pay close attention to any special precautions outlined in this Chapter. It should be noted that the illustrations of the various systems may not exactly match the system installed on your vehicle because of changes made by the manufacturer during production or from year-to-year.

A Vehicle Emissions Control Information (VECI) label is attached to the underside of the hood (see illustration). This label con-

1.6a The Vehicle Emission Control Information (VECI) label contains such essential information as the types of emission control systems installed on the engine, and the valve clearance specifications

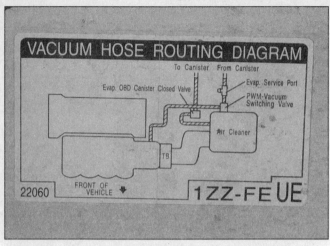

1.6b Vacuum hose routing diagram for a 2003 model

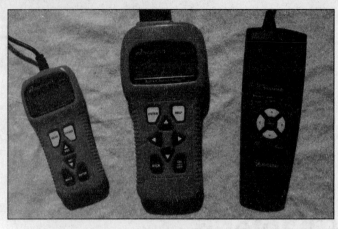

2.2 Scanners like these from Actron Scantool and AutoXray are powerful diagnostic aids - they can tell you just about anything you want to know about your engine management system

tains important emissions specifications and adjustment information. Also under the hood, the Vacuum Hose Routing Diagram **(see illustration)**, provides a vacuum hose schematic with emissions components identified. When servicing the engine or emissions systems, the VECI label and the vacuum hose routing diagram in your particular vehicle should always be checked for up-to-date information.

2 On-Board Diagnostic (OBD) system and trouble codes

Scan tool information

Refer to illustration 2.2

1   Hand-held scanners are the most powerful and versatile tools for analyzing engine management systems used on later model vehicles. Early model scanners handle codes and some diagnostics for many systems. Each brand scan tool must be examined carefully to match the year, make and model of the vehicle you are working on. Often, interchangeable cartridges are available to access the particular manufacturer (Ford, GM, Chrysler, Toyota etc.). Some manufacturers will specify by continent (Asia, Europe, USA, etc.).

2   With the arrival of the Federally mandated emission control system (OBD-II), a specially designed scanner has been developed. Several tool manufacturers have released OBD-II scan tools for the home mechanic **(see illustration)**.

OBD system general description

3   All models are equipped with the second generation OBD-II system. This system consists of an on-board computer known as the Powertrain Control Module (PCM), and information sensors, which monitor various functions of the engine and send data to the PCM. This system incorporates a series of diagnostic monitors that detect and identify fuel injection and emissions control systems

faults and store the information in the computer memory. This updated system also tests sensors and output actuators, diagnoses drive cycles, freezes data and clears codes. This powerful diagnostic computer must be accessed using the new OBD-II scan tool and 16 pin Data Link Connector (DLC) located under the driver's dash area. The PCM is the "brain" of the electronically controlled fuel and emissions system. It receives data from a number of sensors and other electronic components (switches, relays, etc.). Based on the information it receives, the PCM generates output signals to control various relays, solenoids (i.e. fuel injectors) and other actuators. The PCM is specifically calibrated to optimize the emissions, fuel economy and driveability of the vehicle.

4   It isn't a good idea to attempt diagnosis or replacement of the PCM or emission control components at home while the vehicle is under warranty. Because of a Federally mandated warranty which covers the emissions system components and because any owner-induced damage to the PCM, the sensors and/or the control devices may void this warranty, take the vehicle to a dealer service department if the PCM or a system component malfunctions.

Information sensors

5   **Oxygen sensors (O2S)** - The O2S generates a voltage signal that varies with the difference between the oxygen content of the exhaust and the oxygen in the surrounding air.

6   **Crankshaft Position (CKP) sensor** - The crankshaft sensor provides information on crankshaft position and the engine speed signal to the PCM.

7   **Camshaft Position (CMP) sensor** - The camshaft sensor produces a signal in which the PCM uses to identify number 1 cylinder and to time the sequential fuel injection.

8   **Air/Fuel Sensor** - Some vehicles are equipped with an air/fuel ratio sensor mounted upstream of the catalytic converter. These

sensors work similar to the O2 sensors.

9   **Engine Coolant Temperature (ECT) sensor** - The coolant temperature (ECT) sensor monitors engine coolant temperature and sends the PCM a voltage signal that affects PCM control of the fuel mixture, ignition timing, and EGR operation (if equipped).

10   **Throttle Position Sensor (TPS)** - The TPS senses throttle movement and position, then transmits a voltage signal to the PCM. This signal enables the PCM to determine when the throttle is closed, in a cruise position, or wide open. On the 2005 and later models, the TPS is part of the electronic throttle control on the throttle body.

11   **Mass Airflow sensor (MAF)** - The MAF sensor measures the mass of the intake air by detecting volume and weight of the air from samples passing over the hot wire element.

12   **Knock sensor** - The knock sensor is a "piezoelectric" crystal that oscillates in proportion to engine vibration. (The term *piezoelectric* refers to the property of certain crystals that produce a voltage when subjected to a mechanical stress.) The oscillation of the piezoelectric crystal produces a voltage output that is monitored by the PCM, which retards the ignition timing when the oscillation exceeds a certain threshold. When the engine is operating normally, the knock sensor oscillates consistently and its voltage signal is steady. When detonation occurs, engine vibration increases, and the oscillation of the knock sensor exceeds a design threshold. (Detonation is an uncontrolled explosion, after the spark occurs at the spark plug, which spontaneously combusts the remaining air/fuel mixture, resulting in a "pinging" or "knocking" sound.) If allowed to continue, the engine can be damaged. The knock sensor is located on the engine block.

13   **Vehicle Speed Sensor (VSS)** - The vehicle speed sensor provides information to the PCM to indicate vehicle speed.

14   **Vapor pressure sensor** - The vapor pressure sensor is part of the evaporative emission control system and is used to moni-

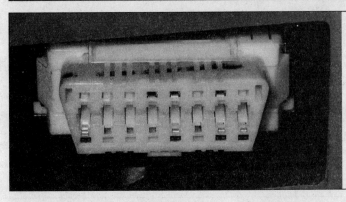

2.23 16-pin Data Link Connector (DLC)

tor vapor pressure in the EVAP system. The PCM uses this information to turn on and off the vacuum switching valves (VSV) of the evaporative emission system.

15   **Power Steering Pressure (PSP) switch** - The PSP switch is used to increase engine idle speed during low-speed vehicle maneuvers.

16   **Transaxle sensors** - In addition to the vehicle speed sensor, the PCM receives input signals from the following sensors inside the transaxle or connected to it: (a) the direct clutch speed sensor (b) the vehicle speed sensor.

17   **Accelerator pedal position sensor** - 2005 and later models do not have a throttle cable, but rather "drive-by-wire" system with an electronically- controlled throttle body. This sensor informs the PCM of the driver's pedal input, which is compared to the operation of the throttle body to check for malfunctions.

18   **Intake air temperature sensor** - The PCM uses information from this sensor to control fuel flow and timing functions. The IAT sensor is part of the MAF sensor module.

Output actuators

19   **EFI main relay** - The EFI main relay activates power to the fuel pump relay (circuit opening relay). It is activated by the ignition switch and supplies battery power to the PCM and the EFI system when the switch is in the Start or Run position. It's located in the underhood fuse/relay box.

20   **Fuel injectors** - The PCM opens the fuel injectors individually in firing order sequence. The PCM also controls the time the injector is open, called the "pulse width." The pulse width of the injector (measured in milliseconds) determines the amount of fuel delivered. For more information on the fuel delivery system and the fuel injectors, including injector replacement, refer to Chapter 4.

21   **EVAP vacuum switching valve (VSV)** - The EVAP vacuum switching valve is a solenoid valve, operated by the PCM to purge the fuel vapor canister and route fuel vapor to the intake manifold for combustion. This valve is also called the purge control valve.

Obtaining trouble codes

Refer to illustration 2.23

22   The PCM will illuminate the CHECK ENGINE light (also called the Malfunction Indicator Light) on the dash if it recognizes a component fault for two consecutive drive cycles. It will continue to set the light until the PCM does not detect any malfunction for three or more consecutive drive cycles.

23   The diagnostic codes for the OBD-II system can be extracted from the PCM by plugging a generic OBD-II scan tool **(see illustration 2.2)** into the PCM's data link connector **(see illustration)**, which is located under the left end of the dash.

24   Plug the scan tool into the 16-pin data link connector (DLC), and then follow the instructions included with the scan tool to extract all the diagnostic codes.

25   After repairs have been made, use your code reader or scan tool to erase the trouble code(s).

Diagnostic Trouble Codes

Trouble code	Code identification
P0010	Camshaft position "A" actuator circuit (bank 1)
P0011	Camshaft position "A" - timing over-advanced or system performance (bank 1)
P0012	Camshaft position "A" - timing over-retarded (bank 1)
P0013	Camshaft position "B" actuator circuit open (bank 1)
P0014	Camshaft position "B" - timing over-advanced or system performance (bank 1)
P0015	Camshaft position "B" - timing over-retarded (bank 1)
P0016	Crankshaft position - camshaft position correlation (bank 1 sensor B)
P0017	Crankshaft position - camshaft position correlation (bank 1 sensor B)
P0031	Oxygen (A/F) sensor heater control circuit low (bank 1 sensor 1)
P0032	Oxygen (A/F) sensor heater control circuit high (bank 1 sensor 1)
P0037	Oxygen sensor heater control circuit low (bank 1 sensor 2)
P0038	Oxygen sensor heater control circuit high (bank 1 sensor 2)
P0100	Mass airflow sensor or circuit fault
P0101	Mass airflow sensor range or performance problem

Diagnostic Trouble Codes (continued)

Trouble code	Code identification
P0102	Mass or volume air flow circuit low input
P0103	Mass or volume air flow circuit high input
P0110 - P0113	Intake air temperature sensor or circuit fault
P0115 - P0118	Engine coolant temperature sensor or circuit fault
P011B	Engine coolant temperature (ECT), intake air temperature (IAT) correlation
P0120 - P0123	Throttle position sensor or circuit fault
P0125	Insufficient coolant temperature for closed loop; O2 sensor heater malfunction
P0128	Thermostat malfunction
P0130	Pre-converter O2 sensor or circuit fault
P0133	Pre-converter O2 sensor circuit slow response fault
P0135	Pre-converter O2 sensor heater fault
P0136 - P0139	Post-converter O2 sensor or circuit fault
P0141	Post-converter Oxygen sensor heater or circuit fault
P0171	Fuel injection system lean
P0172	Fuel injection system rich
P0220 - P0223	Throttle pedal position sensor or switch "B" circuit fault
P0300	Multiple cylinder misfire detected
P0301	Cylinder no. 1 misfire detected
P0302	Cylinder no. 2 misfire detected
P0303	Cylinder no. 3 misfire detected
P0304	Cylinder no. 4 misfire detected
P0325 - P0328	Knock sensor or circuit fault
P0335 - P0339	Crankshaft position sensor or circuit fault
P0340 - P0341	Camshaft position sensor or circuit fault
P0342	Camshaft position sensor "A" circuit low input (bank 1 or single sensor)
P0343	Camshaft position sensor "A" circuit high input (bank 1 or single sensor)
P0351	Ignition coil "A" primary or secondary circuit fault
P0352	Ignition coil "B" primary or secondary circuit fault
P0353	Ignition coil "C" primary or secondary circuit fault
P0354	Ignition coil "D" primary or secondary circuit fault

Trouble code	Code identification
P0365	Camshaft position sensor "B" circuit (bank 1)
P0367	Camshaft position sensor "B" circuit low input (bank 1)
P0368	Camshaft position sensor "B" circuit high input (bank 1)
P0420	Catalytic converter system fault
P043E	EVAP system reference orifice clog up
P043F	EVAP system reference orifice high flow
P0440	EVAP system malfunction
P0441	EVAP system incorrect purge flow detected
P0443	EVAP system purge control valve circuit fault
P0450	EVAP system pressure sensor or circuit fault
P0451	EVAP system pressure sensor range or performance problem
P0452	EVAP pressure sensor or switch low input
P0453	EVAP system pressure sensor or switch high input
P0455	EVAP system leak detected (gross leak)
P0456	EVAP system leak detected (very small leak)
P0500	Vehicle speed sensor or circuit fault
P0504	Brake switch "A" or "B" correlation
P0505	Idle air control valve or circuit fault
P050A	Cold start idle air control system performance
P0560	System voltage
P0601	Internal control memory check sum error
P0604	Random access memory (ram)
P0606	ECM/PCM processor fault
P0607	Control module performance
P060A	ICM monitoring processor performance
P060D	ICM accelerator pedal position performance
P060E	ICM throttle position performance
P0617	Starter relay circuit high
P0630	VIN not programmed or mismatch - ECM/PCM
P0657	Actuator supply voltage circuit fault or open
P0705	Automatic transmission range sensor circuit failure

Diagnostic Trouble Codes (continued)

Trouble code	Code identification
P0710	Automatic transaxle fluid temperature sensor or circuit fault
P0711	Automatic transaxle fluid temperature sensor range performance or circuit fault
P0724	Brake switch "B" circuit high
P0741	Automatic transmission, torque converter clutch solenoid problem
P0750 - P0751	Automatic transaxle shift solenoid A stuck open or closed
P0753	Automatic transaxle shift solenoid A circuit fault
P0755 - P0756	Automatic transaxle shift solenoid B stuck open or closed
P0765	Automatic transaxle shift solenoid D stuck open or closed
P0850	Park/Neutral switch input circuit fault
P0973 - P0974	Automatic transaxle shift solenoid A control circuit
P0976 - P0977	Automatic transaxle shift solenoid B control circuit
P1300	Ignition system malfunction (#1 coil/igniter circuit fault)
P1305	Ignition system malfunction (#2 coil/igniter circuit fault)
P1310	Ignition system malfunction (#3 coil/igniter circuit fault)
P1315	Ignition system malfunction (#4 coil/igniter circuit fault)
P1335	Crankshaft position sensor or circuit fault
P1346	VVT (variable valve timing) sensor circuit fault
P1349	VVT (variable valve timing) system malfunction
P1520	Brake light signal malfunction
P1600	ECM battery supply malfunction
P1607	Cruise control input processor
P1656	OCV (oil control valve) circuit malfunction
P1780	Park/Neutral position switch or circuit fault
P2102	Throttle actuator control motor circuit low
P2103	Throttle actuator control motor circuit high
P2111	Throttle actuator control system - stuck open
P2112	Throttle actuator control system - stuck closed
P2118	Throttle actuator control motor current range or performance
P2119	Throttle actuator control throttle body range or performance
P2120 - P2123	Throttle or pedal position sensor or switch "D" circuit fault

Trouble code	Code identification
P2125 - P2128	Throttle or pedal position sensor or switch "E" circuit fault
P2135	Throttle or pedal position sensor or switch "A" or "B" voltage correlation
P2138	Throttle or pedal position sensor or switch "D" or "E" voltage correlation
P2195	Oxygen (A/F) sensor signal stuck lean (bank 1 sensor 1)
P2196	Oxygen (A/F) sensor signal stuck rich (bank 1 sensor 1)
P2237	Oxygen (A/F) sensor pumping current circuit or open (bank 1 sensor 1)
P2238	Oxygen (A/F) sensor pumping current circuit low (bank 1 sensor 1)
P2239	Oxygen (A/F) sensor pumping current circuit high (bank 1 sensor 1)
P2252	Oxygen (A/F) sensor reference ground circuit low (bank 1 sensor 1)
P2253	Oxygen (A/F) sensor reference ground circuit high (bank 1 sensor 1)
P2401	EVAP leak detection pump stuck off
P2402	EVAP leak detection pump stuck on
P2419	EVAP switching valve control circuit low
P2420	EVAP switching valve control circuit high
P2610	ECM/PCM internal engine off timer performance
P2716	Automatic transaxle, pressure control solenoid D
P2769	Automatic transaxle, DSL solenoid circuit low
P2770	Automatic transaxle, DSL solenoid circuit high
P2A00	A/F sensor circuit slow response (bank 1 sensor 1)

3   Powertrain Control Module (PCM) - removal and installation

Warning: *The models covered by this manual are equipped with Supplemental Restraint systems (SRS), more commonly known as airbags. Always disable the airbag system before working in the vicinity of any airbag system components to avoid the possibility of accidental deployment of the airbag, which could cause personal injury (see Chapter 12).*
Caution: *To avoid electrostatic discharge damage to the PCM, handle the PCM only by its case. Do not touch the electrical terminals during removal and installation. If available, ground yourself to the vehicle with an anti-static ground strap, available at computer supply stores.*

2008 and earlier models

Refer to illustration 3.1

1   The PCM is located inside the passenger compartment under the glove box **(see illustration)**.
2   Disconnect the cable from the negative battery terminal (see Chapter 1).
3   Remove the glove box (see Chapter 11).
4   Use a trim tool to pry up the two clips securing the plastic cover over the PCM.
5   Unplug the electrical connectors from the PCM. **Caution:** *The ignition switch must be turned OFF when pulling out or plugging in the electrical connectors to prevent damage to the PCM.*
6   Remove the two mounting screws, accessing them from the glove box area.
7   Release the two claw-clips and carefully

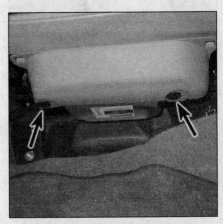

3.1 Typical PCM mounting location under the glove box (there are two push-fasteners securing the cover)

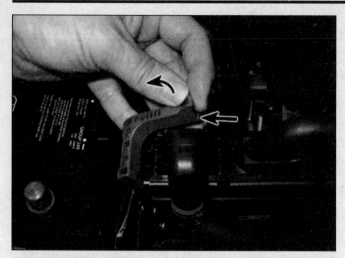

3.14 To release the PCM connectors, push the lever locks in while rotating the lever outwards. Pull out the connectors from the PCM (2009 and later models)

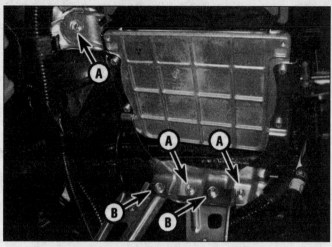

3.15 PCM mounting details (2009 and later models)

A   *PCM bracket-to-body mounting fasteners*
B   *Air filter housing bracket-to-body fasteners*

remove the PCM. **Note:** *Avoid any static electricity damage to the computer by grounding yourself to the body before touching the PCM and using a special anti-static pad to store the PCM on once it is removed.*

8   Installation is the reverse of removal.

2009 and later models

Refer to illustrations 3.14 and 3.15

9   The Powertrain Control Module (PCM) is located in the engine compartment, mounted to the driver's side inner fender panel.

10   Disconnect the cable from the negative battery terminal (see Chapter 5).

11   Remove the engine cover.

12   Remove the air filter cover and intake duct (see Chapter 4).

13   Remove the air filter housing bracket mounting bolts and bracket.

14   To release the PCM connectors, push in the lever locks at the end of each lever while lifting the levers outwards **(see illustration)**,

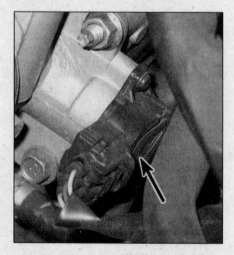

4.1 The TPS is mounted on the firewall-side of the throttle body (2003 and 2004 models)

and pull the PCM connectors out from the PCM. **Caution:** *The ignition switch must be turned OFF when pulling out or plugging in the electrical connectors to prevent damage to the PCM.*

15   Remove the air filter housing bracket fasteners, then the PCM bracket-to-body fasteners **(see illustration)**.

16   Carefully remove the PCM and bracket. **Caution:** *Avoid any static electricity damage to the computer by grounding yourself to the body before touching the PCM and using a special anti-static pad to store the PCM on once it is removed.*

17   Remove the bracket-to-PCM mounting bolts and separate the bracket from the PCM.

18   Installation is the reverse of removal.

4   Throttle Position Sensor (TPS) and throttle control motor - replacement

Refer to illustration 4.1

1   The Throttle Position Sensor (TPS) on 2003 and 2004 models is attached to the firewall side of the throttle body **(see illustration)**. Problems with the TPS and/or motor can cause intermittent bursts of fuel from the injectors and an unstable idle because the PCM thinks the throttle is moving. The PCM is constantly comparing the driver's input from the accelerator pedal position sensor to the actual throttle position at the throttle body. A problem with the TPS circuits will set a diagnostic trouble code (see Section 2).

2   To replace a defective TPS, disconnect the negative battery cable (see Chapter 1).

3   Disconnect the electrical connector at the TPS and remove the two mounting screws.

4   Installation is the reverse of removal.

5   On 2005 and later models, the throttle body is operated by an electric throttle control motor instead of a cable. One these models,

the TPS is part of throttle motor assembly and cannot be replaced separately. If there are problems with the throttle control motor or the TPS, the complete throttle body must be replaced (see Chapter 4).

5   Mass Airflow (MAF) sensor - replacement

Refer to illustrations 5.3

1   The Mass Airflow (MAF) sensor is located on the air filter housing. The MAF system circuit consists of a platinum hot wire, a thermistor and a control circuit inside a plastic housing. The sensor uses a hot-wire sensing element to measure the molecular mass (weight) of air entering the engine. As the throttle opens, increasing volume of air passes over the hot wire, which cools the wire. The MAF sensor circuit is designed to maintain the hot wire at a constant preset temperature by controlling the current flow through the hot wire. So, as the wire cools, the PCM increases the flow of current through the hot wire in order to maintain the wire at a constant temperature. The output voltage signal of the MAF sensor varies in accordance with this current flow. This voltage signal is measured by the PCM, which converts this signal into a digital waveform, calculates the fuel injector pulse width (duration) and turns the injectors on and off accordingly. A problem in the MAF sensor circuit will set a diagnostic trouble code (see Section 2).

2   Make sure the ignition key is in the OFF position.

3   Disconnect the electrical connector from the MAF sensor **(see illustration)**.

4   Remove the two sensor retaining screws and remove the MAF sensor and O-ring from the air filter housing.

5   Installation is the reverse of removal. Be sure to install a new O-ring between the MAF sensor and the filter housing.

5.3 The MAF sensor is located on the air intake housing (intake tube removed for clarity) - note the two mounting screws (A) and the electrical connector (B)

6.4 Location of the Engine Coolant Temperature sensor

6 Engine Coolant Temperature (ECT) sensor - replacement

Refer to illustration 6.4

Warning: *Wait until the engine has cooled completely before beginning this procedure.*

1   The engine coolant temperature (ECT) sensor is a thermistor (a resistor which varies the value of its resistance in accordance with temperature changes). The change in the resistance values will directly affect the voltage signal from the sensor to the PCM. As the sensor temperature DECREASES, the resistance values will INCREASE. As the sensor temperature INCREASES, the resistance values will DECREASE. A problem in the ECT sensor circuit will set a diagnostic trouble code.

2   Make sure the ignition key is in the OFF position.

3   Drain approximately one gallon from the cooling system.

4   Disconnect the electrical connector and carefully unscrew the sensor **(see illustration)**.

5   Wrap the threads of the new sensor with Teflon sealing tape to prevent leakage and thread corrosion.

6   Installation is the reverse of removal. **Caution:** *Handle the coolant sensor with care. Damage to this sensor will affect the operation of the entire fuel injection system.*

7 Crankshaft Position (CKP) sensor - replacement

Refer to illustration 7.4

1   The crankshaft position sensor (CKP) determines the timing for the fuel injection and ignition on each cylinder. The crankshaft sensor is mounted on the timing chain cover next to the crankshaft pulley. A problem in the crankshaft sensor circuit will set a diagnostic trouble code (see Section 2).

2   Loosen the right front wheel lug nuts. Disconnect the cable from the negative battery terminal (see Chapter 1).

3   Raise the front of the vehicle and support it securely on jackstands. Remove the wheel and the inner fender shield (see Chapter 11).

4   Remove the two bolts (one secures the sensor, the other is close by and secures the harness) and detach the sensor **(see illustration)**.

5   At the upper part of the timing chain cover, disconnect the harness connector and remove the harness and sensor.

6   Installation is the reverse of removal. Be sure to use a new O-ring on the sensor, lightly coated with engine oil.

8 Camshaft Position (CMP) sensor - replacement

2008 and earlier models

Refer to illustrations 8.1

1   The camshaft position sensor determines the position of the cylinder for sequential fuel injection signals to each cylinder. The camshaft sensor is mounted on the cylinder head near the intake runner for cylinder no. 4 **(see illustration)**. A problem in the camshaft sensor circuit will set a diagnostic trouble code (see Section 2).

7.4 The Crankshaft Position sensor is mounted on the timing chain cover

8.1 The camshaft position sensor mounts with one bolt to the cylinder head (connector removed for clarity) - 2008 and earlier models

8.7 Intake (A) and exhaust (B) CMP sensor locations (2009 and later models)

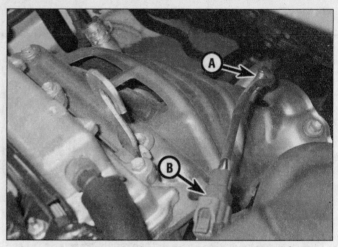

9.2a The upstream oxygen sensor (A) is located in the exhaust manifold, B is the sensor harness connector

2   Make sure the ignition key is in the OFF position.

3   Remove the engine cover (see Chapter 2A, Section 4).

4   Disconnect the harness connector, remove the mounting bolt and remove the camshaft sensor from the cylinder head.

5   Installation is the reverse of the removal. Use a new O-ring, lightly coated with engine oil.

2009 and later models

Refer to illustration 8.7

6   Disconnect the cable from the negative battery terminal (see Chapter 5).

7   The sensors are mounted on the top of the valve cover **(see illustration)**.

8   Disconnect the harness electrical connector.

9   Remove the mounting screws and remove the camshaft sensors from the valve cover.

10   Installation is the reverse of removal.

---

9   Oxygen sensor and air/fuel sensor - general information and replacement

General information

Refer to illustrations 9.2a and 9.2b

1   All vehicles covered by this manual have On-Board Diagnostics II (OBD-II) engine management systems, which means that they have the ability to verify the accuracy of the basic feedback loop between the oxygen sensor and the PCM. They accomplish this by using an oxygen sensor or air/fuel sensor ahead of the catalytic converter and an oxygen sensor behind the catalytic converter. By sampling the exhaust gas before and after the catalytic converter, the PCM can determine the efficiency of the converter and can even predict when it will fail.

2   The primary (upstream) oxygen sensor (sensor 1) is located in the exhaust manifold and the secondary (downstream) oxygen sensor (sensor 2) is located behind the catalytic converter **(see illustrations)**.

3   Special care must be taken whenever a sensor is serviced.

a) *Oxygen sensors and air/fuel sensors have a permanently attached pigtail and electrical connector, which should not be removed from the sensor. Damage or removal of the pigtail or electrical connector can adversely affect operation of the sensor.*

b) *Grease, dirt and other contaminants should be kept away from the electrical connector and the louvered end of the sensor.*

c) *Do not use cleaning solvents of any kind on an oxygen sensor or air/fuel ratio sensor.*

d) *Do not drop or roughly handle an oxygen sensor or air/fuel ratio sensor.*

e) *The silicone boot must be installed in the correct position to prevent the boot from being melted and to allow the sensor to operate properly.*

Replacement

Refer to illustration 9.6

Note: *Because it is installed in the exhaust manifold or pipe, which contracts when cool, the oxygen sensor may be very difficult to loosen when the engine is cold. Rather than risk damage to the sensor (assuming you are planning to reuse it in another manifold or pipe), start and run the engine for a minute or two, then shut it off. Be careful not to burn yourself during the following procedure.*

4   If you're replacing the downstream sensor, raise the vehicle and secure it on jackstands. Follow the oxygen sensor harness through the floor pan, then unplug the electrical connector inside the vehicle.

5   The upstream sensor can be replaced without raising the vehicle. Follow the harness from the sensor (mounted in the exhaust manifold) to the electrical connector, then unplug the connector.

6   Unscrew the sensor from the exhaust manifold or exhaust pipe **(see illustration)**.

Note: *The best tool for removing an oxygen sensor is a special slotted socket, especially if you're planning to reuse a sensor. If you don't*

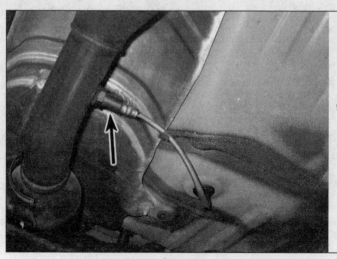

9.2b Location of the downstream oxygen sensor

9.6 Use a slotted socket to remove the oxygen sensors

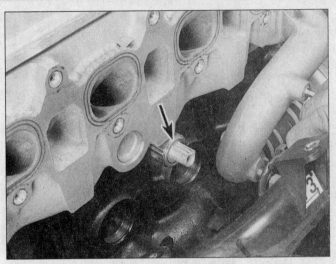

10.5 The knock sensor is screwed into the side of the block below the intake manifold

have this tool, and you plan to reuse the sensor, be extremely careful when unscrewing the sensor.

7   Apply anti-seize compound to the threads of the sensor to facilitate future removal. The threads of new sensors should already be coated with this compound, but if you're planning to reuse an old sensor, recoat the threads. Install the sensor and tighten it securely. **Caution:** *Do not get anti-seize compound on the sensor tip or it could be ruined.*

8   Reconnect the electrical connector of the pigtail lead to the main wiring harness.

9   Lower the vehicle (if it was raised), test drive the car and verify that no trouble codes have been set.

10   Knock sensor - replacement

Refer to illustration 10.5

Warning: *Wait for the engine to cool completely before performing this procedure.*

1   The knock control system is designed to reduce spark knock during periods of heavy detonation. This allows the engine to use optimal spark advance to improve driveability. The knock sensor detects abnormal vibration in the engine and produces a voltage output that increases with the severity of the knock. The voltage signal is monitored by the PCM, which retards ignition timing until the detonation ceases. The knock sensor is located on the backside of the engine block, directly below the cylinder head (facing toward the rear of the engine compartment).

2   Disconnect the cable from the negative terminal of the battery.

3   Drain the cooling system (see Chapter 1).

4   Remove the intake manifold (see Chapter 2A).

5   Disconnect the electrical connector and remove the knock sensor **(see illustration)**.

6   If you're going to reuse the old sensor, coat the threads with thread sealant. New

sensors are pre-coated with thread sealant; do not apply any additional sealant or the operation of the sensor may be affected.

7   Install the knock sensor and tighten it securely. Don't overtighten the sensor or damage may occur. Plug in the electrical connector, refill the cooling system (see Chapter 1) and check for leaks.

11   Vehicle Speed Sensor (VSS) - replacement

Refer to illustration 11.1

1   The Vehicle Speed Sensor (VSS) **(see illustration)** is located on top of the transaxle. This sensor is an electronic component that produces a pulsing voltage signal whenever the sensor shaft is rotated. These voltage pulses are monitored by the PCM, which uses this information to help control the fuel and ignition systems and transaxle shifting.

2   Disconnect the electrical connector from

the VSS.

3   Remove the VSS from the transaxle.

4   Replace the O-ring.

5   Installation is the reverse of removal.

12   Positive Crankcase Ventilation (PCV) system

Refer to illustration 12.1

1   The Positive Crankcase Ventilation (PCV) system reduces hydrocarbon emissions by scavenging crankcase vapors. It does this by circulating fresh air from the air cleaner through the crankcase, where it mixes with blow-by gases and is then rerouted through a PCV valve to the intake manifold **(see illustration)**.

2   The main components of the PCV system are the PCV valve and the vacuum hose connecting the valve to the intake manifold.

3   To maintain idle quality, the PCV valve restricts the flow when the intake manifold vac-

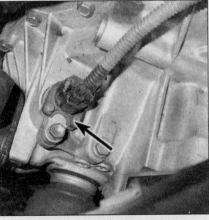

11.1 The VSS is located on top of the transaxle (viewed here looking straight down on the transaxle in the engine compartment)

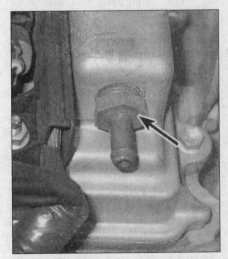

12.1 PCV valve location at the valve cover

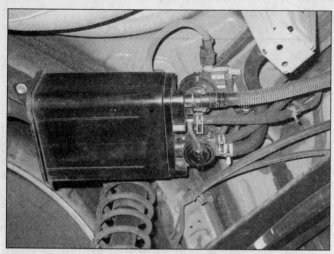

13.1 The EVAP canister is located above the rear crossmember, near the fuel tank

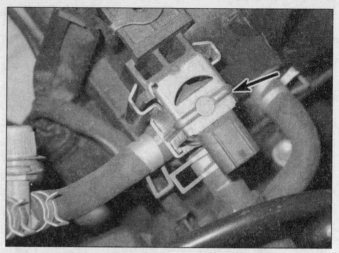

13.6 Two EVAP system vacuum switching valves (purge valve shown) are mounted in the engine compartment

uum is high. If abnormal operating conditions (such as piston ring problems) arise, the system is designed to allow excessive amounts of blow-by gases to flow back through the crankcase vent tube into the air cleaner to be consumed by normal combustion.

4   Checking and replacement of the PCV valve is covered in Chapter 1.

13   Evaporative emissions control (EVAP) system

General description

Refer to illustrations 13.1 and 13.6

1   The fuel evaporative emissions control (EVAP) system absorbs fuel vapors and, during engine operation, releases them into the engine intake where they mix with the incoming air-fuel mixture. The charcoal canister is mounted behind the fuel tank under the vehicle **(see illustration)**.

2   When the engine is not operating, fuel vapors are transferred from the fuel tank, throttle body and intake manifold to the charcoal canister where they are stored. When the engine is running, the fuel vapors are purged from the canister by the purge control valve. The gasses are consumed in the normal combustion process. The electronic purge control valve is directly controlled by the PCM.

3   The fuel filler cap is fitted with a two-way valve as a safety device. The valve vents fuel vapors to the atmosphere if the EVAP system fails.

4   The EVAP system also incorporates a vapor pressure sensor. This sensor detects abnormal vapor pressure in the system. The vapor pressure sensor is mounted in the fuel pump/sending unit assembly on top of the fuel tank.

5   After the engine has been running and warmed up to a pre-set temperature, the vacuum switching valve (VSV) opens. The vacuum switching valve (purge control valve) allows intake manifold vacuum to draw the fuel vapors from the canister to the intake manifold, where they are mixed with intake air before being burned with the air/fuel mixture inside the combustion chambers.

6   The fuel tank vapor pressure sensor monitors changes in pressure inside the tank and, when the pressure exceeds a preset threshold, opens a vacuum switching valve (VSV) **(see illustration)**, which allows a purge port in the canister to admit fuel tank vapors into the canister. These models have three VSV valves, two in the engine compartment and one on the charcoal canister. Also on 2005 and later models, there is a timer in the PCM that operates the pump module to check for fuel vapor leakage five hours after the vehicle has been turned off.

Replacement

7   Disconnect the cable from the negative battery terminal (see Chapter 1).

8   Raise the rear of the vehicle and support it securely on jackstands.

9   Unplug all electrical connectors and clearly label and disconnect the vent hoses to the charcoal canister, remove the bolts and separate the canister from the underside of the vehicle.

10   Installation is the reverse of removal.

14   Catalytic converters

Note: *Because of a Federally mandated extended warranty which covers emissions-related components such as the catalytic converter, check with a dealer service department before replacing the converter at your own expense.*

General description

1   The catalytic converter is an emission control device added to the exhaust system to reduce pollutants from the exhaust gas stream. There are two types of converters. The conventional oxidation catalyst reduces the levels of hydrocarbon (HC) and carbon monoxide (CO). The three-way catalyst lowers the levels of oxides of nitrogen (NOx) as well as hydrocarbons (HC) and carbon monoxide (CO). These models are equipped only with three-way catalytic converters.

Check

2   The test equipment for a catalytic converter is expensive and highly sophisticated. If you suspect that the converter on your vehicle is malfunctioning, take it to a dealer or authorized emissions inspection facility for diagnosis and repair.

3   Whenever the vehicle is raised for servicing of underbody components, check the converter for leaks, corrosion, dents and other damage. Check the welds/flange bolts that attach the front and rear ends of the converter to the exhaust system. If damage is discovered, the converter should be replaced.

4   Although catalytic converters don't break too often, they can become plugged. The easiest way to check for a restricted converter is to use a vacuum gauge to diagnose the effect of a blocked exhaust on intake vacuum.

a) *Connect a vacuum gauge to an intake manifold vacuum source (see Chapter 2B).*

b) *Warm the engine to operating temperature, place the transaxle in Park (automatic) or Neutral (manual) and apply the parking brake.*

c) *Note and record the vacuum reading at idle.*

d) *Quickly open the throttle to near full throttle and release it shut. Note and record the vacuum reading.*

e) *Perform the test three more times, recording the reading after each test.*

f) *If the reading after the fourth test is more than one in-Hg lower than the reading*

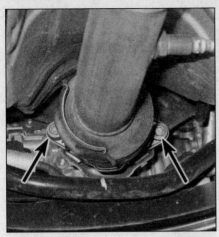

14.6 Remove the two spring-loaded bolts at the front of the catalytic converter

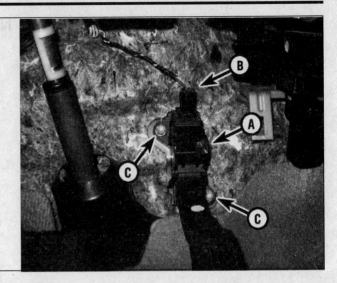

17.2 Typical Accelerator Pedal Position (APP) sensor details

A   APP sensor
B   Electrical connector
C   Mounting fasteners

recorded at idle, the exhaust system may be restricted (the catalytic converter could be plugged or an exhaust pipe or muffler could be restricted).

Replacement

Refer to illustration 14.6

5   Be sure to spray the nuts on the exhaust flange studs before removing them from the front of the catalytic converter.
6   Remove the nuts and separate the catalytic converter from the exhaust manifold **(see illustration)**. The rear of the converter is welded to the exhaust pipe and must be cut off for replacement. A new converter must be welded in.
7   Installation is the reverse of removal. Install new gaskets where required.

15   Transmission Range (TR) sensor - replacement

Even though the Society of Automotive Engineers (SAE) has recommended since 1996 that all manufacturers refer to the Park/ Neutral Position (PNP) switch as the Transmission Range (TR) sensor, Toyota continues to refer to the TR sensor as the PNP switch. To avoid confusion, we have therefore included the TR sensor/PNP switch in Chapter 7B.

16   Variable Valve Timing-intelligent system - description and component replacement

Description

1   See Chapter 2A, Section 5 for a description of the VVT-i system.

Camshaft timing oil control valve(s) replacement

Note: *2008 and earlier 1.8L models use one camshaft timing control valve, while 2009 and later models use two.*
2   Disconnect the cable from the negative battery terminal (see Chapter 5).
3   Remove the engine cover(s).
4   Remove the engine harness mounting fasteners and move the harness to the side. Disconnect the electrical connector from the camshaft timing oil control valve.
5   Remove the camshaft timing oil control valve mounting bolt and remove the oil control valve from the valve cover.
6   Installation is the reverse of removal.

17   Accelerator Pedal Position (APP) sensor - replacement

Refer to illustration 17.2
Note: *The APP sensor and the accelerator pedal are removed as a single assembly*
1   Disconnect the cable from the negative battery terminal (see Chapter 5).
2   Working under the dash, disconnect the APP sensor electrical connector **(see illustration)**.
3   Remove the accelerator pedal/APP sensor assembly mounting bolts and sensor assembly.
4   Installation is the reverse of removal. Be sure to tighten the accelerator pedal assembly mounting bolts securely.

Notes

Chapter 7 Part A
Manual transaxle

Contents

Specifications

Torque specifications

Ft-lbs (unless otherwise indicated)

Note: *One foot-pound (ft-lb) of torque is equivalent to 12 inch-pounds (in-lbs) of torque. Torque values below approximately 15 ft-lbs are expressed in inch-pounds, since most foot-pound torque wrenches are not accurate at these smaller values.*

Back-up light switch	30
Drain and filler plugs	29
Exhaust manifold brace	31
Floor pan brace nuts	22
Shift lever mounting bolts	108 in-lbs
Subframe crossmember **(see illustration 5.22)**	
Bolt A	116
Bolt B	83
Bolts/nuts C	38
Balljoint bolts/nuts D	66
Transaxle-to-engine bolts **(see illustration 5.32)**	
2008 and earlier models (C59 and MK5)	
Bolt A	47
Bolt B	35
Bolt C	17
2009 and later models (C59)	24
Mount bracket bolts	
2008 and earlier models	47
2009 and later models	33

1 General information

The vehicles covered by this manual are equipped with either a 5-speed manual or a 4-speed automatic transaxle. The 5-speed manual transaxle used in these models is named the C59. Information on the manual transaxle is included in this Part of Chapter 7. Service procedures for the automatic transaxle are contained in Chapter 7, Part B.

The manual transaxle is a compact, two-piece, lightweight aluminum alloy housing containing both the transmission and differential assemblies.

Because of the complexity, unavailability of replacement parts and special tools necessary, internal repair procedures for the manual transaxle are not recommended for the home mechanic. The bulk of information in this Chapter is devoted to removal and installation procedures.

2 Shift and select cables - replacement

2008 and earlier models

1 Disconnect the cable from the negative terminal of the battery.

2 Remove the center floor console (see Chapter 11).

3 Remove the large clips and disconnect

4.1 The backup light switch is threaded into the top of the transaxle case

5.15 Support the engine with an engine support fixture (these are available at most tool rental yards and some auto parts stores)

the cable ends at the shifter mechanism.

4   Pull back the carpeting and remove the three bolts securing the airbag ECU to the floor and set the ECU aside.

5   Remove the plastic shield at the lower-left of the heating/air conditioning unit. Remove the nuts securing the shift cable plate and grommet to the floor.

6   Remove the large clips that secure the cable ends to the transaxle, then separate the cables from the cable bracket on the transaxle.

7   Under the vehicle, remove the two nuts securing the cable bracket to the floor, then pull the cables/grommet through the floor and out.

8   Installation is the reverse of the removal procedure.

2009 and later models

Replacement

9   Unscrew the shift lever knob from the shift lever.

10   Remove the center console and center trim panels (see Chapter 11).

11   Carefully pry the shift and select cable ends from the ballstuds.

12   Using a small screwdriver, pry the stop open, but not off of the control cable.

13   Rotate each of the cable housing lock nuts 180-degrees, then hold the nut in this position and disconnect the cable(s) from the bracket. **Caution:** *If the lock nut is rotated more than 180-degrees, the housing will be damaged and the cable will need to be replaced.*

14   To gain access to the transaxle end of the cable, remove the battery, battery tray and carrier (see Chapter 5).

15   Remove the air cleaner assembly (see Chapter 4).

16   Remove the wire clips that attach the cable ends to the transaxle and separate the cables from the transaxle.

17   Remove the front exhaust pipe assembly (see Chapter 4).

18   Remove the floor heat shield mount-

ing screws and remove the heat shield from under the vehicle.

19   Remove the cable bracket retaining nut and cable assembly nuts, and remove the cable assembly from under the vehicle.

20   Installation is the reverse of removal.

21   Adjust the select cable (see Steps 22 through 26).

Adjustment

22   Place the shift lever in the neutral position.

23   Push in the two tabs at the top and bottom of the select cable lock piece.

24   While holding the select cable lock piece in this position, push the two lugs on each side of the lock piece inwards and upwards, then pull out the lock piece.

25   With the lock piece extending out, install the select cable on to the ballstud of the shifter, and press the lock into place.

26   Installation is the reverse of removal.

---

3   Shift lever - removal and installation

---

1   Remove the center console (see Chapter 11).

2   Remove the shift and select cable retainers and disconnect both cables from the shift lever (see Section 2).

3   Remove the retaining bolts and detach the shift lever assembly from the floor.

4   Installation is the reverse of removal.

---

4   Back-up light switch - check and replacement

Refer to illustration 4.1

1   The backup light switch is mounted on the transaxle **(see illustration)**. With the ignition key in the On position, place the shift lever in Reverse. The back-up lights should come on.

a) *If the lights don't come on, check the ignition switch, the GAUGE fuse, the bulbs and the wire harness (see Chapter 12).*

b) *If the lights remain on all the time, even when the shift lever is not in REVERSE, the switch is most likely defective.*

c) *If only one light comes on, but not the other, check the bulb for that light and check the harness.*

2   To check the operation of the back-up light switch itself, disconnect the electrical connector and unscrew the switch from the top of the transaxle, then use an ohmmeter to verify that there's continuity when the plunger is depressed, and no continuity when the plunger is released.

3   If the switch doesn't operate as described, replace it. Disconnect the electrical connector from the switch and unscrew it from the case.

4   Test the new switch before installation by depressing the plunger with an ohmmeter connected across the switch terminals. There should be continuity only when the plunger is depressed.

5   Install the new switch and tighten it securely.

---

5   Manual transaxle - removal and installation

Note: *This procedure applies to 2008 and earlier models only. On 2009 and later models, the manufacturer recommends removing the engine and transaxle as an assembly (see Chapter 2B).*

Removal

Refer to illustrations 5.15 and 5.22

1   Place protective covers on the fenders and cowl and remove the hood (see Chapter 11).

2   Relieve the fuel system pressure (see Chapter 4).

5.22 Remove the front suspension subframe bolts (with an overhead support for the engine and a floorjack under the transaxle) - refer to the letter designations for torque specs when installing fasteners for the subframe (A and B), engine mount crossmember (C) and the lower control arm balljoint bolts (D)

3   Disconnect the negative cable from the battery and drain the transaxle lubricant (see Chapter 1).

4   If the vehicle is equipped with cruise control, unplug the electrical connector for the actuator and remove the actuator (see Chapter 12).

5   Remove the battery and the battery tray (see Chapter 5).

6   Remove the air intake duct and the air cleaner housing (see Chapter 4).

7   Release the residual fuel pressure in the tank by removing the gas cap, then disconnect the fuel lines connecting the engine to the chassis (see Chapter 4). Plug or cap all open fittings.

8   Remove the starter (see Chapter 5).

9   Disconnect the ground cable from the transaxle.

10   Disconnect the clutch release cylinder mounting bolts from the transaxle but do NOT disconnect the hydraulic line. Remove the two mounting bolts from the clutch line bracket.

11   Clearly label, then disconnect all vacuum lines, coolant and emissions hoses, wiring

harness connectors (VSS and back-up light switch) and ground straps.

12   Masking tape and/or a touch-up paint applicator work well for marking items. Take instant photos or sketch the locations of components and brackets.

13   Disconnect the shift and select cables (see Section 2).

14   Remove the exhaust manifold brace.

15   Loosen but do NOT remove the front wheel lug nuts. Also loosen the driveaxle/hub nuts (see Chapter 8). Raise the vehicle and support it securely on jackstands. Secure the engine using an engine support fixture that is installed above the engine compartment **(see illustration)**. If an engine support fixture is not available, install an engine lift and a lifting chain assembly. This will keep the engine stable during the transaxle removal procedure. Remove the front wheels.

16   Detach the exhaust pipe from the manifold and separate the front exhaust pipe from the underside of the vehicle (see Chapter 4). Remove the floorpan brace to allow the exhaust to drop out of the way.

17   Remove the splash shields.

18   Remove the driveaxles (see Chapter 8).

19   Disconnect the two power steering fluid lines from the steering gear. Also detach the tie-rod ends from the steering knuckles (see Chapter 10).

20   Disconnect the stabilizer bar from the links (see Chapter 10).

21   Remove the mounting bolts from the engine/transaxle mounts to the subframe. Refer to Chapter 2A for engine and transaxle mount replacement procedures.

22   Remove the subframe mounting bolts from the chassis, using a floor jack to lower the subframe **(see illustration)**. Be sure to note exactly the size and location of each nut and bolt to insure correct reassembly. **Note:** *The transaxle should be supported by a floor jack immediately after the subframe is removed from the vehicle. The transaxle will tilt slightly but should remain steady if the engine is properly secured with the engine support fixture.*

23   Support the transaxle with a floor jack, preferably a floor jack with a transmission

adapter head. Safety chains will help steady the transaxle on the jack.

24   Remove the transaxle-to-engine bolts.

25   Recheck to be sure nothing is connecting the engine to the vehicle or to the transaxle. Disconnect and label anything still remaining.

26   Slowly lower the transaxle assembly out of the vehicle. Keep the transaxle level as you're separating it from the engine to prevent damage to the input shaft. It may be necessary to pry the mounts away from the frame brackets. **Caution:** *Do not depress the clutch pedal while the transaxle is removed from the vehicle.* **Warning**: *Do not place any part of your body under the transaxle as it's being removed.*

27   Move the transaxle assembly away from the vehicle and carefully place the transaxle assembly on the floor onto wood blocks. Leave enough room for a floor jack underneath the transaxle.

28   The clutch components can now be inspected (see Chapter 8). In most cases, new clutch components should be routinely installed whenever the transaxle is removed.

29   Check the engine and transaxle mounts and the transaxle shock absorber. If any of these components are worn or damaged, replace them.

Installation

Refer to illustration 5.32

30   If removed, install the clutch components (see Chapter 8). Apply a thin film of high temperature grease to the input shaft splines and the surface of the input shaft bearing retainer.

31   With the transaxle secured to the jack as on removal, raise it into position and then carefully slide it forward, engaging the input shaft with the clutch splines. Do not use excessive force to install the transaxle - if the input shaft does not slide into place, readjust the angle of the transaxle so it is level and/or turn the input shaft so the splines engage properly with the clutch. **Caution:** *Do NOT use transaxle-to-engine bolts to force the engine and transaxle into alignment. Doing so could crack or damage major components. If you experience difficulties, have an assistant help you line up the dowel pins on the block with the transaxle. Some wiggling of the engine and/or the transaxle will probably be necessary to secure proper alignment of the two.*

32   Install the transaxle-to-engine bolts and

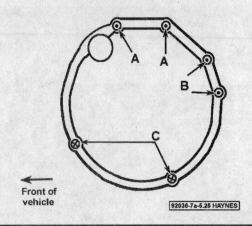

5.32   Refer to these letter designations for torque specs on the transaxle-to-engine bolts (2008 and earlier models)

the engine-to-transaxle bolt. Tighten the bolts to the torque listed in this Chapter's Specifications **(see illustration)**.

33   Install the right engine mount, the front engine mount, the left transaxle mount and the rear engine mount. Tighten all mounting bolts and nuts securely.

34   Reinstall the remaining components in the reverse order of removal. When installing the subframe, use a rod of the same diameter as the four subframe to-chassis bolts to align each side until that side's bolts can be inserted one at a time. Do not tighten any of the bolts until all have been installed finger tight, then tighten to the Specifications in this Chapter.

35   Remove the jack and support fixture and lower the vehicle. Tighten the wheel lug nuts to the torque listed in the Chapter 1 Specifications. Tighten the driveaxle/hub nuts to the torque listed in the Chapter 8 Specifications.

36   Refill the transaxle with the proper lubricant (see Chapter 1).

37   Road test the vehicle to check for proper transaxle operation and check for leakage.

6   Manual transaxle overhaul - general information

1   Overhauling a manual transaxle is a difficult job for the do-it-yourselfer. It involves the disassembly and reassembly of many small parts. Numerous clearances must be precisely measured and, if necessary, changed with select-fit spacers and snap-rings. As a result, if transaxle problems arise, it can be

removed and installed by a competent do-it-yourselfer, but overhaul should be left to a transmission repair shop. Rebuilt transaxles may be available - check with your dealer parts department and auto parts stores. At any rate, the time and money involved in an overhaul is almost sure to exceed the cost of a rebuilt unit.

2   Nevertheless, it's not impossible for an inexperienced mechanic to rebuild a transaxle if the special tools are available and the job is done in a deliberate step-by-step manner so nothing is overlooked.

3   The tools necessary for an overhaul include internal and external snap-ring pliers, a bearing puller, a slide hammer, a set of pin punches, a dial indicator and possibly a hydraulic press. In addition, a large, sturdy workbench and a vise or transaxle stand will be required.

4   During disassembly of the transaxle, make careful notes of how each component was removed, where it fits in relation to other components and what holds it in place. Noting how they are installed when you remove the components will make it much easier to get the transaxle back together correctly.

5   Before taking the transaxle apart for repair, it will help if you have some idea what area of the transaxle is malfunctioning. Certain problems can be closely tied to specific areas in the transaxle, which can make component examination and replacement easier. Refer to the *Troubleshooting* section at the front of this manual for information regarding possible sources of trouble.

Chapter 7 Part B
Automatic transaxle

Contents

Specifications

Torque specifications

	Ft-lbs
Drain plug	See Chapter 1
Subframe crossmember	See Chapter 7A
Transaxle-to-engine bolts **(see illustrations 7.21a and 7.21b)**	
2008 and earlier models	
Bolt A	47
Bolt B	34
Bolt C	17
2009 and later models	24
Bolt A	47
Bolt B	34
Bolt C	34
Bolt D	32
Torque converter-to-driveplate bolts	
2008 and earlier models	20
2009 and later models	30

1   General information

2008 and earlier automatic transaxle models are equipped with the electronically-controlled, four-speed A245E transaxle. 2009 and later models are equipped with the U250E five-speed automatic transaxle. Information on the automatic transaxle is included in this Part of Chapter 7. Service procedures for the manual transaxle are contained in Chapter 7, Part A.

Due to the complexity of the automatic transaxles covered in this manual and to the specialized equipment necessary to perform most service operations, this Chapter contains only those procedures related to general diagnosis, routine maintenance, adjustment and removal and installation.

If the transaxle requires major repair work, it should be left to a dealer service department or an automotive or transmission shop. You can, however, remove and install the transaxle yourself and save the expense, even if a transmission shop does the repair

work (but be sure a proper diagnosis has been made before removing the transaxle).

2   Diagnosis - general

Automatic transaxle malfunctions may be caused by five general conditions:

a) Poor engine performance
b) Improper adjustments
c) Hydraulic malfunctions
d) Mechanical malfunctions
e) Malfunctions in the computer or its signal network

Diagnosis of these problems should always begin with a check of the easily repaired items: fluid level and condition (see Chapter 1) and shift cable adjustment. Next, perform a road test to determine if the problem has been corrected or if more diagnosis is necessary. If the problem persists after the preliminary tests and corrections are completed, additional diagnosis should be done by a dealer service department or transmis-

sion shop. Refer to the Troubleshooting section at the front of this manual for information on symptoms of transaxle problems.

Preliminary checks

1   Drive the vehicle to warm the transaxle to normal operating temperature.
2   Check the fluid level as described in Chapter 1:

a) If the fluid level is unusually low, add enough fluid to bring the level within the designated area of the dipstick, then check for external leaks (see below).
b) If the fluid level is abnormally high, drain off the excess, then check the drained fluid for contamination by coolant. The presence of engine coolant in the automatic transaxle fluid indicates that a failure has occurred in the internal radiator walls that separate the coolant from the transaxle fluid (see Chapter 3).
c) If the fluid is foaming, drain it and refill the transaxle, then check for coolant in the fluid, or a high fluid level.

3.3 Before adjusting the shift cable, loosen the nut (A) that connects the shift cable to the manual lever on the transaxle - B is the clip securing the cable to the bracket on the transaxle

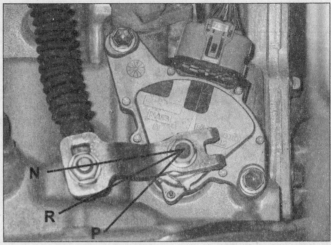

3.4 To adjust the shift cable, push the manual lever all the way DOWN, return it two clicks to the Neutral position, place the shift lever inside the vehicle at the Neutral position and tighten the swivel nut

3   Check the engine idle speed. **Note:** *If the engine is malfunctioning, do not proceed with the preliminary checks until it has been repaired and runs normally.*

4   Inspect the shift cable (see Section 3). Make sure that it's properly adjusted and that it operates smoothly.

Fluid leak diagnosis

5   Most fluid leaks are easy to locate visually. Repair usually consists of replacing a seal or gasket. If a leak is difficult to find, the following procedure may help.

6   Identify the fluid. Make sure it's transmission fluid and not engine oil or brake fluid (automatic transmission fluid is a deep red color).

7   Try to pinpoint the source of the leak. Drive the vehicle several miles, then park it over a large sheet of cardboard. After a minute or two, you should be able to locate the leak by determining the source of the fluid dripping onto the cardboard.

8   Make a careful visual inspection of the suspected component and the area immediately around it. Pay particular attention to gasket mating surfaces. A mirror is often helpful for finding leaks in areas that are hard to see.

9   If the leak still cannot be found, clean the suspected area thoroughly with a degreaser or solvent, then dry it.

10   Drive the vehicle for several miles at normal operating temperature and varying speeds. After driving the vehicle, visually inspect the suspected component again.

11   Once the leak has been located, the cause must be determined before it can be properly repaired. If a gasket is replaced but the sealing flange is bent, the new gasket will not stop the leak. The bent flange must be straightened.

12   Before attempting to repair a leak, check to make sure that the following conditions are corrected or they may cause another leak.

Note: *Some of the following conditions cannot be fixed without highly specialized tools and expertise. Such problems must be referred to a transmission shop or a dealer service department.*

Gasket leaks

13   Check the pan periodically. Make sure the bolts are tight, no bolts are missing, the gasket is in good condition and the pan is flat (dents in the pan may indicate damage to the valve body inside).

14   If the pan gasket is leaking, the fluid level or the fluid pressure may be too high, the vent may be plugged, the pan bolts may be too tight, the pan sealing flange may be warped, the sealing surface of the transaxle housing may be damaged, the gasket may be damaged or the transaxle casting may be cracked or porous. If sealant instead of gasket material has been used to form a seal between the pan and the transaxle housing, it may be the wrong sealant.

Seal leaks

15   If a transaxle seal is leaking, the fluid level or pressure may be too high, the vent may be plugged, the seal bore may be damaged, the seal itself may be damaged or improperly fitted, the surface of the shaft protruding through the seal may be damaged or a loose bearing may be causing excessive shaft movement.

16   Make sure the dipstick tube seal is in good condition and the tube is properly seated. Periodically check the area around the vehicle speed sensor for leakage. If fluid is evident, check the O-ring for damage.

Case leaks

17   If the case itself appears to be leaking, the casting is porous and will have to be repaired or replaced.

18   Make sure the oil cooler hose fittings are tight and in good condition.

Fluid comes out vent pipe or fill tube

19   If this condition occurs, the transaxle is overfilled, there is coolant in the fluid, the case is porous, the dipstick is incorrect, the vent is plugged or the drain-back holes are plugged.

---

3   Shift cable - adjustment and replacement

Adjustment

Refer to illustrations 3.3 and 3.4

1   When the shift lever inside the vehicle is moved from the Neutral position to other positions, it should move smoothly and accurately to each position and the shift indicator should indicate the correct gear position.

2   If the indicator isn't aligned with the correct position, adjust the shift cable as follows:

3   Loosen the nut on the manual shift lever at the transaxle **(see illustration)**.

4   Move the manual lever down into Park (counterclockwise), then return it (clockwise) two notches to the Neutral position **(see illustration)**.

5   Move the shift lever inside the vehicle to the Neutral position.

6   While holding the lever with a slight force toward the REVERSE position, tighten the swivel nut securely.

7   Check the operation of the transaxle in each shift lever position (try to start the engine in each gear - the starter should operate in the Park and Neutral positions only).

Replacement

2008 and earlier models

Refer to illustrations 3.11, 3.12 and 3.13

8   Disconnect the negative battery cable.

3.11 Remove the three bolts at the airbag ECU (two are shown here) and set the unit aside - the shift cable is under the ECU

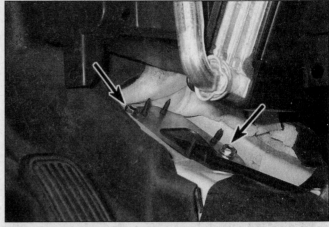

3.12 To detach the cable boot seal from the floor under the heater housing, remove the mounting bolts

Warning: *The models covered by this manual are equipped with Supplemental Restraint systems (SRS), more commonly known as airbags. Always disable the airbag system before working in the vicinity of the impact sensors, steering column or instrument panel to avoid the possibility of accidental deployment of the airbag, which could cause personal injury (see Chapter 12).*

9   Disconnect the cable from the manual lever and remove the large C-clip cable retainer from the bracket above the manual lever **(see illustration 3.3)**.

10   Refer to Chapter 11 and remove the floor console, then pull back the carpeting at the front of the floor tunnel.

11   Remove the three bolts securing the airbag ECU to the floor and set it aside **(see illustration)**.

12   Remove the bolts from the cable-housing retainer on the floor inside the vehicle **(see illustration)**.

13   Pry off the cable ends from the shift housing and disconnect the cable eye from the shifter **(see illustration)**.

14   Pull the cable and grommet through the floor pan.

15   Installation is the reverse of removal.

16   Adjust the cable (see Steps 1 through 7).

2009 and later models

17   Place the shift lever in the neutral position.

18   Remove the center console and center trim panels (see Chapter 11).

19   Carefully pry the control cable end from the shift lever ballstud.

20   Using a small screwdriver, pry the control cable stop open, but not off of the control cable.

21   Rotate the cable housing lock nut 180-degrees counterclockwise, then hold the nut in this position and disconnect the cable from the shift lever retainer. **Caution:** *If the lock nut is rotated more than 180-degrees, the housing will be damaged and the cable will need to be replaced.*

22   Push in the two tabs at the top and bot-

3.13 To detach the shift cables from the shift lever assembly, twist the flange (A) to release its clips, then remove the clips and pry the cable eye (B) from the shifter arm

tom of the control cable lock piece. While holding the control cable lock piece in this position, push the two lugs on each side of the lock piece inwards and upwards, then pull out the lock piece.

23   Rotate the cable housing lock nut 180-degrees counterclockwise, then hold the nut in place. Push the stop in until the stop clicks twice.

24   Install the control cable into the shift lever retainer, making sure the spring faces outwards, and push in the stop. **Note:** *If the stop can't be pushed in, rotate the housing lock nut slightly clockwise and push in the stop.*

25   Install the control cable onto the shift lever ballstud, and press the lock into place.

26   Installation is the reverse of removal.

27   To gain access to the transaxle end of the cable, remove the battery, battery tray and carrier (see Chapter 5).

28   Remove the air cleaner assembly (see Chapter 4).

29   Disconnect the cable from the manual lever and remove the large clip cable retainer from the bracket above the lever **(see illustration 3.3)**.

30   Remove the front exhaust pipe assembly (see Chapter 4).

31   Remove the floor heat shield mounting

screws and shield from under the vehicle.

32   Installation is the reverse of removal. Adjust the shift cable (see Steps 1 through 7).

---

4   Transmission range sensor - replacement and adjustment

1   The transmission range sensor incorporates the Park/Neutral function as well as the back-up light switch and inputs transmission gear position information to the PCM. The Park/Neutral function of the switch prevents the engine from starting in any gear other than Park or Neutral. If the engine starts with the shift lever in any position other than Park or Neutral, adjust the switch. The transmission position switch is also an information sensor for the Electronic Controlled Transaxle (ECT) Powertrain Control Module (PCM). When the shift lever is placed in position, the Park/Neutral position switch sends a voltage signal to the PCM.

Replacement

Refer to illustration 4.4

2   Raise the front of the vehicle and place it securely on jackstands.

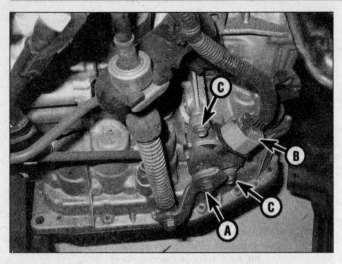

4.4 Remove the manual shift lever retaining nut (A), disconnect the electrical connector (B), and remove the mounting bolts (C)

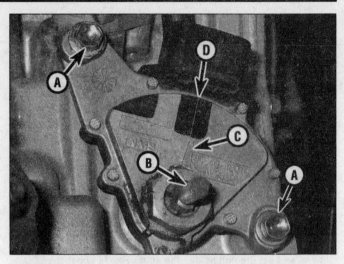

4.8 Detach the manual lever then loosen the switch retaining bolts (A) - the flat on the shaft (B) and the pointer (C) should align with the Neutral line on the switch (D) when installing the switch

3   Disconnect the electrical connector.
4   Remove the manual lever retaining nut and its lock plate **(see illustration)**. **Note:** *If equipped, bend the tabs flat on the lock plate before removing it.*
5   Disconnect the electrical connector from the switch.
6   Remove the retaining bolts and the switch **(see illustration 4.4)**.
7   Installation is the reverse of removal. Be sure to adjust the switch.

Adjustment

Refer to illustration 4.8

8   Loosen the switch retaining bolts and rotate the switch until the flat on the shaft and the neutral basic line on the switch are aligned **(see illustration)**. Hold the switch in this position and tighten the bolts. **Note:** *The pointer on the sheetmetal lock plate will indicate the alignment of the flat on the shaft with the Neutral line on the body of the switch.*

9   Refer to Section 3 for the cable adjustment procedure.

5   Shift lock system - description and component replacement

Description

1   The shift lock system prevents the shift lever from being shifted out of Park until the brake pedal is applied. The system consists of the brake light switch, a key interlock cable, a shift lock override button, a shift lock solenoid, and a shift lock control computer.

Component replacement

Refer to illustrations 5.3, 5.4 and 5.5

2   Remove the center console (see Chapter 11).
3   To disconnect the cable, push in the locking tab and separate the cable end **(see illustration)**.

4   Refer to Chapter 11 and remove the steering column covers. Where the cable mounts at the steering column, disconnect the clip and detach the cable from the lock cylinder housing **(see illustration)**. **Note:** *Whenever this end of the cable is connected or disconnected, the ignition switch must be in the ACC position*.
5   The shift lock control computer is located at the bottom of the shift lever base on the right side **(see illustration)**. Disconnect the electrical connector and unclip the shift-lock computer from the shifter assembly.

6   Oil seal replacement

1   Fluid leaks frequently occur due to wear of the driveaxle oil seals and/or the speedometer drive gear oil seal and O-rings. Replacement of these seals is relatively easy, since the repairs can usually be performed without removing the transaxle from the vehicle.

5.3 Disconnect the shift lock cable at the shifter end - squeeze the clip (A), then pry the cable eye off the stud (B)

5.4 Use a screwdriver to release the clip securing the cable at the top of the ignition lock cylinder housing on the steering column

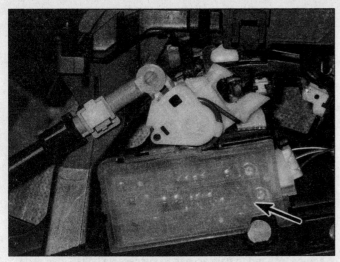

5.5 Shift lock system computer location

6.4 Carefully pry out the old driveaxle seal with a prybar, screwdriver or a special seal removal tool; make sure you don't gouge or nick the surface of the seal bore

Driveaxle seals

Refer to illustrations 6.4 and 6.6

2   The driveaxle oil seals are located in either sides of the transaxle, where the drive-axle shaft is splined into the differential. If leakage at the seal is suspected, raise the vehicle and support it securely on jackstands. If the seal is leaking, fluid will be found on the side of the transaxle.

3   Remove the driveaxle assembly (see Chapter 8).

4   Using a screwdriver or prybar, carefully pry the oil seal out of the transaxle bore **(see illustration)**.

5   If the oil seal cannot be removed with a screwdriver or prybar, a special oil seal removal tool (available at auto parts stores) will be required.

6   Using a seal driver (preferably) or a large deep socket as a drift, install the new oil seal. Drive it into the bore squarely and make sure that it is completely seated **(see illustration)**. Lubricate the lip of the new seal with multi-purpose grease.

7   Install the driveaxle assembly (see Chap-

ter 8). Be careful not to damage the lip of the new seal.

Speed sensor

Refer to illustration 6.10

8   The vehicle speed sensor is located on the case of the transaxle. Look for lubricant around the sensor housing to determine if an O-ring is leaking.

9   Disconnect the electrical connector from the vehicle or transmission speed sensor and remove it from the transaxle (see Chapter 6 for VSS location).

10   Remove the O-ring **(see illustration)**.

11   Install a new O-ring and reinstall the vehicle speed sensor. Tighten the hold-down bolt securely.

---

7   Automatic transaxle - removal and installation

Note: *This procedure applies to 2008 and earlier models only. On 2009 and later models, the manufacturer recommends removing*

the engine and transaxle as an assembly (see Chapter 2B).

Removal

Refer to illustrations 7.12, 7.20, 7.21a and 7.21b

1   Place protective covers on the fenders and cowl and remove the hood (see Chapter 11).

2   Relieve the fuel system pressure (see Chapter 4), and drain the transaxle fluid (see Chapter 1).

3   Disconnect the negative cable from the battery.

4   Remove the battery and the battery tray (see Chapter 5).

5   Remove the air filter housing (see Chapter 4).

6   Remove the starter (see Chapter 5).

7   Remove the fluid cooler hoses from the rigid lines at the transaxle. Be sure to position a pan below the line connections to catch any residual fluid. From the fluid cooler lines, remove the bolts and bracket securing the transmission fluid filler pipe to the cooler lines, then pull the filler tube from the transmission case.

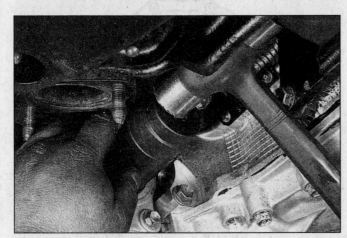

6.6 Drive in the new driveaxle seal with a large socket or a special seal installer

6.10 Remove the O-ring from the speed sensor

7.12 Support the engine with an engine support fixture (these are available at most tool rental yards and some auto parts stores)

7.20 Remove the torque converter-to-driveplate bolts - rotate the engine by hand to gain access to successive bolts - also seen clearly here are the lower transaxle-to-engine bolts

8   Disconnect the transmission range sensor electrical connector (see Section 4).

9   Disconnect the vehicle speed sensor (VSS) electrical connector.

10   Clearly label, then disconnect all vacuum lines, hoses, wiring harness connectors and ground straps. Masking tape and/or a touch-up paint applicator works well for marking items. Take instant photos or sketch the locations of components and brackets.

11   Disconnect the shift cable (see Section 3) from the transaxle.

12   Loosen but do NOT remove the front wheel lug nuts. Also loosen the driveaxle/hub nuts (see Chapter 8). Secure the engine using an engine support fixture that is installed above the engine compartment **(see illustration)**. If an engine support fixture is not available, install an engine lift and a lifting chain assembly. This will keep the engine stable during the transaxle removal procedure. Raise the vehicle and support it securely on jackstands, then remove the front wheels.

Warning: *Be sure the engine/transaxle is securely supported by the support fixture or hoist. If it is not securely supported, it could fall during the removal procedure, causing injury or death.*

13   Detach the exhaust pipe from the manifold (see Chapter 4). Remove the floor pan brace under the car and drop the exhaust system out of the way.

14   Remove the under-vehicle splash shields.

15   Disconnect the two power steering fluid lines from the steering gear. Also separate the tie-rod ends from the steering knuckles (see Chapter 10).

16   Disconnect the stabilizer bar from the links (see Chapter 10).

Remove the stabilizer bar bracket bolts (see Chapter 10).

17   Remove the mounting bolts from the engine/transaxle mounts to the subframe. Refer to Chapter 2A for engine and transaxle mount replacement procedures.

18   Remove the subframe mounting bolts from the chassis, using a floor jack to lower the subframe **(see illustration 5.22 in Chapter 7, Part A)**. Be sure to note exactly the size and location of each nut and bolt to insure correct reassembly. **Note:** *The transaxle should be supported by a floor jack immediately after the subframe is removed from the vehicle. The transaxle will tilt slightly but should remain steady if the engine is properly secured with the engine compartment brace.*

19   Support the transaxle with an approved transaxle jack and safety chains. Floor jacks are often not stable enough to support and lower the transaxle from the vehicle.

20   Remove the access cover in the bellhousing and rotate the engine until all of the six converter-to-driveplate bolts can be removed **(see illustration)**. Have an assistant keep the engine from turning by using a socket and breaker bar on the crankshaft pulley bolt.

21   Remove the transaxle-to-engine bolts **(see illustrations)**.

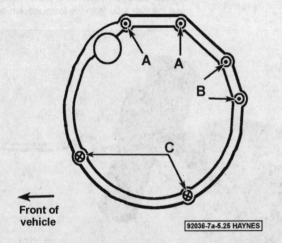

Front of vehicle

92036-7a-5.25 HAYNES

7.21a Transaxle-to-engine mounting bolts (2008 and earlier models)

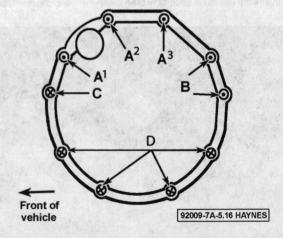

Front of vehicle

92009-7A-5.16 HAYNES

7.21b Transaxle-to-engine mounting bolts (2009 and later models)

22   Recheck to be sure nothing is connecting the engine to the vehicle or to the transaxle. Disconnect and label anything still remaining.

23   Slowly lower the transaxle assembly out of the vehicle. Keep the transaxle level as you're separating it from the engine to prevent damage to the input shaft. **Caution:** *Do not allow the transaxle to tilt forward very much (toward the engine) or the converter may slide out.* **Warning:** *Do not place any part of your body under the transaxle assembly when it's being removed.*

24   Check the engine and transaxle mounts and the transaxle shock absorber. If any of these components are worn or damaged, replace them.

Installation

25   If removed, install the torque converter on the transaxle input shaft. Make sure the converter hub splines are properly engaged with the splines on the transaxle input shaft.

26   With the transaxle secured to the jack as on removal, and with an assistant holding the torque converter in place, raise the transaxle into position and turn the converter to align the bolt holes in the converter with the bolt holes in the driveplate. Install the converter-to-driveplate bolts, starting with the green bolt. **Note:** *Install all of the bolts before tightening any of them.* Do not use excessive force to install the transaxle - if something binds and

the transaxle won't mate with the engine, alter the angle of the transaxle slightly until it does mate.

27   Install the transaxle-to-engine bolts. Tighten the bolts to the torque listed in this Chapter's Specifications **(see illustration 7.21a or 7.21b)**. **Caution:** *Do NOT use transaxle-to-engine bolts to force the engine and transaxle into alignment. Doing so could crack or damage major components. If you experience difficulties, have an assistant help you line up the dowel pins on the block with the transaxle. Some wiggling of the engine and/or the transaxle will probably be necessary to secure proper alignment of the two.*

28   Install the right engine mount, the front engine mount, the left transaxle mount and the rear engine mount. Tighten all mounting bolts and nuts securely.

29   Reinstall the remaining components in the reverse order of removal. When installing the subframe, use a rod of the same diameter as the four subframe-to-chassis bolts to align each side until that side's bolts can be inserted and started. Do not tighten any of the four bolts until all have been installed finger tight, then tighten to the Specifications in this Chapter **(see illustration 5.22 in Chapter 7, Part A)**.

30   Remove the jack and support fixture and lower the vehicle. Tighten the wheel nuts to the torque listed in the Chapter 1 Specifications.

31   Add the specified amount of new transaxle fluid (see Chapter 1).

32   Connect the negative battery cable. Road test the vehicle to check for proper transmission operation and check for leakage.

33   Recheck the fluid level. **Note:** *Since this an electronically-controlled transaxle, the manufacturer recommends that when a transaxle has been replaced, you should take the vehicle to a dealer or other service facility with a scan tool to perform a "reset memory" procedure for optimum transmission performance.*

8   Electronic control system

Trouble codes

1   The electronic control system for the transaxle has some self-diagnostic capabilities. If certain kinds of system malfunctions occur, the PCM stores the appropriate diagnostic trouble code in its memory and the CHECK ENGINE indicator light illuminates to inform the driver. The diagnostic trouble codes can only be extracted from the PCM using a scan tool that can be linked to the On Board Diagnostic (OBD II) computer via the 16-pin diagnostic link. Codes are listed below for reference (refer to Chapter 6 for additional information).

Trouble code	Code identification
P0500	Vehicle speed sensor or circuit failure
P0705	Transmission range sensor circuit malfunction
P0710	Transmission fluid temperature sensor "A" Circuit
P0711	Transmission fluid temperature sensor, range or performance fault
P0712	Transmission fluid temperature sensor "A" Circuit (low) input
P0713	Transmission fluid temperature sensor "A" Circuit (high) input
P0715	Input/turbine speed sensor circuit malfunction
P0717	Turbine speed sensor circuit No Signal
P0724	Brake switch "B" circuit High
P0741	Torque converter clutch solenoid performance malfunction
P0746	Pressure control solenoid "A" performance malfunction
P0748	Pressure control solenoid "A" electrical malfunction
P0750 - P0751	Shift solenoid "A" performance (Shift Solenoid Valve S1)
P0756	Shift solenoid "B" performance (Shift Solenoid Valve S2)
P0766	Shift solenoid "D" performance malfunction

Trouble code	Code identification
P0771	Shift solenoid "E" performance malfunction
P0776	Pressure control solenoid "B" performance malfunction
P0778	Pressure control solenoid "B" electrical malfunction
P0787	Shift/timing solenoid low (Shift Solenoid Valve ST)
P0788	Shift/timing solenoid high (Shift Solenoid Valve ST)
P0791	Intermediate shaft speed sensor "A" circuit malfunction
P0793	Intermediate shaft speed sensor "A" circuit malfunction
P0796	Pressure control solenoid "C" performance malfunction
P0798	Pressure control solenoid "C" electrical malfunction
P0850	Park/Neutral function performance
P0973	Shift solenoid "A" control circuit low (Shift Solenoid Valve S1)
P0974	Shift solenoid "A" control circuit high (Shift Solenoid Valve S1)
P0976	Shift solenoid "B" control circuit low (Shift Solenoid Valve S2)
P0977	Shift solenoid "B" control circuit high (Shift Solenoid Valve S2)
P0982	Shift solenoid "D" control circuit (low) problem
P0983	Shift solenoid "D" control circuit (high) problem
P0985	Shift solenoid "E" control circuit (low) problem
P0986	Shift solenoid "E" control circuit (high) problem
P2714	Pressure control solenoid "D" performance malfunction
P2716	Pressure control solenoid "D" electrical malfunction
P2757	Torque converter clutch pressure control solenoid performance (Shift Solenoid Valve SLU)
P2759	Torque converter clutch pressure control solenoid control circuit electrical (Shift Solenoid Valve SLU)
P2769	Torque converter clutch solenoid, circuit (low) problem
P2770	Torque converter clutch solenoid, circuit (high) problem

Other Electronic Control System checks

Preliminary checks

2   Check the fluid level and condition. If the fluid smells burned, replace it (see Chapter 1).
3   Check for fluid leaks (see Section 2).
4   Check and, if necessary, adjust the shift cable (see Section 3).
5   Check and, if necessary, adjust the transmission range sensor (see Section 5).

O/D OFF indicator light check

6   Turn the ignition switch to ON.
7   Verify that the O/D OFF indicator light comes on when the O/D main switch is in the Off (up) position, and goes out when the O/D main switch is pushed to the On position.
8   If the O/D OFF indicator light does not light up, or remains on all the time, have the circuit checked out by a dealer service department or other qualified repair shop.

Chapter 8
Clutch and driveaxles

Contents

Specifications

Clutch

Fluid type	See Chapter 1
Pedal freeplay	See Chapter 1
Driveaxle standard length	
Left driveaxle	22.2 to 22.6 inches
Right driveaxle	33.2 to 33.6 inches

Torque specifications

Ft-lbs (unless otherwise indicated)

Note: *One foot-pound (ft-lb) of torque is equivalent to 12 inch-pounds (in-lbs) of torque. Torque values below approximately 15 ft-lbs are expressed in inch-pounds, since most foot-pound torque wrenches are not accurate at these smaller values.*

Clutch master cylinder mounting nuts	108 in-lbs
Clutch pressure plate-to-flywheel bolts	168 in-lbs
Clutch release cylinder mounting bolts	108 in-lbs
Clutch release cylinder line fitting	132 in-lbs
Driveaxle/hub nut	159
Wheel lug nuts	See Chapter 1

1   General information

The information in this Chapter deals with the components from the rear of the engine to the front wheels, except for the transaxle, which is dealt with in Chapters 7A and 7B. For the purposes of this Chapter, these components are grouped into two categories: clutch and driveaxles. Separate Sections within this Chapter offer general descriptions and checking procedures for both groups.

Since nearly all the procedures covered in this Chapter involve working under the vehicle, make sure it's securely supported on sturdy jackstands or a hoist where the vehicle can be easily raised and lowered.

2   Clutch - description and check

Refer to illustration 2.1

1   All vehicles with a manual transaxle use a single dry plate, diaphragm spring type clutch **(see illustration)**. The clutch disc has a splined hub that allows it to slide along the splines of the transaxle input shaft. The clutch

and pressure plate are held in contact by spring pressure exerted by the diaphragm in the pressure plate.

2   The clutch release system is operated by hydraulic pressure. The hydraulic release system consists of the clutch pedal, a master cylinder and fluid reservoir, the hydraulic line, a slave cylinder which actuates the clutch release lever and the clutch release (or throw-out) bearing.

3   When pressure is applied to the clutch pedal to release the clutch, hydraulic pressure is exerted against the outer end of the clutch release lever. As the lever pivots, the shaft fingers push against the release bearing. The bearing pushes against the fingers of the diaphragm spring of the pressure plate assembly, which in turn releases the clutch plate.

4   Terminology can be a problem regarding the clutch components because common names have in some cases changed from that used by the manufacturer. For example, the driven plate is also called the clutch plate or disc, the pressure plate assembly is sometimes referred to as the clutch cover, the clutch release bearing is sometimes called a throw-out bearing, and the release cylinder is sometimes called the operating or slave cylinder.

5   Other than replacing components that have obvious damage, some preliminary checks should be performed to diagnose a clutch system failure.

a) *The first check should be of the fluid level in the clutch master cylinder (see Chapter 1). If the fluid level is low, add fluid as necessary and inspect the hydraulic clutch system for leaks. If the master cylinder reservoir has run dry, bleed the system (see Section 7) and retest the clutch operation.*

b) *To check "clutch spin down time," run the engine at normal idle speed with the transaxle in Neutral (clutch pedal up - engaged). Disengage the clutch (pedal down), wait several seconds and shift the transaxle into Reverse. No grinding noise should be heard. A grinding noise would most likely indicate a problem in the pressure plate or the clutch disc.*

c) *To check for complete clutch release, run the engine (with the parking brake applied to prevent movement) and hold the clutch pedal approximately 1/2-inch from the floor. Shift the transaxle between 1st gear and Reverse several times. If the shift is not smooth, component failure is indicated. Check the release cylinder pushrod travel. With the clutch pedal depressed completely the release cylinder pushrod should extend substantially. If it doesn't, check the fluid level in the clutch master cylinder.*

d) *Visually inspect the clutch pedal bushing at the top of the clutch pedal to make sure there is no sticking or excessive wear.*

e) *Under the vehicle, check that the clutch release lever is solidly mounted on the ball stud.*

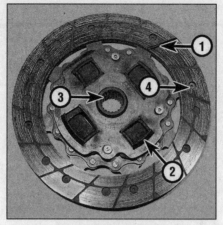

2.1 Typical clutch disc

1   *Lining* - this will wear down in use
2   *Springs or dampers* - check for cracking and deformation
3   *Splined hub* - the splines must not be worn and should slide smoothly on the transaxle input shaft splines
4   *Rivets* - these secure the lining and will damage the flywheel or pressure plate if allowed to contact the surfaces

3   Clutch components - removal, inspection and installation

Warning: *Dust produced by clutch wear and deposited on clutch components is hazardous to your health. DO NOT blow it out with compressed air and DO NOT inhale it. DO NOT use gasoline or petroleum based solvents to remove the dust. Brake system cleaner should be used to flush the dust into a drain pan. After the clutch components are wiped clean with a rag, dispose of the contaminated rags and cleaner in a labeled, covered container.*

Removal

Refer to illustration 3.6

1   Access to the clutch components is normally accomplished by removing the transaxle, leaving the engine in the vehicle. If, of course, the engine is being removed for major overhaul, then the opportunity should always be taken to check the clutch for wear and replace worn components as necessary. However, the relatively low cost of the clutch components compared to the time and labor involved in gaining access to them warrants their replacement any time the engine or transaxle is removed, unless they are new or in near-perfect condition. The following procedures assume that the engine will stay in place.

2   Remove the release cylinder (see Section 6). Hang it out of the way with a piece of wire - it isn't necessary to disconnect the hose.

3   Remove the transaxle from the vehicle (see Chapter 7A). Support the engine while the transaxle is out. Preferably, an engine

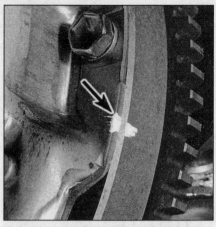

3.6 Mark the relationship of the pressure plate to the flywheel (in case you're going to reuse the same pressure plate)

hoist or support fixture should be used to support it from above. However, if a jack is used underneath the engine, make sure a piece of wood is used between the jack and oil pan to spread the load. **Caution:** *The pick-up for the oil pump is very close to the bottom of the oil pan. If the pan is bent or distorted in any way, engine oil starvation could occur.*

4   The release fork and release bearing can remain attached to the transaxle for the time being.

5   To support the clutch disc during removal, install a clutch alignment tool through the clutch disc hub.

6   Carefully inspect the flywheel and pressure plate for indexing marks. The marks are usually an X, an O or a white letter. If they cannot be found, scribe marks yourself so the pressure plate and the flywheel will be in the same alignment during installation **(see illustration).**

7   Slowly loosen the pressure plate-to-flywheel bolts. Work in a diagonal pattern and loosen each bolt a little at a time until all spring pressure is relieved. Then hold the pressure plate securely and completely remove the bolts, followed by the pressure plate and clutch disc.

Inspection

Refer to illustrations 3.10, 3.12a and 3.12b

8   Ordinarily, when a problem occurs in the clutch, it can be attributed to wear of the clutch driven plate assembly (clutch disc). However, all components should be inspected at this time.

9   Inspect the flywheel for cracks, heat checking, score marks and other damage. If the imperfections are slight, a machine shop can resurface it to make it flat and smooth. Refer to Chapter 2 for the flywheel removal procedure.

10   Inspect the lining on the clutch disc. There should be at least 1/32-inch of lining above the rivet heads **(see illustration 2.1).** Check for loose rivets, distortion, cracks, broken springs and other obvious damage **(see**

3.10 Examine the clutch disc for evidence of excessive wear, such as smeared friction material, loose rivets, worn hub splines and distorted damper cushions or springs

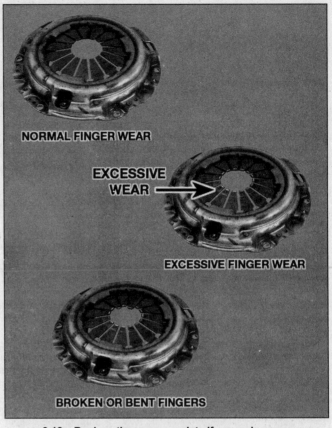

NORMAL FINGER WEAR

EXCESSIVE WEAR

EXCESSIVE FINGER WEAR

BROKEN OR BENT FINGERS

3.12a Replace the pressure plate if excessive wear or damage are noted

3.12b Examine the pressure plate friction surface for score marks, cracks and evidence of overheating (blue spots)

3.14 Center the clutch disc in the pressure plate with a clutch alignment tool

illustration). As mentioned above, ordinarily the clutch disc is replaced as a matter of course, so if in doubt about the condition, replace it with a new one.

11   The release bearing should be replaced along with the clutch disc (see Section 4).

12   Check the machined surface and the diaphragm spring fingers of the pressure plate **(see illustrations)**. If the surface is grooved or otherwise damaged, replace the pressure plate assembly. Also check for obvious damage, distortion, cracking, etc. Light glazing can be removed with emery cloth or sandpaper. If a new pressure plate is indicated, new or factory rebuilt units are available.

Installation

Refer to illustration 3.14

13   Before installation, carefully wipe the flywheel and pressure plate machined surfaces clean. It's important that no oil or grease is on these surfaces or the lining of the clutch disc. Handle these parts only with clean hands.

14   Position the clutch disc and pressure plate with the clutch held in place with an alignment tool **(see illustration)**. Make sure it's installed properly (most replacement clutch plates will be marked "flywheel side" or something similar - if not marked, install the clutch disc with the damper springs or cushion toward the transaxle).

15   Tighten the pressure plate-to-flywheel bolts only finger tight, working around the pressure plate.

16   Center the clutch disc by ensuring the alignment tool is through the splined hub and into the recess in the crankshaft. Wiggle the tool up, down or side-to-side as needed to bottom the tool. Tighten the pressure plate-to-flywheel bolts a little at a time, working in a criss-cross pattern to prevent distortion of the cover. After all of the bolts are snug, tighten them to the torque listed in this Chapter's Specifications. Remove the alignment tool.

17   Using high-temperature grease, lubricate the inner groove of the release bearing (see Section 4). Also place grease on the release lever contact areas and the transaxle input-shaft bearing retainer.

18   Install the clutch release bearing (see Section 4).

19   Install the transaxle, release cylinder and all components removed previously, tightening all fasteners to the proper torque specifications.

4.4 To check the operation of the bearing, hold it by the outer race and rotate the inner race while applying pressure - the bearing should turn smoothly - if it doesn't, replace it

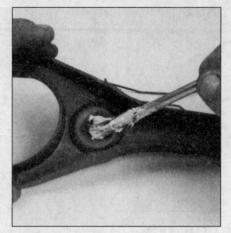

4.6a Using high temperature grease, lubricate the ball stud socket in the back of the release lever . . .

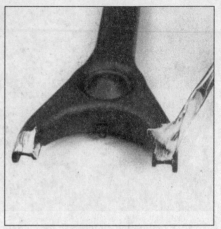

4.6b . . . the lever ends and the depression for the cylinder pushrod

4 Clutch release bearing and lever - removal, inspection and installation

Warning: *Dust produced by clutch wear and deposited on clutch components is hazardous to your health. DO NOT blow it out with compressed air and DO NOT inhale it. DO NOT use gasoline or petroleum-based solvents to remove the dust. Brake system cleaner should be used to flush it into a drain pan. After the clutch components are wiped clean with a rag, dispose of the contaminated rags and cleaner in a labeled, covered container.*

Removal

1   Disconnect the negative cable from the battery.
2   Remove the transaxle (see Chapter 7).
3   Remove the clutch release lever from the ball stud by pulling on the retention spring, then remove the bearing and the lever.

Inspection

Refer to illustration 4.4

4   Hold the bearing by the outer race and rotate the inner race while applying pressure **(see illustration)**. If the bearing doesn't turn smoothly or if it's noisy, replace the bearing/ hub assembly with a new one. Wipe the bearing with a clean rag and inspect it for damage, wear and cracks. Don't immerse the bearing in solvent - it's sealed for life and to do so would ruin it. Also check the release lever for cracks and bends.

Installation

Refer to illustrations 4.6a and 4.6b

5   Fill the inner groove of the release bearing with high-temperature grease. Also apply a light coat of the same grease to the transaxle input shaft splines and the front bearing retainer.

6   Lubricate the release lever ball socket, lever ends and release cylinder pushrod socket with high-temperature grease **(see illustrations)**.
7   Attach the release bearing to the release lever. On models that use a retaining clip, make sure it engages properly with the lever.
8   Slide the release bearing onto the transaxle input shaft front bearing retainer while passing the end of the release lever through the opening in the clutch housing. Push the clutch release lever onto the ball stud until it's firmly seated.
9   Apply a light coat of high-temperature grease to the face of the release bearing where it contacts the pressure plate diaphragm fingers.
10   The remainder of installation is the reverse of the removal procedure.

5 Clutch master cylinder - removal and installation

Removal

Refer to illustration 5.2

1   Disconnect the negative cable from the battery.
2   Remove the driver's side knee bolster (see Chapter 11). Under the dashboard, disconnect the pushrod from the top of the clutch pedal. It's held in place with a clevis pin. To remove the clevis pin, remove the clip **(see illustration)**.
3   On 2008 and earlier models, remove the brake master cylinder and the power brake booster (see Chapter 9).
4   Disconnect the hydraulic line at the clutch master cylinder. If available, use a flarenut wrench on the fitting, to protect the fitting from being rounded off. Have rags handy as some fluid will be lost as the line is removed.
Caution: *Don't allow brake fluid to come into contact with paint, as it will damage the finish.*
5   From under the dash, remove the nuts which attach the master cylinder to the

firewall. Remove the master cylinder, again being careful not to spill any of the fluid.

Installation

6   Position the master cylinder on the firewall, installing the mounting nuts fingertight.
7   Connect the hydraulic line to the master cylinder, moving the cylinder slightly as necessary to thread the fitting properly into the bore. Don't cross-thread the fitting as it's installed.
8   Tighten the mounting nuts and the hydraulic line fitting securely.
9   Connect the pushrod to the clutch pedal.
10   Install the power brake booster and master cylinder (see Chapter 9). Connect the clutch fluid feed line to the brake fluid reservoir.
11   Fill the brake fluid reservoir with the proper brake fluid (see Chapter 1) and bleed the clutch system (see Section 7) and the brake system (see Chapter 9).
12   Check the clutch pedal height and freeplay (see Chapter 1).

5.2 To release the clutch pushrod from the clutch pedal, remove this clip and the clevis pin

6 Clutch release cylinder - removal and installation

Removal

Refer to illustration 6.3

1   Disconnect the negative cable from the battery.
2   Raise the vehicle and support it securely on jackstands.
3   Disconnect the hydraulic line at the release cylinder. If available, use a flare-nut wrench on the fitting, which will prevent the fitting from being rounded off **(see illustration)**. Have a small can and rags handy, as some fluid will be spilled as the line is removed.
4   Remove the release cylinder mounting bolts.
5   Remove the release cylinder.

Installation

6   Install the release cylinder on the clutch housing. Make sure the pushrod is seated in the release fork pocket.
7   Connect the hydraulic line to the release cylinder. Tighten the connection securely.
8   Fill the brake master cylinder with the proper brake fluid (see Chapter 1).
9   Bleed the system (see Section 7).
10 Lower the vehicle and connect the negative battery cable.

7 Clutch hydraulic system - bleeding

1   The hydraulic system should be bled of all air whenever any part of the system has been removed or if the fluid level has been allowed to fall so low that air has been drawn into the master cylinder. The procedure is similar to bleeding a brake system.
2   Fill the brake master cylinder with new brake fluid of the proper type (see Chapter 1). **Caution:** *Do not re-use any of the fluid coming from the system during the bleeding operation or use fluid which has been inside an open container for an extended period of time.*
3   Raise the vehicle and place it securely on jackstands to gain access to the release cylinder, which is located on the left side of the clutch housing.
4   Locate the bleeder valve on the clutch release cylinder (right above the fitting for the hydraulic fluid line). Remove the dust cap that fits over the bleeder valve and push a length of clear tubing over the valve. Place the other end of the hose into a clear container with about two inches of brake fluid in it. The hose end must be submerged in the fluid.
5   Have an assistant depress the clutch pedal and hold it. Open the bleeder valve on the release cylinder, allowing fluid to flow through the hose. Close the bleeder valve when fluid stops flowing from the hose. Once closed, have your assistant release the pedal.

6.3 Use a flare-nut wrench when disconnecting the hydraulic line fitting (left) to prevent rounding off the corners of the tubing nut, then remove the mounting bolts (typical installation)

6   Continue this process until all air is evacuated from the system, indicated by a full, solid stream of fluid being ejected from the bleeder valve each time and no air bubbles in the hose or container. Keep a close watch on the fluid level inside the clutch master cylinder reservoir; if the level drops too low, air will be sucked back into the system and the process will have to be started all over again.
7   Install the dust cap and lower the vehicle. Check carefully for proper operation before placing the vehicle in normal service.

8 Clutch start switch - check and replacement

1   Check the pedal height, pedal freeplay and pushrod play (see Chapter 1).
2   Verify that the engine will not start when the clutch pedal is released.
3   Verify that the engine will start when the clutch pedal is depressed all the way.
4   The clutch start switch is located on a bracket forward of the clutch pedal (under the dash).
5   If the switch fails either of the tests, replace it. This is accomplished by removing the nut nearest the plunger end of the switch and unscrewing the switch. Disconnect the wire harness. Installation is the reverse of removal.
6   To adjust the clutch start switch, depress the clutch pedal completely and turn the switch in or out to achieve the spacing of the original switch.
7   Verify that the switch operates properly by performing Steps 2 and 3 again.

9 Driveaxles - general information and inspection

1   Power is transmitted from the transaxle to the wheels through a pair of driveaxles. The inner end of each driveaxle is splined into the differential side gears. The outer ends of the driveaxles are splined to the axle hubs and locked in place by a large nut.

2   The inner ends of the driveaxles are equipped with sliding constant velocity joints, which are capable of both angular and axial motion. Each inner joint assembly consists of a tripod bearing and a joint housing (outer race) in which the joint is free to slide in and out as the driveaxle moves up and down with the wheel. The joints can be disassembled and cleaned in the event of a boot failure (see Section 11), but if any parts are damaged, the joints must be replaced as a unit. When buying parts for a driveaxle, or a complete replacement driveaxle assembly, make sure you get the right components. Some Corollas may have Toyota-made axles, and some may have axles from other suppliers to Toyota.
3   The outer CV joints consist of ball bearings running between an inner race and an outer cage, and are capable of angular but not axial movement. The outer joints should be cleaned, inspected and repacked, but they cannot be disassembled. If an outer joint is damaged, it must be replaced along with the axleshaft (the outer joint and axleshaft are sold as a single component).
4   The boots should be inspected periodically for damage and leaking lubricant. Torn CV joint boots must be replaced immediately or the joints can be damaged. Boot replacement involves removal of the driveaxle (see Section 10). **Note:** *Some auto parts stores carry split-type replacement boots, which can be installed without removing the driveaxle from the vehicle. This is a convenient alternative; however, the driveaxle should be removed and the CV joint disassembled and cleaned to ensure the joint is free from contaminants such as moisture and dirt which will accelerate CV joint wear.* The most common symptom of worn or damaged CV joints, besides lubricant leaks, is a clicking noise in turns, a clunk when accelerating after coasting and vibration at highway speeds. To check for wear in the CV joints and driveaxle shafts, grasp each axle (one at a time) and rotate it in both directions while holding the CV joint housings, feeling for play indicating worn splines or sloppy CV joints. Also check the driveaxle shafts for cracks, dents and distortion.

10   Driveaxle - removal and installation

Caution: *The manufacturer states that a new driveaxle/hub nut must be installed whenever it is removed.*

Removal

Refer to illustrations 10.4, 10.5, 10.6, 10.9 and 10.10

1   Disconnect the cable from the negative terminal of the battery.
2   Set the parking brake.
3   Loosen the front wheel lug nuts, raise the vehicle and support it securely on jackstands. Remove the wheel.
4   Unstake the driveaxle/hub nut **(see illustration)**.
5   Remove the driveaxle/hub nut. To prevent the hub from turning, wedge a prybar between two of the wheel studs and allow the prybar to rest against the ground or the floor pan of the vehicle **(see illustration)**.
6   To loosen the driveaxle from the hub splines, tap the end of the driveaxle with a soft-faced hammer or a hammer and a brass punch **(see illustration)**. **Note:** *Don't attempt to push the end of the driveaxle through the hub yet. Applying force to the end of the driveaxle, beyond just breaking it loose from the hub, can damage the driveaxle or transaxle.* If the driveaxle is stuck in the hub splines and won't move, it may be necessary to remove the brake disc (see Chapter 9) and push it from the hub with a two-jaw puller after Step 8 is performed.
7   Remove the engine splash shields (see Chapter 1). Place a drain pan underneath the transaxle to catch any lubricant that may spill out when the driveaxle is removed.
8   Remove the nuts and bolt securing the balljoint to the control arm, then pry the control arm down to separate the components (see Chapter 10).

10.4 Using a hammer and punch, unstake the driveaxle/hub nut

10.5 Use a large prybar to immobilize the hub while loosening the driveaxle/hub nut

10.6 Using a brass punch, strike the end of the driveaxle sharply with a hammer; when it breaks free, it will move noticeably

9   Pull out on the steering knuckle and detach the driveaxle from the hub **(see illustration)**. Don't let the driveaxle hang by the inner CV joint after the outer end has been detached from the steering knuckle, as the inner joint could become damaged. Support the outer end of the driveaxle with a piece of wire, if necessary.
10   Carefully pry the inner CV joint out of the transaxle **(see illustration)**.
11   If necessary, refer to Chapter 7 for the driveaxle oil seal replacement procedure.

10.9 Pull the steering knuckle out and slide the end of the driveaxle out of the hub

10.10 To separate the inner end of the driveaxle from the transaxle, pry on the CV joint housing like this with a large screwdriver or prybar - you may need to give the prybar a sharp rap with a brass hammer

11.3 Lift the tabs on all the boot clamps with a screwdriver, then open the clamps

11.4 Remove the boot from the inner CV joint and slide the joint housing from the tripod

Installation

12   Installation is the reverse of the removal procedure, but with the following additional points:

a) *Push the driveaxle sharply in to seat the retaining ring on the inner CV joint in the groove in the differential side gear.*

b) *Tighten the **new** driveaxle/hub nut to the torque listed in this Chapter's Specifications, then stake the collar of the nut into the groove in the driveaxle.*

c) *Tighten the lug nuts to the torque listed in the Chapter 1 Specifications.*

d) *Check the transaxle lubricant and add, if necessary, to bring it to the proper level (see Chapter 1).*

11   Driveaxle boot replacement

Note: *If the CV joint boots must be replaced, explore all options before beginning the job. Complete rebuilt driveaxles are available on an exchange basis, which eliminates much time and work. Whichever route you choose to take, check on the cost and availability of parts before disassembling the vehicle.*

1   Remove the driveaxle (see Section 10).

Disassembly

Refer to illustrations 11.3, 11.4 and 11.6

2   Mount the driveaxle in a vise with wood lined jaws (to prevent damage to the axleshaft). Check the CV joint for excessive play in the radial direction, which indicates worn parts. Check for smooth operation throughout the full range of motion for each CV joint. If a boot is torn, disassemble the joint, clean the components and inspect for damage due to loss of lubrication and possible contamination by foreign matter.

3   Using a small screwdriver, pry the retaining tabs on the clamps up to loosen them and slide them off **(see illustration)**.

4   Using a screwdriver, carefully pry up on the edge of the outer boot and push it away from the CV joint. Old and worn boots can be cut off. Pull the inner CV joint boot back from the housing and slide the housing from the tripod **(see illustration)**.

5   Mark the tripod and axleshaft to ensure that they are reassembled properly.

6   Remove the tripod joint snap-ring with a pair of snap-ring pliers **(see illustration)**.

7   Remove the tripod joint from the driveaxle, then remove the inner stop-ring from its groove on the shaft.

8   If you haven't already cut them off, remove both boots. If you're working on a right-side driveaxle, you'll also have to cut off the clamp for the dynamic damper and slide the damper off. **Note:** *Before removing the damper, measure its distance from the end of the driveaxle - when reassembling, it must be returned to the same spot.*

Check

9   Thoroughly clean all components, including the outer CV joint assembly, with solvent until the old CV joint grease is completely removed. Inspect the bearing surfaces of the inner tripods and housings for cracks, pitting, scoring and other signs of wear. It's very difficult to inspect the bearing surfaces of the inner and outer races of the outer CV joint, but you can at least check the surfaces of the ball bearings themselves. If they're in good shape, the races probably are too; if they're not, neither are the races. If the inner CV joint is worn, you can buy a new inner CV joint and install it on the old axleshaft; if the outer CV joint is worn, you'll have to purchase a new outer CV joint *and* axleshaft (they're sold pre-assembled).

Reassembly

Refer to illustrations 11.10a, 11.10b, 11.10c, 11.12a and 11.12b

10   Wrap the splines on the end the axleshaft with electrical tape to protect the boots from the sharp edges of the splines **(see illustration)**. Slide the clamps and boot(s) onto the axleshaft, then place the inner stop-ring and the tripod on the shaft, aligning the marks

11.6 Remove the snap-ring with a pair of snap-ring pliers

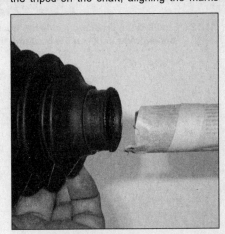

11.10a Wrap the splined area of the axleshaft with tape to prevent damage to the boots when removing or installing them

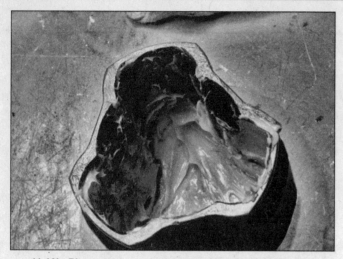

11.10b Place grease at the bottom of the CV joint housing

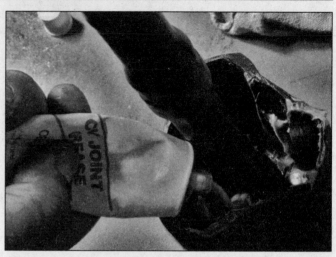

11.10c Install the boot and clamps onto the axleshaft, then insert the tripod into the housing, followed by the rest of the grease

made before removal. **Note:** *If you removed the dynamic damper, be sure to install it in its original location and secure it with a new clamp before installing the inner boot.* Pack the CV joint(s) with CV joint grease, and also apply some to the inside of the boot(s).

Insert the tripod into the housing and pack the remainder of the grease around the tripod **(see illustrations)**. **Caution:** *Use CV joint grease only.*

11   Slide the boot into place, making sure both ends seat in their grooves. When install-

ing the inner boot, position the CV joint mid-way through its travel, then proceed to the next Step.

12   Equalize the pressure in the boot, then tighten and secure the boot clamps **(see illustrations)**.

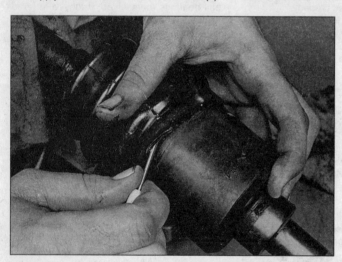

11.12a Equalize the pressure inside the boot by inserting a small screwdriver between the boot and the outer race

11.12b You'll need a special boot clamp installation tool like this one to tighten the new clamps; follow the instructions provided by the tool manufacturer

Notes

Notes

Chapter 9   Brakes

Contents

Specifications

General
Brake fluid type	See Chapter 1
Brake pedal height	
Manual transmission models	5-5/16 to 5-45/64 inches
Automatic transmission models	5-11/32 to 5-3/4 inches
Brake pedal freeplay	3/64 to 1/4 inch
Power brake booster pushrod-to-master cylinder piston clearance	0.0 inch
Brake light switch plunger protrusion (from threaded portion of switch)	1/32 to 3/32 inch

Disc brakes
Minimum brake pad thickness	See Chapter 1
Front disc thickness	
Standard	0.984 inch
Minimum*	0.906 inch
Rear disc thickness	
Standard	0.354 inch
Minimum	0.295 inch
Disc runout limit	
Front	0.002 inch
Rear	0.006 inch
Parking brake shoe minimum thickness	1/32 inch

Drum brakes
Brake shoe minimum lining thickness	See Chapter 1
Drum inside diameter	
Standard	7.874 inches
Maximum*	7.913 inches

* Note: *If different specifications are cast into the disc or drum, they supersede information printed here.*

Torque specifications
Ft-lbs (unless otherwise indicated)

Note: *One foot-pound (ft-lb) of torque is equivalent to 12 inch-pounds (in-lbs) of torque. Torque values below approximately 15 ft-lbs are expressed in inch-pounds, since most foot-pound torque wrenches are not accurate at these smaller values.*

Caliper mounting bolts	
Front	25
Rear	26
Caliper torque plate bolts	
Front	79
Rear	46
Brake hose-to-caliper banjo bolt	21
Wheel cylinder mounting bolt	87 in-lbs
Master cylinder-to-brake booster nuts	108 in-lbs
Power brake booster mounting nuts	108 in-lbs
Wheel lug nuts	See Chapter 1

1   General information

The vehicles covered by this manual are equipped with hydraulically operated front and rear brake systems. The front brakes are disc type and the rear brakes are drum type. Both the front and rear brakes are self-adjusting. The disc brakes automatically compensate for pad wear, while the drum brakes incorporate an adjustment mechanism that is activated as the parking brake is applied.

Hydraulic system

The hydraulic system consists of two separate circuits. The master cylinder has separate reservoirs for the two circuits, and, in the event of a leak or failure in one hydraulic circuit, the other circuit will remain operative. A dual proportioning valve on the firewall provides brake balance between the front and rear brakes.

Power brake booster

The power brake booster, utilizing engine manifold vacuum and atmospheric pressure to provide assistance to the hydraulically operated brakes, is mounted on the firewall in the engine compartment.

Parking brake

The parking brake lever operates the rear brakes only, through cable actuation. It's mounted in the center console.

Service

After completing any operation involving disassembly of any part of the brake system, always test-drive the vehicle to check for proper braking performance before resuming normal driving. When testing the brakes, perform the tests on a clean, dry, flat surface. Conditions other than these can lead to inaccurate test results.

Test the brakes at various speeds with both light and heavy pedal pressure. The vehicle should stop evenly without pulling to one side or the other. Avoid locking the brakes, because this slides the tires and diminishes braking efficiency and control of the vehicle.

Tires, vehicle load and wheel alignment are factors which also affect braking performance.

2   Anti-lock Brake System (ABS) - general information

1   The Anti-lock Brake System (ABS) is designed to maintain vehicle steerabilty, directional stability and optimum deceleration under severe braking conditions and on most road surfaces. It does so by monitoring the rotational speed of each wheel and controlling the brake line pressure to each wheel during braking. This prevents the wheel from locking up.

The ABS system is primarily designed to prevent wheel lockup during heavy braking, but the information provided by the wheel speed sensors of the ABS system is shared with an optional system that uses the data to control vehicle handling. EBD (Electronic Brakeforce Distribution), varies the front-to-rear and side-to-side braking balance under different vehicle loads.

Components
Actuator assembly

2   The actuator assembly is mounted in the right front corner of the engine compartment (behind the headlight housing), and consists of the master cylinder, an electric hydraulic pump and four solenoid valves. **Note:** *The actuator assembly for ABS brakes and ABS-with EBD are similar, but the configuration of actuator and ECU differ.*

a) *The electric pump provides hydraulic pressure to charge the reservoirs in the actuator, which supplies pressure to the braking system. The pump and reservoirs are housed in the actuator assembly.*

b) *The solenoid valves modulate brake line pressure during ABS operation. The body contains four valves - one for each wheel.*

Speed sensors

3   These sensors are located at each wheel and generate small electrical pulsations when the toothed sensor rings are turning, sending a signal to the electronic controller indicating wheel rotational speed.

4   The front speed sensors are mounted to the front steering knuckle in close relationship to the toothed sensor rings, which are integral with the front driveaxle outer CV joints.

5   The rear wheel sensors are bolted to the axle carriers. The sensor rings are integral with the rear hub assemblies.

ABS computer

6   The ABS computer is mounted with the actuator and is the "brain" for the ABS system. The function of the computer is to accept and process information received from the wheel speed sensors to control the hydraulic line pressure, avoiding wheel lock up. The computer also constantly monitors the system, even under normal driving conditions, to find faults within the system.

Diagnosis and repair

7   If a problem develops within the system, an "ABS" light will glow on the dashboard. If the dashboard warning light comes on and stays on while the vehicle is in operation, the ABS system requires attention. Here are few simple checks you can perform:

a) *Check the brake fluid level in the master cylinder reservoir.*

b) *Check that all electrical connectors are securely connected.*

c) *Check all the applicable fuses.*

If the above preliminary checks do not rectify the problem, the vehicle should be diagnosed and repaired by a dealer service department or other qualified repair shop.

3.5 Before removing the front caliper, be sure to depress the piston into its bore in the caliper with a large C-clamp to make room for the new pads

3   Disc brake pads - replacement

Warning: *Disc brake pads must be replaced on both front wheels at the same time - never replace the pads on only one wheel. Also, the dust created by the brake system is harmful to your health. Never blow it out with compressed air and don't inhale any of it. An approved filtering mask should be worn when working on the brakes. Do not, under any circumstances, use petroleum-based solvents to clean brake parts. Use brake system cleaner only!*
Note: *The manufacturer recommends replacing the pad shims and wear-indicators whenever the pads are replaced.*

1   Remove the cap from the brake fluid reservoir.

2   Loosen the wheel lug nuts, raise the front or rear of the vehicle and support it securely on jackstands. Block the wheels at the opposite end.

3   Remove the wheels. Work on one brake assembly at a time, using the assembled brake for reference if necessary.

4   Inspect the brake disc carefully as outlined in Section 5. If machining is necessary, follow the information in that Section to remove the disc, at which time the pads can be removed as well.

Front brake pads

Refer to illustrations 3.5 and 3.6a through 3.6r

5   Push the piston back into its bore to provide room for the new brake pads. A C-clamp can be used to accomplish this **(see illustration)**. As the piston is depressed to the bottom of the caliper bore, the fluid in the master cylinder will rise. Make sure that it doesn't overflow. If necessary, siphon off some of the fluid.

6   Follow the accompanying photos, beginning with **illustration 3.6a**. Be sure to stay in order and read the caption under each illustration, then proceed to Step 12.

3.6a Always wash the brakes with brake cleaner before disassembling anything

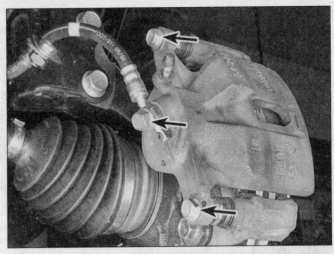

3.6b To remove the caliper, remove the bolts indicated by the upper and lower arrows (the center arrow points to the brake hose banjo bolt, which shouldn't be unscrewed unless the caliper is being completely removed from the vehicle)

3.6c Remove the caliper . . .

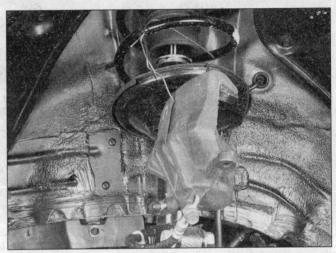

3.6d . . . and hang it from the strut coil spring with a piece of wire; do not allow the caliper to hang by the flexible brake hose

3.6e Remove the outer shim . . .

3.6f . . . and the inner shim from the outer brake pad

3.6g Remove the outer brake pad

3.6h Remove the outer shim . . .

3.6i . . . and the inner shim from the inner brake pad

3.6j Remove the inner brake pad

3.6k Remove the upper and lower pad support plates; inspect them for damage and replace as necessary (the supports should "snap" into place in the torque plate; if they're weak or distorted, they should be replaced)

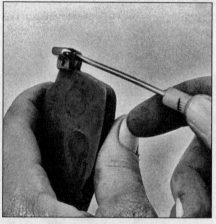

3.6l If equipped, pry the wear indicator off the old inner brake pad and transfer it to the new inner pad (if the wear indicator is worn or bent, replace it)

3.6m Install the upper and lower pad support plates, the new inner brake pad and the shims; make sure the ears on the pad are properly engaged with the pad support plate as shown

Rear brake pads

Refer to illustration 3.9

7   Wash the caliper and disc with brake sys-tem cleaner **(see illustration 3.6a)**. Remove the caliper mounting bolts, then lift off the cali-per. Support the caliper with a length of wire - don't let it hang by the brake hose **(see illus-**tration 3.6d).

8   Follow **illustrations 3.6e through 3.6r** to replace the pads.

9   Using a caliper piston retracting tool (or

3.6n Install the outer pad and the shims, engaging the pad with the support plates

3.6o Pull out the upper and lower sliding pins and clean them off (if either rubber boot is damaged, remove it by levering the flange of the metal bushing that retains the boot) . . .

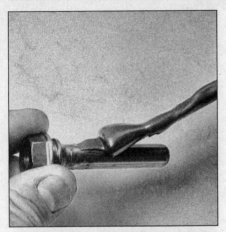

3.6p . . . apply a coat of high-temperature grease to the pins and install them

3.6q Install the caliper and tighten the caliper bolts to the torque listed in this Chapter's Specifications

3.6r If you have difficulty installing the caliper over the new pads, use a C-clamp to bottom the piston in its bore, then try again - it should now slip over the pads

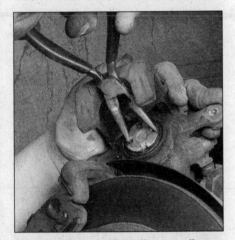

3.9 Using a pair of needle-nose pliers, turn the piston to retract it into the caliper. Make sure the piston is positioned so that one of the notches in the piston face will engage with the projection on the brake pad backing plate

needle-nose pliers), rotate the piston to retract it to make room for the new pads **(see illustration)**. On the left side caliper, turn the piston counterclockwise; on the right side caliper, turn the piston clockwise. Once the piston has bottomed in the bore, turn it back the other way far enough to position one of the notches in the piston face point straight up towards the center of the caliper frame (90-degrees from the centerline of the mounting bolt holes.

10   Install the caliper over the brake pads, making sure the projection on the inner pad engages with the slot in the caliper piston face.

11   Install the caliper mounting bolts and tighten them to the torque listed in this Chapter's Specifications, then proceed to the next Step.

Front or rear brake pads

12   When reinstalling the caliper, be sure to tighten the mounting bolts to the torque listed in this Chapter's Specifications. After the job has been completed, firmly depress the brake pedal a few times to bring the pads into

contact with the disc. Check the level of the brake fluid, adding some if necessary. Tighten the wheel lug nuts to the torque listed in the Chapter 1 Specifications. Check the operation of the brakes carefully before placing the vehicle into normal service.

4   Disc brake caliper - removal and installation

Warning: *Dust created by the brake system is harmful to your health. Never blow it out with compressed air and don't inhale any of it. An approved filtering mask should be worn when working on the brakes. Do not, under any circumstances, use petroleum-based solvents to clean brake parts. Use brake system cleaner only!*
Note: *Always replace the calipers in pairs - never replace just one of them.*

Removal

Refer to illustration 4.2

1   Loosen the wheel lug nuts, raise the vehicle and support it securely on jackstands. Remove the wheels.

2   Remove the brake hose banjo bolt and disconnect the hose from the caliper. Plug the hose to keep contaminants out of the brake system and to prevent losing any more brake fluid than is necessary **(see illustration)**. If you are removing the rear brake caliper, loosen the parking brake cable adjustment from inside the vehicle (see Section 12), then remove the bolt holding the parking brake cable clamp to the control arm. Detach the cable end from the lever on the caliper. **Note:** *If you're just removing the caliper for access to other components, don't disconnect the hose.*

3   Remove the caliper mounting bolts **(see illustration 3.6b).**

4   Remove the caliper. If necessary, remove the caliper torque plate from the steering knuckle **(see illustration 5.2).**

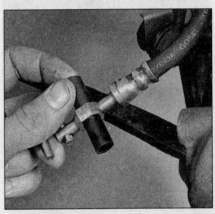

4.2 Using a piece of rubber hose of the appropriate size, plug the brake line banjo fitting to prevent brake fluid from leaking out and to prevent dirt and moisture from contaminating the fluid in the hose

Installation

5   Install the caliper by reversing the removal procedure. Remember to install new sealing washers on either side of the brake hose banjo fitting (they should be included with the rebuild kit). Tighten the caliper mounting bolts (and torque plate bolts, if removed) to the torque listed in this Chapter's Specifications.

6   If the hose was disconnected, bleed the brake system (see Section 10).

7   Install the wheels and lug nuts. Lower the vehicle and tighten the lug nuts to the torque listed in the Chapter 1 Specifications.

5   Brake disc - inspection, removal and installation

Inspection

Refer to illustrations 5.2, 5.3, 5.4a, 5.4b, 5.5a and 5.5b

1   Loosen the wheel lug nuts, raise the vehicle and support it securely on jackstands.

5.2 To remove the caliper torque plate from the steering knuckle, remove these two bolts

5.3 The brake pads on this vehicle were obviously neglected, as they wore down completely and cut deep grooves into the disc - wear this severe means the disc must be replaced

5.4a Use a dial indicator to check disc runout; if the reading exceeds the maximum allowable runout limit, the disc will have to be machined or replaced

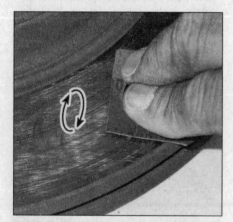

5.4b Using a swirling motion, remove the glaze from the disc surface with sandpaper or emery cloth

5.5a The minimum wear dimension is cast into the back side of the disc (typical)

5.5b Use a micrometer to measure disc thickness

Remove the wheel and install the lug nuts to hold the disc in place.

2   Remove the brake caliper as outlined in Section 4. It isn't necessary to disconnect the brake hose. After removing the caliper bolts, suspend the caliper out of the way with a piece of wire **(see illustration 3.6d)**. Remove the torque plate mounting bolts and detach the torque plate **(see illustration)**.

3   Visually inspect the disc surface for score marks and other damage. Light scratches and shallow grooves are normal after use and may not always be detrimental to brake operation, but deep scoring requires disc removal and refinishing by an automotive machine shop. Be sure to check both sides of the disc **(see illustration)**. If pulsating has been noticed during application of the brakes, suspect disc runout.

4   To check disc runout, place a dial indicator at a point about 1/2-inch from the outer edge of the disc **(see illustration)**. Set the indicator to zero and turn the disc. The indicator reading should not exceed the specified allowable runout limit. If it does, the disc should be refinished by an automotive machine shop. **Note:** *The discs should be resurfaced regardless of the dial indicator*

reading, as this will impart a smooth finish and ensure a perfectly flat surface, eliminating any brake pedal pulsation or other undesirable symptoms related to questionable discs. At the very least, if you elect not to have the discs resurfaced, remove the glaze from the surface with sandpaper or emery cloth using a swirling motion **(see illustration)**.

5   It's absolutely critical that the disc not be machined to a thickness under the specified minimum allowable refinish thickness. The minimum wear (or discard) thickness is cast into the inside of the disc **(see illustration)**. The disc thickness can be checked with a micrometer **(see illustration)**.

Removal

6   Remove the lug nuts that were put on to hold the disc in place and slide the disc from the hub.

Installation

7   Place the disc in position over the threaded studs.

8   Install the torque plate, tightening the bolts to the torque listed in this Chapter's Specifications.

9   Install the caliper, tightening the bolts to the torque listed in this Chapter's Specifications. Bleeding won't be necessary unless the brake hose was disconnected from the caliper.

10   Install the wheel and lug nuts. Lower the vehicle and tighten the lug nuts to the torque listed in the Chapter 1 Specifications. Depress the brake pedal a few times to bring the brake pads into contact with the disc. Check the operation of the brakes carefully before driving the vehicle.

6   Drum brake shoes - replacement

Refer to illustrations 6.4a through 6.4y and 6.5

Warning: *Drum brake shoes must be replaced on both wheels at the same time - never replace the shoes on only one wheel. Also, the dust created by the brake system is harmful to your health. Never blow it out with compressed air and don't inhale any of it. An approved filtering mask should be worn when working on the brakes. Do not, under any cir-*

6.4a Mark the relationship of the drum to the hub to insure that the dynamic balance is unaltered

6.4b Before removing anything, clean the brake assembly with brake cleaner and allow it to dry (position a drain pan under the brake to catch the fluid and residue); **DO NOT USE COMPRESSED AIR TO BLOW OFF BRAKE DUST!**

6.4c This is the complete rear brake assembly, refer to this photo during your disassembly/assembly procedure (NUMMI/TMMC-manufactured brake)

6.4d Unhook the return spring from the adjuster lever (**Note:** *This is a NUMMI/TMMC brake - on 2005 models with a TMC brake, the return spring is wound around the adjuster screw assembly, and the adjuster lever is on the front shoe*)

6.4e Remove the brake adjuster lever from the stud at the top of the rear shoe (**Note:** *This is a NUMMI/TMMC brake - on 2005 models with a TMC brake, the adjuster lever is on the front shoe*)

6.4f Remove the lower spring between the primary and secondary shoes

cumstances, use petroleum-based solvents to clean brake parts. Use brake system cleaner only!

Caution: *Whenever the brake shoes are replaced, the return and hold-down springs should also be replaced. Due to the continuous heating/cooling cycle the springs are subjected to, they lose tension over a period of time and may allow the shoes to drag on the drum and wear at a much faster rate than normal.*

Note: *The accompanying photo sequence illustrates a drum brake shoe replacement procedure on a NUMMI/TMMC-manufactured drum brake, which is the most common type of drum brake on the models covered by this manual. Some 2005 models are equipped with a TMC-manufactured drum brake. The differences lie in the adjuster mechanism and the upper return spring.*

1   Loosen the wheel lug nuts, raise the rear of the vehicle and support it securely on jackstands. Block the front wheels to keep the vehicle from rolling.

2   Release the parking brake.

3   Remove the wheel. **Note:** *All four rear brake shoes must be replaced at the same time, but to avoid mixing up parts, work on the brake assembly for only one side at a time.*

4   Follow the accompanying illustrations for the brake shoe replacement procedure (**see illustrations 6.4a through 6.4y**). Be sure to stay in order and read the caption under each illustration. **Note:** *If the brake drum cannot be easily removed, make sure the parking brake is completely released. If the drum still cannot be pulled off, the brake shoes will have to be retracted. This is done by first removing the plug from the backing plate. With the plug removed, push the lever off the adjuster star wheel with a narrow screwdriver while turning the adjuster wheel with another screwdriver, moving the shoes away from the drum. The drum should now come off.*

6.4g Depress the hold-down spring and turn the retainer 90-degrees, then release it; a pair of pliers will work, but a special hold-down spring removal tool makes the job easier (these inexpensive tools are available at most auto parts stores)

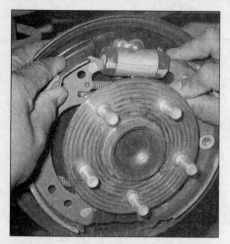

6.4h Pull the front shoe away from the adjuster mechanism and the wheel cylinder while holding the adjuster mechanism back - twist the shoe until the spring end comes free of the shoe

6.4i With the front shoe removed, disconnect the other end of the upper return spring and remove it (Note: *On 2005 models with a TMC brake, the spring comes out with the adjuster screw assembly*)

6.4j Remove the hold-down spring from the rear shoe

6.4k Remove the rear shoe and adjuster assembly from the backing plate, then use pliers to remove the clip holding the park brake lever to the stud on the rear shoe

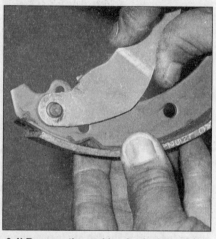

6.4l Remove the parking brake lever from the rear shoe

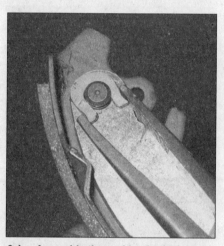

6.4m Assemble the parking brake lever to the new rear shoe and crimp the C-washer closed with a pair of pliers (always use a new C-washer)

6.4n These points of shoe contact on the backing plate should receive a small dab of high-temperature grease before installing the new shoes

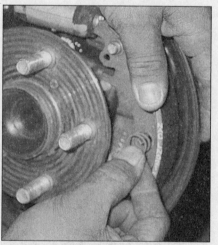

6.4o Guide the hold-down pin through while positioning the rear shoe

6.4p Secure the rear shoe with the hold-down cup/spring/ outer cup over the pin

6.4q Lubricate the moving parts of the adjuster screw with a light coat of high-temperature grease; the screw portion of the adjuster will need to be threaded in further than before to allow the drum to fit over the new shoes

6.4r Install the adjuster assembly on the rear shoe (make sure the end fits properly into the slot in the shoe

6.4s Hook the spring into the hole in the rear shoe (Note: *NUMMI/TMMC brake shown; on 2005 models with a TMC brake, the spring is installed with the adjuster and connects to the shoe from the front side)*

6.4t Hold the front end of the spring with pliers while guiding it through the front shoe (Note: *NUMMI/TMMC brake shown; on 2005 models with a TMC brake, the spring connects to the shoe from the front side)*

6.4u Align the top of the front shoe with the adjuster and the slot in the piston on the wheel cylinder

6.4v Wiggle the shoe to make sure it's seated properly against the backing plate, then secure it with the hold-down spring

6.4w Install the lever for the automatic adjuster (Note: *NUMMI/TMMC brake shown; on 2005 models with a TMC brake, the adjuster lever is on the front shoe)*

6.4x Install the upper spring and connect it to the adjuster lever (Note: *NUMMI/ TMMC brake shown; on 2005 models with a TMC brake, the adjuster lever is on the front shoe)*

6.4y Install the lower spring between the two shoes

6.5 The maximum drum diameter is cast into the inside of the rear drums (typical)

7.4 To remove the wheel cylinder, unscrew the hydraulic line-to-wheel cylinder threaded fitting (1), then remove the mounting bolt (2)

5   Before reinstalling the drum, it should be checked for cracks, score marks, deep scratches and hard spots, which will appear as small discolored areas. If the hard spots cannot be removed with fine emery cloth or if any of the other conditions listed above exist, the drum must be taken to an automotive machine shop to have it resurfaced. **Note:** *Professionals recommend resurfacing the drums each time a brake job is done. Resurfacing will eliminate the possibility of out-of-round drums. If the drums are worn so much that they can't be resurfaced without exceeding the maximum allowable diameter (stamped into the drum), then new ones will be required* **(see illustration)**. *At the very least, if you elect not to have the drums resurfaced, remove the glaze from the surface with emery cloth using a swirling motion.*
6   Install the brake drum on the axle flange.
7   Install the wheel and lug nuts, then lower the vehicle. Tighten the lug nuts to the torque listed in the Chapter 1 Specifications.
8   Make a number of forward and reverse stops and operate the parking brake to adjust the brakes until satisfactory pedal action is obtained.
9   Check the operation of the brakes carefully before driving the vehicle.

7   Wheel cylinder - removal and installation

Note: *Never replace only one wheel cylinder - always replace both of them at the same time.*

Removal

Refer to illustration 7.4

1   Raise the rear of the vehicle and support it securely on jackstands. Block the front wheels to keep the vehicle from rolling.
2   Remove the brake shoe assembly (see Section 6).

3   Remove all dirt and foreign material from around the wheel cylinder.
4   Disconnect the brake line with a flare-nut wrench, if available **(see illustration)**. Don't pull the brake line away from the wheel cylinder.
5   Remove the wheel cylinder mounting bolt.
6   Detach the wheel cylinder from the brake backing plate and place it on a clean workbench. Immediately plug the brake line to prevent fluid loss and contamination.

Installation

7   Place the wheel cylinder in position and install the bolt finger tight. Connect the brake line to the cylinder, being careful not to cross-thread the fitting. Tighten the wheel cylinder bolt to the torque listed in this Chapter's Specifications.
8   Tighten the brake line fitting and install the brake shoes and drum.
9   Bleed the brakes (see Section 10). Install the wheel and lug nuts. Lower the vehicle to the ground and tighten the lug nuts to the torque listed in this Chapter's Specifications.
10   Check the operation of the brakes carefully before driving the vehicle.

8   Master cylinder - removal and installation

Warning: *On 2009 and later models, do not drop or hit the master cylinder. If the master cylinder is dropped, it may not be reused.*
Caution: *On 2009 and later models, the master cylinder is designed to allow the piston to pop out and be exposed. Hold the master cylinder by the body, not the piston, or the master cylinder could be damaged. Do not try to remove the piston or allow the piston to be scratched or damaged.*

Removal

Refer to illustration 8.1

1   Remove the cover from the air filter housing. Unplug the electrical connector for the brake fluid level warning switch **(see illustration)**. On 2009 and later models, remove the windshield wiper arms, linkage, wiper motor (see Chapter 12) and the upper and lower cowl (see Chapter 11).
2   Remove as much fluid as possible from the reservoir with a syringe. If the vehicle is equipped with a manual transaxle, clamp off the fluid feed hose to the clutch master cylin-

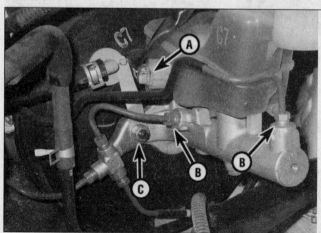

8.1 Master cylinder installation details

A   *Electrical connector*
B   *Brake line fittings*
C   *Mounting nut (right shown)*

8.10 The best way to bleed air from the master cylinder before installing it on the vehicle is with a pair of bleed tubes (typical master cylinder)

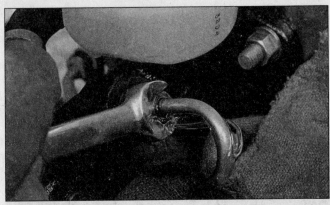

8.18 Have an assistant depress the brake pedal and hold it down, then loosen the fitting nut, allowing the air and fluid to escape; repeat this procedure on both fittings until the fluid is clear of air bubbles

der, then detach the hose from the brake fluid reservoir.

3   Place rags under the fittings and prepare caps or plastic bags to cover the ends of the lines once they're disconnected. **Caution:** *Brake fluid will damage paint. Cover all body parts and be careful not to spill fluid during this procedure.*

4   Loosen the fittings at the ends of the brake lines where they enter the master cylinder. To prevent rounding off the flats, use a flare-nut wrench, which wraps around the fitting hex.

5   Pull the brake lines away from the master cylinder and plug the ends to prevent contamination.

6   Remove the nuts attaching the master cylinder to the power booster **(see illustration 8.1)**. Pull the master cylinder off the studs to remove it. Again, be careful not to spill the fluid as this is done.

Installation

Refer to illustrations 8.10 and 8.18

Note: *On 2009 and later models, when installing the master cylinder, remove the piston and port protective caps. Apply only the grease supplied to the piston and brake booster.*

Note: *On 2009 and later models, If the piston gets dirty, clean it with a rag or cloth and apply lithium soap based glycol grease, evenly, around the sliding portion of the piston.* **Warning:** *Do not use any other type of grease.*

7   On 2008 and earlier models, bench bleed the new master cylinder before installing it. On 2009 and later models, the master cylinder must be bled in the vehicle.

8   On 2008 and earlier models, it is recommended that the master cylinder be mounted in a vise, with the jaws of the vise clamping on the mounting flange.

9   On 2009 and later models, install the reservoir cover, then install the master cylinder over the studs on the power brake booster and tighten the attaching nuts only finger tight at this time. **Caution:** *Keep the master cylinder level or piston end up as much as possible to prevent the piston from falling out.*

10   Attach a pair of master cylinder bleeder tubes to the outlet ports of the master cylinder **(see illustration)**.

11   Fill the reservoir with brake fluid of the recommended type (see Chapter 1).

12   On 2008 and earlier models, use a Phillips screwdriver to slowly push the piston into the master cylinder. On 2009 and later models, have an assistant slowly push the brake pedal down inside the vehicle. Air will be expelled from the pressure chambers and into the reservoir. Because the tubes are submerged in fluid, air can't be drawn back into the master cylinder when you release the pedal. **Caution:** *Have plenty of rags on hand to catch the fluid - brake fluid will ruin painted surfaces.*

13   Repeat the procedure until no more air bubbles are present.

14   On 2008 and earlier models, remove the bleed tubes, one at a time, and install plugs in the open ports to prevent fluid leakage and air from entering. If installing a new master cylinder, adjust the booster push-rod length (see Section 11). Also install a new O-ring on the master cylinder body.

15   On 2008 and earlier models, install the master cylinder on the power brake booster in the same manner as Step 9.

16   Thread the brake line fittings into the master cylinder. Since the master cylinder is finger tight, the nuts can be easily loosened and moved slightly in order for the fittings to thread in easily. Do not strip the threads as the fittings are tightened.

17   Fully tighten the mounting nuts, then tighten the brake line fittings.

18   Fill the master cylinder reservoir with fluid, then bleed the master cylinder and the brake system as described in Section 10. To bleed the cylinder on the vehicle, have an assistant depress the brake pedal slowly and then hold the pedal to the floor. Loosen the fitting nut to allow air and fluid to escape **(see illustration)**. Repeat this procedure on both fittings until the fluid is clear of air bubbles. **Caution:** *Have plenty of rags on hand to catch the fluid - brake fluid will ruin painted surfaces.*

19   Test the operation of the brake system carefully before placing the vehicle into normal service. **Warning:** *Do not operate the vehicle if you are in doubt about the effectiveness of the brake system.*

9   Brake hoses and lines - inspection and replacement

Inspection

1   About every six months, with the vehicle raised and supported securely on jackstands, the rubber hoses which connect the steel brake lines with the front and rear brake assemblies should be inspected for cracks, chafing of the outer cover, leaks, blisters and other damage. These are important and vulnerable parts of the brake system and inspection should be complete. A light and mirror will be helpful for a thorough check. If a hose exhibits any of the above conditions, replace it with a new one.

Replacement
Front brake hose

Refer to illustrations 9.3 and 9.4

2   Loosen the wheel lug nuts, raise the vehicle and support it securely on jackstands. Remove the wheel.

3   At the frame bracket, unscrew the brake

9.3 Unscrew the brake line threaded fitting with a flare-nut wrench to protect the fitting corners from being rounded off

9.4 Remove the brake hose-to-brake line U-clip (A) with a pair of pliers - B is the brake hose bracket bolt on the strut

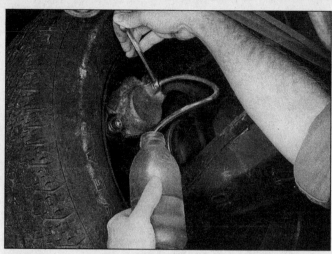

10.8 When bleeding the brakes, a hose is connected to the bleeder valve at the caliper or wheel cylinder and then submerged in brake fluid. Air will be seen as bubbles in the tube and container. All air must be expelled before moving to the next wheel

line fitting from the hose **(see illustration)**. Use a flare-nut wrench to prevent rounding off the corners.

4   Remove the U-clip from the female fitting at the bracket with a pair of pliers **(see illustration)**, then pass the hose through the bracket.

5   At the caliper end of the hose, remove the banjo fitting bolt **(see illustration 3.6b)**, then separate the hose from the caliper. Note that there are two copper sealing washers on either side of the fitting - they should be replaced with new ones during installation.

6   Remove the U-clip from the strut bracket, then feed the hose through the bracket.

7   To install the hose, pass the caliper fitting end through the strut bracket, then connect the fitting to the caliper with the banjo bolt and copper washers. Make sure the locating lug on the fitting is engaged with the hole in the caliper, then tighten the bolt to the torque listed in this Chapter's Specifications.

8   Push the metal support into the strut bracket and install the U-clip. Make sure the hose isn't twisted between the caliper and the strut bracket.

9   Route the hose into the frame bracket, again making sure it isn't twisted, then connect the brake line fitting, starting the threads by hand. Install the clip and E-ring, if equipped, then tighten the fitting securely.

10   Bleed the caliper (see Section 10).

11   Install the wheel and lug nuts, lower the vehicle and tighten the lug nuts to the torque specified in Chapter 1.

Rear brake hose

12   Perform Steps 2, 3 and 4 above, then repeat Steps 3 and 4 at the other end of the hose. Be sure to bleed the wheel cylinder (see Section 10).

Metal brake lines

13   When replacing brake lines, be sure to use the correct parts. Don't use copper tubing for any brake system components. Purchase genuine steel brake lines from a dealer or auto parts store.

14   Prefabricated brake line, with the tube ends already flared and fittings installed, is available at auto parts stores and dealer parts departments.

15   When installing the new line, make sure it's securely supported in the brackets and has plenty of clearance between moving or hot components.

16   After installation, check the master cylinder fluid level and add fluid as necessary. Bleed the brake system (see Section 10) and test the brakes carefully before driving the vehicle in traffic.

10   Brake hydraulic system - bleeding

Refer to illustration 10.8

Warning: *Wear eye protection when bleeding the brake system. If the fluid comes in contact with your eyes, immediately rinse them with water and seek medical attention.*

Note: *Bleeding the hydraulic system is necessary to remove any air that manages to find its way into the system when it's been opened during removal and installation of a hose, line, caliper or master cylinder.*

1   You'll probably have to bleed the system at all four brakes if air has entered it due to low fluid level, or if the brake lines have been disconnected at the master cylinder.

2   If a brake line was disconnected only at a wheel, then only that caliper or wheel cylinder must be bled.

3   If a brake line is disconnected at a fitting located between the master cylinder and any of the brakes, that part of the system served by the disconnected line must be bled.

4   Remove any residual vacuum from the brake power booster by applying the brake several times with the engine off.

5   Remove the master cylinder reservoir cover and fill the reservoir with brake fluid. Reinstall the cover. **Note:** *Check the fluid level often during the bleeding operation and add fluid as necessary to prevent the fluid level from falling low enough to allow air bubbles into the master cylinder.*

6   Have an assistant on hand, as well as a supply of new brake fluid, a clear container partially filled with clean brake fluid, a length of tubing to fit over the bleeder valve and a wrench to open and close the bleeder valve.

7   Beginning at the right rear wheel, loosen the bleeder valve slightly, then tighten it to a point where it's snug but can still be loosened quickly and easily.

8   Place one end of the tubing over the bleeder valve and submerge the other end in brake fluid in the container **(see illustration)**.

9   Have the assistant depress the brake pedal slowly, then hold the pedal down firmly.

10   While the pedal is held down, open the bleeder valve just enough to allow a flow of fluid to leave the valve. Watch for air bubbles to exit the submerged end of the tube. When the fluid flow slows after a couple of seconds, close the valve and have your assistant release the pedal.

11   Repeat Steps 9 and 10 until no more air is seen leaving the tube, then tighten the bleeder valve and proceed to the left rear wheel, the right front wheel and the left front wheel, in that order, and perform the same procedure. Be sure to check the fluid in the master cylinder reservoir frequently.

12   Never use old brake fluid. It contains moisture that will deteriorate the brake system components.

13   Refill the master cylinder with fluid at the end of the operation.

14   Check the operation of the brakes. The

11.11 To disconnect the power brake booster pushrod from the brake pedal, remove the retaining clip and clevis pin (center); to detach the booster from the firewall, remove the four mounting nuts (three seen here)

11.14a Measure the distance that the pushrod protrudes from the brake booster at the master-cylinder mounting surface (including the gasket)

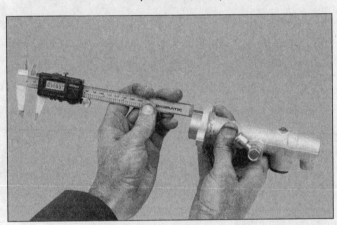

11.14b Measure the distance from the mounting flange to the end of the master cylinder

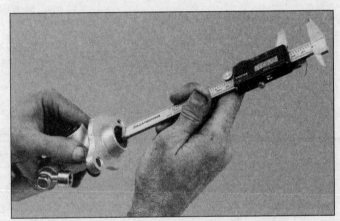

11.14c Measure the distance from the piston pocket to the end of the master cylinder

pedal should feel solid when depressed, with no sponginess. If necessary, repeat the entire process. **Warning:** *Do not operate the vehicle if you're in doubt about the effectiveness of the brake system.*

11 Power brake booster - check, removal and installation

Operating check

1   Depress the brake pedal several times with the engine off and make sure there's no change in the pedal reserve distance.
2   Depress the pedal and start the engine. If the pedal goes down slightly, operation is normal.

Airtightness check

3   Start the engine and turn it off after one or two minutes. Depress the brake pedal slowly several times. If the pedal depresses less each time, the booster is airtight.

4   Depress the brake pedal while the engine is running, then stop the engine with the pedal depressed. If there's no change in the pedal reserve travel after holding the pedal for 30 seconds, the booster is airtight.

Removal

Refer to illustration 11.11

5   Power brake booster units shouldn't be disassembled. They require special tools not normally found in most automotive repair stations or shops. They're fairly complex and, because of their critical relationship to brake performance, should be replaced with a new or rebuilt one.
6   Remove the brake master cylinder (see Section 8).
7   Remove the air filter housing (see Chapter 4).
8   In the engine compartment, disconnect the vacuum hose from the booster.
9   On models with cruise control, remove the cruise control actuator and bracket.
10   Unclip and/or detach any brake lines

around the booster, as necessary, to allow the booster to be removed without damaging the lines.
11   Using a flashlight, locate the clevis which connects the booster pushrod to the top of the brake pedal. Remove the clevis pin retaining clip with pliers and pull out the pin **(see illustration)**.
12   Remove the four nuts and washers holding the brake booster to the firewall (you may need a light to see them). Slide the booster straight out from the firewall until the studs clear the holes.

Installation

Refer to illustrations 11.14a, 11.14b, 11.14c and 11.14d

13   Installation procedures are basically the reverse of removal. Tighten the clevis locknut securely and the booster mounting nuts to the torque listed in this Chapter's Specifications.
14   If a new power brake booster unit is being installed, the booster pushrod-to-master cylinder piston clearance must beat zero

11.14d To adjust the length of the booster pushrod, hold the serrated portion of the rod with a pair of pliers and turn the adjusting screw in or out, as necessary, to achieve the desired setting

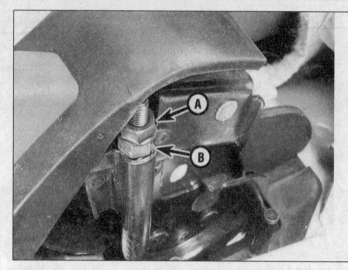

12.3 Loosen the locknut (A), then turn the adjusting nut (B) until the desired handle travel is obtained

- if there is interference between the two, the brakes may drag. If there is too much clearance, there will be excessive brake pedal travel. Check the pushrod clearance as follows:

a) *Measure the distance that the pushrod protrudes from the master cylinder mounting surface on the front of the power brake booster, including the gasket. Write down this measurement* **(see illustration)**. *This is "dimension A."*

b) *Measure the distance from the mounting flange to the end of the master cylinder* **(see illustration)**. *Write down this measurement. This is "dimension B."*

c) *Measure the distance from the end of the master cylinder to the bottom of the pocket in the piston* **(see illustration)**. *Write down this measurement. This is "dimension C."*

d) *Subtract measurement B from measurement C, then subtract measurement A from the difference between B and C. This is the pushrod clearance.*

e) *Compare your calculated pushrod clearance to the pushrod clearance listed in this Chapter's Specifications. If necessary, adjust the pushrod length to achieve the correct clearance* **(see illustration 11.14d)**.

15   After the final installation of the master cylinder and brake hoses and lines, the brake pedal height and freeplay must be adjusted and the system must be bled. See the appropriate Sections of this Chapter for the procedures.

12   Parking brake - adjustment

Refer to illustration 12.3

1   The parking brake lever, when properly adjusted, should travel six to nine clicks when a moderate pulling force is applied. If it travels less than six clicks, there's a chance the parking brake might not be releasing completely and might be dragging on the drum or disc.

If the lever can be pulled up more than nine clicks, the parking brake may not hold adequately on an incline, allowing the car to roll.
2   To gain access to the parking brake cable adjuster, remove the center console (see Chapter 11).
3   Loosen the locknut (the upper nut) while holding the adjusting nut (lower nut) with a wrench **(see illustration)**. Tighten the adjusting nut until the desired travel is attained. Tighten the locknut.
4   Install the console.

13   Brake pedal - adjustment

Pedal height

Refer to illustration 13.1

1   The height of the brake pedal is the distance the pedal sits off the floor **(see illustration)**. If the pedal height is not within Specifications, it must be adjusted.
2   Loosen the locknut on the brake light switch and unscrew the switch until it doesn't contact the pedal arm. **(see illustration 14.2)**. Before measuring the brake pedal height, make sure the pedal is in the fully-returned position. Measure the pedal height and, if necessary, adjust it by loosening the locknut on the pedal pushrod and turning the pushrod to achieve the proper height. When the proper height has been obtained, tighten the locknut securely.
3   Adjust the brake light switch (see Section 14).

Pedal freeplay

4   The freeplay is the pedal slack, or the distance the pedal can be depressed before it begins to have any effect on the brake system **(see illustration 13.1)**. Before checking brake pedal freeplay, depress the brake pedal several times (with the engine off).
5   If the pedal freeplay is not within the specified range, check the adjustment of the brake light switch (see Section 14).
6   If the brake light switch is properly

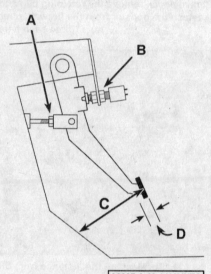

92037-9-13.1 HAYNES

13.1 Brake pedal adjusting details

A   *Pedal height adjusting point*
B   *Brake light switch locknut*
C   *Pedal height measurement point*
D   *Freeplay measurement point*

adjusted, troubleshoot the brake system for the cause of excessive freeplay (suspect either air in the hydraulic system [see Section 10], excessive clearance between the booster pushrod and the master cylinder piston [see Section 11]), or excessive clearance between the rear brake shoes and the brake drums.

Brake pedal reserve distance

7   With the parking brake released and the engine running, depress the pedal with normal braking effort and have an assistant measure the distance from the center of the pedal pad to the floor. If the distance is less than specified, troubleshoot the brake system (see Step 6).

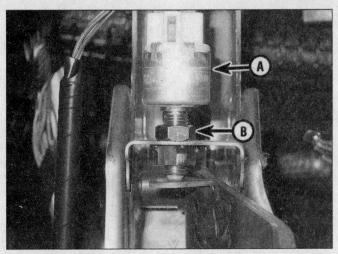

14.7 The brake light switch (A) is located at the top of the brake pedal - B is the adjusting locknut

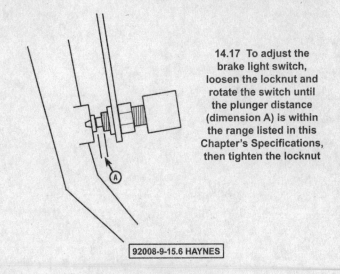

14.17 To adjust the brake light switch, loosen the locknut and rotate the switch until the plunger distance (dimension A) is within the range listed in this Chapter's Specifications, then tighten the locknut

92008-9-15.6 HAYNES

14   Brake light switch - check, removal, installation and adjustment

Check

1   The brake light switch is located on the brake pedal bracket. You'll need to remove the trim panel beneath the steering column to get to the switch and connector (see Chapter 11).

2   With the brake pedal in the fully released position, the switch opens the brake light circuit. When the brake pedal is depressed, the switch closes the circuit and sends current to the brake lights.

3   If the brake lights are inoperative, check the fuse and the bulbs (see Chapter 12).

4   If the fuse and bulbs are okay, verify that voltage is available at the switch.

5   If there's no voltage to the switch, search for an open circuit condition between the fuse block and the switch. If there is voltage to the switch, close the switch (depress the brake pedal) and verify that there's voltage on the other side of the switch.

6   If there's no voltage on the other side of the switch, replace the switch. If there is voltage but the brake lights still don't work, look for an open circuit condition between the switch and the brake lights. **Note:** *There is always the remote possibility that all of the brake light bulbs are burned out, but this is not very likely.*

Removal and installation
2008 and earlier models

Refer to illustration 14.7

7   The brake light switch **(see illustration)** is located on a bracket at the top of the brake pedal.

8   Disconnect the wiring harness at the brake light switch.

9   Loosen the locknut and unscrew the switch from the pedal bracket.

10   Installation is the reverse of removal.

2009 and later models

11   Disconnect the electrical connector from the brake light switch.

12   Rotate the switch counterclockwise 90-degrees, so that it unlocks from its holder, then pull it directly out of the holder.

13   To install the switch, insert it into its holder and push it in until the switch body contacts the rubber stop on the brake pedal bracket. Hold the brake pedal up while placing the switch in position. Rotate the switch 90-degrees clockwise to lock it into place. It will achieve the proper clearance (0.020 to 0.102 inch) to the rubber stop automatically. **Caution:** *Do not press in on the switch while turning it.*

14   Plug the electrical connector into the switch.

15   Confirm that the brake lights work properly before placing the vehicle into normal service.

Adjustment

Refer to illustration 14.17

16   Check and, if necessary, adjust brake pedal height (see Chapter 1).

17   Loosen the switch locknut, adjust the switch so that the distance the plunger protrudes **(see illustration)** is within the range listed in this Chapter's Specifications. (If you're unable to measure this distance, adjust the plunger so that it lightly contacts the pedal stop.) Tighten the locknut.

18   Plug the electrical connector into the switch and reconnect the battery. Make sure the brake lights come on when the brake pedal is depressed and go off when the pedal is released. If not, repeat the adjustment procedure until the brake lights function properly.

Notes

Chapter 10
Suspension and steering systems

Contents

Specifications

Torque specifications
Ft-lbs (unless otherwise indicated)

Note: *One foot-pound (ft-lb) of torque is equivalent to 12 inch-pounds (in-lbs) of torque. Torque values below approximately 15 ft-lbs are expressed in inch-pounds, since most foot-pound torque wrenches are not accurate at these smaller values.*

Front suspension
Balljoints
- Balljoint-to-control arm bolt/nuts ... 66
- Balljoint-to-steering knuckle nut ... 76
- Control arm-to-cross member ... 101

Stabilizer bar
- Bracket-to-cross member bolts
  - 2008 and earlier models ... 168 in-lbs
  - 2009 and later models ... 18

Struts
- Strut-to-steering knuckle bolts/nuts
  - 2008 and earlier models ... 113
  - 2009 and later models ... 177
- Strut upper mounting nuts
  - 2008 and earlier models ... 29
  - 2009 and later models ... 37
- Damper shaft nut ... 35

Subframe crossmember **(see illustration 4.6)**
- Bolt A ... 116
- Bolt B ... 83
- Bolts/nuts C ... 38

Rear suspension
Axle beam pivot bolts
- 2008 and earlier models ... 66
- 2009 and later models ... 63

Hub and bearing assembly-to-rear axle beam bolts
- 2008 and earlier models ... 45
- 2009 and later models ... 74

Stabilizer bar-to-rear axle beam bolts/nuts
- 2008 and earlier models ... 144
- 2009 and later models ... 184

Shock absorber/coil spring assembly
- Lower mounting nut ... 59
- Upper mounting nuts/bolt ... 59
- Damper shaft nut
  - 2008 and earlier models ... 41
  - 2009 and later models ... 29

Torque specifications (continued)

Ft-lbs (unless otherwise indicated)

Note: *One foot-pound (ft-lb) of torque is equivalent to 12 inch-pounds (in-lbs) of torque. Torque values below approximately 15 ft-lbs are expressed in inch-pounds, since most foot-pound torque wrenches are not accurate at these smaller values.*

Steering

Airbag module Torx screws	78 in-lbs
Steering gear-to-crossmember bolts	43
Steering wheel nut	37
Tie-rod end-to-steering knuckle nut	36
Tie-rod end locknuts	55
U-joint-to-pinion shaft pinch bolt	26
Power steering pressure line fitting-to-pump	30
Power steering pump mounting bolts	27
Pressure lines to steering gear	108 in-lbs

1   General information

Refer to illustrations 1.1 and 1.2

The front suspension **(see illustration)** is a MacPherson strut design. The upper end of each strut/coil spring assembly is attached to the vehicle's body strut support. The lower end of the strut assembly is connected to the upper end of the steering knuckle. The steering knuckle is attached to a balljoint mounted on the outer end of the suspension control arm. A stabilizer bar reduces body roll.

The rear suspension **(see illustration)** utilizes shock absorber/coil spring assemblies. The upper end of each assembly is attached to the vehicle body. The lower ends are attached to a beam axle. The axle has two integral forward arms located to the chassis by bolts through pivot bushings.

The rack-and-pinion steering gear is

1.1 Front suspension and steering components

1	*Front stabilizer bar*	*3*	*Balljoint*	*5*	*Support brace*
2	*Control arm*	*4*	*Strut/coil spring assembly*	*6*	*Suspension crossmember*

located behind the engine/transaxle assembly on the firewall and actuates the tie-rods, which are attached to the steering knuckles. The inner ends of the tie-rods are protected by rubber boots, which should be inspected periodically for secure attachment, tears and leaking lubricant.

The power assist system consists of a belt-driven pump and associated lines and hoses. The fluid level in the power steering pump reservoir should be checked periodically (see Chapter 1).

The steering wheel operates the steering shaft, which actuates the steering gear through universal joints. Looseness in the steering can be caused by wear in the steering shaft universal joints, the steering gear, the tie-rod ends and loose retaining bolts.

Precautions

Frequently, when working on the suspension or steering system components, you may come across fasteners that seem impossible to loosen. These fasteners on the underside of the vehicle are continually subjected to water, road grime, mud, etc., and can become rusted or "frozen," making them extremely difficult to remove. In order to unscrew these stubborn fasteners without damaging them (or other components), be sure to use lots of penetrating oil and allow it to soak in for a while. Using a wire brush to clean exposed threads will also ease removal of the nut or bolt and prevent damage to the threads. Sometimes a sharp blow with a hammer and punch will break the bond between a nut and bolt threads, but care must be taken to prevent the punch from slipping off the fastener and ruining the threads. Heating the stuck fastener and surrounding area with a torch sometimes helps too, but isn't recommended because of the obvious dangers associated with fire. Long breaker bars and extension, or "cheater," pipes will increase leverage, but never use an extension pipe on a ratchet - the ratcheting mechanism could be damaged.

Sometimes tightening the nut or bolt first will help to break it loose. Fasteners that require drastic measures to remove should always be replaced with new ones.

Since most of the procedures dealt with in this Chapter involve jacking up the vehicle and working underneath it, a good pair of jackstands will be needed. A hydraulic floor jack is the preferred type of jack to lift the vehicle, and it can also be used to support certain components during various operations. **Warning:** *Never, under any circumstances, rely on a jack to support the vehicle while working on it. Whenever any of the suspension or steering fasteners are loosened or removed they must be inspected and, if necessary, replaced with new ones of the same part number or of original equipment quality and design. Torque specifications must be followed for proper reassembly and component retention. Never attempt to heat or straighten any suspension or steering components. Instead, replace any bent or damaged part with a new one.*

1.2 Typical rear suspension components

1	Rear axle beam	3	Shock absorber/coil spring assembly
2	Rear axle beam pivots	4	Rear stabilizer bar (inside axle beam)

2.3 To detach the strut assembly from the steering knuckle, remove the two nuts, then knock out the bolts with a hammer and punch - note marks of bolt/strut relationship

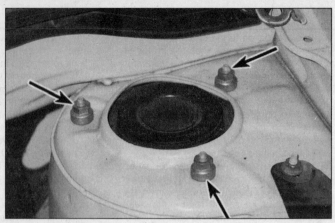

2.5 To detach the upper end of the strut assembly from the body, remove the upper mounting nuts

2   Strut assembly (front) - removal, inspection and installation

Removal

Refer to illustrations 2.3 and 2.5

Note: *On 2009 and later models, it is necessary to remove the windshield wiper motor and link assembly to perform this procedure (see Chapter 12).*

1   Loosen the wheel lug nuts, raise the vehicle and support it securely on jackstands. Remove the wheel.

2   Unbolt the brake hose bracket from the strut. If the vehicle is equipped with ABS, detach the speed sensor wiring harness from the strut by removing the clamp bracket bolt. Refer to Section 4 and disconnect the stabilizer link from the strut.

3   Mark the relationship of the strut to the steering knuckle. **Note:** *Also mark the positions of the bolts, as special camber adjusting bolts may have been fitted at some point.* Remove the strut-to-knuckle nuts **(see illustration)** and knock the bolts out with a hammer and punch.

4   Separate the strut from the steering knuckle. Be careful not to overextend the inner CV joint. Also, don't let the steering knuckle fall outward and strain the brake hose.

5   Support the strut and spring assembly (an assistant would be helpful here) and remove the three strut-to-body nuts **(see illustration)**. Remove the assembly out from the fenderwell.

Inspection

6   Check the strut body for leaking fluid, dents, cracks and other obvious damage that would warrant repair or replacement.

7   Check the coil spring for chips or cracks in the spring coating (this will cause premature spring failure due to corrosion). Inspect the spring seat for cuts, hardness and general deterioration.

8   If any undesirable conditions exist, proceed to the strut disassembly procedure (see Section 3).

Installation

9   Guide the strut assembly up into the fenderwell and insert the upper mounting studs through the holes in the body. Once the studs protrude, install the nuts so the strut won't fall back through. This is most easily accomplished with the help of an assistant, as the strut is quite heavy and awkward.

10   Slide the steering knuckle into the strut flange and insert the two bolts. Install the nuts, align the previously made match-marks and tighten them to the torque listed in this Chapter's Specifications.

11   Connect the brake hose bracket to the strut and tighten the bolt securely. If the vehicle is equipped with ABS, install the speed sensor wiring harness bracket.

12   Install the wheel and lug nuts, then lower the vehicle and tighten the lug nuts to the torque listed in the Chapter 1 Specifications.

13   Tighten the upper mounting nuts to the torque listed in this Chapter's Specifications.

14   Drive the vehicle to an alignment shop to have the front-end alignment checked, and if necessary, adjusted.

3   Strut or shock absorber/coil spring assembly - replacement

1   If the struts or coil springs exhibit the tell-tale signs of wear (leaking fluid, loss of damping capability, chipped, sagging or cracked coil springs) explore all options before beginning any work. The strut/shock absorber assemblies are not serviceable and must be replaced if a problem develops. However, strut assemblies complete with springs may be available on an exchange basis, which eliminates much time and work. Whichever route you choose to take, check on the cost and availability of parts before disassembling your vehicle. **Warning:** *Disassembling a strut is potentially dangerous and utmost attention must be directed to the job, or serious injury may result. Use only a high-quality spring compressor and carefully follow the manufacturer's instructions furnished with the tool. After removing the coil spring from the strut assembly, set it aside in a safe, isolated area.*

Disassembly

Refer to illustrations 3.3, 3.4, 3.5, 3.6 and 3.7

2   Remove the strut assembly following the procedure described in Section 2 (front) or if you're working on a rear shock absorber/ coil spring assembly, Section 10. Mount the assembly in a vise. Line the vise jaws with wood or rags to prevent damage to the unit and don't tighten the vise excessively.

3   Following the tool manufacturer's instructions, install the spring compressor (which

3.3 Install the spring compressor according to the tool manufacturer's instructions and compress the spring until all pressure is relieved from the upper spring seat

3.4 Remove the damper shaft nut - if the upper spring seat turns while loosening the nut, immobilize it with a chain wrench or strap wrench

3.5 Lift the suspension support off the damper shaft

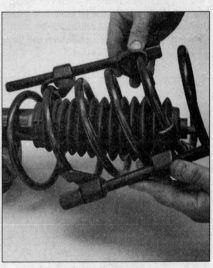

3.6 Remove the spring seat from the damper shaft

3.7 Remove the compressed spring assembly - keep the ends of the spring pointed away from your body

can be obtained at most auto parts stores or equipment yards on a daily rental basis) on the spring and compress it sufficiently to relieve all pressure from the upper spring seat **(see illustration)**. This can be verified by wiggling the spring.

4   Mark the positions of the upper and lower spring seats and suspension support to each other. Loosen the damper shaft nut with a socket **(see illustration)**.

5   Remove the nut and suspension support **(see illustration)**. Inspect the bearing in the suspension support for smooth operation. If it doesn't turn smoothly, replace the suspension support. Check the rubber portion of the suspension support for cracking and general deterioration. If there is any separation of the rubber, replace it.

6   Lift the spring seat and upper insulator from the damper shaft **(see illustration)**. Check the rubber spring seat for cracking and hardness, replacing it if necessary.

7   Carefully lift the compressed spring from the assembly **(see illustration)** and set it in a safe place. **Warning:** *Never place your head near the end of the spring!*

8   Slide the rubber bumper off the damper shaft.

9   Check the lower insulator (if equipped) for wear, cracking and hardness and replace it if necessary.

Reassembly

Refer to illustrations 3.11 and 3.12

10   If the lower insulator is being replaced, set it into position with the dropped portion seated in the lowest part of the seat. Extend the damper rod to its full length and install the rubber bumper.

11   Carefully place the coil spring onto the lower insulator, with the end of the spring resting in the lowest part of the insulator **(see illustration)**.

12   Install the upper insulator and spring seat, making sure that the flats in the hole in the seat match up with the flats on the damper shaft **(see illustration)**.

13   Install the dust seal and suspension support to the damper shaft. Make sure all of the marks made in Step 4 are in alignment.

14   Install a new nut and tighten it to the torque listed in this Chapter's Specifications. **Warning:** *The manufacturer states that a new damper shaft nut must be installed.*

15   Install the strut assembly following the procedure outlined in Section 2 (front), or the rear shock absorber/coil spring as described in Section 10.

4   Stabilizer bar and bushings (front) - removal and installation

Note: *This is a difficult procedure for the novice mechanic, since the engine/transaxle must be supported from above with an engine support fixture or hoist, while the front suspension crossmember is unbolted and lowered.*

Removal

Refer to illustrations 4.2, 4.6 and 4.7

1   Loosen the front wheel lug nuts. Raise the front of the vehicle and support it securely on jackstands. Apply the parking brake and block the rear wheels to keep the vehicle

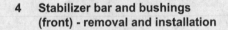

3.11 When installing the spring, make sure the end fits into the recessed portion of the lower seat

3.12 The flats on the damper shaft must match up with the flats in the spring seat

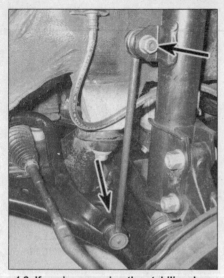

4.2 If you're removing the stabilizer bar, detach the bar from the link by removing the lower nut; if you're removing the strut, remove the upper nut and detach the link from the strut

from rolling off the stands. Remove the front wheels.

2   Detach the stabilizer bar link from the bar **(see illustration)**. If the ballstud turns with the nut, use an Allen wrench to hold the stud.

3   Remove the steering shaft pinch bolt (see Section 17).

4   Support the engine/transaxle assembly from above with an engine hoist or support fixture **(see illustration 17.3)**.

5   Remove the mounting bolts from the engine/transaxle mounts to the crossmember. Refer to Chapter 2A for engine and transaxle mount replacement procedures.

6   Remove the subframe/crossmember mounting bolts from the chassis, using a floor jack to lower the crossmember enough to access the stabilizer bar clamps **(see illustration)**. Be sure to note exactly the size and location of each nut and bolt to insure correct reassembly. **Note:** *The transaxle should be supported by a floor jack immediately after the subframe is removed from the vehicle. The transaxle will tilt slightly but should remain steady if the engine is properly secured with the engine compartment brace.*

7   Unbolt the stabilizer bar bushing clamps and remove the stabilizer bar **(see illustration)**.

8   While the stabilizer bar is off the vehicle, slide off the retainer bushings and inspect them. If they're cracked, worn or deteriorated, replace them. It's also a good idea to inspect the stabilizer bar link. To check it, flip the balljoint stud side-to-side five or six times, then install the nut. Using an inch-pound torque wrench, turn the nut continuously one turn every two to four seconds and note the torque reading on the fifth turn. It should be about 0.4 to 8.7 in-lbs. If it isn't, replace the link.

9   Clean the bushing area of the stabilizer bar with a stiff wire brush to remove any rust or dirt.

Installation

10   Lubricate the inside and outside of the new bushing with vegetable oil (used in cooking) to simplify reassembly. **Caution:** *Don't use petroleum or mineral-based lubricants or brake fluid - they will lead to deterioration of the bushings.*

4.6 Remove the front suspension subframe bolts (with an overhead support for the engine/transaxle and a floor jack under the subframe - refer to the letter designations for torque specs when installing fasteners for the subframe (A and B), engine mount crossmember (C) and the lower control arm balljoint bolts (D)

11   Installation is the reverse of removal. Tighten all fasteners to the torque values listed in this Chapter's Specifications. **Note:** *When installing the subframe, use a rod of the same diameter as the four subframe to-chassis bolts to align each side until that side's bolts can be inserted one at a time. Do not tighten any of the four bolts until all have been installed finger tight, then tighten to the Specifications in this Chapter.*

12   Install the wheel and lug nuts, lower the vehicle and tighten the lug nuts to the torque listed in the Chapter 1 Specifications.

13   It's a good idea to have the front wheel alignment checked, and if necessary, adjusted after this job has been performed.

5   Control arm - removal, inspection and installation

Removal

Refer to illustrations 5.2a and 5.2b

1   Loosen the wheel lug nuts on the side to be dismantled, raise the front of the vehicle, support it securely on jackstands and remove the wheel.

2   Remove the bolt and two nuts holding the control arm to the steering knuckle. Use a prybar to disconnect the control arm from the steering knuckle **(see illustrations)**.

3   Refer to Section 4 and unbolt and lower the front suspension crossmember with a floor jack.

4   Remove the control arm front pivot bolt.

5   Remove the rear bushing bolt.

6   Remove the control arm.

Inspection

7   Check the control arm for distortion and the bushings for wear, replacing parts as necessary. Do not attempt to straighten a bent control arm.

Installation

8   Installation is the reverse of removal.

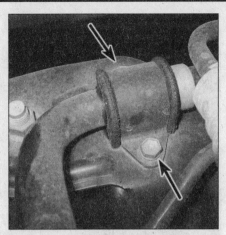

4.7 Remove the bolts and the stabilizer clamps

Tighten all of the fasteners to the torque values listed in this Chapter's Specifications, but don't tighten the front pivot bolt until the outer end of the control arm has been raised with a floor jack to simulate normal ride height. **Note:** *When installing the subframe, use a rod of the same diameter as the four subframe to-chassis bolts to align each side until that side's bolts can be inserted one at a time. Do not tighten any of the four bolts until all have been installed finger tight, then tighten to the Specifications in this Chapter.*

9   Install the wheel and lug nuts, lower the vehicle and tighten the lug nuts to the torque listed in the Chapter 1 Specifications.

10   It's a good idea to have the front wheel alignment checked, and if necessary, adjusted after this job has been performed.

6   Balljoint - replacement

Refer to illustration 6.3

1   Loosen the wheel lug nuts, raise the vehicle and support it securely on jackstands. Remove the wheel.

2   Remove the cotter pin from the balljoint

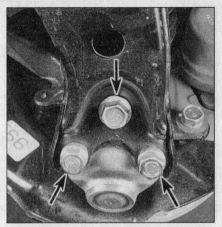

5.2a To detach the control arm from the steering knuckle balljoint, remove this bolt and these two nuts . . .

stud and loosen the nut (but don't remove it yet).

3   Separate the balljoint from the steering knuckle with a picklefork-type balljoint separator **(see illustration)**. Remove the balljoint stud nut. The clearance between the balljoint stud and the CV joint is very tight. To remove the stud nut, you'll have to alternately back off the nut a turn or two, pull down the stud, turn the nut another turn or two, etc. until the nut is off.

4   Remove the bolt and nuts securing the balljoint to the control arm, then separate the balljoint from the control arm with a prybar **(see illustrations 5.2a and 5.2b)**.

5   To install the balljoint, insert the balljoint stud through the hole in the steering knuckle and install the nut, but don't tighten it yet. Don't push the balljoint stud all the way up into and through the hole; instead, thread the nut onto the stud as soon as the stud protrudes through the hole, then turn the nut to draw the stud up through the hole.

6   Attach the balljoint to the control arm and install the bolt and nuts, tightening them to the torque listed in this Chapter's Specifications.

7   Tighten the balljoint stud nut to the

5.2b . . . and pry the control arm and balljoint apart with a large prybar or screwdriver

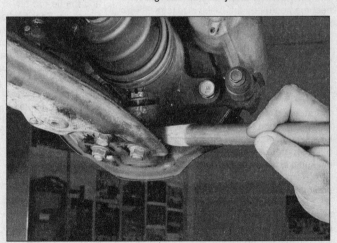

6.3 Separate the balljoint from the steering knuckle with a picklefork-type balljoint separator

7.8 Use a balljoint removal tool or small puller to remove the balljoint

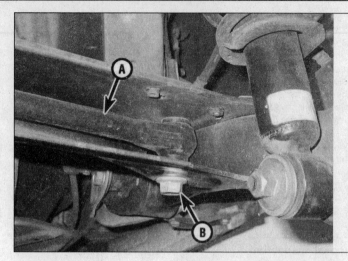

9.2 To detach the rear stabilizer bar (A) from the axle beam, remove the bolts/nuts (B, right side shown)

torque listed in this Chapter's Specifications and install a new cotter pin. If the cotter pin hole doesn't line up with the slots on the nut, tighten the nut additionally until it does line up - don't loosen the nut to insert the cotter pin.

8   Install the wheel and lug nuts. Lower the vehicle and tighten the lug nuts to the torque listed in the Chapter 1 Specifications.

7   Steering knuckle and hub - removal and installation

Warning: *Dust created by the brake system is harmful to your health. Never blow it out with compressed air and don't inhale any of it. Do not, under any circumstances, use petroleum-based solvents to clean brake parts. Use brake system cleaner only.*

Removal

Refer to illustration 7.8

1   Loosen the wheel lug nuts, raise the vehicle and support it securely on jackstands, then remove the wheel.

2   Remove the brake caliper (don't disconnect the hose) and the brake disc (see Chapter 9), and disconnect the brake hose from the strut. Hang the caliper from the coil spring with a piece of wire - don't let it hang by the brake hose.

3   If the vehicle is equipped with ABS, disconnect and remove the wheel speed sensor.

4   Mark the relationship of the strut to the steering knuckle **(see illustration 2.3)**. Loosen, but don't remove the strut-to-steering knuckle nuts and bolts (see Section 2).

5   Separate the tie-rod end from the steering knuckle arm (see Section 15).

6   Remove the balljoint-to-lower arm bolt and nuts **(see illustrations 5.2a and 5.2b)**.

7   Remove the driveaxle/hub nut and push the driveaxle from the hub as described in Chapter 8. Support the end of the driveaxle with a piece of wire.

8   Since the axle is out in this case, you can use a balljoint removal tool **(see illustration)**

or a small puller to remove the balljoint from the steering knuckle. **Note:** *If you're removing the steering knuckle to replace the hub bearings, and the balljoint is in good condition, the balljoint can remain attached.*

9   The strut-to-knuckle bolts can now be removed.

10   Carefully separate the steering knuckle from the strut.

Installation

11   Guide the knuckle and hub assembly into position, inserting the driveaxle into the hub.

12   Push the knuckle into the strut flange and install the bolts and nuts, but don't tighten them yet.

13   If you removed the balljoint from the old knuckle, and are planning to use it with the new knuckle, connect the balljoint to the knuckle and tighten the balljoint stud nut to the torque listed in this Chapter's Specifications. Install a new cotter pin.

14   Attach the balljoint to the control arm, but don't tighten the bolt and nuts yet.

15   Attach the tie-rod to the steering knuckle arm (see Section 15). Tighten the strut bolt nuts, the balljoint-to-control arm bolt and nuts and the tie-rod nut to the torque listed in this Chapter's Specifications.

16   Place the brake disc on the hub and install the caliper as outlined in Chapter 9.

17   Install the driveaxle/hub nut and tighten it to the torque listed in the Chapter 8 Specifications.

18   Install the wheel and lug nuts. Lower the vehicle and tighten the lug nuts to the torque listed in the Chapter 1 Specifications.

19   Have the front-end alignment checked and, if necessary, adjusted.

8   Hub and bearing assembly (front) - removal and installation

Due to the special tools and expertise required to press the hub and bearing from the steering knuckle, this job should be left to a professional shop. However, the steer-

ing knuckle and hub may be removed and the assembly taken to an automotive machine shop or other qualified repair facility equipped with the necessary tools. See Section 7 for the steering knuckle and hub removal procedure.

9   Stabilizer bar and bushings (rear) - removal and installation

Refer to illustration 9.2

1   Loosen the rear wheel lug nuts. Raise the rear of the vehicle and place it securely on jackstands.

2   Remove the stabilizer bar-to-axle beam bolts/nuts **(see illustration)**.

3   The stabilizer bar is mounted inside the open back of the U-channel axle beam. Once the bolts are removed, you may have to use a prybar to remove the stabilizer bar from the axle beam.

4   Installation is the reverse of the removal procedure. When reinstalling the bar to the axle beam, look for a distinctive mark on the top of the bar at one side. When properly installed, this mark will face Up and be on the left side of the axle beam.

5   Tighten the bolts/nuts to the Specifications listed in this Chapter.

10   Shock absorber/coil spring assembly (rear) - removal, inspection and installation

Note: *Shock absorber/coil spring assemblies should only be replaced in pairs.*

Removal

Refer to illustrations 10.4 and 10.6

1   Open the trunk and remove the spare tire.

2   Refer to Chapter 11 and remove the left and right inner trim panels at the sides of the trunk compartment, and the floor trim panel ahead of the spare tire well.

3   Raise the rear of the vehicle and sup-

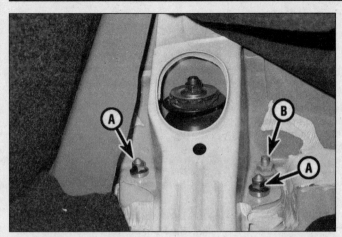

10.4 Inside the trunk, remove the two nuts (A) securing the upper part of the shock absorber - the bolt (B) is removed from below

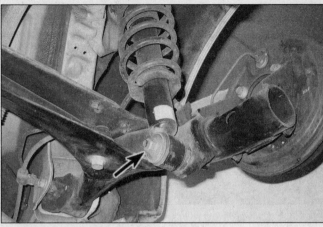

10.6 To detach the rear shock absorber from the axle beam, remove the nut and washer then pull the shock off the stud

port it securely on jackstands. Support the axle beam with a floor jack, nearest the shock absorber being removed.

4   From inside the trunk remove the two nuts at the upper mount **(see illustration)**. **Note:** *The shock absorber is still secured by one bolt, which is accessed from below.*

5   From below, remove the bolt securing the upper part of the shock absorber to the body.

6   Remove the shock absorber lower mounting nut and washer **(see illustration)**.

7   Remove the shock absorber assembly. It may be necessary to lower the floor jack far enough to disengage the upper mount before pulling the shock off the lower mounting stud.

Inspection

8   Follow the inspection procedures described in Section 3. If you determine that the shock absorber assembly must be disassembled for replacement of the shock body or the coil spring, refer to Section 3.

Installation

9   Maneuver the assembly up into the fenderwell and install the lower mount onto the stud and guide the upper mounting studs into the holes in the body. Install the bolt from below, tightening it to the torque listed in this Chapter's Specifications.

10   Install the lower washer and nut. Raise the axle beam with the floor jack to simulate normal ride height, then tighten the nut to the torque listed in this Chapter's Specifications.

11   Install the two upper mounting nuts and tighten them to the torque listed in this Chapter's Specifications.

12   Install the spare tire and the trim panels in the trunk.

11   Hub and bearing assembly (rear) - removal and installation

Warning: *Dust created by the brake system is harmful to your health. Never blow it out with compressed air and don't inhale any of it.*

11.3 Remove the four bolts that attach the hub and bearing assembly to the rear axle beam

Do not, under any circumstances, use petroleum-based solvents to clean brake parts. Use brake system cleaner only.

Removal

Refer to illustration 11.3

1   Loosen the wheel lug nuts, raise the vehicle and support it securely on jackstands. Remove the wheel.

2   Remove the brake drum (see Chapter 9). On models with ABS, disconnect the wheel sensor.

3   Remove the four hub-to-axle beam bolts, accessed from behind the brake backing plate **(see illustration)**.

4   Remove the hub and bearing assembly from its seat, maneuvering it out through the brake assembly.

5   If the hub exhibits looseness or excessive runout, the hub and bearing assembly must be replaced as a unit.

Installation

6   Position the hub and bearing assembly on the axle carrier and align the holes in the backing plate. After all four bolts have been installed, tighten them to the torque listed in this Chapter's Specifications.

7   Install the brake drum (and ABS sensor if equipped) and the wheel. Lower the vehicle

and tighten the lug nuts to the torque listed in the Chapter 1 Specifications.

12   Rear axle beam - removal and installation

Warning: *Dust created by the brake system is harmful to your health. Never blow it out with compressed air and don't inhale any of it. Do not, under any circumstances, use petroleum-based solvents to clean brake parts. Use brake system cleaner only.*

Removal

Refer to illustration 12.7

1   Loosen the rear wheel lug nuts, raise the vehicle and support it on jackstands. Block the front wheels and remove the rear wheels.

2   On models with ABS, disconnect the sensors and unbolt the ABS wire harness on each side from the axle beam.

3   Remove the rear stabilizer bar (see Section 9).

4   Remove the rear hub and bearing assembly on each side (see Section 11).

5   Detach the backing plate and rear brake assembly and brake lines from the axle beam. It isn't necessary to disassemble the brake shoe assembly or disconnect the parking

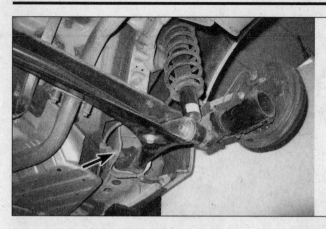

12.7 On each side, remove the bolt and nut securing the axle beam to the body (right side shown)

14.2 Back out the Torx screws until the airbag module is free, but don't try to remove them from the screw case (left side shown)

brake cable from the backing plate. Suspend the backing plate and brake assembly from the coil spring with a piece of wire. Be careful not to kink the brake line.

6   Support the axle beam with a floor jack, then disconnect the shock absorbers from the studs on the axle beam (see Section 10).

7   Lower the axle beam down, then remove the two bolts/nuts through the pivot bushings and remove the axle beam **(see illustration)**.

Installation

8   Inspect the axle beam bushings for cracks, deformation and signs of wear. If either is worn out, take the beam to a dealer service department or other repair shop to have the old ones pressed out and new ones pressed in. **Note:** *Only replace the bushings as a pair.*

9   Push the axle beam up to the vehicle until the bolts can be inserted into the front bushings and body. Install the nuts, but do not tighten yet.

10   Raise the axle beam and push the bottom of the shock absorbers onto the axle beam studs and secure with the washers and nuts.

11   Raise the axle beam to simulate normal ride height, then tighten the bushing bolts/nuts and the shock absorber lower mounting nuts to the torque listed in this Chapter's Specifications.

12   The remainder of the installation is the reverse of the removal procedure. Install the wheel and lug nuts. Lower the vehicle and tighten the lug nuts to the torque listed in the Chapter 1 Specifications.

13 Steering system - general information

All models are equipped with rack-and-pinion steering. The steering gear operates the steering knuckles via tie-rods. The inner ends of the tie-rods are protected by rubber boots that should be inspected periodically for secure attachment, tears and leaking lubricant.

On 2008 and earlier models, the power assist system consists of a belt-driven pump and associated lines and hoses. The fluid level in the power steering pump reservoir should be checked periodically (see Chapter 1).

On 2009 and later models, an electronic power steering system is used, consisting of a non-serviceable electro-mechanical motor incorporated into the steering column, an ECM, a torque sensor and an angle rotation sensor.

The steering wheel operates the steering shaft, which actuates the steering gear through universal joints. Looseness in the steering can be caused by wear in the steering shaft universal joints, the steering gear, the tie-rod ends, or loose retaining bolts.

14 Steering wheel - removal and installation

Warning: *These models are equipped with airbags. Always disable the airbag system*

before working in the vicinity of any airbag system component to avoid the possibility of accidental deployment of the airbag(s), which could cause personal injury (see Chapter 12).

Removal

Refer to illustrations 14.2, 14.3, 14.5 and 14.6

1   Turn the ignition key to Off, then disconnect the cable from the negative terminal of the battery. Wait at least two minutes before proceeding.

2   Turn the steering wheel so the wheels are pointing straight ahead, then loosen the Torx screws that attach the airbag module to the steering wheel **(see illustration)**. **Note:** *On 2009 and later models, use a small screwdriver to pry off the plastic cover from each side of the steering wheel to remove the Torx screws. Loosen each screw until the groove in the circumference of the screw catches on the screw case.*

3   Pull the airbag module off the steering wheel and disconnect the module electrical connectors **(see illustration)**. To disconnect the connectors, use a small screwdriver to pry up the locks (center part), then disconnect the connectors. Set the airbag module in a safe,

14.3 Lift the airbag module straight out from the steering wheel, then disconnect the electrical connectors at the back of the module

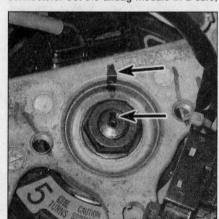

14.5 Mark the relationship of the steering wheel to the shaft before removing the wheel

14.6 If the steering wheel is difficult to remove from the shaft, use a steering wheel puller to remove it

14.8 After properly centering the spiral cable as described in the text, make sure the pointers are aligned

15.2 Remove the cotter pin from the castle nut and loosen - but don't remove - the nut

isolated area. **Warning:** *Carry the airbag module with the trim side facing away from you, and set the airbag module down with the trim side facing up. Don't place anything on top of the airbag module.*

4   Unplug the electrical connector for the cruise control (if equipped).

5   Mark the relationship of the steering shaft to the hub (if marks don't already exist or don't line up) to simplify installation and ensure steering wheel alignment, then remove the steering wheel retaining nut **(see illustration)**.

6   Use a puller to disconnect the steering wheel from the shaft **(see illustration)**. **Warning:** *Do not hammer on the shaft or the puller in an attempt to loosen the wheel from the shaft. Also, don't allow the steering shaft to turn with the steering wheel removed. If the shaft turns, the airbag spiral cable will become uncentered, which may cause the wire inside to break when the vehicle is returned to service.*

7   If it is necessary to remove the airbag spiral cable, follow the spiral cable wiring harness and unplug the electrical connector, then disengage the three claws and detach it from the combination switch.

Installation

Refer to illustration 14.8

8   Make sure that the front wheels are pointing straight ahead. Depress the lock tab

or hub of the spiral cable and turn the spiral cable counterclockwise by hand until it stops (don't apply too much force). Rotate the cable clockwise about 2-1/2 turns and align the two pointers **(see illustration)**.

9   To install the wheel, align the mark on the steering wheel hub with the mark on the shaft and slip the wheel onto the shaft. Install the nut and tighten it to the torque listed in this Chapter's Specifications.

10   Plug in the cruise control connector.

11   Plug in the electrical connectors for the airbag module and press down the locking tab.

12   Make sure the airbag module electrical connector is positioned correctly and that the wires don't interfere with anything, then install the airbag module and tighten the retaining screws to the torque listed in this Chapter's Specifications.

13   Connect the negative battery cable.

15   Tie-rod ends - removal and installation

Removal

Refer to illustrations 15.2, 15.3a, 15.3b and 15.4

1   Loosen the wheel lug nuts. Raise the front of the vehicle, support it securely on

15.3a Loosen the jam nut . . .

jackstands, block the rear wheels and set the parking brake. Remove the front wheel.

2   Remove the cotter pin **(see illustration)** and loosen the nut on the tie-rod end stud.

3   Hold the tie-rod with a pair of locking pliers or wrench and loosen the jam nut enough to mark the position of the tie-rod end in relation to the threads **(see illustrations)**.

4   Disconnect the tie-rod from the steering

15.3b . . . then mark the position of the tie-rod end in relation to the threads

15.4 Disconnect the tie-rod from the steering knuckle arm with a puller

16.3a The outer ends of the steering gear boots are secured by spring-type clamps; they're easily released with a pair of pliers

16.3b The inner ends of the steering gear boots are retained by boot clamps, which must be cut off and discarded

knuckle arm with a puller **(see illustration)**. Remove the nut and detach the tie-rod.

5   Unscrew the tie-rod end from the tie-rod.

Installation

6   Thread the tie-rod end on to the marked position and insert the tie-rod stud into the steering knuckle arm. Tighten the jam nut securely.

7   Install the castle nut on the stud and tighten it to the torque listed in this Chapter's Specifications. Install a new cotter pin. If the hole for the cotter pin doesn't line up with one of the slots in the nut, turn the nut an additional amount until it does.

8   Install the wheel and lug nuts. Lower the vehicle and tighten the lug nuts to the torque listed in the Chapter 1 Specifications.

9   Have the alignment checked and, if necessary, adjusted.

16   Steering gear boots - replacement

Refer to illustrations 16.3a and 16.3b

1   Loosen the lug nuts, raise the vehicle and

support it securely on jackstands. Remove the wheel.

2   Remove the tie-rod end and jam nut (see Section 15).

3   Remove the outer steering gear boot clamp with a pair of pliers **(see illustration)**. Cut off the inner boot clamp with a pair of diagonal cutters **(see illustration)**. Slide off the boot.

4   Before installing the new boot, wrap the threads and serrations on the end of the steering rod with a layer of tape so the small end of the new boot isn't damaged.

5   Slide the new boot into position on the steering gear until it seats in the groove in the steering rod and install new clamps.

6   Remove the tape and install the tie-rod end (see Section 15).

7   Install the wheel and lug nuts. Lower the vehicle and tighten the lug nuts to the torque listed in the Chapter 1 Specifications.

17   Steering gear - removal and installation

Refer to illustrations 17.3, 17.5, 17.6a and 17.6b

Warning: *These models are equipped with airbags. Always disable the airbag system*

before working in the vicinity of any airbag system component to avoid the possibility of accidental deployment of the airbag(s), which could cause personal injury (see Chapter 12).

1   Disconnect the cable from the negative terminal of the battery.

2   Remove the steering wheel (see Section 14). **Note:** *This will prevent the spiral cable from being damaged in the event the steering gear is not centered when it is installed.*

3   Support the engine from above with an engine support fixture **(see illustration)**. This tool can be obtained at most equipment rental yards.

4   Loosen the front wheel lug nuts, raise the front of the vehicle and support it securely on jackstands. Apply the parking brake and remove the wheels. Remove the engine under covers.

5   Place a drain pan under the steering gear. Detach the power steering pressure and return lines **(see illustration)** and cap the ends to prevent excessive fluid loss and contamination. Also unbolt the line clamp from the top of the steering gear.

6   Remove the universal joint cover **(see illustration)**. Mark the relationship of the lower universal joint to the steering gear input shaft and remove the lower intermediate shaft pinch-bolt **(see illustration)**. Loosen the

17.3 Support the engine from above with an engine support fixture

17.5 Disconnect the power steering line fittings

17.6a Pull back the carpeting at the bottom of the steering column and remove the universal joint cover

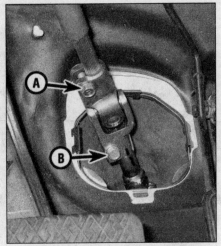

17.6b Mark the relationship of the universal joint to the steering gear input shaft, loosen the upper U-joint pinch bolt (A), then remove the lower bolt (B) and detach the joint from the steering gear input shaft

upper universal joint bolt, then slide the joint up and disconnect it from the steering gear input shaft.

7   Separate the tie-rod ends from the steering knuckle arms (see Section 15). Separate the stabilizer bar links from the bar (see Section 4).

8   Disconnect the balljoints from the control arms **(see illustrations 5.2a and 5.2b)**.

9   Remove the front section of the exhaust pipe. Unbolt the suspension crossmember and lower it along with the control arms **(see illustration 4.6)**.

10   Remove the bolts securing the steering gear to the crossmember **(see illustration)**.

11   Installation is the reverse of removal, noting the following points:

a) *Tighten all steering and suspension fasteners to the torque listed in this Chapter's Specifications.*

b) *Install the wheels and lug nuts. Lower the vehicle and tighten the lug nuts to the torque listed in the Chapter 1 Specifications.*

c) *Set the front wheels in the straight-ahead position, then center the spiral cable and install the steering wheel and airbag module (see Section 14).*

d) *Fill the power steering fluid reservoir with the recommended fluid (see Chapter 1). Bleed the steering system (see Section 19).*

18   Power steering pump - removal and installation

Refer to illustration 18.4

Removal

1   Disconnect the cable from the negative battery terminal.

2   Using a large syringe or suction gun, suck as much fluid out of the power steering fluid reservoir as possible. Place a drain pan under the vehicle to catch any fluid that spills out when the hoses are disconnected.

3   Remove the drivebelt (see Chapter 1). Loosen the right front wheel lug nuts, raise the front of the vehicle and support it securely on jackstands. Remove the wheel and the right side engine under cover.

18.4 Power steering pump mounting details

A   *Power steering pressure switch connector*

B   *Pressure line fitting*

4   Unplug the electrical connector from the power steering fluid pressure switch **(see illustration)**.

5   Unscrew the pressure line-to-pump fitting, using a flare-nut wrench, if available, to avoid rounding-off the corners of the fitting.

6   Loosen the hose clamp and detach the return hose from the pump.

7   Remove the two mounting nuts and detach the power steering pump from the engine. **Note:** *The pump-to-mounting bracket nuts are accessible through the holes in the pump pulley, using a short extension and socket.*

Installation

8   Installation is the reverse of removal. Be sure to tighten the mounting bolts/nuts and the pressure line fitting to the torque listed in this Chapter's Specifications.

9   Install the engine under cover, wheel and lug nuts. Lower the vehicle and tighten the lug nuts to the torque listed in the Chapter 1 Specifications.

10   Install the drivebelt (see Chapter 1).

11   Top up the fluid level in the reservoir (see Chapter 1) and bleed the system (see Section 19).

19   Power steering system - bleeding

1   Following any operation in which the power steering fluid lines have been disconnected, the power steering system must be bled to remove all air and obtain proper steering performance.

2   With the front wheels in the straight ahead position, check the power steering fluid level and, if low, add fluid until it reaches the Cold mark on the reservoir.

3   Start the engine and allow it to run at fast idle. Recheck the fluid level and add more if necessary to reach the Cold mark.

4   Bleed the system by turning the wheels from side to side, without hitting the stops. This will work the air out of the system. Keep the reservoir full of fluid as this is done.

5   When the air is worked out of the system, return the wheels to the straight-ahead position and leave the vehicle running for several more minutes before shutting it off.

6   Road test the vehicle to be sure the steering system is functioning normally and noise free.

7   Recheck the fluid level to be sure it is up to the Hot mark on the reservoir while the engine is at normal operating temperature. Add fluid if necessary (see Chapter 1).

20   Wheel studs - replacement

Refer to illustrations 20.3 and 20.4

Note: *This procedure applies to both the front and rear wheel studs.*

1   Loosen the wheel lug nuts, raise the

20.3 Use a press tool to push the stud out of the flange

1	Hub flange	2	Lug nut on stud	3	Press tool

20.4 Install a spacer and a lug nut on the stud, then tighten the nut to draw the stud into place

1	Hub flange	2	Spacer

vehicle and support it securely on jackstands. Remove the wheel.

2   Remove the brake disc or drum (see Chapter 9).

3   Install a lug nut part way onto the stud being replaced. Push the stud out of the hub flange with a press tool **(see illustration)**.

4   Insert the new stud into the hub flange from the back side and install some flat washers and a lug nut on the stud **(see illustration)**.

5   Tighten the lug nut until the stud is seated in the flange.

6   Reinstall the brake drum or disc. Install the wheel and lug nuts. Lower the vehicle and tighten the lug nuts to the torque listed in the Chapter 1 Specifications.

21   Wheels and tires - general information

Refer to illustration 21.1

1   All vehicles covered by this manual are equipped with metric-sized steel belted radial tires **(see illustration)**. Use of other size or type of tires may affect the ride and handling of the vehicle. Don't mix different types of tires, such as radials and bias belted on the same vehicle, as handling may be seriously affected. It's recommended that tires be replaced in pairs on the same axle, but if only one tire is being replaced, be sure it's the same size, structure and tread design as the other.

2   Because tire pressure has a substantial effect on handling and wear, the pressure on all tires should be checked at least once a month or before any extended trips (see Chapter 1).

3   Wheels must be replaced if they are bent, dented, leak air, have elongated bolt holes, are heavily rusted, out of vertical symmetry or if the lug nuts won't stay tight. Wheel

repairs that use welding or peening are not recommended.

4   Tire and wheel balance is important in the overall handling, braking and performance of the vehicle. Unbalanced wheels can adversely affect handling and ride characteristics as well as tire life. Whenever a tire is installed on a wheel, the tire and wheel should be balanced by a shop with the proper equipment.

22   Wheel alignment - general information

Refer to illustration 22.1

A wheel alignment refers to the adjustments made to the wheels so they are in proper angular relationship to the suspension and the ground. Wheels that are out of proper alignment not only affect vehicle control, but

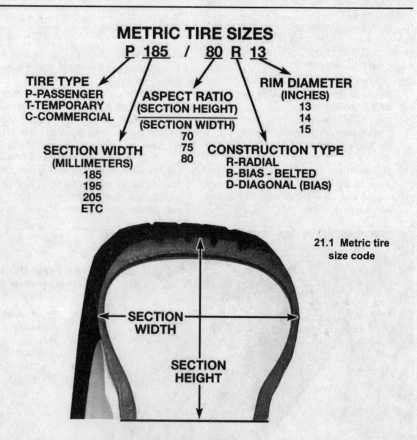

METRIC TIRE SIZES
P 185 / 80 R 13

TIRE TYPE
P-PASSENGER
T-TEMPORARY
C-COMMERCIAL

ASPECT RATIO
(SECTION HEIGHT)
─────────────
(SECTION WIDTH)
70
75
80

RIM DIAMETER
(INCHES)
13
14
15

SECTION WIDTH
(MILLIMETERS)
185
195
205
ETC

CONSTRUCTION TYPE
R-RADIAL
B-BIAS - BELTED
D-DIAGONAL (BIAS)

SECTION WIDTH

SECTION HEIGHT

21.1 Metric tire size code

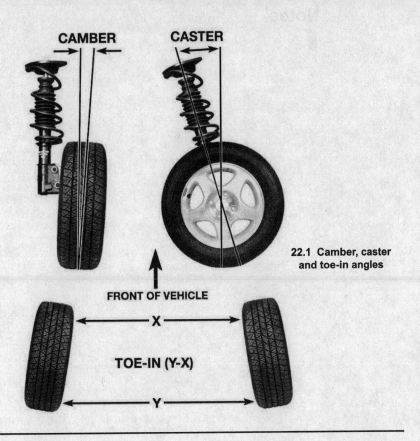

22.1 Camber, caster and toe-in angles

also increase tire wear. The alignment angles normally measured are camber, caster and toe-in **(see illustration)**. Toe-in and camber are the only adjustable angles on the front. Caster should be measured to check for bent or worn suspension parts. Camber and toe-in should be measured on the rear to check for a bent axle.

Getting the proper wheel alignment is a very exacting process, one in which complicated and expensive machines are necessary to perform the job properly. Because of this, you should have a technician with the proper equipment perform these tasks. We will, how-

ever, use this space to give you a basic idea of what is involved with a wheel alignment so you can better understand the process and deal intelligently with the shop that does the work.

Toe-in is the turning in of the wheels. The purpose of a toe specification is to ensure parallel rolling of the wheels. In a vehicle with zero toe-in, the distance between the front edges of the wheels will be the same as the distance between the rear edges of the wheels. The actual amount of toe-in is normally only a fraction of an inch. On the front end, toe-in is controlled by the tie-rod end position on the tie-rod. On the rear end, it's not adjustable. Incorrect toe-in will cause the tires to wear improperly by making them scrub against the road surface.

Camber is the tilting of the wheels from vertical when viewed from one end of the vehicle. When the wheels tilt out at the top, the camber is said to be positive (+). When the wheels tilt in at the top the camber is negative (-). The amount of tilt is measured in degrees from vertical and this measurement is called the camber angle. This angle affects the amount of tire tread which contacts the road and compensates for changes in the suspension geometry when the vehicle is cornering or traveling over an undulating surface. On the front end, camber is adjusted by altering the position of the steering knuckle in the strut flange. If camber can't be adjusted within the specified range, special adjuster bolts, which replace the standard strut-to-knuckle bolts, are available. On the rear end, camber is not adjustable.

Caster is the tilting of the front steering axis from the vertical. A tilt toward the rear is positive caster and a tilt toward the front is negative caster. Caster is not adjustable on these vehicles

Notes

Chapter 11   Body

Contents

1   General information

The models covered by this manual feature a unibody construction, using a floor pan with front and rear frame side rails which support the body components, front and rear suspension systems and other mechanical components. Certain components are particularly vulnerable to accident damage and can be unbolted and repaired or replaced. Among these parts are the body moldings, bumpers, hood and trunk lids and all glass.

Only general body maintenance practices and body panel repair procedures within the scope of the do-it-yourselfer are included in this Chapter.

2   Body - maintenance

1   The condition of your vehicle's body is very important, because the resale value depends a great deal on it. It's much more difficult to repair a neglected or damaged body than it is to repair mechanical components. The hidden areas of the body, such as the wheel wells, the frame and the engine compartment, are equally important, although they don't require as frequent attention as the rest of the body.
2   Once a year, or every 12,000 miles, it's a good idea to have the underside of the body steam cleaned. All traces of dirt and oil will be removed and the area can then be inspected carefully for rust, damaged brake lines, frayed electrical wires, damaged cables and other problems. The front suspension components should be greased after completion of this job.
3   At the same time, clean the engine and the engine compartment with a steam cleaner or water soluble degreaser.
4   The wheel wells should be given close attention, since undercoating can peel away and stones and dirt thrown up by the tires can cause the paint to chip and flake, allowing rust to set in. If rust is found, clean down to the bare metal and apply an anti-rust paint.
5   The body should be washed about once a week. Wet the vehicle thoroughly to soften the dirt, then wash it down with a soft sponge and plenty of clean soapy water. If the surplus dirt is not washed off very carefully, it can wear down the paint.
6   Spots of tar or asphalt thrown up from the road should be removed with a cloth soaked in solvent.
7   Once every six months, wax the body and chrome trim. If a chrome cleaner is used to remove rust from any of the vehicle's plated parts, remember that the cleaner also removes part of the chrome, so use it sparingly.

3   Vinyl trim - maintenance

Don't clean vinyl trim with detergents, caustic soap or petroleum-based cleaners. Plain soap and water works just fine, with a soft brush to clean dirt that may be ingrained. Wash the vinyl as frequently as the rest of the vehicle.

After cleaning, application of a high quality rubber and vinyl protectant will help prevent oxidation and cracks. The protectant can also be applied to weather-stripping, vacuum lines and rubber hoses, which often fail as a result of chemical degradation, and to the tires.

4 Upholstery and carpets - maintenance

1 Every three months remove the carpets or mats and clean the interior of the vehicle (more frequently if necessary). Vacuum the upholstery and carpets to remove loose dirt and dust.

2 Leather upholstery requires special care. Stains should be removed with warm water and a very mild soap solution. Use a clean, damp cloth to remove the soap, then wipe again with a dry cloth. Never use alcohol, gasoline, nail polish remover or thinner to clean leather upholstery.

3 After cleaning, regularly treat leather upholstery with a leather wax. Never use car wax on leather upholstery.

4 In areas where the interior of the vehicle is subject to bright sunlight, cover leather seats with a sheet if the vehicle is to be left out for any length of time.

5 Body repair - minor damage

See photo sequence

Repair of minor scratches

1 If the scratch is superficial and does not penetrate to the metal of the body, repair is very simple. Lightly rub the scratched area with a fine rubbing compound to remove loose paint and built-up wax. Rinse the area with clean water.

2 Apply touch-up paint to the scratch, using a small brush. Continue to apply thin layers of paint until the surface of the paint in the scratch is level with the surrounding paint. Allow the new paint at least two weeks to harden, then blend it into the surrounding paint by rubbing with a very fine rubbing compound. Finally, apply a coat of wax to the scratch area.

3 If the scratch has penetrated the paint and exposed the metal of the body, causing the metal to rust, a different repair technique is required. Remove all loose rust from the bottom of the scratch with a pocket knife, then apply rust inhibiting paint to prevent the formation of rust in the future. Using a rubber or nylon applicator, coat the scratched area with glaze-type filler. If required, the filler can be mixed with thinner to provide a very thin paste, which is ideal for filling narrow scratches. Before the glaze filler in the scratch hardens, wrap a piece of smooth cotton cloth around the tip of a finger. Dip the cloth in thinner and then quickly wipe it along the surface of the scratch. This will ensure that the surface of the filler is slightly hollow. The scratch can now be painted over as described earlier in this section.

Repair of dents

4 When repairing dents, the first job is to pull the dent out until the affected area is as close as possible to its original shape. There is no point in trying to restore the original shape completely as the metal in the damaged area will have stretched on impact and cannot be restored to its original contours. It is better to bring the level of the dent up to a point that is about 1/8-inch below the level of the surrounding metal. In cases where the dent is very shallow, it is not worth trying to pull it out at all.

5 If the back side of the dent is accessible, it can be hammered out gently from behind using a soft-face hammer. While doing this, hold a block of wood firmly against the opposite side of the metal to absorb the hammer blows and prevent the metal from being stretched.

6 If the dent is in a section of the body which has double layers, or some other factor makes it inaccessible from behind, a different technique is required. Drill several small holes through the metal inside the damaged area, particularly in the deeper sections. Screw long, self-tapping screws into the holes just enough for them to get a good grip in the metal. Now the dent can be pulled out by pulling on the protruding heads of the screws with locking pliers.

7 The next stage of repair is the removal of paint from the damaged area and from an inch or so of the surrounding metal. This is done with a wire brush or sanding disk in a drill motor, although it can be done just as effectively by hand with sandpaper. To complete the preparation for filling, score the surface of the bare metal with a screwdriver or the tang of a file, or drill small holes in the affected area. This will provide a good grip for the filler material. To complete the repair, see the subsection on filling and painting later in this Section.

Repair of rust holes or gashes

8 Remove all paint from the affected area and from an inch or so of the surrounding metal using a sanding disk or wire brush mounted in a drill motor. If these are not available, a few sheets of sandpaper will do the job just as effectively.

9 With the paint removed, you will be able to determine the severity of the corrosion and decide whether to replace the whole panel, if possible, or repair the affected area. New body panels are not as expensive as most people think and it is often quicker to install a new panel than to repair large areas of rust.

10 Remove all trim pieces from the affected area except those which will act as a guide to the original shape of the damaged body, such as headlight shells, etc. Using metal snips or a hacksaw blade, remove all loose metal and any other metal that is badly affected by rust. Hammer the edges of the hole in to create a slight depression for the filler material.

11 Wire brush the affected area to remove the powdery rust from the surface of the metal. If the back of the rusted area is accessible, treat it with rust inhibiting paint.

12 Before filling is done, block the hole in some way. This can be done with sheet metal riveted or screwed into place, or by stuffing the hole with wire mesh.

13 Once the hole is blocked off, the affected area can be filled and painted. See the following subsection on filling and painting.

Filling and painting

14 Many types of body fillers are available, but generally speaking, body repair kits which contain filler paste and a tube of resin hardener are best for this type of repair work. A wide, flexible plastic or nylon applicator will be necessary for imparting a smooth and contoured finish to the surface of the filler material. Mix up a small amount of filler on a clean piece of wood or cardboard (use the hardener sparingly). Follow the manufacturer's instructions on the package, otherwise the filler will set incorrectly.

15 Using the applicator, apply the filler paste to the prepared area. Draw the applicator across the surface of the filler to achieve the desired contour and to level the filler surface. As soon as a contour that approximates the original one is achieved, stop working the paste. If you continue, the paste will begin to stick to the applicator. Continue to add thin layers of paste at 20-minute intervals until the level of the filler is just above the surrounding metal.

16 Once the filler has hardened, the excess can be removed with a body file. From then on, progressively finer grades of sandpaper should be used, starting with a 180-grit paper and finishing with 600-grit wet-or-dry paper. Always wrap the sandpaper around a flat rubber or wooden block, otherwise the surface of the filler will not be completely flat. During the sanding of the filler surface, the wet-or-dry paper should be periodically rinsed in water. This will ensure that a very smooth finish is produced in the final stage.

17 At this point, the repair area should be surrounded by a ring of bare metal, which in turn should be encircled by the finely feathered edge of good paint. Rinse the repair area with clean water until all of the dust produced by the sanding operation is gone.

18 Spray the entire area with a light coat of primer. This will reveal any imperfections in the surface of the filler. Repair the imperfections with fresh filler paste or glaze filler and once more smooth the surface with sandpaper. Repeat this spray-and-repair procedure until you are satisfied that the surface of the filler and the feathered edge of the paint are perfect. Rinse the area with clean water and allow it to dry completely.

19 The repair area is now ready for painting. Spray painting must be carried out in a warm, dry, windless and dust free atmosphere. These conditions can be created if you have access to a large indoor work area, but if you are forced to work in the open, you will have to pick the day very carefully. If you are working indoors, dousing the floor in the work area with water will help settle the dust that would otherwise be in the air. If the repair area is confined to one body panel, mask off the surrounding

panels. This will help minimize the effects of a slight mismatch in paint color. Trim pieces such as chrome strips, door handles, etc., will also need to be masked off or removed. Use masking tape and several thickness of newspaper for the masking operations.

20   Before spraying, shake the paint can thoroughly, then spray a test area until the spray painting technique is mastered. Cover the repair area with a thick coat of primer. The thickness should be built up using several thin layers of primer rather than one thick one. Using 600-grit wet-or-dry sandpaper, rub down the surface of the primer until it is very smooth. While doing this, the work area should be thoroughly rinsed with water and the wet-or-dry sandpaper periodically rinsed as well. Allow the primer to dry before spraying additional coats.

21   Spray on the top coat, again building up the thickness by using several thin layers of paint. Begin spraying in the center of the repair area and then, using a circular motion, work out until the whole repair area and about two inches of the surrounding original paint is covered. Remove all masking material 10 to 15 minutes after spraying on the final coat of paint. Allow the new paint at least two weeks to harden, then use a very fine rubbing compound to blend the edges of the new paint into the existing paint. Finally, apply a coat of wax.

6   Body repair - major damage

1   Major damage must be repaired by an auto body shop specifically equipped to perform unibody repairs. These shops have the specialized equipment required to do the job properly.

2   If the damage is extensive, the body must be checked for proper alignment or the vehicle's handling characteristics may be adversely affected and other components may wear at an accelerated rate.

3   Due to the fact that all of the major body components (hood, fenders, etc.) are separate and replaceable units, any seriously damaged components should be replaced rather than repaired. Sometimes the components can be found in a wrecking yard that specializes in used vehicle components, often at considerable savings over the cost of new parts.

7   Hinges and locks - maintenance

Once every 3000 miles, or every three months, the hinges and latch assemblies on the doors, hood and trunk should be given a few drops of light oil or lock lubricant. The door latch strikers should also be lubricated with a thin coat of grease to reduce wear and ensure free movement. Lubricate the door and trunk locks with spray-on graphite lubricant.

8   Windshield and fixed glass - replacement

Replacement of the windshield and fixed glass requires the use of special fast-setting adhesive/caulk materials and some specialized tools. It is recommended that these operations be left to a dealer or a shop specializing in glass work.

9   Hood - removal, installation and adjustment

Refer to illustrations 9.1, 9.10 and 9.11
Note: *The hood is heavy and somewhat awkward to remove and install - at least two people should perform this procedure.*

Removal and installation

1   Make marks around the hinge plate to ensure proper alignment during installation **(see illustration)**.

2   Use blankets or pads to cover the cowl area of the body and fenders. This will protect the body and paint as the hood is lifted off.

3   Disconnect any cables or wires that will interfere with removal. On some models, it may be necessary to remove the lower two hood insulation retaining pins and peel the insulation back enough to disconnect the windshield washer hoses.

4   Have an assistant support one side of the hood while you support the other. Simultaneously remove the hinge-to-hood bolts.

5   Lift off the hood.

6   Installation is the reverse of removal.

Adjustment

Note: *On 2009 and later models, centering bolts are used to mount the hood and hood latch. The hood and hood latch cannot be adjusted with the centering bolts in place. Replace the centering bolts with standard bolts and washers when making adjustments.*

7   Fore-and-aft and side-to-side adjustment of the hood is done by moving the hinge plate slot after loosening the bolts.

8   Scribe a line around the entire hinge plate so you can judge the amount of movement **(see illustration 9.1)**

9   Loosen the bolts or nuts and move the hood into correct alignment. Move it only a little at a time. Tighten the hinge bolts and carefully lower the hood to check the position.

10   If necessary after installation, the entire hood latch assembly can be adjusted up-and-down as well as from side-to-side on the radiator support so the hood closes securely, flush with the fenders. To make the adjustment, scribe a line around the hood latch mounting bolts to provide a reference point, then loosen them and reposition the latch assembly, as necessary **(see illustration)**. Following adjustment, retighten the mounting bolts.

11   Finally, adjust the hood bumpers on the radiator support so the hood, when closed, is flush with the fenders **(see illustration)**.

12   The hood latch assembly, as well as the hinges, should be periodically lubricated with white, lithium-base grease to prevent binding and wear.

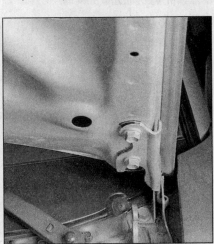

9.1 Before removing the hood, make marks around the hinge plate

9.10 Loosen the hood latch bolts, move the latch and retighten bolts, then close the hood to check the fit - repeat the procedure until the hood is flush with the fenders

9.11 Adjust the hood height by screwing the hood bumpers in-or-out

These photos illustrate a method of repairing simple dents. They are intended to supplement *Body repair - minor damage* in this Chapter and should not be used as the sole instructions for body repair on these vehicles.

1 If you can't access the backside of the body panel to hammer out the dent, pull it out with a slide-hammer-type dent puller. In the deepest portion of the dent or along the crease line, drill or punch hole(s) at least one inch apart . . .

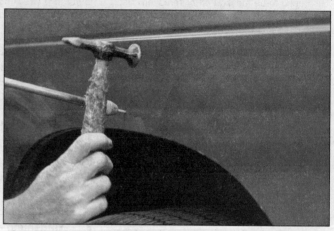

2 . . . then screw the slide-hammer into the hole and operate it. Tap with a hammer near the edge of the dent to help 'pop' the metal back to its original shape. When you're finished, the dent area should be close to its original contour and about 1/8-inch below the surface of the surrounding metal

3 Using coarse-grit sandpaper, remove the paint down to the bare metal. Hand sanding works fine, but the disc sander shown here makes the job faster. Use finer (about 320-grit) sandpaper to feather-edge the paint at least one inch around the dent area

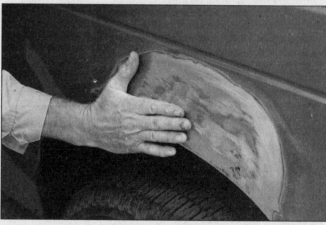

4 When the paint is removed, touch will probably be more helpful than sight for telling if the metal is straight. Hammer down the high spots or raise the low spots as necessary. Clean the repair area with wax/silicone remover

5 Following label instructions, mix up a batch of plastic filler and hardener. The ratio of filler to hardener is critical, and, if you mix it incorrectly, it will either not cure properly or cure too quickly (you won't have time to file and sand it into shape)

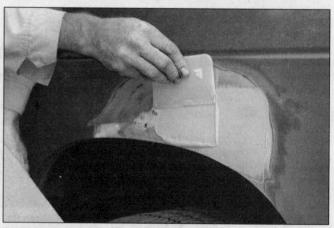

6 Working quickly so the filler doesn't harden, use a plastic applicator to press the body filler firmly into the metal, assuring it bonds completely. Work the filler until it matches the original contour and is slightly above the surrounding metal

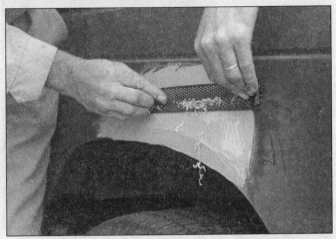

7 Let the filler harden until you can just dent it with your fingernail. Use a body file or Surform tool (shown here) to rough-shape the filler

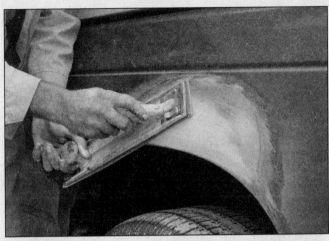

8 Use coarse-grit sandpaper and a sanding board or block to work the filler down until it's smooth and even. Work down to finer grits of sandpaper - always using a board or block - ending up with 360 or 400 grit

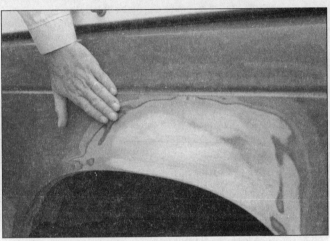

9 You shouldn't be able to feel any ridge at the transition from the filler to the bare metal or from the bare metal to the old paint. As soon as the repair is flat and uniform, remove the dust and mask off the adjacent panels or trim pieces

10 Apply several layers of primer to the area. Don't spray the primer on too heavy, so it sags or runs, and make sure each coat is dry before you spray on the next one. A professional-type spray gun is being used here, but aerosol spray primer is available inexpensively from auto parts stores

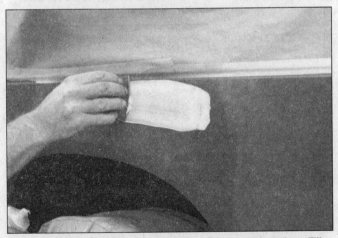

11 The primer will help reveal imperfections or scratches. Fill these with glazing compound. Follow the label instructions and sand it with 360 or 400-grit sandpaper until it's smooth. Repeat the glazing, sanding and respraying until the primer reveals a perfectly smooth surface

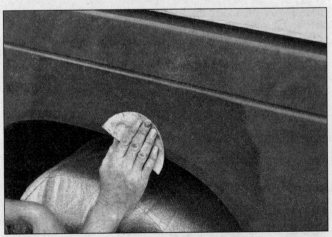

12 Finish sand the primer with very fine sandpaper (400 or 600-grit) to remove the primer overspray. Clean the area with water and allow it to dry. Use a tack rag to remove any dust, then apply the finish coat. Don't attempt to rub out or wax the repair area until the paint has dried completely (at least two weeks)

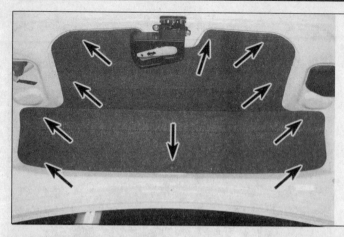

10.2 Remove the plastic retainers and the trunk lid trim panel

10.3 Draw a mark around the bolt heads to help with lid realignment on installation

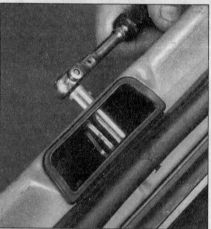

10.8 Loosen the bolts, then adjust the latch and striker position

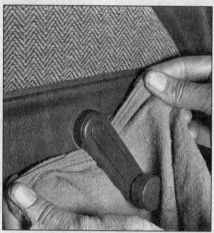

11.2a Work a cloth up behind the regulator handle and move it back-and-forth . . .

3   Make alignment marks around the hinge mounting bolts **(see illustration)**.
4   While an assistant supports the lid, remove the lid-to-hinge bolts on both sides and lift it off.
5   Installation is the reverse of removal.
Note: *When reinstalling the trunk lid, align the lid-to-hinge bolts with the marks made during removal.*
6   After installation, close the lid and make sure it's in proper alignment with the surrounding panels.
7   Forward-and-backward and side-to-side adjustments are made by loosening the hinge-to-lid bolts and gently moving the lid into correct alignment.
8   To adjust the lid so it is flush with the body when closed, loosen the mounting bolts and move the lock and striker **(see illustration)**.

10 Trunk lid - removal, installation and adjustment

Refer to illustrations 10.2, 10.3 and 10.8
Note: *On 2009 and later models, centering bolts are used to mount the trunk and trunk latch. The trunk and trunk latch cannot be adjusted with the centering bolts in place. Replace the centering bolts with standard*

bolts and washers when making adjustments.
1   Open the trunk lid and cover the edges of the trunk compartment with pads or cloths to protect the painted surfaces when the lid is removed.
2   Open the trunk lid and remove the trunk lid trim cover **(see illustrations)**. Follow the wiring harness into the trunk lid, mark and disconnect all electrical connectors, then pull the harness out of the lid.

11 Door trim panel - removal and installation

Removal

Refer to illustrations 11.2a, 11.2b, 11.2c, 11.5a, 11.5b, 11.6 and 11.8
1   Disconnect the negative cable from the battery.
2   On manual window regulator equipped models, remove the window crank by working a cloth back-and-forth behind the handle to dislodge the retaining clip **(see illustrations)**. A special tool is available for this purpose but it's not essential. With the retainer removed, pull off the handle. On power window models, pry out the switch assembly, unplug the electrical connector and remove it **(see illustration)**.
3   Remove the outside mirror trim cover (see Section 16).
4   On 2008 and earlier models, remove the screw in the inside handle trim. On 2009 and later models, carefully pry the inside trim panel out using a trim tool.

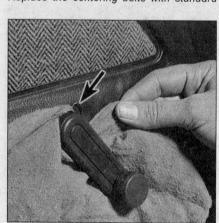

11.2b . . . until the retaining clip is pushed up so you can remove it

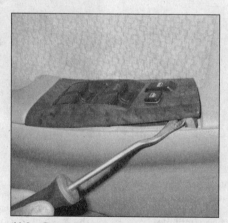

11.2c Pry up on the power window switch and disconnect the electrical connector

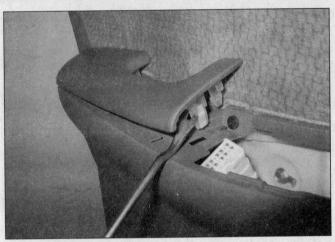

11.5a Pry the armrest up with a screwdriver or trim tool . . .

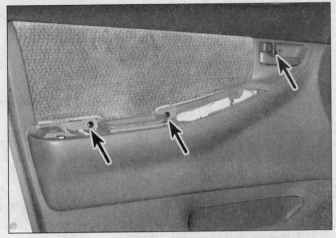

11.5b . . . and remove the door panel screws

5   Pry up the armrest panel with a trim tool and remove the two door panel screws under the armrest **(see illustrations)**.

6   Insert a wide putty knife, a thin screwdriver or a special trim panel removal tool between the trim panel and door to disengage the retaining clips. Work around the outer edge until the panel is free **(see illustration)**.

7   Once all of the clips are disengaged, detach the trim panel, unplug any electrical connectors and remove the trim panel from the vehicle by gently pulling it up and out.

8   For access to the inner door remove the plastic watershield. Peel back the plastic cover, taking care not to tear it **(see illustration)**. Remove the plastic grommets, if necessary.

Installation

9   To install the trim panel, first press the watershield back into place. If necessary, add more sealant to hold it in place.

10   Prior to installation of the door panel, be sure to reinstall any clips in the panel which may have come out during the removal procedure and stayed in the door.

11   Plug in any electrical connectors and place the panel in position. Press it into place until the clips are seated and install any retaining screws and armrest/door pulls. Install the manual regulator window crank or power switch assembly.

12   Door - removal, installation and adjustment

Removal and installation

Refer to illustrations 12.2, 12.3 and 12.4

1   Remove the door trim panel (see Section 11). Disconnect any electrical connectors and push them through the door opening so they won't interfere with removal.

2   Position a jack or jackstands under the door or have an assistant on hand to support the door when the hinge bolts are removed **(see illustration)**. **Note:** *If a jack or stand is used, place a rag between it and the door to protect the door's paint.*

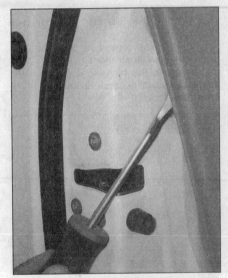

11.6 Use a trim panel removal tool to detach the trim panel retaining clips, then pull the door trim up and out to remove it

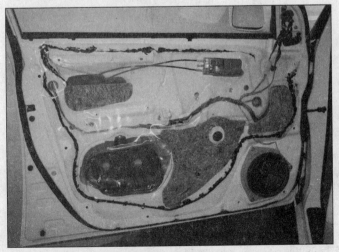

11.8 If the plastic watershield is peeled off carefully it can be reused

12.2 Use two jackstands padded with rags (to protect the paint) to support the door during the removal and installation procedures

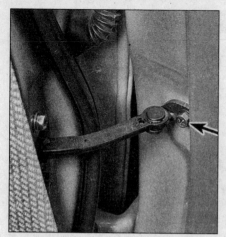

12.3 Remove the bolt and detach the stop strut

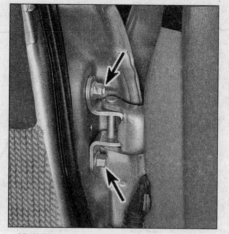

12.4 Mark the position of each hinge to the door, then remove the hinge bolts

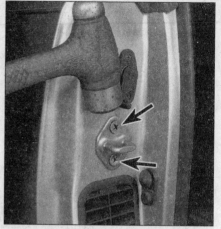

12.6 Adjust the door lock striker by loosening the mounting screws and gently tapping the striker in the desired direction

3   Remove the door stop strut bolt **(see illustration)**.
4   Draw a mark around the hinges to aid in alignment **(see illustration)**.
5   Remove the hinge-to-door bolts and carefully detach the door. Installation is the reverse of removal.

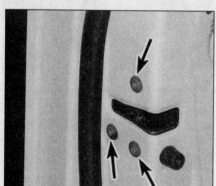

13.3 Remove the latch screws from the end of the door

13.7 Remove the plastic cover, and the outside handle cover/lock cylinder retention screw can be reached through the access in the door frame

Adjustment

Refer to illustration 12.6

Note: *On 2009 and later models, centering bolts are used to mount the door hinge. The hinge cannot be adjusted with the centering bolts in place. Replace the centering bolts with standard bolts and washers when making adjustments.*

6   Following installation, make sure the door is aligned properly. Adjust it if necessary as follows:

a) Up-and-down and forward-and-backward adjustments are made by loosening the hinge-to-body bolts and moving the door, as necessary. A special offset tool may be required to reach some of the bolts.
b) In-and-out and up-and-down adjustments are made by loosening the door side hinge bolts and moving the door, as necessary. A special offset tool may be required to reach some of the bolts.
c) The door lock striker can also be adjusted both up-and-down and sideways to provide a positive engagement

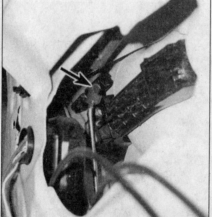

13.8 Disconnect the rod and fasteners from the outside handle (shown inside door)

with the locking mechanism. This is done by loosening the screws and moving the striker, as necessary **(see illustration)**.

---

13 Door latch, lock cylinder and handles - removal and installation

1   Remove the door trim panel and the plastic watershield (see Section 11).

Door latch

Refer to illustration 13.3

2   Reach inside the door and disconnect the control links from the latch.
3   Remove the latch retaining screws from the end of the door **(see illustration)**.
4   Detach the door latch and (if equipped) the door lock solenoid.
5   Installation is the reverse of removal.

Lock cylinder and outside handle

Refer to illustrations 13.7 and 13.8

6   Working through the access holes in the door, disconnect the control rods from the lock cylinder and outside handle.
7   Loosen the screw with a Torx bit and pull the lock cover and lock cylinder from the outside of the door **(see illustration)**.
8   To remove the outside handle, disconnect the control rod and remove the two mounting screws inside the door **(see illustration)**.
9   If the outside handle assembly is to be replaced, disconnect the rod and door operating cable from the handle assembly and transfer them to the new handle.
10   Use a screwdriver to pry the retaining clip off or remove the lock cylinder retaining bolt and remove the lock cylinder from the handle.
11   Installation is the reverse of removal.

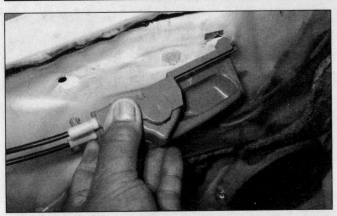

13.13a Rotate the handle clips out of the door and pull the handle assembly away

13.13b Detach the control cables with a small screwdriver

Inside handle

Refer to illustrations 13.13a and 13.13b

12   Remove the retaining screw **(see illustration 11.5b)**.

13   Pull the handle free, disconnect the cables from the inside handle control and remove the handle from the door **(see illustrations)**.

14   Installation is the reverse of removal.

14   Door window glass - removal and installation

Refer to illustrations 14.2 and 14.4

1   Remove the door trim panel and the plastic watershield (see Section 11).

2   Lower the window glass. Remove the door access plate from the door frame **(see illustration)**.

3   Carefully pry the inner weatherstrip out of the door window opening.

4   Place a rag inside the door panel to help prevent scratching the glass, then remove the two glass mounting bolts **(see illustration)**.

5   Remove the glass by pulling it up.

6   Installation is the reverse of the removal procedure.

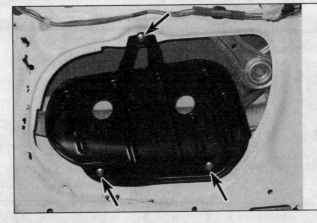

14.2 Remove the screws and this plate for access to one of the glass mounting bolts

15   Bumper covers - removal and installation

Warning: *The models covered by this manual are equipped with Supplemental Restraint systems (SRS), more commonly known as airbags. Always disable the airbag system before working in the vicinity of any airbag system component to avoid the possibility of accidental deployment of the airbag, which could cause personal injury (see Chapter 12).*

Front bumper

Refer to illustrations 15.3a, 15.3b, 15.3c and 15.4

1   Apply the parking brake, raise the vehicle and support it securely on jackstands.

2   Disconnect the negative battery cable, then the positive battery cable and wait two minutes before proceeding any further. On models equipped with fog lights, disconnect the electrical connectors at the fog lights on the back of the bumper fascia.

3   Detach the screws and/or pushpins

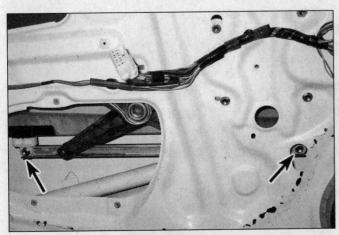

14.4 Location of glass mounting bolts

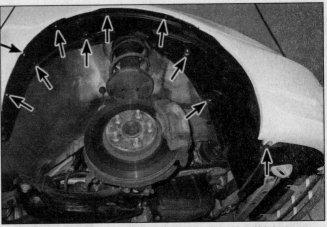

15.3a Remove the fasteners and the inner fenderwell liner

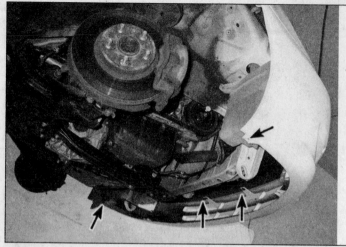

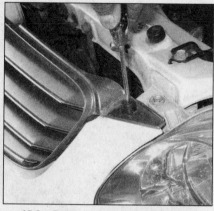

15.3b From below (shown without engine splash panels) remove the screws and plastic pins securing the bumper cover

15.3c Remove the two screws (one shown) at either side of the grille - these screws also secure the bumper cover

15.4 Front bumper beam mounting nuts (access through holes)

15.6 Remove the fasteners securing the bottom lip of the rear bumper cover

securing the top, bottom, sides and top of the bumper cover **(see illustrations)**. **Note 1:** *Use a small screwdriver to pop the center button up on the plastic fasteners, but do not try to remove the center buttons. They stay in the ferrules.* **Note 2:** *Don't try to remove the cover until all fasteners have been located and removed.*

4   If the bumper beam itself is to be replaced, remove the nuts and pull the beam off its mounts **(see illustration)**.

5   Installation is the reverse of removal. Make sure the tabs on the back of the bumper cover fit into the corresponding clips on the body before attaching the bolts and screws. An assistant would be helpful at this point.

Rear bumper

Refer to illustrations 15.6, 15.7, 15.8a and 15.8b

6   Working under the vehicle, detach the plastic clips and screws securing the lower edge of the bumper cover **(see illustration)**.

7   In the rear fenderwells, remove the fas-

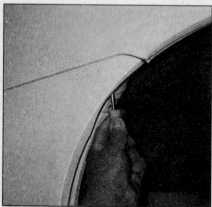

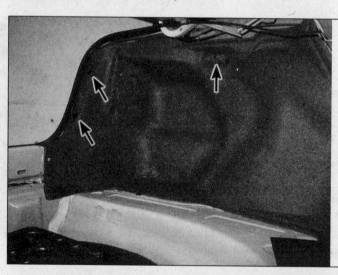

15.7 With the rear of the fenderwell liner pulled back, you can access the one bumper cover screw on each side

15.8a Pry out the plastic fasteners (three shown) and remove the left and right side trim panels in the trunk

15.8b With a socket and extension remove the rear bumper cover mounting nuts through the body holes (three of the four are seen here)

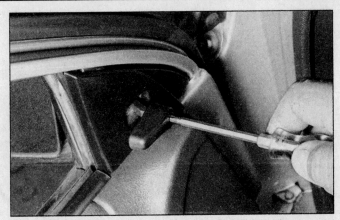

16.1a On manually operated side view mirrors, remove the screw and detach the mirror control handle

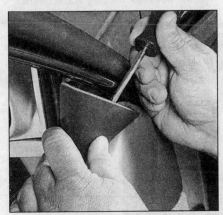

16.1b Detach the cover and lift it out (power mirror shown)

16.2a Remove the three nuts securing the outside mirror to the door - on some models, the nuts also secure a small speaker

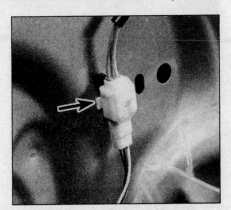

16.2b On vehicles equipped with power side view mirrors, unplug the electrical connector

teners securing the rear of the fenderwell liner, pull back the liner and remove the screw securing the front edge of the bumper cover to the fenderwell **(see illustration)**.

8   Remove the fasteners securing the bumper cover in each corner inside the trunk, and those behind the rear trunk trim panel **(see illustrations)**. To access these fasteners, pull up the trunk mat, then use a trim tool to release the clips securing the rear trunk trim panel and the left and right rear corner panels.

9   Installation is the reverse of removal.

16 Outside mirror - removal and installation

Refer to illustrations 16.1a, 16.1b, 16.2a and 16.2b

1   On manually operated mirrors, remove the control handle **(see illustration)**. On all models, detach the mirror cover by using a small screwdriver to pry the retainers free from the door **(see illustration)**.

2   Remove the three retaining nuts and detach the mirror **(see illustration)**. On power mirrors, unplug the electrical connector **(see illustration)**.

3   Installation is the reverse of removal.

17 Seats - removal and installation

Warning: *These models are equipped with airbags. Always disable the airbag system before working in the vicinity of any airbag system component to avoid the possibility of*

accidental deployment of the airbag(s), which could cause personal injury (see Chapter 12).

Front seats

Refer to illustration 17.1a and 17.1b

1   Pry off the seat bolt covers, if equipped, and remove the retaining bolts, unplug any electrical connectors and lift the seats from the vehicle **(see illustrations)**.

2   Installation is the reverse of removal.

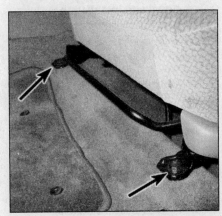

17.1a Slide the seat rearward and remove the front mounting bolts

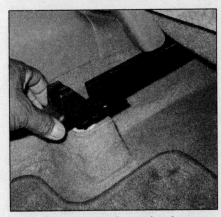

17.1b Slide the seat forward and remove the two covers over the tracks, then remove the two seat mounting bolts

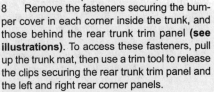

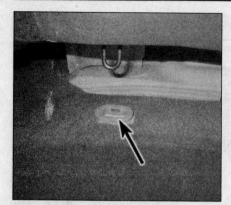

17.3 Pull up on the seat bottom to release the one clip at each side

17.5 On split-back models, pull the release cables for each half of the seatback

17.6a With the split seat-backs folded down, pull back the carpet and remove this trim piece

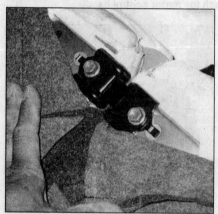

17.6b Remove the mounting bolts securing the seat-backs to the floor - center bolts shown

18.2a Remove the one pushpin fastener at the center-top of the instrument bezel

Rear seats

Refer to illustrations 17.3, 17.5. 17.6a and 17.6b

3   Lift the front of the cushion up, then pull it out toward the front of the vehicle **(see illustration)**.

4   On models with a one-piece seatback, remove the seat back retaining bolts at the floor, then lift up on the back to release the seat back from the body.

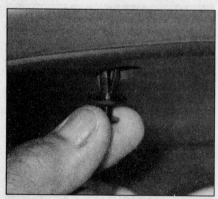

18.2b Pop the center out of the pushpin, then remove it from the bezel (2008 and earlier models)

5   On models with a split-back rear seat, open the trunk and release the two seatback cables, allowing the seatbacks to fold down **(see illustrations)**.

6   Remove the bolts in the middle securing the seat-back assembly to the floor **(see illustration)**. Lift each section up and out to disengage its pins from the brackets at each side.

7   Installation is the reverse of removal.

18   Instrument cluster bezel - removal and installation

Refer to illustrations 18.2a and 18.2b

Warning: *These models are equipped with airbags. Always disable the airbag system before working in the vicinity of any airbag system component to avoid the possibility of accidental deployment of the airbag(s), which could cause personal injury* (see Chapter 12).

1   Disconnect the cable from the negative battery terminal.

2   Tilt the steering column to its lowest position. Remove the one pushpin at the top of the bezel, then detach the bezel clips at the lower edges by prying with a screwdriver to release the clips **(see illustrations)**.

3   Grasp the bezel securely and remove it.

4   Installation is the reverse of the removal procedure.

19   Glove box - removal and installation

Refer to illustration 19.1

Warning: *These models are equipped with airbags. Always disable the airbag system before working in the vicinity of any airbag system component to avoid the possibility of accidental deployment of the airbag(s), which could cause personal injury* (see Chapter 12).

1   Open the glove box and remove the screw

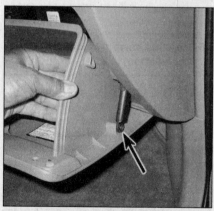

19.1 Remove the stop screw at the right side of the glove box (2008 and earlier models)

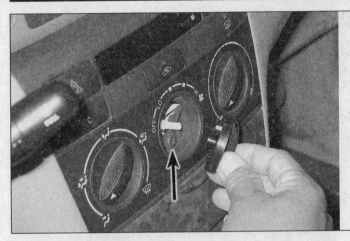

20.3 Pull off this knob for access to the panel screw behind it

20.4a Use a trim tool to release the clips holding the lower trim panel and pull it out

20.4b After the lower center trim panel is detached from the instrument panel, disconnect the electrical connectors at the back

20.8 Remove the four bolts at the bottom of the upper trim panel - the other fasteners are clips

at the lower right corner **(see illustration)**.

2   Squeeze the sides of the glove box toward the center enough to clear the stoppers on each side. Remove the glove box.

3   Installation is the reverse of removal.

20   Center trim panels - removal and installation

Warning: *These models are equipped with airbags. Always disable the airbag system before working in the vicinity of any airbag system component to avoid the possibility of accidental deployment of the airbag(s), which could cause personal injury* (see Chapter 12).

1   Disconnect the cable from the negative battery terminal.

Lower trim panel
2008 and earlier models

Refer to illustrations 20.3, 20.4a and 20.4b

2   Refer to Section 23 and remove the top trim panel at the front of the floor console.

3   Remove the center knob from the heating/air-conditioning control panel, then remove the screw behind it **(see illustration)**.

4   Using a small screwdriver, detach the retaining clips at each corner, then remove

the panel and unplug the electrical connectors **(see illustrations)**.

2009 and later models

5   Remove the upper center trim and driver's side trim panels (see Section 23). If equipped with a tilt steering column, tilt the column all the way down.

6   Using a screwdriver with the tip taped with masking tape, start at the bottom of the bezel and carefully pry the outer edges of the bezel away from the instrument panel until the clips are released. Take care not to scratch the surrounding trim on the instrument panel.

Upper trim panel

Refer to illustrations 20.8 and 20.9

7   Follow Steps 2 through 4 or Steps 5 and 6 to remove the lower trim panel.

8   Remove the screws at the bottom of the panel, then pry the panel from its clips with a trim tool or taped screwdriver **(see illustration)**.

9   Pull the upper trim panel out and unplug the electrical connectors and antenna cable from the radio **(see illustration)**.

10   Installation is the reverse of the removal procedure.

20.9 Pull the upper panel out far enough to disconnect the electrical connectors and the antenna cable

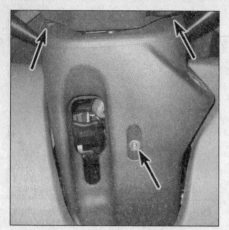

21.1 Remove the lower column cover screws (steering wheel removed for clarity)

21 Steering column covers - removal and installation

Refer to illustration 21.1

Warning: *These models are equipped with airbags. Always disable the airbag system*

22.3a Carefully pry up the shift bezel to release the clips . . .

before working in the vicinity of any airbag system component to avoid the possibility of accidental deployment of the airbag(s), which could cause personal injury (see Chapter 12).

2008 and earlier models

1   Remove the screws securing the lower steering column cover **(see illustration)**. **Note:** *These models have three screws in the lower cover (two mounted horizontally and one mounted vertically). It will be necessary to rotate the steering wheel in order to access the forward facing (horizontally mounted) screws on the lower cover.*

2   Separate the cover halves and detach them from the steering column.

3   Disconnect any electrical connections and the covers.

4   Installation is the reverse of the removal procedure.

2009 and later models

5   Push in on the right and left sides of the lower steering column cover, and disengage the claws.

6   Insert your fingers into the opening of the tilt lever of the lower steering column cover and spread the claw to disengage it.

7   Insert the tip of a screwdriver into the ser-

vice slots at the front of the cover (facing you) and unclip the claws, then remove the cover.

8   Reaching under the upper cover, unclip the claw and two pins to release the cover.

9   Installation is the reverse of removal.

22 Console - removal and installation

Refer to illustrations 22.2, 22.3a, 22.3b and 22.4

Note: *On 2009 and earlier models, it is necessary to remove the lower center trim panel (see Section 20) prior to removing the console.*

Warning: *These models are equipped with airbags. Always disable the airbag system before working in the vicinity of any airbag system component to avoid the possibility of accidental deployment of the airbag(s), which could cause personal injury* (see Chapter 12).

1   Disconnect the cable from the negative battery terminal.

2   Lift up the console armrest and remove the retaining screws from the storage compartment, then remove the mounting screws **(see illustration)**.

3   Detach the shift bezel, using a plastic trim tool, then disconnect the 12-volt power

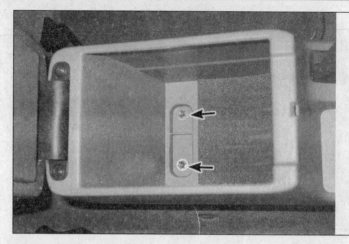

22.2 Remove the retaining screws in the console storage box

22.3b . . . then pull up the bezel and disconnect the electrical connector

22.4 Remove the four screws securing the front portion of the console to the floor, then disconnect the electrical connector

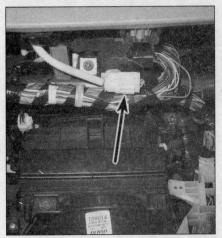

23.3 Typical passenger side airbag module electrical connector

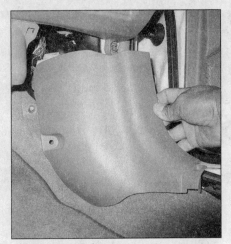

23.8 Pry up the scuff plate from the sill, then remove the one screw and the kick panel (right-side shown)

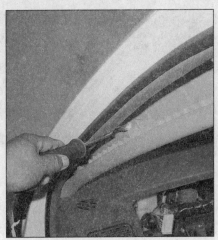

23.10 Carefully pry off the windshield pillar trim panels

source connector **(see illustrations)**.

4   Remove the four screws, disconnect the electrical connector and remove the floor console **(see illustration)**.

5   Installation is the reverse of the removal procedure.

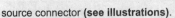

23   Instrument panel - removal and installation

Warning: *These models are equipped with airbags. Always disable the airbag system before working in the vicinity of any airbag system component to avoid the possibility of accidental deployment of the airbag(s), which could cause personal injury (see Chapter 12).*
Note: *This procedure requires the removal of the instrument panel, the cross-cowl support tube and steering column. This involves disconnecting numerous electrical connectors and there is the potential for breakage of delicate plastic tabs on various components. This is a difficult job for the average home mechanic.*

Instrument panel

Refer to illustrations 23.3, 23.8, 23.10, 23.11, 23.12, 23.13 and 23.14

1   Disconnect the cable from the negative battery terminal.

2   Remove the driver's airbag module and the steering wheel (see Chapter 10).

3   Remove the glove box assembly (see Section 19), disconnect the passenger airbag module electrical connector **(see illustration)**. The electrical connectors used in the airbag system are a twin-lock design; use the proper method for disconnecting these connectors or damage to the connector may occur (see Chapter 12).

4   Remove the instrument cluster bezel (see Section 18) and remove the instrument cluster (see Chapter 12).

5   Remove the center trim panels (see Section 20) and the heater and air conditioning control panel (see Chapter 3).

6   Remove the steering column covers (see Section 21).

7   Remove the center console (see Sec-

tion 22).

8   Remove the front door scuff plates and the kick panels from both sides **(see illustration)**.

9   Pry out the left and right air vents in the upper instrumentv panel.

10   Use a trim tool to remove the left and right trim pieces along the inside of the windshield pillars **(see illustration)**. Cover the entire length of the curtain shield airbag with a protective cover as soon as the front pillar trim is removed.

11   Remove the three fasteners and release the clips, then remove the upper instrument panel **(see illustration)**. Be sure to disconnect any electrical connectors attached behind the upper instrument panel.

12   On the left side of the lower instrument panel, disconnect and remove the release handle for the hood **(see illustration)**. Also, separate the diagnostic connector under the left edge of the instrument panel.

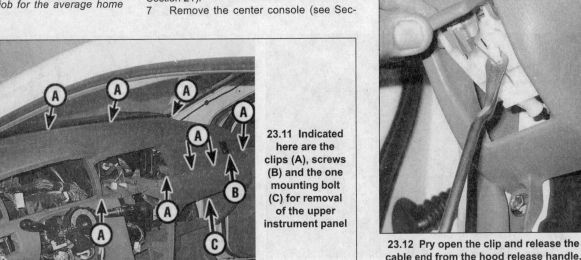

23.11 Indicated here are the clips (A), screws (B) and the one mounting bolt (C) for removal of the upper instrument panel

23.12 Pry open the clip and release the cable end from the hood release handle, then pry the plastic housing from the lower instrument panel

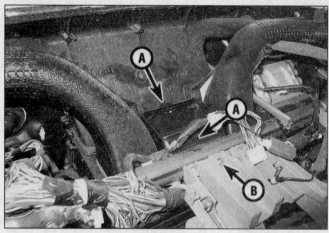

23.13 Remove the pins (A) securing the left, right and center (shown) ducts - also remove the center bolt (B) securing the lower instrument panel to the reinforcement tube

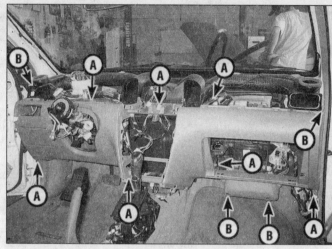

23.14 Location of lower instrument panel screws (A) and pins (B)

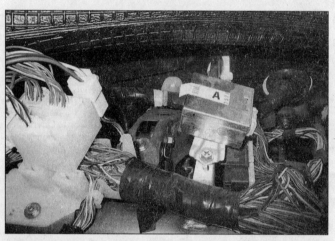

23.16 Go along the width of the beam, disconnecting electrical components bolted to the beam and harnesses attached with pins

23.17a Remove the bolts and this reinforcement plate below the steering column

13   Pry up the plastic pins securing the vent ducts at the center and each side of the lower instrument panel (see illustration).

14   Remove the fasteners and remove the lower instrument panel (see illustration). Do not force the panel off, make sure you have found all the fasteners first. Make notes and use plastic bags to keep track of which fasten-ers go where.

15   The remainder of installation is the reverse of removal.

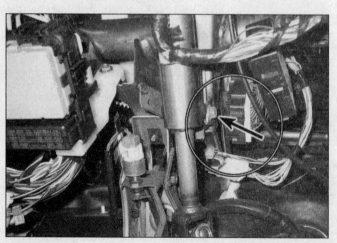

23.17b Remove the lower steering column mounting bolt . . .

23.17c . . . and the two upper mounting bolts (upper captive nuts indicated, bolt heads are below bracket)

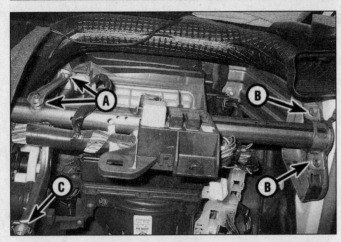

23.18 At the right side of the beam, disconnect the brace to the blower housing (A), the two end mounting bolts (B), and the bottom screw (C). Then move to the left side and detach the braces and mounting bolts

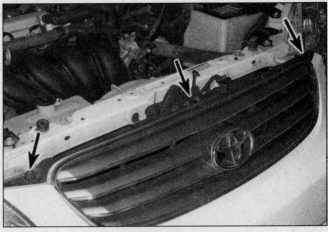

24.1 Along the top of the grille, remove the screws at each side and the pushpin at the center, then disengage the clips at the bottom and pull the grille forward and out

Cowl reinforcement beam

Refer to illustrations 23.16, 23.17a, 23.17b, 23.17c and 23.18

16   If the cowl reinforcement beam must be removed for a service procedure, follow Steps 1 through 15, then proceed to disconnect all components fastened to the reinforcement beam **(see illustration)**.

17   Disconnect the electrical connectors at the steering column and remove the bolts securing the column to the beam **(see illustrations)**.

18   At the left and right sides of the beam, remove the bolts holding braces from the tube to other components, then remove the two bolts holding the beam into the body saddles at either end **(see illustration)**. Remove the beam from the vehicle.

19   Installation is the reverse of removal.

24   Radiator grille - removal and installation

2008 and earlier models

Refer to illustration 24.1

1   Remove three fasteners along the top of the grille **(see illustration)**.

2   Pull the top of the grille out for access and disengage the lower retaining clips with a screwdriver.

3   Installation is the reverse of removal.

2009 and later models

4   Remove the six clips along the top edge of the grille.

5   Using a flat tipped screwdriver, release the claws and guides, and remove the radiator grille.

6   Installation is the reverse of removal.

25   Cowl louver panels - removal and installation

1   Mark the position of the windshield wiper blades on the windshield with a wax marking pen.

2   Remove the wiper arms (see Chapter 12).

3   With a trim tool, release the clips and peel up the cowl-to-hood rubber seal.

4   Remove the cowl louver retaining pins, disconnect the windshield washer hoses and detach the cowl louver panels from the vehicle. **Note:** *Remove the right-side panel first, then the left.*

5   Installation is the reverse of removal. Make sure to align the wiper blades with the marks made during removal.

26   Seat belts - check

1   Check the seat belts, buckles, latch plates and guide loops for any obvious damage or signs of wear.

2   Make sure the seat belt reminder light comes on when the key is turned on.

3   The seat belts are designed to lock up during a sudden stop or impact, yet allow free movement during normal driving. The retractors should hold the belt against your chest while driving and rewind the belt when the buckle is unlatched.

4   If any of the above checks reveal problems with the seat-belt system, replace parts as necessary.

27   Front fender - removal and installation

1   Raise the vehicle, support it securely on jackstands and remove the front wheel.

2   Remove the headlight housing (see Chapter 12).

3   Detach the inner fenderwell screws and clips, then remove the inner fenderwell liner **(see illustration 15.3a)**.

4   Open the front door, and remove the upper fender-to-body bolt and the one bolt inside the fenderwell.

5   Under the headlight housing area, remove the two fender fasteners.

6   Remove the cowl louver panel and the rubber hood sealing strip along the top of the fender, then remove the remaining fender mounting bolts.

7   Lift off the fender. It's a good idea to have an assistant support the fender while it's being moved away from the vehicle to prevent damage to the surrounding body panels.

8   Installation is the reverse of removal. Check the alignment of the fender to the hood and front edge of the door before final tightening of the fender fasteners.

Notes

Chapter 12
Chassis electrical system

Contents

1 General information

The electrical system is a 12-volt, negative ground type. Power for the lights and all electrical accessories is supplied by a lead/acid-type battery, which is charged by the alternator.

This Chapter covers repair and service procedures for the various electrical components not associated with the engine. Information on the battery, alternator and starter motor can be found in Chapter 5.

It should be noted that when portions of the electrical system are serviced, the cable should be disconnected from the negative battery terminal to prevent electrical shorts and/or fires.

2 Electrical troubleshooting - general information

Refer to illustrations 2.5a, 2.5b, 2.6 and 2.9

A typical electrical circuit consists of an electrical component, any switches, relays, motors, fuses, fusible links or circuit breakers related to that component and the wiring and connectors that link the component to both the battery and the chassis. To help you pinpoint an electrical circuit problem, wiring diagrams are included at the end of this Chapter.

Before tackling any troublesome electrical circuit, first study the appropriate wiring diagrams to get a complete understanding of what makes up that individual circuit.

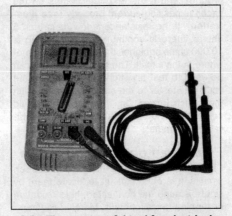

2.5a The most useful tool for electrical troubleshooting is a digital multimeter that can check volts, amps, and test continuity

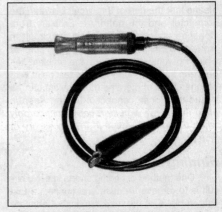

2.5b A simple test light is a very handy tool for testing voltage

Trouble spots, for instance, can often be narrowed down by noting if other components related to the circuit are operating properly. If several components or circuits fail at one time, chances are the problem is in a fuse or ground connection, because several circuits are often routed through the same fuse and ground connections.

Electrical problems usually stem from simple causes, such as loose or corroded connections, a blown fuse, a melted fusible link or a failed relay. Visually inspect the condition of all fuses, wires and connections in a problem circuit before troubleshooting the circuit.

If test equipment and instruments are going to be utilized, use the diagrams to plan ahead of time where you will make the necessary connections in order to accurately pinpoint the trouble spot.

The basic tools needed for electrical troubleshooting include a circuit tester or voltmeter (a 12-volt bulb with a set of test leads can also be used), a continuity tester, which includes a bulb, battery and set of test leads, and a jumper wire, preferably with a circuit breaker incorporated, which can be used to bypass electrical components **(see illustrations)**. Before attempting to locate a problem with test instruments, use the wiring diagram(s) to decide where to make the connections.

2.6 In use, a basic test light's lead is clipped to a known good ground, then the pointed probe can test connectors, wires or electrical sockets - if the bulb lights, the circuit being tested has battery voltage

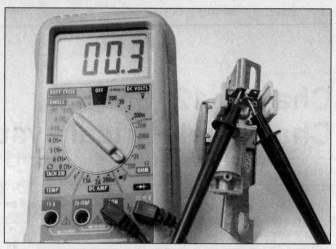

2.9 With a multimeter set to the ohms scale, resistance can be checked across two terminals - when checking for continuity, a low reading indicates continuity, a high reading or infinity indicates lack of continuity

Voltage checks

Voltage checks should be performed if a circuit is not functioning properly. Connect one lead of a circuit tester to either the negative battery terminal or a known good ground. Connect the other lead to a connector in the circuit being tested, preferably nearest to the battery or fuse **(see illustration)**. If the bulb of the tester lights, voltage is present, which means that the part of the circuit between the connector and the battery is problem free. Continue checking the rest of the circuit in the same fashion. When you reach a point at which no voltage is present, the problem lies between that point and the last test point with voltage. Most of the time the problem can be traced to a loose connection. **Note:** *Keep in mind that some circuits receive voltage only when the ignition key is in the Accessory or Run position.*

Finding a short

One method of finding shorts in a live circuit is to remove the fuse and connect a test light in place of the fuse terminals (fabricate two jumper wires with small spade terminals, plug the jumper wires into the fuse box and connect the test light). There should be voltage present in the circuit. Move the suspected wiring harness from side-to-side while watching the test light. If the bulb goes off, there is a short to ground somewhere in that area, probably where the insulation has rubbed through.

Ground check

Perform a ground test to check whether a component is properly grounded. Disconnect the battery and connect one lead of a continuity tester or multimeter (set to the ohms scale), to a known good ground. Connect the other lead to the wire or ground connection being tested. If the resistance is low (less than 5 ohms), the ground is good. If the bulb on a self-powered test light does not go on, the ground is not good.

Continuity check

A continuity check is done to determine if there are any breaks in a circuit - if it is passing electricity properly. With the circuit off (no power in the circuit), a self-powered continuity tester or multimeter can be used to check the circuit. Connect the test leads to both ends of the circuit (or to the "power" end and a good ground), and if the test light comes on the circuit is passing current properly **(see illustration)**. If the resistance is low (less than 5 ohms), there is continuity; if the reading is 10,000 ohms or higher, there is a break somewhere in the circuit. The same procedure can be used to test a switch, by connecting the continuity tester to the switch terminals. With the switch turned On, the test light should come on (or low resistance should be indicated on a meter).

Finding an open circuit

When diagnosing for possible open circuits, it is often difficult to locate them by sight because the connectors hide oxidation or terminal misalignment. Merely wiggling a connector on a sensor or in the wiring harness may correct the open circuit condition. Remember this when an open circuit is indicated when troubleshooting a circuit. Intermittent problems may also be caused by oxidized or loose connections.

Electrical troubleshooting is simple if you keep in mind that all electrical circuits are basically electricity running from the battery, through the wires, switches, relays, fuses and fusible links to each electrical component (light bulb, motor, etc.) and to ground, from which it is passed back to the battery. Any electrical problem is an interruption in the flow of electricity to and from the battery.

Connectors

Most electrical connections on these vehicles are made with multi-wire plastic connectors. The mating halves of many connectors are secured with locking clips molded into the plastic connector shells. The mating halves of large connectors, such as some of those under the instrument panel, are held together by a bolt through the center of the connector.

To separate a connector with locking clips, use a small screwdriver to pry the clips apart carefully, then separate the connector halves. Pull only on the shell, never pull on the wiring harness as you may damage the individual wires and terminals inside the connectors. Look at the connector closely before trying to separate the halves. Often the locking clips are engaged in a way that is not immediately clear. Additionally, many connectors have more than one set of clips.

Each pair of connector terminals has a male half and a female half. When you look at the end view of a connector in a diagram, be sure to understand whether the view shows the harness side or the component side of the connector. Connector halves are mirror images of each other, and a terminal shown on the right side end-view of one half will be on the left side end view of the other half.

3   Fuses and fusible links - general information

Fuses

Refer to illustrations 3.1a, 3.1b and 3.3

The electrical circuits of the vehicle are protected by a combination of fuses, circuit breakers and fusible links. The fuse blocks are located under the instrument panel and in the engine compartment **(see illustrations)**.

Each of the fuses is designed to protect a specific circuit, and the various circuits are identified on the fuse panel cover.

Miniaturized fuses are employed in the fuse blocks. These compact fuses, with blade terminal design, allow fingertip removal and

3.1a The interior fuse box is tucked up under the instrument panel, to the left of the steering column - it's fairly difficult to reach

3.1b The main engine compartment fuse/relay box is located near the left strut tower

replacement. If an electrical component fails, always check the fuse first. The best way to check a fuse is with a test light. Check for power at the exposed terminal tips of each fuse. If power is present on one side of the fuse but not the other, the fuse is blown. A blown fuse can also be confirmed by visually inspecting it **(see illustration)**.

Be sure to replace blown fuses with the correct type. Fuses of different ratings are physically interchangeable, but only fuses of the proper rating should be used. Replacing a fuse with one of a higher or lower value than specified is not recommended. Each electrical circuit needs a specific amount of protection. The amperage value of each fuse is molded into the fuse body.

If the replacement fuse immediately fails, don't replace it again until the cause of the problem is isolated and corrected. In most cases, this will be a short circuit in the wiring caused by a broken or deteriorated wire.

Fusible links

Some circuits are protected by fusible links. The links are used in circuits which are not ordinarily fused, such as the ignition circuit, or which carry high current.

Cartridge type fusible links are located in the engine compartment fuse box and are similar to a large fuse. After disconnecting the negative battery cable, simply unplug and replace it with a fusible link of the same amperage.

A wire-type fusible link, installed in the harness between the battery and the fuse/relay blocks, protects the entire chassis electrical system. It's located near the positive battery terminal. If the fusible link melts, the cause of the short must first be repaired, then the fusible link must be replaced with a fusible link of the same gauge. Never substitute a regular wire for a fusible link.

To replace a wire-type fusible link, disconnect the cable from the negative terminal of the battery, cut the damaged link out and solder a new one in its place. Cover the exposed wires with shrink-wrap tubing or plenty of electrical tape.

4 Circuit breakers - general information

Circuit breakers protect certain circuits, such as the power windows or heated seats. Depending on the vehicle's accessories, there may be one or two circuit breakers, located in the fuse/relay box in the engine compartment **(see illustration 3.1b)**.

Because the circuit breakers reset automatically, an electrical overload in a circuit-breaker-protected system will cause the circuit to fail momentarily, then come back on. If the circuit does not come back on, check it immediately.

For a basic check, pull the circuit breaker up out of its socket on the fuse panel, but just far enough to probe with a voltmeter. The breaker should still contact the sockets.

With the voltmeter negative lead on a good chassis ground, touch each end prong of the circuit breaker with the positive meter probe. There should be battery voltage at each end. If there is battery voltage only at one end, the circuit breaker must be replaced.

Some circuit breakers must be reset manually.

5 Relays - general information and testing

General information

1   Several electrical accessories in the vehicle, such as the fuel injection system, horns, starter, and fog lamps use relays to transmit the electrical signal to the component. Relays use a low-current circuit (the control circuit) to open and close a high-current circuit (the power circuit). If the relay is defective, that component will not operate properly. Most relays are mounted in the engine compartment fuse/relay box. If a faulty relay is suspected, it can be removed and tested using the procedure below or by a dealer service department or a repair shop. Defective relays must be replaced as a unit. Identification of the circuit the relay controls is often marked on the top of the relay, but the decal or imprint inside the cover of the relay box should also indicate which circuits they control. **Note:** *Some relays are an integral part of the interior fuse box. These include the starter relay, the IG1 relay, the defroster relay, the power window relay, the circuit opening relay and the integration relay.*

Testing

Refer to illustrations 5.3a, 5.3b and 5.6

2   Refer to the wiring diagrams for the circuit to determine the proper connections for the relay you're testing. If you can't determine the correct connection from the wiring diagrams, however, you may be able to determine the test connections from the information that follows.

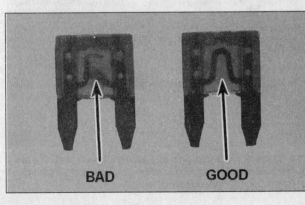

3.3 When a fuse blows, the element between the terminals melts

BAD   GOOD

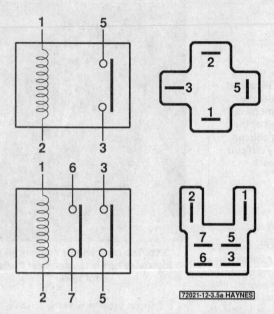

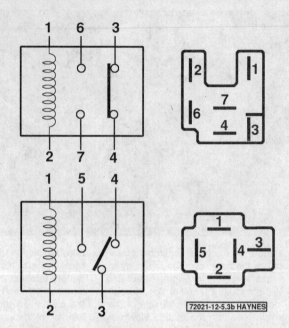

5.3a These two relays are typical normally open types; the one above completes a single circuit (terminal 5 to terminal 3) when energized - the lower relay type completes two circuits (6 and 7, and 3 and 5) when energized

5.3b These relays are normally closed types, where current flows though one circuit until the relay is energized, which interrupts that circuit and completes the second circuit

3   There are four basic types of relays used on these models **(see illustrations)**. Some are normally open type and some normally closed, while others include a circuit of each type.

4   On most relays, two of the terminals are the relay control circuit (they connect to the relay coil which, when energized, closes the large contacts to complete the circuit). The other terminals are the power circuit (they are connected together within the relay when the control-circuit coil is energized).

5   Some relays may be marked as an aid to help you determine which terminals make up the control circuit and which make up the power circuit. If the relay is not marked, refer to the wiring diagrams at the end of this Chap-

ter to determine the proper hook-ups for the relay you're testing.

6   To test a relay, connect an ohmmeter across the two terminals of the power circuit, continuity should not be indicated **(see illustration)**. Now connect a fused jumper wire between one of the two control circuit terminals and the positive battery terminal. Connect another jumper wire between the other control circuit terminal and ground. When the connections are made, the relay should click and continuity should be indicated on the meter. On some relays, polarity may be critical, so, if the relay doesn't click, try swapping the jumper wires on the control circuit terminals.

7   If the relay fails the above test, replace it.

6   Turn signal and hazard flasher - check and replacement

Refer to illustration 6.1

Warning: *The models covered by this manual are equipped with Supplemental Restraint Systems (SRS), more commonly known as airbags. Always disable the airbag system before working in the vicinity of any airbag system components to avoid the possibility of accidental deployment of the airbags, which could cause personal injury (see Section 26).*

1   The turn signal and hazard flasher is a single combination unit, located on the interior fuse/relay box **(see illustration)**.

2   When the flasher unit is functioning prop-

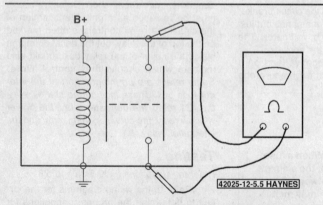

5.6 To test a typical four-terminal normally open relay, connect an ohmmeter to the two terminals of the power circuit - the meter should indicate continuity with the relay energized and no continuity with the relay not energized

6.1 Location of the turn signal and hazard flasher (seen here through the opening for the small utility compartment to the left of the steering wheel)

7.4 Release the switch retaining claw with a plastic tool - wiper/washer switch shown, headlight/turn signal switch similar (steering wheel removed for clarity, but it isn't necessary to remove the steering wheel for switch removal)

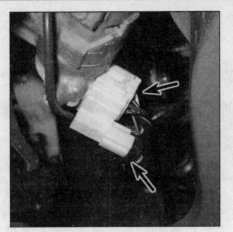

8.3 Disconnect the electrical connectors at the bottom of the ignition switch housing

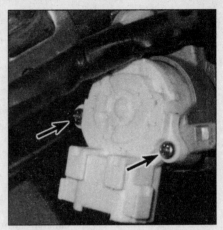

8.4 Unscrew the retaining screws to remove the electrical portion of the ignition switch

erly, an audible click can be heard during its operation. If the turn signals fail on one side or the other and the flasher unit does not make its characteristic clicking sound, or if a bulb on one side of the vehicle flashes much faster than normal but the bulb at the other end of the vehicle (on the same side) doesn't light at all, a faulty turn signal bulb may be indicated.

3   If both turn signals fail to blink, the problem may be due to a blown fuse, a faulty flasher unit, a defective switch or a loose or open connection. If a quick check of the fuse box indicates that the turn signal fuse has blown, check the wiring for a short before installing a new fuse.

4   To replace the flasher, disconnect the electrical connector and remove the flasher unit from the electrical center.

5   Make sure that the replacement unit is identical to the original. Compare the old one to the new one before installing it.

6   Installation is the reverse of removal.

---

7   Steering column switches - replacement

Refer to illustration 7.4

Warning: *The models covered by this manual are equipped with Supplemental Restraint Systems (SRS), more commonly known as airbags. Always disable the airbag system before working in the vicinity of any airbag system components to avoid the possibility of accidental deployment of the airbag(s), which could cause personal injury (see Section 26).*

1   Disconnect the cable from the negative terminal of the battery.

2   Remove the steering column covers (see Chapter 11).

3   The steering column switches on these models are two separate switch units connected to a central plastic housing. The left-side switch is for the headlight and turn sig-

nal control, while the right-side switch is for the washer/wiper control. Either switch can be replaced separately. Unplug the electrical connectors from the combination switch to be replaced.

4   Depress the claw in the switch, then pull the switch from the steering column **(see illustration)**. **Note:** *Excessive force may break the claw.*

5   Installation is the reverse of removal.

---

8   Ignition switch and key lock cylinder - replacement

Warning: *The models covered by this manual are equipped with Supplemental Restraint Systems (SRS), more commonly known as airbags. Always disable the airbag system before working in the vicinity of any airbag system components to avoid the possibility of accidental deployment of the airbag(s), which could cause personal injury (see Section 26).*

1   Disconnect the cable from the negative terminal of the battery.

2   Remove the steering column covers (see Chapter 11).

Ignition switch

Refer to illustrations 8.3 and 8.4

3   Unplug the ignition switch wiring harness connectors **(see illustration)**.

4   Remove the switch retaining screws **(see illustration)** then pull the switch from the lock cylinder housing.

5   Installation is reverse of the removal.

Lock cylinder

Refer to illustration 8.8

6   On models equipped with the engine immobilizer system, gently pry off the plastic shroud around the key-lock cylinder and disconnect the electrical connector. Lift the shroud edge from the locating tab only enough to slip the shroud off. The shroud houses the amplifier for the special transponder keys. Pry

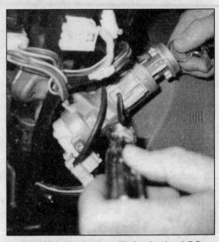

8.8 With the lock cylinder in the ACC position, depress the retaining pin with a small screwdriver, then pull the cylinder straight out

lightly to remove the illumination ring, then remove the unlock arming switch.

7   Insert the key and turn it to the ACC position.

8   Use a small screwdriver or punch to depress the lock cylinder retaining pin, then withdraw the key cylinder **(see illustration)**.

9   To install the lock cylinder, depress the retaining pin and guide the lock cylinder into the housing until the retaining pin extends itself back into the locating hole in the housing.

10   The remainder of the installation is the reverse of removal.

---

9   Instrument panel switches - replacement

Warning: *The models covered by this manual are equipped with Supplemental Restraint Systems (SRS), more commonly known as airbags. Always disable the airbag system before working in the vicinity of any airbag*

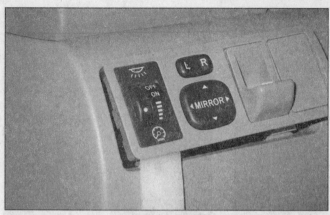

9.5 Use a trim tool to pry the dimmer/mirror switch panel from the left side of the dash

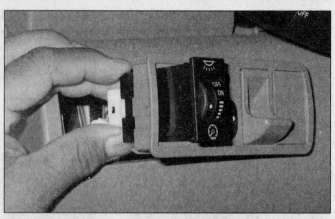

9.6 Disconnect the electrical connector and release the two clips securing the light control switch - mirror switch removal is similar

10.3 Remove this screw at the top of the instrument cluster . . .

10.4 . . . then release the clips and pull the cluster out at the bottom

system components to avoid the possibility of accidental deployment of the airbag(s), which could cause personal injury (see Section 26).

Hazard warning switch

1   Disconnect the negative battery cable (see Chapter 1).
2   Carefully remove the center cluster finish panel (see Chapter 11) from the instrument panel and pull the assembly out until you can disconnect the electrical connector at the rear of the switch.
3   Use two screwdrivers to depress the switch retaining tangs, then remove the switch cluster from the panel.
4   Installation is the reverse of the removal procedure.

Power mirror control switch and dimmer switch

Refer to illustrations 9.5 and 9.6
5   The switches are located in a small panel to the left of the steering column. Carefully pry the panel from the dash with a trim tool **(see illustration)**.
6   Disconnect the electrical connector and remove the switches **(see illustration)**.
7   Installation is the reverse of the removal procedure.

Defogger switch

8   The rear window defogger switch is located in the heating and air conditioning control panel.
9   Refer to Chapter 3 and remove the control panel, then pull the assembly out until you can disconnect the electrical connector at the rear of the switch. Depress the tab and remove the switch from the bezel.
10   Installation is the reverse of the removal procedure.

10   Instrument cluster - removal and installation

Refer to illustrations 10.3, 10.4 and 10.5
Warning: *The models covered by this manual are equipped with Supplemental Restraint Systems (SRS), more commonly known as airbags. Always disable the airbag system before working in the vicinity of any airbag system component to avoid the possibility of accidental deployment of the airbag(s), which could cause personal injury (see Section 26).*
1   Disconnect the negative battery cable. Remove the steering wheel (see Chapter 10).
2   Remove the instrument cluster trim panel (see Chapter 11).

3   Remove the cluster mounting screw at the top **(see illustration)**.
4   Pry at the two bottom clips to release them, then pull the cluster out **(see illustration)**.
5   Disconnect the electrical connectors **(see illustration)**.

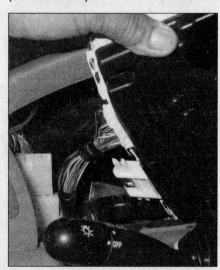

10.5 Disconnect the electrical connectors at the back of the cluster

11.7 Lift the end cap to access the wiper arm nut, remove the nut, then make a reference mark before removing the arm

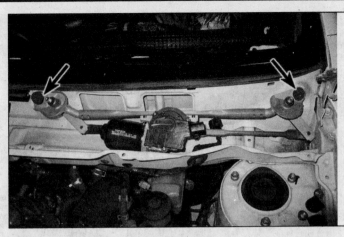

11.9 Location of the wiper linkage mounting bolts

6   Cover the steering column with a cloth to protect the trim covers, then remove the instrument cluster from the vehicle.
7   Installation is the reverse of removal.

11 Wiper motor - check and replacement

Wiper motor circuit check

Note: *Refer to the wiring diagrams for wire colors and locations in the following checks. When checking for voltage, probe a grounded 12-volt test light to each terminal at a connector until it lights; this verifies voltage (power) at the terminal. If the following checks fail to locate the problem, have the system diagnosed by a dealer service department or other properly equipped repair facility.*
1   If the wipers work slowly, make sure the battery is in good condition and has a strong charge (see Chapter 5). If the battery is in good condition, remove the wiper motor (see below) and operate the wiper arms by hand. Check for binding linkage and pivots. Lubricate or repair the linkage or pivots as

necessary. Reinstall the wiper motor. If the wipers still operate slowly, check for loose or corroded connections, especially the ground connection. If all connections look OK, replace the motor.
2   If the wipers fail to operate when activated, check the fuse in the driver's side interior fuse panel. If the fuse is OK, connect a jumper wire between the wiper motor's ground terminal and ground, then retest. If the motor works now, repair the ground connection. If the motor still doesn't work, turn the wiper switch to the HI position and check for voltage at the motor. **Note:** *The cowl cover will have to be removed (see Chapter 11) to access the electrical connector.*
3   If there's voltage at the connector, remove the motor and check it off the vehicle with fused jumper wires from the battery. If the motor now works, check for binding linkage (see Step 1). If the motor still doesn't work, replace it. If there's no voltage to the motor, check for voltage at the wiper control relays. If there's voltage at the wiper control relays and no voltage at the wiper motor, have the switch tested. If the switch is OK, the wiper control relay is probably bad. See Section 5 for relay testing.
4   If the interval (delay) function is inoperative, check the continuity of all the wiring between the switch and wiper control module.
5   If the wipers stop at the position they're

in when the switch is turned off (fail to park), check for voltage at the park feed wire of the wiper motor connector when the wiper switch is OFF but the ignition is ON. If no voltage is present, check for an open circuit between the wiper motor and the fuse panel.

Replacement

Refer to illustrations 11.7, 11.9 and 11.11
6   Disconnect the negative cable from the battery.
7   Remove the covers over the wiper arm mounting nuts. Remove the nuts, mark the relationship of the arms to the spindles, then pry up the wiper arms **(see illustration)**.
8   Remove the cowl louver panels.
9   Disconnect the wiper motor harness connector and remove the windshield wiper motor/linkage assembly mounting bolts **(see illustration)**.
10   Slide the assembly toward the passenger side to detach the rubber pin near the motor from the cowl sheetmetal, then lift the windshield wiper motor assembly from the cowl area.
11   Pry the linkage from the motor arm, remove the wiper motor mounting bolts and separate the motor from the frame **(see illustration)**.
12   Installation is the reverse of removal.

12 Radio and speakers - removal and installation

Warning: *The models covered by this manual are equipped with Supplemental Restraint Systems (SRS), more commonly known as airbags. Always disable the airbag system before working in the vicinity of any airbag system components to avoid the possibility of accidental deployment of the airbag(s), which could cause personal injury (see Section 26).*
1   Disconnect the negative battery cable.

Radio

Refer to illustration 12.3
2   The air conditioning control panel must be removed before the radio mounting screws can be accessed (see Chapter 11).

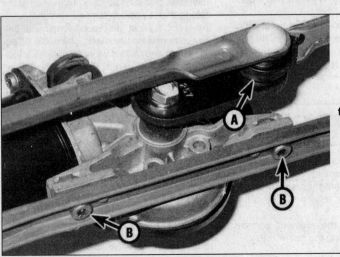

11.11 Pry the link from the motor arm (A), then remove the wiper motor mounting bolts (B)

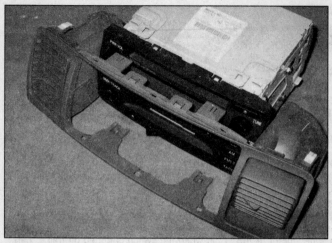

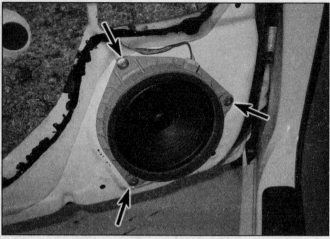

12.3 The radio comes out with this panel and two vents - release the clips top and bottom to remove the radio from the vent panel

12.6 Drill out the rivets securing the door speaker, then pull the speaker out and disconnect the electrical connector

3   Remove the retaining screws and pull the radio panel outward to access the back-side, then disconnect the electrical connectors and the antenna lead. Release the clips and separate the radio from the panel **(see illustration)**.

4   Installation is the reverse of removal.

Door speakers

Refer to illustration 12.6

5   Remove the door trim panel (see Chapter 11). All models have speakers in both front and rear doors. Rear door speakers are mounted similarly to the front door speakers.

6   Remove the speaker mounting rivets **(see illustration)**. Disconnect the electrical connector and remove the speaker from the vehicle

7   Installation is the reverse of removal.

Tweeters

Refer to illustration 12.10

8   In addition to the standard door and rear speakers, some models are equipped with small tweeters for improved high-range sound.

9   The tweeters are mounted in the front of the doors under the mirror cover. Refer to Chapter 11 and remove the outside mirror covers.

10   Remove the tweeter mounting nuts and disconnect the electrical connector **(see illustration)**.

11   Installation is the reverse of removal.

13   Antenna - replacement

1   The vehicles covered by this manual are equipped with a mast-type antenna attached to the rear of the roof.

2   If the antenna mast is damaged, it can be removed by turning it counterclockwise. Wrap the antenna with tape for a good grip and it can be removed by hand.

12.10 The tweeters are the small speakers located behind the outside mirror mounting nut covers. They're secured by two of the mirror mounting nuts

3   The antenna cable runs from the radio up through the passenger-side windshield pillar under the headliner at is joined with a connector at the rear of the roof.

4   It's a difficult job for the home mechanic to remove all the panels and the headliner for access to the cables or replacement of the antenna mast base. This procedure is best left to a qualified shop.

14   Rear window defogger - check and repair

1   The rear window defogger consists of a number of horizontal elements baked onto the glass surface. If the defogger isn't working, first check the defogger relay and fuse in the interior fuse/relay box.

2   Small breaks in the element can be repaired without removing the rear window.

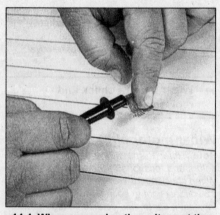

14.4 When measuring the voltage at the rear window defogger grid, wrap a piece of aluminum foil around the positive probe of the voltmeter and press the foil against the wire with your finger

Check

Refer to illustrations 14.4, 14.5 and 14.7

3   Turn the ignition switch and defogger system switches to the ON position. Using a voltmeter, place the positive probe against the defogger grid positive terminal and the negative probe against the ground terminal. If battery voltage is not indicated, check the defogger switch and related wiring. If voltage is indicated, but all or part of the defogger doesn't heat, proceed with the following tests.

4   When measuring voltage during the next two tests, wrap a piece of aluminum foil around the tip of the voltmeter positive probe and press the foil against the heating element with your finger **(see illustration)**. Place the negative probe on the defogger grid ground terminal.

5   Check the voltage at the center of each heating element **(see illustration)**. If the voltage is 5 or 6-volts, the element is okay (there is no break). If the voltage is 0-volts, the element is broken between the center of the element and the positive end. If the voltage is

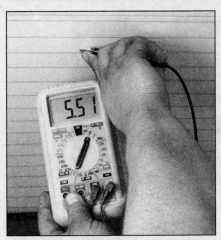

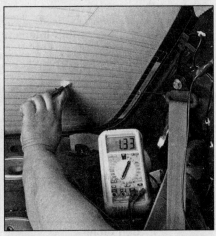

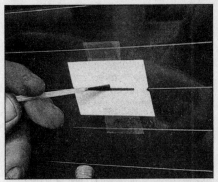

14.5 To determine if a heating element has broken, check the voltage at the center of each element - if the voltage is 5 or 6-volts, the element is unbroken - if the voltage is 10 or 12-volts, the element is broken between the center and the ground side - if there is no voltage, the element is broken between the center and the positive side

14.7 To find the break, place the voltmeter negative lead against the defogger ground terminal, place the voltmeter positive lead with the foil strip against the heating element at the positive terminal end and slide it toward the negative terminal end - the point at which the voltmeter reading changes abruptly is the point at which the element is broken

14.13 To use a defogger repair kit, apply masking tape to the inside of the window at the damaged area, then brush on the special conductive coating

10 to 12-volts the element is broken between the center of the element and ground. Check each heating element.

6   Connect the negative lead to a good body ground. The reading should stay the same. If it doesn't, the ground connection is bad.

7   To find the break, place the voltmeter negative probe against the defogger ground terminal. Place the voltmeter positive probe with the foil strip against the heating element at the positive terminal end and slide it toward the negative terminal end. The point at which the voltmeter deflects from several volts to zero is the point at which the heating element is broken **(see illustration)**.

Repair

Refer to illustration 14.13

8   Repair the break in the element using a

repair kit specifically recommended for this purpose, available at most auto parts stores. Included in this kit is plastic conductive epoxy.

9   Prior to repairing a break, turn off the system and allow it to cool off for a few minutes.

10   Lightly buff the element area with fine steel wool, then clean it thoroughly with rubbing alcohol.

11   Use masking tape to mask off the area being repaired.

12   Thoroughly mix the epoxy, following the instructions provided with the repair kit.

13   Apply the epoxy material to the slit in the masking tape, overlapping the undamaged area about 3/4-inch on either end **(see illustration)**.

14   Allow the repair to cure for 24 hours before removing the tape and using the system.

15   Headlight bulb - replacement

Refer to illustrations 15.1 and 15.2

Warning: *Halogen gas filled bulbs are under pressure and may shatter if the surface is scratched or the bulb is dropped. Wear eye protection and handle the bulbs carefully, grasping only the base whenever possible. Do not touch the surface of the bulb with your fingers because the oil from your skin could cause it to overheat and fail prematurely. If you do touch the bulb surface, clean it with rubbing alcohol.*

1   Open the hood. Reach behind the headlight assembly and unplug the electrical connector, depressing the clip on the harness connector **(see illustration)**. To access the left-side headlight bulbs, remove the battery (see Chapter 5), then remove the pushpin securing the air intake duct and set the duct aside.

2   Grasp the bulb holder securely and rotate it counterclockwise to remove it from the housing **(see illustration)**.

3   Pull straight out on the bulb to remove from it from the bulb holder. Without touching the glass with your bare fingers, insert the new bulb assembly into the headlight housing.

4   Plug in the electrical connector.

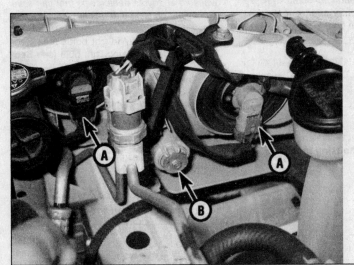

15.1 Location of the two headlight bulbs (A) and the aiming screw (B)

15.2 Disconnect the electrical connector, then twist the bulb holder counterclockwise and pull the holder out

16 Headlights - adjustment

Refer to illustration 16.3

Note: *The headlights must be aimed correctly. If adjusted incorrectly they could blind the driver of an oncoming vehicle and cause a serious accident or seriously reduce your ability to see the road. The headlights should be checked for proper aim every 12 months and any time a new headlight is installed or front-end bodywork is performed. It should be emphasized that the following procedure is only an interim step, which will provide temporary adjustment until the headlights can be adjusted by a properly equipped shop.*

1   The vertical adjustment screws are located behind each headlight housing **(see illustration 15.1)**. (There are no horizontal adjustment screws.)

2   There are several methods for adjusting the headlights. The simplest method requires masking tape, a blank wall and a level floor.

3   Position masking tape vertically on the wall in reference to the vehicle centerline and the centerlines of both headlights **(see illustration)**.

4   Position a horizontal tape line in reference to the centerline of all the headlights.

Note: *It might be easier to position the tape on the wall with the vehicle parked only a few inches away.*

5   Adjustment should be made with the vehicle parked 25 feet from the wall, sitting level, the gas tank half-full and no heavy load in the vehicle.

6   Starting with the low beam adjustment, position the high intensity zone so it is two inches below the horizontal line. Adjustment is made by turning the adjusting screw clockwise to raise the beam and counterclockwise to lower the beam.

7   With the high beams on, the high intensity zone should be vertically centered with the exact center just below the horizontal line.

Note: *It might not be possible to position the headlight aim exactly for both high and low beams. If a compromise must be made, keep in mind that the low beams are the most used and have the greatest effect on safety.*

8   Have the headlights adjusted by a dealer

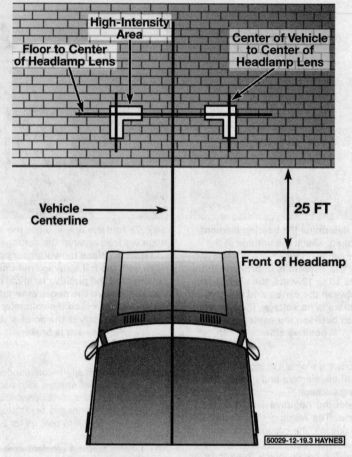

16.3 Headlight adjustment details

service department or service station at the earliest opportunity.

17 Headlight housing - replacement

Refer to illustration 17.2

Warning: *These vehicles are equipped with halogen gas-filled headlight bulbs that are under pressure and may shatter if the surface is damaged or the bulb is dropped. Wear eye protection and handle the bulbs carefully, grasping only the base whenever possible. Do not touch the surface of the bulb with your fingers because the oil from your skin could cause it to overheat and fail prematurely. If you do touch the bulb surface, clean it with rubbing alcohol.*

Note: *Headlight housings are expensive to replace, but on most models repair kits are available at Toyota dealerships that can save a headlight housing that has broken mounting tabs.*

1   Remove the headlight bulbs (see Section 15) and the parking light bulb (see Section 19).

2   The front bumper cover must be removed to access one of the headlight housing fasteners (see Chapter 11). Remove the retaining bolts, detach the housing and withdraw it from the vehicle **(see illustration)**.

3   Installation is the reverse of removal. Be sure to check headlight adjustment (see Section 16).

18 Horn - check and replacement

Warning: *The models covered by this manual are equipped with Supplemental Restraint*

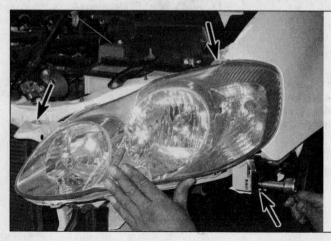

17.2 Headlight housing mounting screws

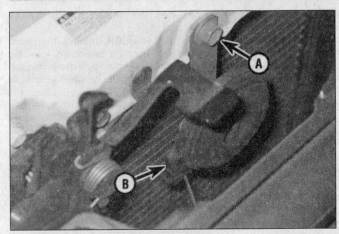

18.9 Location of the horn mounting bolt (A) and electrical connector (B)

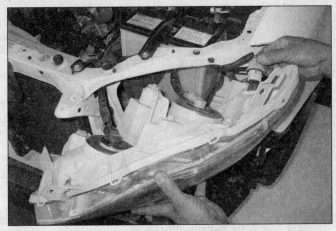

19.2 Rotate the bulb holder counterclockwise to remove the park/turn/marker bulb from the headlight housing

Systems (SRS), more commonly known as airbags. Always disable the airbag system before working in the vicinity of any airbag system components to avoid the possibility of accidental deployment of the airbag(s), which could cause personal injury (see Section 26).

Check

Note: *Check the fuses before beginning electrical diagnosis.*

1   Disconnect the electrical connector from the horn.

2   To test the horn, connect battery voltage to the horn terminal with a jumper wire. If the horn doesn't sound, replace it.

3   If the horn does sound, check for voltage at the terminal when the horn button is depressed. If there's voltage at the terminal, check for a bad ground at the horn.

4   If there's no voltage at the horn, check the relay (see Section 5).

5   If the relay is OK, check for voltage to the relay power and control circuits. If either of the circuits is not receiving voltage, inspect the wiring between the relay and the fuse panel.

6   If both relay circuits are receiving voltage, depress the horn button and check the circuit from the relay to the horn button for continuity to ground. If there's no continuity, check the

circuit for an open. If there's no open circuit, replace the horn button.

7   If there's continuity to ground through the horn button, check for an open or short in the circuit from the relay to the horn.

Replacement

Refer to illustration 18.9

8   To access the horn, open the hood. The horn is located in front of the radiator.

9   To replace the horn, disconnect the electrical connector and remove the bracket bolt **(see illustration)**.

10   Installation is the reverse of removal.

---

19   Bulb replacement

Front park/turn signal lights

Refer to illustration 19.2

1   The park/turn signal lights and side marker lights are all are part of the headlight housing. These bulbs are accessible from behind the headlight housing (in place), although with some difficulty. If you have trouble, refer to Section 17 and remove the headlight housing for access to these bulbs.

2   Rotate the bulb holder counterclockwise and pull the bulb out **(see illustration)**. Remove the bulb from the holder. On some models, the side marker light is a separate unit mounted in the front fender. On these models, access to the bulb is from underneath the fender.

3   Installation is the reverse of removal.

Rear tail light/brake light/turn signal/side marker/backup

Refer to illustrations 19.4 and 19.6

4   The taillight/brake/turn signal bulbs can be accessed by removing access panels in the trunk interior **(see illustration)**.

5   Rotate the bulb holders counterclockwise and pull the bulbs out to remove them. Remove the bulb from the holder.

6   The backup lights in the trunk lid are accessible only after opening a cover on the inside of the trunk lid, using a screwdriver to release it **(see illustration)**. Twist the bulb holder counterclockwise to remove it.

7   Installation is the reverse of removal.

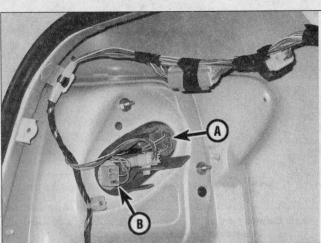

19.4 Open the access panel inside the trunk (panel removed in this photo) to access the bulbs

A   Taillight/stop and rear side marker bulb
B   Turn signal bulb

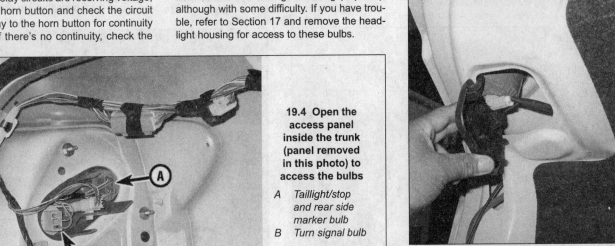

19.6 Swing open this hinged cover on the trunk lid to access the backup light bulb

19.8 Rotate the bulb holder and remove it from the high-mounted brake light assembly

Center high-mounted stop light

Refer to illustration 19.8

8   Open the trunk and crawl in enough to see the underside of the rear package shelf. Reach the bulb through the opening under the CHMSL housing **(see illustration)**.
9   Twist the bulb holder counterclockwise to remove it, then pull the bulb straight out of the holder.
10   Installation is the reverse of removal.

Instrument cluster lights

Refer to illustration 19.12

11   To gain access to the instrument cluster illumination bulbs, the instrument cluster will have to be removed (see Section 10). The bulbs can then be removed and replaced from the rear of the cluster.
12   Rotate the bulb holder counterclockwise to remove it **(see illustration)**.
13   Installation is the reverse of removal.

Interior light

Refer to illustration 19.15

14   Pry the lens off the interior light housing.

15   Detach the bulb from the terminals **(see illustration)**. It may be necessary to pry the bulb out - if this is the case, pry only on the ends of the bulb (otherwise the glass may shatter).
16   Installation is the reverse of removal.

License plate light

17   Remove the trunk lid lock cylinder by disconnecting the rods and removing the two mounting bolts.
18   Release the four clips inside the trunk lid and remove the outside trim panel.
19   On the outside, push the license light bezel to the left to compress the clip, then withdraw the bezel and bulb holder.
20   Installation is the reverse of removal.

Fog light

21   Raise the vehicle and secure it on jackstands.
22   Remove the splash shield.
23   Twist the bulb holder from the housing and replace the bulb.

20   Electric side view mirrors - description

1   Most electric rear view mirrors use two motors to move the glass; one for up and down adjustments and one for left-right adjustments.
2   The control switch has a selector portion that sends voltage to the left or right side mirror. With the ignition ON but the engine OFF, roll down the windows and operate the mirror control switch through all functions (left-right and up-down) for both the left and right side mirrors.
3   Listen carefully for the sound of the electric motors running in the mirrors.
4   If the motors can be heard but the mirror glass doesn't move, there's a problem with the drive mechanism inside the mirror.
5   If the mirrors do not operate and no

sound comes from the mirrors, check the fuse (see Chapter 1).
6   If the fuse is OK, remove the mirror control switch from the dashboard. Have the switch continuity checked by a dealership service department or other qualified automobile repair facility.
7   If the mirror still doesn't work, remove the mirror and check the wires at the mirror for voltage.
8   If there's not voltage in each switch position, check the circuit between the mirror and control switch for opens and shorts.
9   If there's voltage, remove the mirror and test it off the vehicle with jumper wires. Replace the mirror if it fails this test.

21   Cruise control system - description

1   On 2003 and 2004 models the accelerator pedal is linked to the throttle body with a pair of cables; one running to the cruise control actuator and another running from the actuator to the throttle body. 2005 models utilize an electric motor to operate the throttle body, and wiring between the accelerator pedal and the throttle body. The ECM communicates between them. Listed below are some general procedures that may be used to locate common problems.
2   With the ignition switch turned to the On position, turn the cruise control main switch On. The CRUISE light on the instrument panel should light up, and turn off when you turn the cruise control main switch back to Off.
3   Check the fuses (see Section 3).
4   If the check in Step 2 is abnormal, further diagnosis requires a scan tool to read diagnostic trouble codes for the cruise control system. For more information on diagnostic code retrieval, see Chapter 6.
5   The cruise control system uses inputs from the Vehicle Speed Sensor (VSS). Refer to Chapter 6 for more information on the VSS.
6   Test-drive the vehicle to determine if the

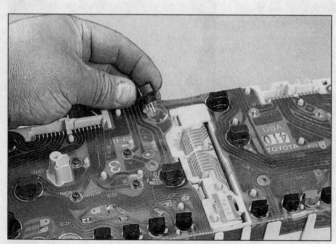

19.12 Twist the bulb holders counterclockwise to remove them from the back of the instrument cluster

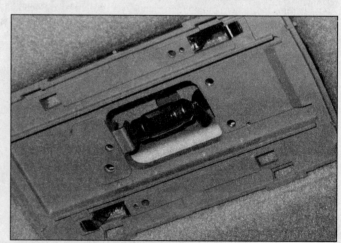

19.15 Carefully pry off the dome light lens using a flat-bladed screwdriver, then remove the bulb

cruise control is now working. If it isn't, take it to a dealer service department or an automotive electrical specialist for further diagnosis.

22   Power window system - description

1   The power window system operates electric motors, mounted in the doors, which lower and raise the windows. The system consists of the control switches, relays, the motors, regulators, glass mechanisms and associated wiring.

2   The power windows can be lowered and raised from the master control switch by the driver or by remote switches located at the individual windows. Each window has a separate motor that is reversible. The position of the control switch determines the polarity and therefore the direction of operation.

3   The circuit is protected by a fuse and a circuit breaker. Each motor is also equipped with an internal circuit breaker; this prevents one stuck window from disabling the whole system.

4   The power window system will only operate when the ignition switch is ON. In addition, many models have a window lockout switch at the master control switch that, when activated, disables the switches at the rear windows and, sometimes, the switch at the passenger's window also. Always check these items before troubleshooting a window problem.

5   These procedures are general in nature, so if you can't find the problem using them, take the vehicle to a dealer service department or other properly equipped repair facility.

6   If the power windows won't operate, always check the fuse and circuit breaker first.

7   If only the rear windows are inoperative, or if the windows only operate from the master control switch, check the rear window lockout switch for continuity in the unlocked position. Replace it if it doesn't have continuity.

8   Check the wiring between the switches and fuse panel for continuity. Repair the wiring, if necessary.

9   If only one window is inoperative from the master control switch, try the other control switch at the window. **Note:** *This doesn't apply to the driver's door window.*

10   If the same window works from one switch, but not the other, check the switch for continuity. Have the switch checked at a dealer service department or other qualified automobile repair facility.

11   If the switch tests OK, check for a short or open in the circuit between the affected switch and the window motor.

12   If one window is inoperative from both switches, remove the trim panel from the affected door and check for voltage at the switch and at the motor while the switch is operated.

13   If voltage is reaching the motor, disconnect the glass from the regulator (see Chapter 11). Move the window up and down by hand while checking for binding and damage. Also check for binding and damage to the regulator. If the regulator is not damaged and the window moves up and down smoothly, replace the motor. If there's binding or damage, lubricate, repair or replace parts, as necessary.

14   If voltage isn't reaching the motor, check the wiring in the circuit for continuity between the switches and motors. You'll need to consult the wiring diagram for the vehicle. If the circuit is equipped with a relay, check that the relay is grounded properly and receiving voltage.

15   Test the windows after you are done to confirm proper repairs.

23   Power door lock system - description

1   A power door lock system operates the door lock actuators mounted in each door. The system consists of the switches, actuators, a control unit and associated wiring. Diagnosis can usually be limited to simple checks of the wiring connections and actuators for minor faults that can be easily repaired.

2   Power door lock systems are operated by bi-directional solenoids located in the doors. The lock switches have two operating positions: Lock and Unlock. When activated, the switch sends a ground signal to the door lock control unit to lock or unlock the doors. Depending on which way the switch is activated, the control unit reverses polarity to the solenoids, allowing the two sides of the circuit to be used alternately as the feed (positive) and ground side.

3   Some vehicles may have an anti-theft system incorporated into the power locks. If you are unable to locate the trouble using the following general Steps, consult a dealer service department or other qualified repair shop.

4   Always check the circuit protection first. Some vehicles use a combination of circuit breakers and fuses.

5   Operate the door lock switches in both directions (Lock and Unlock) with the engine off. Listen for the click of the solenoids operating.

6   Test the switches for continuity. Remove the switches and have them checked by a dealer service department or other qualified automobile repair facility.

7   Check the wiring between the switches, control unit and solenoids for continuity. Repair the wiring if there's no continuity.

8   Check for a bad ground at the switches or the control unit.

9   If all but one lock solenoids operate, remove the trim panel from the affected door (see Chapter 11) and check for voltage at the solenoid while the lock switch is operated One of the wires should have voltage in the Lock position; the other should have voltage in the Unlock position.

10   If the inoperative solenoid is receiving voltage, replace the solenoid.

11   If the inoperative solenoid isn't receiving voltage, check the relay for an open or short in the wire between the lock solenoid and the control unit. **Note:** *It's common for wires to break in the portion of the harness between the body and door (opening and closing the door fatigues and eventually breaks the wires).*

Keyless entry system

Refer to illustrations 23.14 and 23.15

12   The keyless entry system consists of a remote control transmitter that sends a coded infrared signal to a receiver that then operates the door lock system. On models so equipped, the transmitter may also engage the alarm system and provide a "panic" button that flashes the lights and blows the horn for emergencies.

13   Replace the transmitter batteries when the red LED light on the case doesn't light when the button is pushed. As the batteries deteriorate with age, the distance at which the remote transmitter operates will diminish.

14   Use a coin or small screwdriver to carefully separate the case halves for battery replacement **(see illustration)**.

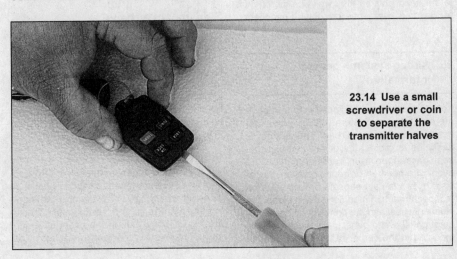

23.14 Use a small screwdriver or coin to separate the transmitter halves

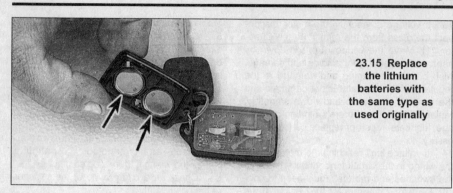

23.15 Replace the lithium batteries with the same type as used originally

15   Replace the two lithium batteries with the same type as originally installed, observing the polarity diagram on the case **(see illustration)**.
16   Snap the case halves together.

24   Power sunroof - description

1   The power sunroof or sliding roof system consists of the control switch, the module, the roof motor and the glass and track mechanism. The sunroof switch is located in a panel in the headliner, above the rear-view mirror. If there is a problem with sunroof operation, first check the 30-amp "Power" and 10-amp "Gauge" fuses in the instrument panel fuse/relay box. If the fuse is OK, check the P/W relay, also in the instrument panel fuse/relay box, as this relay supplies power to the sunroof relay which is located in the module behind the sunroof control switch bezel.

25   Daytime Running Lights (DRL) - general information

The Daytime Running Lights (DRL) system illuminates the headlights whenever the engine is running. The only exception is with the engine running and the parking brake engaged. Once the parking brake is released, the lights will remain on as long as the ignition switch is on, even if the parking brake is later applied.

The DRL system supplies reduced power to the headlights so they won't be too bright for daytime use, while prolonging headlight life.

26   Airbag system - general information

All models are equipped with a Supplemental Restraint System (SRS), more commonly known as an airbag. This system is designed to protect the driver, and the front seat passenger, from serious injury in the event of a head-on or frontal collision. It consists of two impact sensors behind the front bumper, an airbag module in the center of the steering wheel and the right side of the instrument panel and a sensing/diagnostic module mounted in the center of the vehicle, ahead

of the floor console. Additionally, some models are equipped with side impact airbags and side curtain airbags.

Airbag module
Driver's side

The airbag inflator module contains a housing incorporating the cushion (airbag) and inflator unit, mounted in the center of the steering wheel The inflator assembly is mounted on the back of the housing over a hole through which gas is expelled, inflating the bag almost instantaneously when an electrical signal is sent from the system. A spiral cable assembly on the steering column under the steering wheel carries this signal to the module.

This spiral cable assembly can transmit an electrical signal regardless of steering wheel position. The igniter in the airbag converts the electrical signal to heat and ignites the powder, which inflates the bag.

Passenger's side

The airbag is mounted above the glove compartment and designated by the letters SRS (Supplemental Restraint System). It consists of an inflator containing an igniter, a bag assembly, a reaction housing and a trim cover.

The airbag is considerably larger than the steering wheel-mounted unit and is supported by the steel reaction housing. The trim cover is textured and painted to match the instrument panel and has a molded seam that splits when the bag inflates.

Side impact airbags

Extra protection is provided on some models with the addition of optional side-impact airbags. These are smaller devices located in the seat backs on the side toward the exterior of the vehicle. The impact sensors for the side-impact airbags are located at the bottom of the door pillars in the body, in the bottom of the driver and passenger seats, or in the driver and passenger doors.

Side curtain airbags

Extra side-impact protection is provided on some models with the addition of optional side-curtain airbags (in addition to the side-impact airbags in the seatbacks). These are long airbags that, in the event of a side impact, come out of the headliner at each side

of the car and come down between the side windows and the seats. They are designed to protect the heads of both front seat and rear seat passengers.

Sensing and diagnostic module

The sensing and diagnostic module supplies the current to the airbag system in the event of the collision, even if battery power is cut off. It checks this system every time the vehicle is started, causing the "AIR BAG" light to go on then off, if the system is operating properly. If there is a fault in the system, the light will go on and stay on, flash, or the dash will make a beeping sound. If this happens, the vehicle should be taken to your dealer immediately for service.

Disarming the system and other precautions

Warning: *Failure to follow these precautions could result in accidental deployment of the airbag and personal injury.*

Whenever working in the vicinity of the steering wheel, steering column or any of the other SRS system components, the system must be disarmed. To disarm the system:

a) *Point the wheels straight ahead and turn the key to the Lock position.*
b) *Disconnect the cable from the negative battery terminal. Make sure the cable is positioned so that it cannot come into contact with the battery terminal.*
c) *Wait at least two minutes for the back-up power supply to be depleted.*

Whenever handling an airbag module, always keep the airbag opening (the trim side) pointed away from your body. Never place the airbag module on a bench of other surface with the airbag opening facing the surface. Always place the airbag module in a safe location with the airbag opening facing up.

Never measure the resistance of any SRS component. An ohmmeter has a built-in battery supply that could accidentally deploy the airbag.

Never use electrical welding equipment on a vehicle equipped with an airbag without first disconnecting the yellow airbag connector, located under the steering column near the combination switch connector (driver's airbag) and behind the glove box (passenger's airbag).

Never dispose of a live airbag module. Return it to a dealer service department or other qualified repair shop for safe deployment and disposal.

Component removal and installation

Driver's side airbag module and spiral cable

1   Refer to Chapter 10, *Steering wheel - removal and installation*, for the driver's side airbag module and spiral cable removal and installation procedures.

Passenger's side airbag module

Refer to illustration 26.3

2   Disarm the airbag system as describes previously in this Section. Under the right side of the instrument panel, disconnect the yellow connectors for the passenger airbag.

3   Remove the glove box (see Chapter 11). The airbag is bolted to the underside of the instrument panel. Remove the fasteners and detach the airbag module from the instrument panel **(see illustration)**. Be sure to heed the precautions outlined previously in this Section.

4   Installation is the reverse of the removal procedure. Tighten the airbag module mounting fasteners to 15 ft-lbs (20 Nm).

26.3 Remove the bolt and two nuts to remove the passenger airbag from behind the instrument panel

27   Wiring diagrams - general information

Since it isn't possible to include all wiring diagrams for every year covered by this manual, the following diagrams are those that are typical and most commonly needed.

Prior to troubleshooting any circuits, check the fuse and circuit breakers (if equipped) to make sure they're in good condition. Make sure the battery is properly charged and check the cable connections (see Chapter 1).

When checking a circuit, make sure that all connectors are clean, with no broken or loose terminals. When unplugging a connector, do not pull on the wires. Pull only on the connector housings themselves.

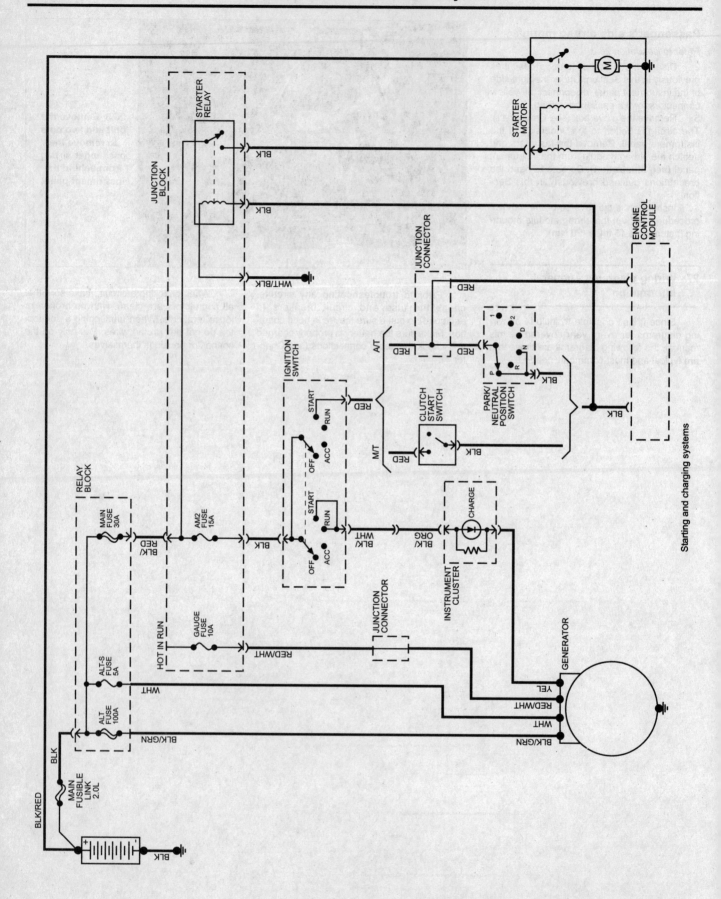

Starting and charging systems

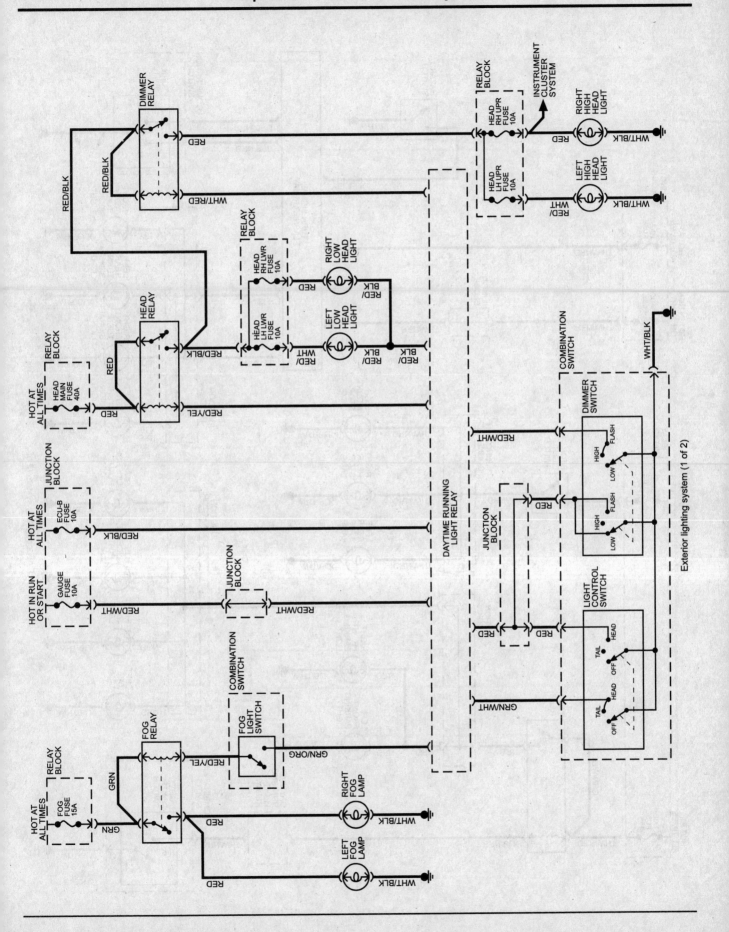

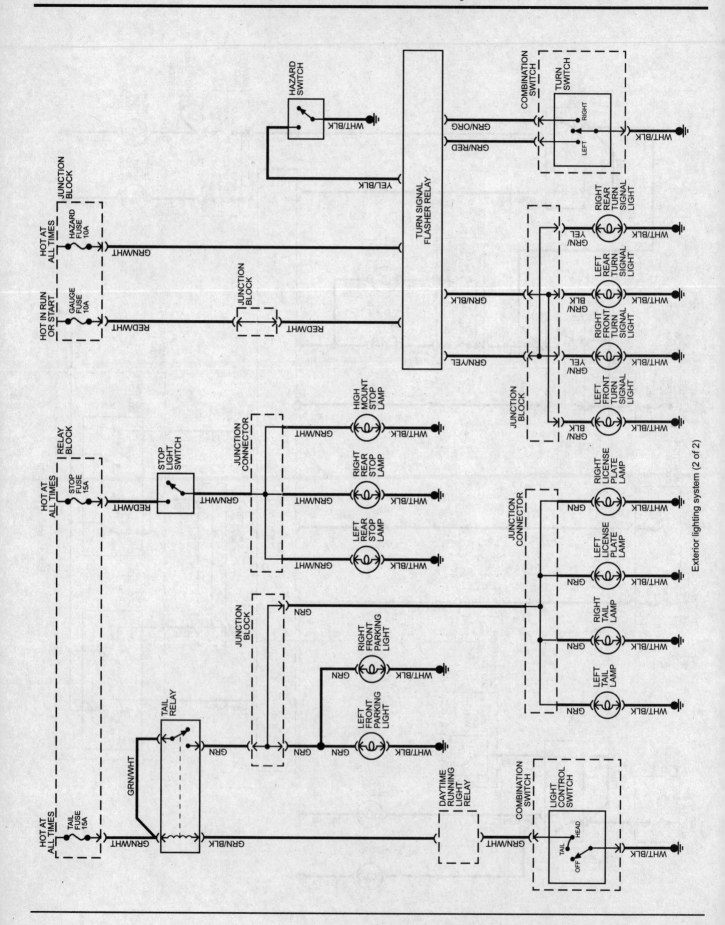

Exterior lighting system (2 of 2)

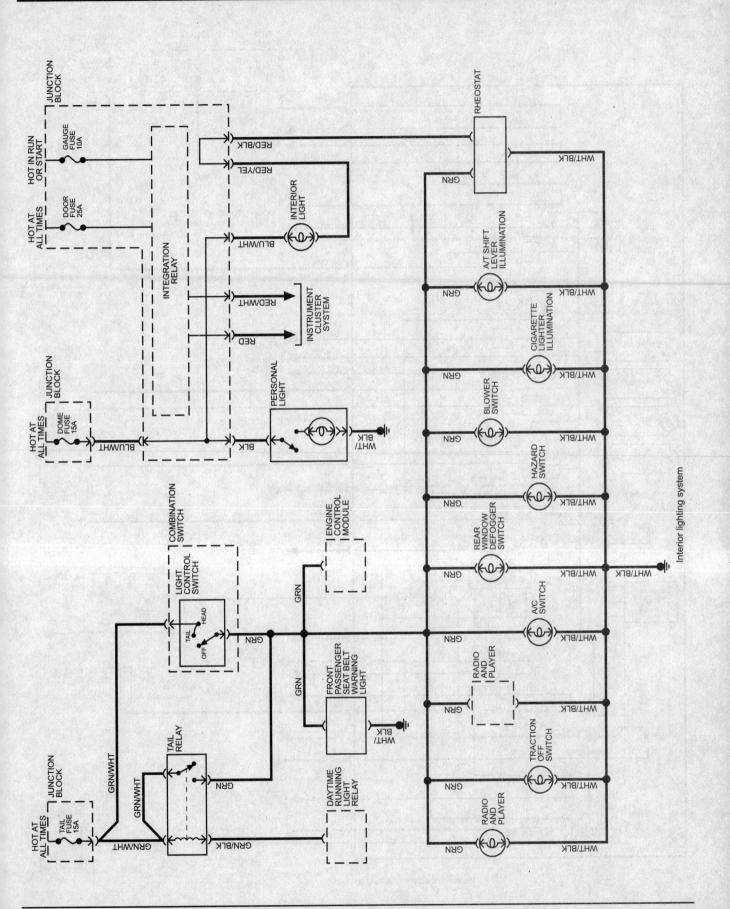

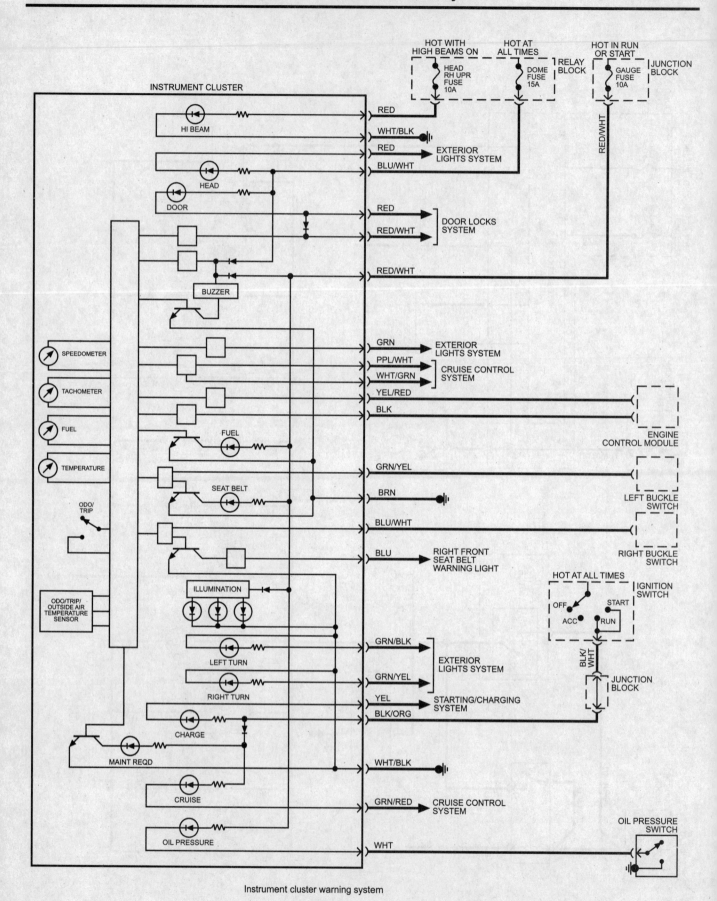

Instrument cluster warning system

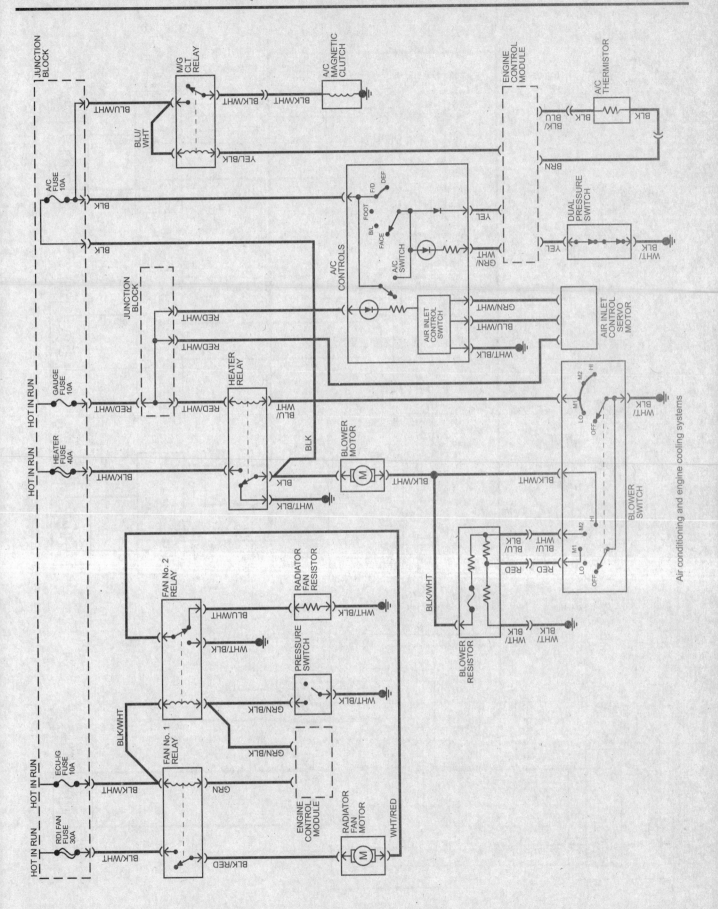

Air conditioning and engine cooling systems

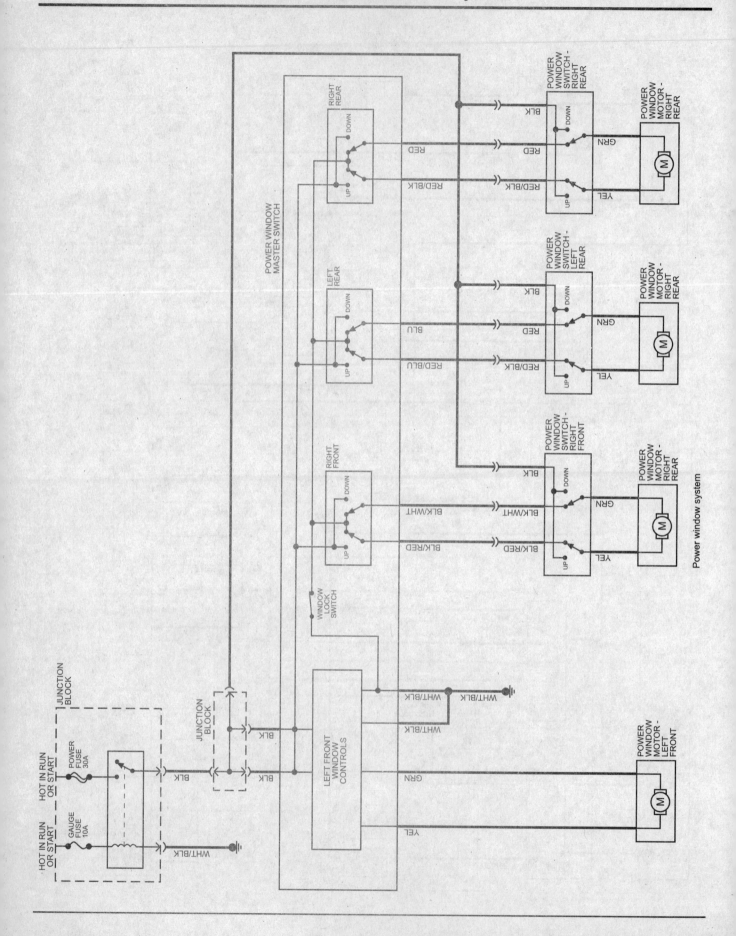

Power window system

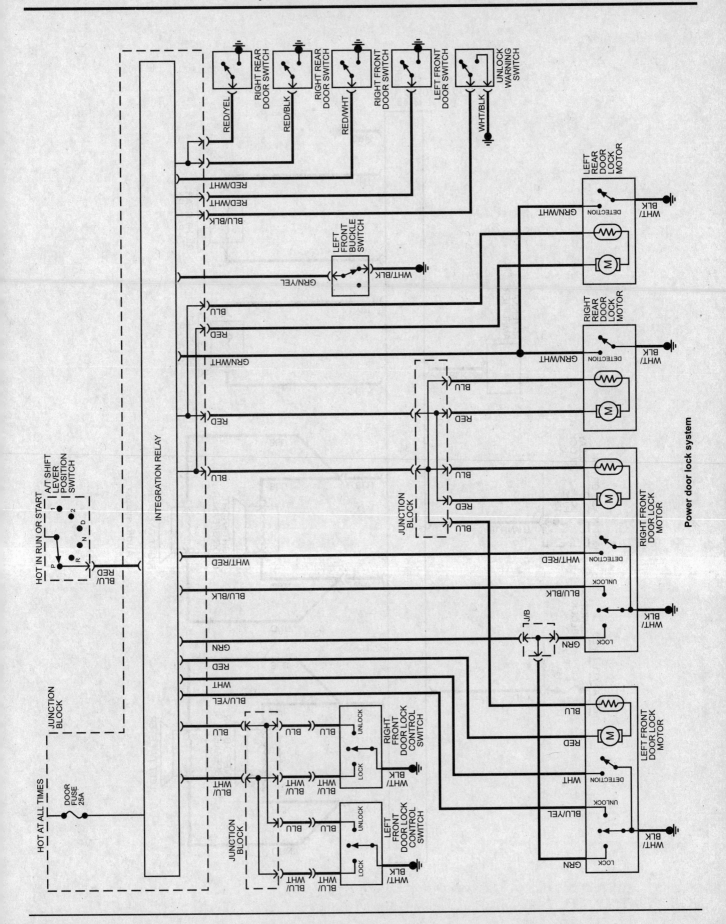

Power door lock system

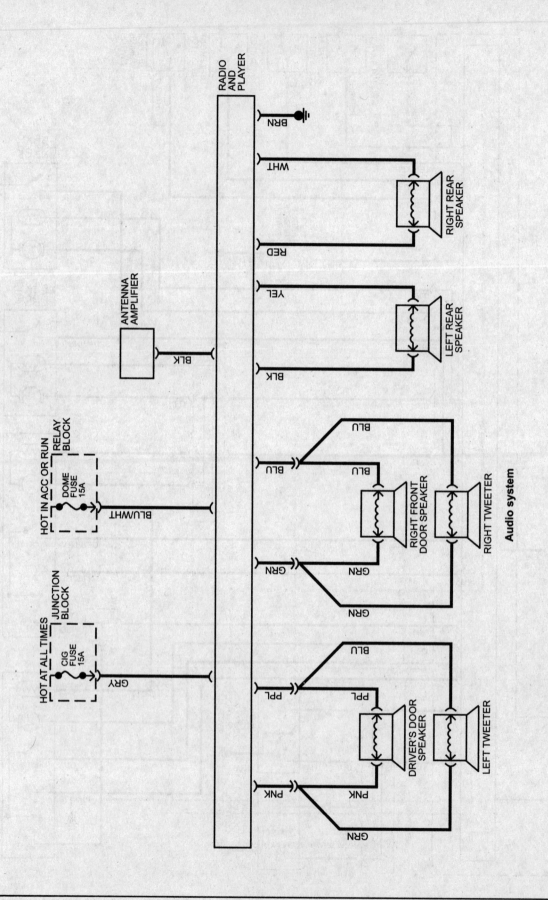

Audio system

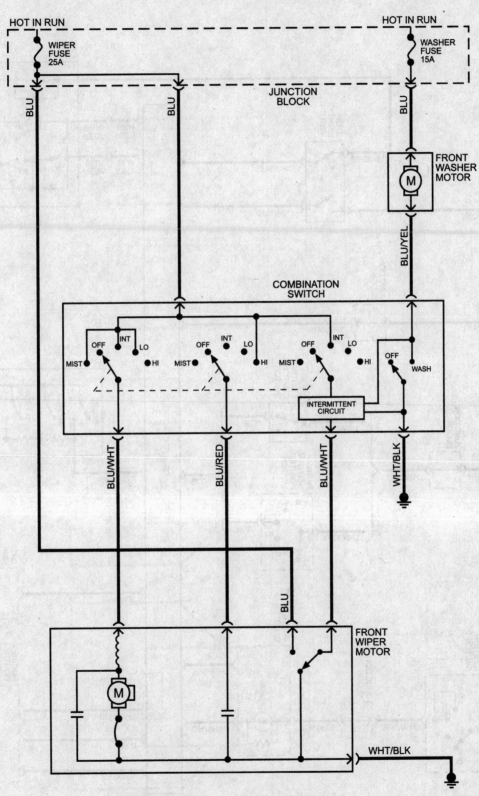

Windshield wiper and washer system

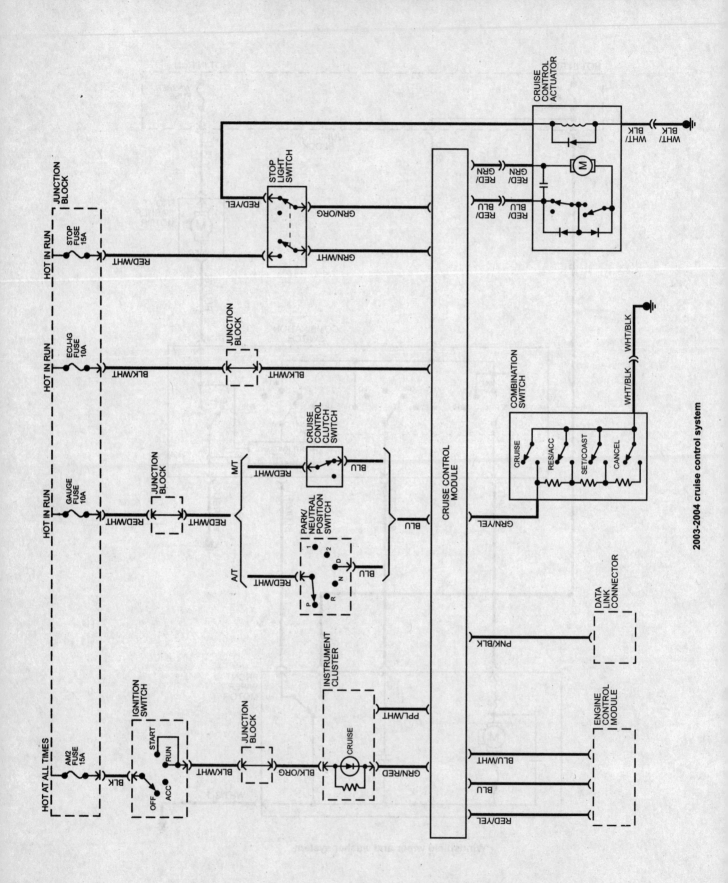

2003-2004 cruise control system

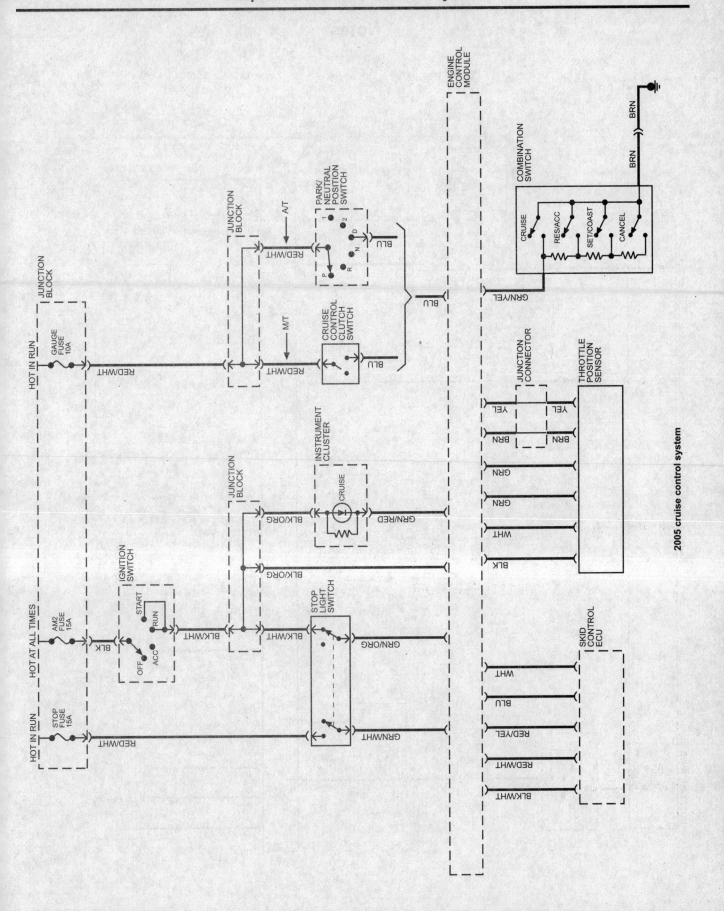

2005 cruise control system

Notes

Index

Haynes Automotive Manuals

NOTE: If you do not see a listing for your vehicle, consult your local Haynes dealer for the latest product information.

ACURA
- **12020** Integra '86 thru '89 & Legend '86 thru '90
- **12021** Integra '90 thru '93 & Legend '91 thru '95
- **12050** Acura TL all models '99 thru '08

AMC
- Jeep CJ - *see JEEP (50020)*
- **14020** Mid-size models '70 thru '83
- **14025** (Renault) Alliance & Encore '83 thru '87

AUDI
- **15020** 4000 all models '80 thru '87
- **15025** 5000 all models '77 thru '83
- **15026** 5000 all models '84 thru '88
- **15030** Audi A4 '02 thru '08

AUSTIN-HEALEY
- Sprite - *see MG Midget (66015)*

BMW
- **18020** 3/5 Series '82 thru '92
- **18021** 3-Series incl. Z3 models '92 thru '98
- **18022** 3-Series, '99 thru '05, Z4 models
- **18025** 320i all 4 cyl models '75 thru '83
- **18050** 1500 thru 2002 except Turbo '59 thru '77

BUICK
- **19010** Buick Century '97 thru '05
  - Century (front-wheel drive) - *see GM (38005)*
- **19020** Buick, Oldsmobile & Pontiac Full-size (Front-wheel drive) '85 thru '05
  - Buick Electra, LeSabre and Park Avenue; Oldsmobile Delta 88 Royale, Ninety Eight and Regency; Pontiac Bonneville
- **19025** Buick, Oldsmobile & Pontiac Full-size (Rear wheel drive) '70 thru '90
  - Buick Estate, Electra, LeSabre, Limited, Oldsmobile Custom Cruiser, Delta 88, Ninety-eight, Pontiac Bonneville, Catalina, Grandville, Parisienne
- **19030** Mid-size Regal & Century all rear-drive models with V6, V8 and Turbo '74 thru '87
  - Regal - *see GENERAL MOTORS (38010)*
  - Riviera - *see GENERAL MOTORS (38030)*
  - Roadmaster - *see CHEVROLET (24046)*
  - Skyhawk - *see GENERAL MOTORS (38015)*
  - Skylark - *see GM (38020, 38025)*
  - Somerset - *see GENERAL MOTORS (38025)*

CADILLAC
- **21030** Cadillac Rear Wheel Drive '70 thru '93
  - Cimarron - *see GENERAL MOTORS (38015)*
  - DeVille - *see GM (38031 & 38032)*
  - Eldorado - *see GM (38030 & 38031)*
  - Fleetwood - *see GM (38031)*
  - Seville - *see GM (38030, 38031 & 38032)*

CHEVROLET
- **10305** Chevrolet Engine Overhaul Manual
- **24010** Astro & GMC Safari Mini-vans '85 thru '05
- **24015** Camaro V8 all models '70 thru '81
- **24016** Camaro all models '82 thru '92
- **24017** Camaro & Firebird '93 thru '02
  - Cavalier - *see GENERAL MOTORS (38016)*
  - Celebrity - *see GENERAL MOTORS (38005)*
- **24020** Chevelle, Malibu & El Camino '69 thru '87
- **24024** Chevette & Pontiac T1000 '76 thru '87
  - Citation - *see GENERAL MOTORS (38020)*
- **24027** Colorado & GMC Canyon '04 thru '08
- **24032** Corsica/Beretta all models '87 thru '96
- **24040** Corvette all V8 models '68 thru '82
- **24041** Corvette all models '84 thru '96
- **24045** Full-size Sedans Caprice, Impala, Biscayne, Bel Air & Wagons '69 thru '90
- **24046** Impala SS & Caprice and Buick Roadmaster '91 thru '96, Impala - *see LUMINA (24048)*
  - Lumina '90 thru '94 - *see GM (38010)*
- **24047** Impala & Monte Carlo all models '06 thru '08
- **24048** Lumina & Monte Carlo '95 thru '05
  - Lumina APV - *see GM (38035)*
- **24050** Luv Pick-up all 2WD & 4WD '72 thru '82
  - Malibu '97 thru '00 - *see GM (38026)*
- **24055** Monte Carlo all models '70 thru '88
  - Monte Carlo '95 thru '01 - *see LUMINA (24048)*
- **24059** Nova all V8 models '69 thru '79
- **24060** Nova and Geo Prizm '85 thru '92
- **24064** Pick-ups '67 thru '87 - Chevrolet & GMC, all V8 & in-line 6 cyl, 2WD & 4WD '67 thru '87; Suburbans, Blazers & Jimmys '67 thru '91
- **24065** Pick-ups '88 thru '98 - Chevrolet & GMC, full-size pick-ups '88 thru '98, C/K Classic '99 & '00, Blazer & Jimmy '92 thru '94; Suburban '92 thru '99; Tahoe & Yukon '95 thru '99

- **24066** Pick-ups '99 thru '06 - Chevrolet Silverado & GMC Sierra '99 thru '06, Suburban/Tahoe/Yukon/Yukon XL/Avalanche '00 thru '06
- **24067** Chevrolet Silverado & GMC Sierra '07 thru '09
- **24070** S-10 & S-15 Pick-ups '82 thru '93, Blazer & Jimmy '83 thru '94,
- **24071** S-10 & Sonoma Pick-ups '94 thru '04, including Blazer, Jimmy & Hombre
- **24072** Chevrolet TrailBlazer, GMC Envoy & Oldsmobile Bravada '02 thru '09
- **24075** Sprint '85 thru '88 & Geo Metro '89 thru '01
- **24080** Vans - Chevrolet & GMC '68 thru '96
- **24081** Chevrolet Express & GMC Savana Full-size Vans '96 thru '07

CHRYSLER
- **10310** Chrysler Engine Overhaul Manual
- **25015** Chrysler Cirrus, Dodge Stratus, Plymouth Breeze '95 thru '00
- **25020** Full-size Front-Wheel Drive '88 thru '93
  - K-Cars - *see DODGE Aries (30008)*
  - Laser - *see DODGE Daytona (30030)*
- **25025** Chrysler LHS, Concorde, New Yorker, Dodge Intrepid, Eagle Vision, '93 thru '97
- **25026** Chrysler LHS, Concorde, 300M, Dodge Intrepid, '98 thru '04
- **25027** Chrysler 300, Dodge Charger & Magnum '05 thru '09
- **25030** Chrysler & Plymouth Mid-size front wheel drive '82 thru '95
  - Rear-wheel Drive - *see Dodge (30050)*
- **25035** PT Cruiser all models '01 thru '09
- **25040** Chrysler Sebring, Dodge Avenger '95 thru '05 Dodge Stratus '01 thru 05

DATSUN
- **28005** 200SX all models '80 thru '83
- **28007** B-210 all models '73 thru '78
- **28009** 210 all models '79 thru '82
- **28012** 240Z, 260Z & 280Z Coupe '70 thru '78
- **28014** 280ZX Coupe & 2+2 '79 thru '83
  - 300ZX - *see NISSAN (72010)*
- **28018** 510 & PL521 Pick-up '68 thru '73
- **28020** 510 all models '78 thru '81
- **28022** 620 Series Pick-up all models '73 thru '79
  - 720 Series Pick-up - *see NISSAN (72030)*
- **28025** 810/Maxima all gasoline models, '77 thru '84

DODGE
- **400 & 600** - *see CHRYSLER (25030)*
- **30008** Aries & Plymouth Reliant '81 thru '89
- **30010** Caravan & Plymouth Voyager '84 thru '95
- **30011** Caravan & Plymouth Voyager '96 thru '02
- **30012** Challenger/Plymouth Saporro '78 thru '83
- **30013** Caravan, Chrysler Voyager, Town & Country '03 thru '07
- **30016** Colt & Plymouth Champ '78 thru '87
- **30020** Dakota Pick-ups all models '87 thru '96
- **30021** Durango '98 & '99, Dakota '97 thru '99
- **30022** Durango '00 thru '03 Dakota '00 thru '04
- **30023** Durango '04 thru '06, Dakota '05 and '06
- **30025** Dart, Demon, Plymouth Barracuda, Duster & Valiant 6 cyl models '67 thru '76
- **30030** Daytona & Chrysler Laser '84 thru '89
  - Intrepid - *see CHRYSLER (25025, 25026)*
- **30034** Neon all models '95 thru '99
- **30035** Omni & Plymouth Horizon '78 thru '90
- **30036** Dodge and Plymouth Neon '00 thru '05
- **30040** Pick-ups all full-size models '74 thru '93
- **30041** Pick-ups all full-size models '94 thru '01
- **30042** Pick-ups full-size models '02 thru '08
- **30045** Ram 50/D50 Pick-ups & Raider and Plymouth Arrow Pick-ups '79 thru '93
- **30050** Dodge/Plymouth/Chrysler RWD '71 thru '89
- **30055** Shadow & Plymouth Sundance '87 thru '94
- **30060** Spirit & Plymouth Acclaim '89 thru '95
- **30065** Vans - Dodge & Plymouth '71 thru '03

EAGLE
- Talon - *see MITSUBISHI (68030, 68031)*
- Vision - *see CHRYSLER (25025)*

FIAT
- **34010** 124 Sport Coupe & Spider '68 thru '78
- **34025** X1/9 all models '74 thru '80

FORD
- **10320** Ford Engine Overhaul Manual
- **10355** Ford Automatic Transmission Overhaul
- **36004** Aerostar Mini-vans all models '86 thru '97
- **36006** Contour & Mercury Mystique '95 thru '00

- **36008** Courier Pick-up all models '72 thru '82
- **36012** Crown Victoria & Mercury Grand Marquis '88 thru '10
- **36016** Escort/Mercury Lynx all models '81 thru '90
- **36020** Escort/Mercury Tracer '91 thru '02
- **36022** Escape & Mazda Tribute '01 thru '07
- **36024** Explorer & Mazda Navajo '91 thru '01
- **36025** Explorer/Mercury Mountaineer '02 thru '10
- **36028** Fairmont & Mercury Zephyr '78 thru '83
- **36030** Festiva & Aspire '88 thru '97
- **36032** Fiesta all models '77 thru '80
- **36034** Focus all models '00 thru '07
- **36036** Ford & Mercury Full-size '75 thru '87
- **36044** Ford & Mercury Mid-size '75 thru '86
- **36048** Mustang V8 all models '64-1/2 thru '73
- **36049** Mustang II 4 cyl, V6 & V8 models '74 thru '78
- **36050** Mustang & Mercury Capri '79 thru '86
- **36051** Mustang all models '94 thru '04
- **36052** Mustang '05 thru '07
- **36054** Pick-ups & Bronco '73 thru '79
- **36058** Pick-ups & Bronco '80 thru '96
- **36059** F-150 & Expedition '97 thru '09, F-250 '97 thru '99 & Lincoln Navigator '98 thru '09
- **36060** Super Duty Pick-ups, Excursion '99 thru '10
- **36061** F-150 full-size '04 thru '09
- **36062** Pinto & Mercury Bobcat '75 thru '80
- **36066** Probe all models '89 thru '92
- **36070** Ranger/Bronco II gasoline models '83 thru '92
- **36071** Ranger '93 thru '10 & Mazda Pick-ups '94 thru '09
- **36074** Taurus & Mercury Sable '86 thru '95
- **36075** Taurus & Mercury Sable '96 thru '05
- **36078** Tempo & Mercury Topaz '84 thru '94
- **36082** Thunderbird/Mercury Cougar '83 thru '88
- **36086** Thunderbird/Mercury Cougar '89 and '97
- **36090** Vans all V8 Econoline models '69 thru '91
- **36094** Vans full size '92 thru '05
- **36097** Windstar Mini-van '95 thru '07

GENERAL MOTORS
- **10360** GM Automatic Transmission Overhaul
- **38005** Buick Century, Chevrolet Celebrity, Oldsmobile Cutlass Ciera & Pontiac 6000 all models '82 thru '96
- **38010** Buick Regal, Chevrolet Lumina, Oldsmobile Cutlass Supreme & Pontiac Grand Prix (FWD) '88 thru '07
- **38015** Buick Skyhawk, Cadillac Cimarron, Chevrolet Cavalier, Oldsmobile Firenza & Pontiac J-2000 & Sunbird '82 thru '94
- **38016** Chevrolet Cavalier & Pontiac Sunfire '95 thru '05
- **38017** Chevrolet Cobalt & Pontiac G5 '05 thru '09
- **38020** Buick Skylark, Chevrolet Citation, Olds Omega, Pontiac Phoenix '80 thru '85
- **38025** Buick Skylark & Somerset, Oldsmobile Achieva & Calais and Pontiac Grand Am all models '85 thru '98
- **38026** Chevrolet Malibu, Olds Alero & Cutlass, Pontiac Grand Am '97 thru '03
- **38027** Chevrolet Malibu '04 thru '07
- **38030** Cadillac Eldorado, Seville, Oldsmobile Toronado, Buick Riviera '71 thru '85
- **38031** Cadillac Eldorado & Seville, DeVille, Fleetwood & Olds Toronado, Buick Riviera '86 thru '93
- **38032** Cadillac DeVille '94 thru '05 & Seville '92 thru '04 Cadillac DTS '06 thru '10
- **38035** Chevrolet Lumina APV, Olds Silhouette & Pontiac Trans Sport all models '90 thru '96
- **38036** Chevrolet Venture, Olds Silhouette, Pontiac Trans Sport & Montana '97 thru '05
  - General Motors Full-size Rear-wheel Drive - *see BUICK (19025)*
- **38040** Chevrolet Equinox '05 thru '09 Pontiac Torrent '06 thru '09

GEO
- Metro - *see CHEVROLET Sprint (24075)*
- Prizm - '85 thru '92 *see CHEVY (24060)*, '93 thru '02 *see TOYOTA Corolla (92036)*
- **40030** Storm all models '90 thru '93
- Tracker - *see SUZUKI Samurai (90010)*

GMC
- Vans & Pick-ups - *see CHEVROLET*

HONDA
- **42010** Accord CVCC all models '76 thru '83
- **42011** Accord all models '84 thru '89
- **42012** Accord all models '90 thru '93

(Continued on other side)

Haynes North America, Inc., 861 Lawrence Drive, Newbury Park, CA 91320-1514 • (805) 498-6703 • http://www.haynes.com

Haynes Automotive Manuals (continued)

NOTE: If you do not see a listing for your vehicle, consult your local Haynes dealer for the latest product information.

42013 Accord all models '94 thru '97
42014 Accord all models '98 thru '02
42015 Accord models '03 thru '07
42020 Civic 1200 all models '73 thru '79
42021 Civic 1300 & 1500 CVCC '80 thru '83
42022 Civic 1500 CVCC all models '75 thru '79
42023 Civic all models '84 thru '91
42024 Civic & del Sol '92 thru '95
42025 Civic '96 thru '00, CR-V '97 thru '01, Acura Integra '94 thru '00
42026 Civic '01 thru '10, CR-V '02 thru '09
42035 Odyssey all models '99 thru '04
42037 Honda Pilot '03 thru '07, Acura MDX '01 thru '07
42040 Prelude CVCC all models '79 thru '89

HYUNDAI
43010 Elantra all models '96 thru '06
43015 Excel & Accent all models '86 thru '09
43050 Santa Fe all models '01 thru '06
43055 Sonata all models '99 thru '08

ISUZU
Hombre - see CHEVROLET S-10 (24071)
47017 Rodeo, Amigo & Honda Passport '89 thru '02
47020 Trooper & Pick-up '81 thru '93

JAGUAR
49010 XJ6 all 6 cyl models '68 thru '86
49011 XJ6 all models '88 thru '94
49015 XJ12 & XJS all 12 cyl models '72 thru '85

JEEP
50010 Cherokee, Comanche & Wagoneer Limited all models '84 thru '01
50020 CJ all models '49 thru '86
50025 Grand Cherokee all models '93 thru '04
50026 Grand Cherokee '05 thru '09
50029 Grand Wagoneer & Pick-up '72 thru '91 Grand Wagoneer '84 thru '91, Cherokee & Wagoneer '72 thru '83, Pick-up '72 thru '88
50030 Wrangler all models '87 thru '08
50035 Liberty '02 thru '07

KIA
54070 Sephia '94 thru '01, Spectra '00 thru '09

LEXUS
ES 300 - see TOYOTA Camry (92007)

LINCOLN
Navigator - see FORD Pick-up (36059)
59010 Rear-Wheel Drive all models '70 thru '10

MAZDA
61010 GLC Hatchback (rear-wheel drive) '77 thru '83
61011 GLC (front-wheel drive) '81 thru '85
61015 323 & Protegé '90 thru '00
61016 MX-5 Miata '90 thru '09
61020 MPV all models '89 thru '98
Navajo - see Ford Explorer (36024)
61030 Pick-ups '72 thru '93
Pick-ups '94 thru '00 - see Ford Ranger (36071)
61035 RX-7 all models '79 thru '85
61036 RX-7 all models '86 thru '91
61040 626 (rear-wheel drive) all models '79 thru '82
61041 626/MX-6 (front-wheel drive) '83 thru '92
61042 626, MX-6/Ford Probe '93 thru '01

MERCEDES-BENZ
63012 123 Series Diesel '76 thru '85
63015 190 Series four-cyl gas models, '84 thru '88
63020 230/250/280 6 cyl sohc models '68 thru '72
63025 280 123 Series gasoline models '77 thru '81
63030 350 & 450 all models '71 thru '80
63040 C-Class: C230/C240/C280/C320/C350 '01 thru '07

MERCURY
64200 Villager & Nissan Quest '93 thru '01
All other titles, see FORD Listing.

MG
66010 MGB Roadster & GT Coupe '62 thru '80
66015 MG Midget, Austin Healey Sprite '58 thru '80

MITSUBISHI
68020 Cordia, Tredia, Galant, Precis & Mirage '83 thru '93
68030 Eclipse, Eagle Talon & Ply. Laser '90 thru '94
68031 Eclipse '95 thru '05, Eagle Talon '95 thru '98
68035 Galant '94 thru '03
68040 Pick-up '83 thru '96 & Montero '83 thru '93

NISSAN
72010 300ZX all models including Turbo '84 thru '89
72011 350Z & Infiniti G35 all models '03 thru '08
72015 Altima all models '93 thru '06
72020 Maxima all models '85 thru '92
72021 Maxima all models '93 thru '04
72030 Pick-ups '80 thru '97 Pathfinder '87 thru '95
72031 Frontier Pick-up, Xterra, Pathfinder '96 thru '04
72032 Frontier & Xterra '05 thru '08
72040 Pulsar all models '83 thru '86
Quest - see MERCURY Villager (64200)
72050 Sentra all models '82 thru '94
72051 Sentra & 200SX all models '95 thru '06
72060 Stanza all models '82 thru '90
72070 Titan pick-ups '04 thru '09
Armada '05 thru '10

OLDSMOBILE
73015 Cutlass V6 & V8 gas models '74 thru '88
For other OLDSMOBILE titles, see BUICK, CHEVROLET or GENERAL MOTORS listing.

PLYMOUTH
For PLYMOUTH titles, see DODGE listing.

PONTIAC
79008 Fiero all models '84 thru '88
79018 Firebird V8 models except Turbo '70 thru '81
79019 Firebird all models '82 thru '92
79025 G6 all models '05 thru '09
79040 Mid-size Rear-wheel Drive '70 thru '87
For other PONTIAC titles, see BUICK, CHEVROLET or GENERAL MOTORS listing.

PORSCHE
80020 911 except Turbo & Carrera 4 '65 thru '89
80025 914 all 4 cyl models '69 thru '76
80030 924 all models including Turbo '76 thru '82
80035 944 all models including Turbo '83 thru '89

RENAULT
Alliance & Encore - see AMC (14020)

SAAB
84010 900 all models including Turbo '79 thru '88

SATURN
87010 Saturn all S-series models '91 thru '02
87011 Saturn Ion '03 thru '07
87020 Saturn L-series models '00 thru '04
87040 Saturn VUE '02 thru '07

SUBARU
89002 1100, 1300, 1400 & 1600 '71 thru '79
89003 1600 & 1800 2WD & 4WD '80 thru '94
89100 Legacy all models '90 thru '99
89101 Legacy & Forester '00 thru '06

SUZUKI
90010 Samurai/Sidekick & Geo Tracker '86 thru '01

TOYOTA
92005 Camry all models '83 thru '91
92006 Camry all models '92 thru '96
92007 Camry, Avalon, Solara, Lexus ES 300 '97 thru '01
92008 Toyota Camry, Avalon and Solara and Lexus ES 300/330 all models '02 thru '06
92015 Celica Rear Wheel Drive '71 thru '85
92020 Celica Front Wheel Drive '86 thru '99
92025 Celica Supra all models '79 thru '92
92030 Corolla all models '75 thru '79
92032 Corolla all rear wheel drive models '80 thru '87
92035 Corolla all front wheel drive models '84 thru '92
92036 Corolla & Geo Prizm '93 thru '02
92037 Corolla '03 thru '08
92040 Corolla Tercel all models '80 thru '82
92045 Corona all models '74 thru '82
92050 Cressida all models '78 thru '82
92055 Land Cruiser FJ40, 43, 45, 55 '68 thru '82
92056 Land Cruiser FJ60, 62, 80, FZJ80 '80 thru '96
92060 Matrix & Pontiac Vibe '03 thru '08
92065 MR2 all models '85 thru '87
92070 Pick-up all models '69 thru '78
92075 Pick-up all models '79 thru '95
92076 Tacoma, 4Runner, & T100 '93 thru '04
92077 Tacoma '05 thru '09
92078 Tundra '00 thru '06 & Sequoia '01 thru '07
92079 4Runner all models '03 thru '09
92080 Previa all models '91 thru '95
92081 Prius all models '01 thru '08
92082 RAV4 all models '96 thru '05

92085 Tercel all models '87 thru '94
92090 Sienna all models '98 thru '09
92095 Highlander & Lexus RX-330 '99 thru '06

TRIUMPH
94007 Spitfire all models '62 thru '81
94010 TR7 all models '75 thru '81

VW
96008 Beetle & Karmann Ghia '54 thru '79
96009 New Beetle '98 thru '05
96016 Rabbit, Jetta, Scirocco & Pick-up gas models '75 thru '92 & Convertible '80 thru '92
96017 Golf, GTI & Jetta '93 thru '98 & Cabrio '95 thru '02
96018 Golf, GTI, Jetta '99 thru '05
96020 Rabbit, Jetta & Pick-up diesel '77 thru '84
96023 Passat '98 thru '05, Audi A4 '96 thru '01
96030 Transporter 1600 all models '68 thru '79
96035 Transporter 1700, 1800 & 2000 '72 thru '79
96040 Type 3 1500 & 1600 all models '63 thru '73
96045 Vanagon all air-cooled models '80 thru '83

VOLVO
97010 120, 130 Series & 1800 Sports '61 thru '73
97015 140 Series all models '66 thru '74
97020 240 Series all models '76 thru '93
97040 740 & 760 Series all models '82 thru '88
97050 850 Series all models '93 thru '97

TECHBOOK MANUALS
10205 Automotive Computer Codes
10206 OBD-II & Electronic Engine Management
10210 Automotive Emissions Control Manual
10215 Fuel Injection Manual, 1978 thru 1985
10220 Fuel Injection Manual, 1986 thru 1999
10225 Holley Carburetor Manual
10230 Rochester Carburetor Manual
10240 Weber/Zenith/Stromberg/SU Carburetors
10305 Chevrolet Engine Overhaul Manual
10310 Chrysler Engine Overhaul Manual
10320 Ford Engine Overhaul Manual
10330 GM and Ford Diesel Engine Repair Manual
10333 Engine Performance Manual
10340 Small Engine Repair Manual, 5 HP & Less
10341 Small Engine Repair Manual, 5.5 - 20 HP
10345 Suspension, Steering & Driveline Manual
10355 Ford Automatic Transmission Overhaul
10360 GM Automatic Transmission Overhaul
10405 Automotive Body Repair & Painting
10410 Automotive Brake Manual
10411 Automotive Anti-lock Brake (ABS) Systems
10415 Automotive Detailing Manual
10420 Automotive Electrical Manual
10425 Automotive Heating & Air Conditioning
10430 Automotive Reference Manual & Dictionary
10435 Automotive Tools Manual
10440 Used Car Buying Guide
10445 Welding Manual
10450 ATV Basics
10452 Scooters 50cc to 250cc

SPANISH MANUALS
98903 Reparación de Carrocería & Pintura
98904 Carburadores para los modelos Holley & Rochester
98905 Códigos Automotrices de la Computadora
98910 Frenos Automotriz
98913 Electricidad Automotriz
98915 Inyección de Combustible 1986 al 1999
99040 Chevrolet & GMC Camionetas '67 al '87
99041 Chevrolet & GMC Camionetas '88 al '98
99042 Chevrolet & GMC Camionetas Cerradas '68 al '95
99043 Chevrolet/GMC Camionetas '94 thru '04
99055 Dodge Caravan & Plymouth Voyager '84 al '95
99075 Ford Camionetas y Bronco '80 al '94
99077 Ford Camionetas Cerradas '69 al '91
99088 Ford Modelos de Tamaño Mediano '75 al '86
99091 Ford Taurus & Mercury Sable '86 al '95
99095 GM Modelos de Tamaño Grande '70 al '90
99100 GM Modelos de Tamaño Mediano '70 al '88
99106 Jeep Cherokee, Wagoneer & Comanche '84 al '00
99110 Nissan Camioneta '80 al '96, Pathfinder '87 al '95
99118 Nissan Sentra '82 al '94
99125 Toyota Camionetas y 4Runner '79 al '95

Over 100 Haynes motorcycle manuals also available

8-10

Haynes North America, Inc., 861 Lawrence Drive, Newbury Park, CA 91320-1514 • (805) 498-6703 • http://www.haynes.com